Object-Oriented Development

Building CASE Tools with C++

DAVID E. BRUMBAUGH

John Wiley & Sons, Inc.

New York • Chichester • Brisbane • Toronto • Singapore

Associate Publisher: Katherine Schowalter
Senior Acquisitions Editor: Diane Cerra
Associate Editor: Terri Hudson
Managing Editor: Jacqueline A. Martin
Editorial Production: Pageworks

This test is printed on acid-free paper.

This publication is designed to provide accurate and authoritative information in regard to the subject matter covered. It is sold with the understanding that the publisher is not engaged in rendering legal, accounting, or other professional service. If legal advice or other expert assistance is required, the services of a competent professional person should be sought. FROM A DECLARATION OF PRINCIPLES JOINTLY ADOPTED BY A COMMITTEE OF THE AMERICAN BAR ASSOCIATION AND A COMMITTEE OF PUBLISHERS.

Library of Congress Cataloging-in-Publication Data:

Brumbaugh, David E.
    Object-oriented development : building CASE tools with C++ / David
Brumbaugh.
        p.   cm.
    Includes index.
    ISBN 0-471-58371-5 (alk. paper)
    1. Object-oriented programming (Computer science).   2. C++ (Computer program language.   3. Computer-aided software engineering.   I. Title.
    QA76.64.B78   1994
    005.1'1—dcx20   93-2025
                                                                                CIP

Printed in the United States of America

10 9 8 7 6 5 4 3 2 1

To Kathleen for her love and commitment.

To Mom, Dad, my grandparents, and siblings for believing in me when I didn't believe in myself.

To Gary B., George M., and David C., my mentors.

To Charlie M., for the dream we never fulfilled, and all we learned along the way.

To Mike Y., for friendship and the first object-oriented success.

About the Author

David Brumbaugh is a project manager for Advanced Information Services, a systems integrator in Peoria, IL. He has a B.A. in computer information science from Jusdon College in Elgin, IL. He has been developing programs professionally since 1985. Since 1989 he has had five articles published in various professional journals. Also in 1989, he discovered C++ and Object-Oriented Programming and has been hooked ever since. He has been developing programs professionally since 1985. In that time he has been active in all phases of software development: management, analysis, design, and programming. His projects have included an interactive exhibit for the Money Center at the Museum of Science and Industry in Chicago, an image identification system for a Chicago bank, a weld planning system for a major international manufacturer, and a Windows-based document storage and retrieval system.

In 1989, David began programming in C++. Since then he has had over one hundred hours of formal Object-Oriented or C++ training. He has served on the Object-Oriented steering committee at AIS. Before this book project, he had designed and written several OO programs in C++ for simulation, design, and planning.

David began writing technical articles in 1989 with a report on the ORACLE DBMS for the *C User's Journal*. He has had three other articles published in the *C User's Journal*. These include articles on how to do OOP in C, how to port C libraries to C++ using class wrappers, and a report on the Zinc C++ user interface library. In 1992, *PCTechniques* published an article by him about practical software design. This is his first book.

Preface

"The industry is ready to move from the introductory and research stages into practical applications. We need to see object-oriented projects developed from concept to completion."

David Brumbaugh

I consider this a "second generation" object-oriented book. The first generation of books were introductions to the "Object-Oriented Paradigm." Most of them were about OOP (Object-Oriented Programming). Many were written by academic researchers. The industry is ready to move from the introductory and research stages into practical applications. We need to see object-oriented projects developed from concept to completion.

A lot of myths have sprung up regarding object-oriented programming. If you discover that some of these myths aren't entirely true, you may be tempted to reject OOP entirely. It is my goal to find the real benefits and drawbacks in OO development.

In this book, we will explore the entire OO development process while developing the CASE tools. The book comes with a disk containing the source code and executable programs developed in the book.

TARGET AUDIENCE

This is a book for PC software developers who want to become more familiar with object-oriented development and for anyone who needs more than theory presented in text books, but knows better than to jump into a project without thinking it through.

This book should appeal to the managers, designers, and programmers of object-oriented software projects. Often, those three roles are assumed by one or two people. In other cases, those roles may be shared among many people. In any of these cases, this book should be helpful.

There have been a lot of promises made by object-oriented evangelists. This book is targeted at developers who want to have those promises fulfilled.

To get the most from this book you should have a working knowledge of the C++ programming language; I used Borland C++ to develop the tools and source code examples. You should also have at least a passing familiarity with traditional structured analysis and structured design methods. If you have used traditional design methods, it is even better.

WHAT MAKES THIS BOOK UNIQUE?

Before discussing what this book is, I think I should tell you what it is not. It is not a rehash of existing manuals. It is not a book with a deep theoretical treatment of the subject. It is a book that addresses the real problems you will encounter in the relatively new field of object-oriented development, and it provides you with real, workable solutions to those problems. The feature that makes this book unique is its method of solving these problems. It treats theory and practice as a single entity. When you are done with this book, you will have a set of CASE tools you can use in your development and a solid set of examples you can refer to during your own projects.

WHAT PROBLEMS DOES THIS BOOK SOLVE?

There are plenty of introductory books on object-oriented design. One notable example is Grady Booch's *Object-Oriented Design with Applications*. According to Booch, three things are needed for a smooth transition to an object oriented mind set: training, a low-risk first project, and a good set of examples. He goes on to suggest that software development tools are good candidates for first projects.

This book helps smooth the transition to object-oriented development because it provides you with an opportunity to train yourself. It also could serve as a text for classroom training. It presents a case study of a first project, building software development tools, that you could follow from start to finish, giving plenty of examples. You could develop the project as you read, or simply use the examples in your own project.

WHAT ARE THE BENEFITS OF READING THIS BOOK?

Object-oriented technology is more than just the latest fad in software development. It is a relevant, practical method of development that will make software more reliable, make programmers more productive, and lessen the impact of changes during development. It is not a magic solution, however. Developers need to understand it, and they need the tools to use it.

This book solves several problems at once: it provides you with valuable CASE tools, and it also has the complete design of those CASE tools as examples for you to study.

SUBJECTS COVERED

This book covers the following subjects in varying detail:

- The Fundamentals of OO Design, Analysis, and Programming
- Management and Documentation of OO Development Projects
- CASE Tools Needed for OO Development
- Building Certain CASE Tools

BUILDING CASE TOOLS

CASE is an acronym for Computer Aided Software Engineering. The term CASE usually brings to mind charting and diagraming programs. However, any software that saves time, increases quality, or enhances communication during software development is a CASE tool. "One definition of CASE is the use of tools that provide leverage at any point in the software development cycle." [Fisher 1988] Since different CASE tools are targeted at different parts of the software development cycle, they are used by analysts, designers, programmers, and managers. I work for a small company where these jobs overlap, and I have needed to be all four simultaneously. This is not uncommon, so many CASE tools address a variety of these needs. Additional, many CASE tools assume you use the Structured Life Cycle, or something similar to develop your software. The older, structured techniques don't consider many of the issues in OOD, so we need new tools. Also, since certain CASE tools are missing from the shelves of software vendors, we will build the tools we need. I will discuss these new CASE tools in this book. There's no need to type in all the code in the building chapters; the executable programs are included on the disk that comes with this book.

There are actually four complete CASE tools on this disk. The first is a small DOS command line program. The other three require Microsoft Windows 3.1 or higher to run.

1. The first CASE tool is defined in Chapter 6. This is the code template generator. This can be run on any PC or MS-DOS compatible machine. It's been tested with DOS 5, but any version of DOS after 3.0 should work. Full source is included. There is also a Borland MAKE file.

2. The second CASE tool is the Class Librarian. It keeps track of classes you are building or have built. It is defined in Chapters 8 through 10. This requires MS Windows 3.1 or higher to run. It was tested on a 386SX with 4 Meg of RAM. All of the source I created is included. It uses two commercial libraries as noted in the text of the book. There is also a Borland MAKE file.

3. The third CASE tool is a class Browser. It is defined in Chapter 11. This requires MS Windows 3.1 or higher to run. It was tested on a 386SX with 4 Meg of RAM. All of the source I created is included. It uses two

commercial libraries as noted in the text of the book. There is also a Borland MAKE file.

4. The final CASE tool is the Graphic Designer. One of the new implementations of the list definitions uses some classes from the book *Practical Data Structures in C++* by Bryan Flamig, also published by John Wiley & Sons. (You can get the code by getting that book, or change the implementation to another list.) All of the source I created is included. It uses two commercial libraries as noted in the text of the book. There is also a Borland MAKE file.

If I enhance any of the CASE tools, I will make them available on CompuServe. I will put it in the OOP Alley library of the Computer Language (soon to be Software Development) forum. (GO CLMFOR or GO SDFORUM). Use any of the following Keywords: "SSOOT", "BRUMBAUGH", "CASE", "OOBOOK" to find any of the files I upload.

I will monitor that forum for messages addressed to me about the book. Unless it's a very private matter, feel free to make the messages public—the discussion may help other readers. Suggestions for SSOOT CASE improvements or bug reports are also welcome.

The install program for this disk will create the following directory structure on the disk you choose. (This of course assumes you install the whole thing).

```
\OOBOOK
\OOBOOK\CHAP06
\OOBOOK\CHAP08
\OOBOOK\CHAP09
\OOBOOK\CHAP10
\OOBOOK\CHAP11
\OOBOOK\CHAP12
```

Each of the subdirectories contains the files appropriate to the chapter it is named after.

The code in the CHAP08, CHAP10, CHAP11, and CHAP12 cannot be linked into a complete program without a user interface library and a database library. To link without changing the code you will need to purchase the Zink User Interface Library and the Pinnacle Relationship Engine.

I have designed the classes so you should be able to substitute your own user interface library and database library without a major impact on the rest of the program. (This is by necessity less true with the Graphic Tool.)

The details, reasons, and philosophies behind this are discussed in the book in section 1.4.4, 3.2.4, 7.7, and Appendix A.

HOW THIS BOOK IS ORGANIZED

I've tried to make each section of this book as independent from the others are possible, while maintaining a cohesive whole. Chapter 1 is a detailed introduction to this book. It gives a complete idea about what to expect in the rest of this book, introducing methodologies, OO development tools, and the components of software development.

Chapters 2 through 7 address issues such as the fundamentals, analysis, design, programming, and management. These are not "the theory chapters," instead they are insights and experience gained while developing object-oriented systems.

Chapters 8 through 12 present the requirements, design and construction of some CASE tools. Each tool is developed using the same general strategy:

- Figure out what you want to do.
- Figure out how to do it.
- Do it.
- Make it better.

Chapter 13 contains a summary of the major points of the book and some ideas for further exploration.

The appendices will serve as valuable reference tools. They list sources of information on object-oriented development and where you can find object-oriented development tools and components. Appendix D contains the source code for the examples in Chapter 6 and the librarian in Chapter 10. The rest of the codes and the executables are on the disk that accompanies this book. Appendix D also contains detailed instructions for the installation of the software that comes with the book.

There is a standard index to help you find your way around in this book and an index to source code so that you can find exactly the class and function definitions you need.

I've tried to keep the book personal and informal. Sometimes technical books get esoteric and cerebral, so I've tried to use a straightforward, common-sense approach to my explanations. I hope you enjoy this book and hope it helps you to become more productive and helps you to enjoy your work more.

About the Software

WHAT IS ON THIS DISK?

The accompanying diskette contains the complete and latest code that is referenced in the book. Each chapter's code will be placed in it's own directory on the disk where you choose to install this product. Each directory contains a README file which contains an overview of the contents of the directory, and any significant changes to the files.

HARDWARE REQUIREMENTS

- 386SX or better CPU
- 2 Megabytes RAM
- Hard Drive with about 3 megabytes free (Librarian only)
- MS-DOS 5.0 or higher
- Mouse supported but not required

MAKING A BACKUP COPY

Before you start to use the enclosed disk, we strongly recommend that you make a backup copy of the original. Remember, however, that a backup disk is for your own personal use only. Any other use of the backup disk violates copyright law. Please take the time now to make the backup, using the instructions below:

1. Assuming your floppy drive is "A," insert your DOS disk into drive A of your computer.
2. At the A:>, type DISKCOPY A: A: and press Return. You will be prompted by DOS to place the disk to be copied into drive A.
3. Place the *Object-Oriented Development* disk into drive A.

Follow the direction on the screen to complete the copy. When you are through, remove the new copy of the disk and label it immediately. Remove the original disk and store it in a safe place.

INSTALLING THE DISK

The enclosed diskette contained 79 individual files in compressed format. In order to use the files, you must run the installation program from the diskette.
You can install the diskette onto your computer by following these simple steps:

1. Assuming your floppy drive is "A," insert the *Object-Oriented Development* disk into drive A of your computer.
2. At the A:> type INSTALL and press Return.

The installation program will be loaded. After the title screen appears, you will be given the options shown in Figure P.1.
To change any of the default settings, type the highlighted letter or move the menu bar to the desired option and press Enter.

3. To start the installation type "S" or move the menu bar to the **Start Installation** option and press Enter.

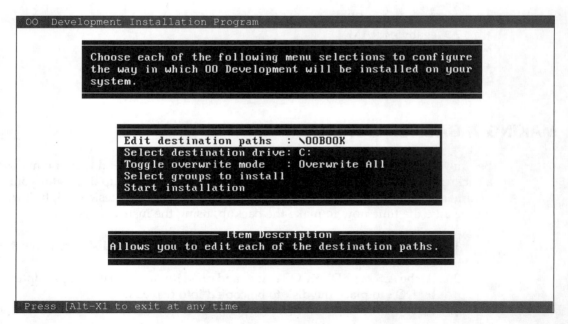

```
 OO  Development Installation Program

    Choose each of the following menu selections to configure
    the way in which OO Development will be installed on your
    system.


        Edit destination paths  : \OOBOOK
        Select destination drive: C:
        Toggle overwrite mode   : Overwrite All
        Select groups to install
        Start installation


              ───── Item Description ─────
        Allows you to edit each of the destination paths.



 Press [Alt-X] to exit at any time
```

FIGURE P.1   Object-Oriented Development Installation Program Startup Screen.

After the installation is complete, remove your original diskette and store it in a safe place.

USER ASSISTANCE AND INFORMATION

John Wiley & Sons, Inc. is please to provide assistance to users of this software package. Should you have questions regarding the use of this package, please call our technical support number at (212) 850-6194 weekdays between 9 am and 4 pm Eastern Standard Time.

To place additional orders or to request information about other Wiley products, please call (800) 879-4539.

For more information or to place an order for the **Class Library Sources** used in the product, please refer to Appendix A in the user documentation.

Contents

CHAPTER 1
Introduction

"Theory and practice. Not only are the inseparable, *they are the same thing*: Reflections of one another in the product under development."

Jeff Duntemann, *PC Techniques*, Dec/Jan 1991.

1.1   WHY OBJECT ORIENTATION?

I sincerely believe that the successful software developers of this decade will be the ones that learn the secrets of productivity. One of those secrets is object-oriented development, not just programming, but analysis and design as well.

We've all heard about the promise of massive productivity gains from object-oriented programming. Usually, we hear about this boost coming from reusability. There are other, unsung, productivity benefits from object-oriented development. One such benefit is the reduction of overhead through minimization of the semantic gap between the "real world" and the program. The productivity bonuses from the reduced semantic gaps come in all the activities of development: analysis, design, and programming.

Object orientation is not a programming language. It is not a magic solution to all programming problems. It does not even require an object-oriented programming language. Object orientation is a style. Instead of treating a program as a series of tasks that work on data, the object engineer treats the program as a collection of independent objects cooperating with one another. In a way, each object is like a miniature program with its own data, functions, and purpose.

1.2   ABOUT METHODOLOGIES, STRATEGIES, NOTATIONS, AND STUFF LIKE THAT

I hear the word "methodology" about a hundred times a month. I still haven't been able to pin down a definition that captures the essence of the word. A methodology encompasses notations, strategies, development models, philosophies, and techniques.

Because object orientation is a new idea, there is not yet a single predominant "object-oriented methodology." Computer professionals still have a multitude of opinions on "the best" notation, strategy, development model, or life cycle mode for object-oriented development. Instead of presenting "the best" or "only real" object-oriented methodology, I'll present some alternatives, where to find more information on those alternatives, and focus on the similarities among the choices rather than the differences. Then I'll present my personal favorite notations and discuss strategies for using them in the development of the programs in this book.

1.3   THE NEED FOR OO TOOLS

There are plenty of introductory books on object-oriented design. One notable example is Grady Booch's *Object-Oriented Design With Applications*. According to Booch, three things are needed for a smooth transition to an object-oriented mindset: training, a low-risk first project, and a good set of examples. He goes on to suggest that software development tools are good candidates for first projects.

Booch also provides a list of tools useful in object-oriented design. He suggests:

1. A graphics system that supports object-oriented notation
2. A class browser
3. An incremental compiler
4. A debugger with knowledge of classes
5. A version control tool
6. A class librarian

When I started writing this book, some of these tools for the PC were either not available, too expensive, or inadequate for the serious professional. These included:

- Graphic systems that support object-oriented notation
- Class browsers for C++
- Class librarian

This book provides examples by solving this tool problem. It also presents the design and development of these three tools.

1.4   COMPONENTS OF DEVELOPMENT

Professional programming does not occur in a vacuum. One of the early criticisms of OO programming was the lack of full software engineering support. Object Engineering, the application of software engineering to object-oriented development, is comprised of components which are similar to those of traditional development.

1.4.1   Analysis

Analysis, figuring out what the system is supposed to do, is key to the success of any software development progress. Some of the most frustrating experiences I've had in software development could be traced back to a lack of understanding of exactly what the system was supposed to be accomplishing.

One of the biggest complaints I've had with structured analysis is that the users and domain experts had to be trained in basic "computerese" to read data flow diagrams. An understanding of these diagrams was necessary to catch problems with perceptions of what the system was supposed to do. Object-Oriented Analysis (OOA) techniques address system issues with terms that "non-computer people" can understand. Some of the most significant work to date in the field of Object-Oriented Analysis has been done by Peter Coad and Ed Yourdon.

1.4.2   Design

In 1990, I went to Borland's OOP World Tour in Chicago. While presenting the differences between traditional software development and OO development, the speaker, David Intersimone, said that about 50% more time should be spent on design when using OO techniques. He couldn't give us much guidance on HOW design was done, though; he said that the technology was too young.

When I started my first OO project I read as much about object-oriented design (OOD) as I could get my hands on. I made two discoveries:

1.   Everyone did basically the same thing
2.   They all had different ways of expressing what they did

So I did what everyone else did at the time. I made up an OO notation. My colleagues liked the notation and it worked, but we were the only ones using it. When we began sharing our designs with developers from outside of our group, we discovered that *they* had found a notation that they liked in a magazine [Wasserman, Pircher, Muller]. We decided to use the one from the magazine because it was more likely to be known by more people. A design is no good unless people can understand it.

OOD has matured since 1990, but it is still a maturing technology. In this book I will explain not only the elements of OOD but a few of the common notations for expressing OOD so you can understand and be understood.

1.4.3   OO Programming in C++

In the interest of completeness, I'll give a brief overview of C++ for those readers who don't know the language. It will not be a full tutorial, but after reading that chapter you should be able to read the examples in this book. I'll show how to map the results of OOD to C++ code.

1.4.4   Management and Documentation of OO Projects

OO projects should be managed differently than traditional projects. I'll talk about issues like budgets, schedules, training, and planning. I'll also discuss some of the issues involved in documenting the OO development process discussed, including how the tools in this book can help.

One of the most important parts of managing OO projects is the selection and purchase of software components. In the early days of America, owning your own home meant taking an ax, chopping down a few trees, cutting off the branches, and stacking them together to make a log cabin. People don't do that much any more. Their time is too valuable. Even people who build log cabins for fun use a chain saw.

We cannot afford to build major systems from scratch. The very premise of reusable software parts through object-oriented development is that it will be unnecessary: It is silly to spend hundreds of hours on developing and documenting (and even sillier NOT to document) standard libraries that can be purchased for a few hundred dollars.

If I were building a house, I would get my materials from a lumber yard, not a forest. I'm not about to spend 10,000 hours and eight chapters building database systems and user interface libraries. (They wouldn't be as good as the ones I ended up buying anyway.) If you want to modify and rebuild some of the executable programs provided with this book, you'll need to purchase certain libraries or rewrite some of interfaces for other libraries you choose to purchase. I'll discuss the separation of interface and problem domain classes to facilitate this. I will also discuss the issues involved in the purchase of programs and libraries for OO software development, and I'll show design techniques that will avoid tying your classes to any one vendor's library.

1.5   SUMMARY

Productivity gains from object-oriented development come not only from reusability but from the reduction of the semantic gap between the "real world" and the program.

There is not yet a predominant OO methodology. Several options are available. Later in this book we'll discuss the options in detail.

This book will provide examples of object-oriented development by building the following tools:

- A graphic tool that supports object-oriented notation
- A class browser for C++
- A class librarian

The components of Object Engineering are similar to those of traditional development:

- Analysis
- Object-Oriented Design
- Object-Oriented Programming
- Management and Documentation

CHAPTER 2
The Fundamentals of OO Analysis, Design, and Programming

"Programming is mirroring the world inside a computer."

Larry O'Brien, *Computer Language*, October, 1991.

2.1 INTRODUCTION

This chapter describes Object Engineering. Object Engineering is the application of software engineering principles to object-oriented development. This chapter presents an introduction to the fundamentals of OO Development: classes, objects, inheritance, and polymorphism. The principles of OO system development are discussed with a focus on class design.

Engineers love to build models of things. They build mathematical models, computer models, and physical models. Object orientation is a powerful modeling tool. This chapter presents the basics for using that tool.

2.2 THE MOVE TO OBJECT-ORIENTED TECHNIQUES:

Electrical engineers have Ohm's law. Chemical engineers have the laws of thermodynamics. Mechanical engineers have Newton's laws. Software engineers have Wirth's law: Program = Algorithms + Data Structures. Just as a chemical engineer cannot devise a system in which matter and energy are created or destroyed, a software engineer cannot create a non-trivial program that violates Wirth's law.

Earlier software development techniques, such as structured analysis and design, treated Wirth's law like this:

Program = (Algorithms) + (Data Structures)

The two parts were designed separately with the primary emphasis on the processing performed in the algorithm part. Experience began to show that it was unwise to trivialize the data part. Data flow diagrams and structure charts that focused on the processing and transformation of data proved to be inadequate. As time went on, more and more attention was given to data modeling techniques using tools like entity relationship diagrams. Ultimately treating the data and the functionality as totally separate entities sometimes proved to be unworkable in practice [Coad, Yourdon, 1990, 1991], and some software developers began to treat Wirth's law like this:

Programs = (Algorithms + Data Structures)

This is the basis of object-oriented design and programming. The only thing really new about object-oriented programs is the way they're packaged. (Let's face it, no matter how we perceive the system, when the compiler's done with it, all that's left is nibbles and bits.) This new "packaging" is not a trivial change. Problems are often solved when they're looked at in a different way.

Finally, the "object engineer" describes Wirth's laws like this:

Object = (Algorithms + Data Structures)

Programs = (Object+Object+....)

2.3   OBJECT-ORIENTED TERMS

You should be familiar with the following OO terms. For more details on these terms I refer you to the recommended reading list at the end of this book.

2.3.1   Class

A class describes what something is and what it does. In formal terms, it encapsulates the attributes and behavior of an object. In C++, a class is treated like a user-defined data type.

Classes can be abstract or concrete. Abstract classes are used to describe data and behavior of a family of classes. They are not intended to be used to instantiate objects. In C++, if a class is a purely abstract class, you cannot declare any variables of that type. Abstract classes are sometimes called formal classes.

Concrete classes are where masons go to school. Just kidding. Concrete classes can be used to instantiate objects. For example, in C++ a concrete class can have variables of that type declared.

2.3.2   Attributes

Attributes are the data parts of a class. In C++ these are sometimes called data members. Attributes are the "data structure" part of Wirth's Law.

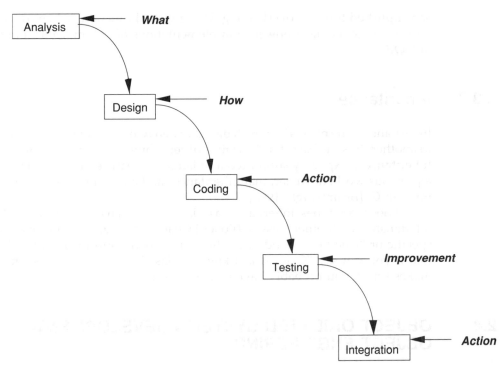

FIGURE 2-1   Traditional waterfall development model.

Note that all three models have the elements I have identified. Since each software project is in some way unique, no single model accurately represents "the best" way to develop software. There are certain development models that support object-oriented styles better than others, but there are always tradeoffs. A good software engineer will pick the model that offers the best representation of the particular problem in question, rather than dogmatically adhering to a method for the method's own sake. Coad and Yourdon point out that their OO techniques can be used with any development model [Coad, Yourdon 1991].

2.4.1.1   Figure Out What You Want to Do

Other engineers have their laws; these are the Laws of Initial Requirements for the software engineer:

1. Users generally start out with only a vague notion of what they want.
2. Even if users think they know what they want, you probably won't understand it.
3. You must help the users figure out what they really want and communicate their requirements to you.

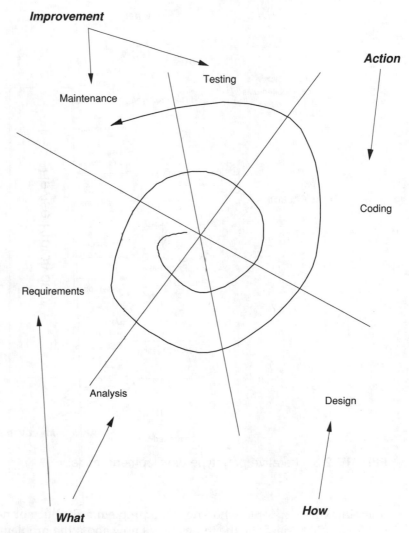

FIGURE 2-2 The spiral model.

4. After you and the users agree on what they want, the users will change their minds.

How do we help users figure out what they want and tell us about it? The process of figuring out what the system is supposed to do is called *analysis*. Analysis typically starts with some sort of list of initial requirements. The analyst (who may or may not also be the designer and programmer) helps the users clarify their needs.

In object-oriented analysis (OOA), the analyst asks the potential users and

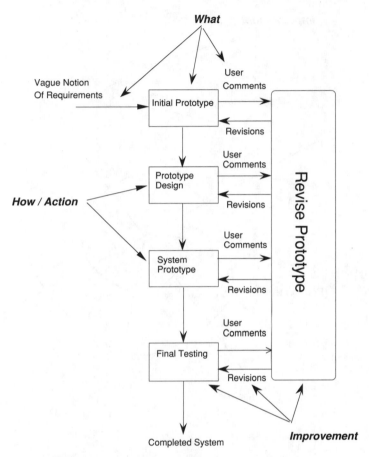

FIGURE 2-3   Iterative prototype development model.

domain experts (people who know the problem area, but not necessarily "computer stuff"), to describe the things they know about the problem. These "things" are candidates for classes and objects. The descriptions of the things become the attributes. The analyst also asks, "What do these things do?" and "What needs to be done to these things?" The answers to these questions will provide clues to methods and services. Analysis will be discussed in more detail in Chapter 3.

2.4.1.2   Figure Out How You Want to Do It

After you figure out what you want to do, you must figure out how you want to do it. This is called design.

When I do OOD, my first step is to get the initial list of candidate classes. Depending on how the analysis is done, this may mean I have to create the list from the analysis documents. When I make this list, I always come up with a lot of questions that I didn't think about during the analysis, so I generally go back and ask more questions about the requirements. Booch calls this "Identifying Classes and Objects" [Booch 1991].

Next, I make a first stab at exactly what the objects are and what they do. Booch calls this the "Identification of Semantics" [Booch]. Please note that if the analysis is done well, these two steps should take very little time.

Now that I have some idea of the candidate classes and objects, I begin to revise the list and the things in the list. I play with potential class hierarchies. Up until now, I've been adding things to the list. Now I look for things to take out. Booch suggests identifying relationships at this point.

Once the list is fairly stable, I get into a little more detail about the design of the individual classes. In the Chapter 4, I'll go into more detail about design in general and object-oriented design in particular.

2.4.1.3   Do It

A design without a program is at best an academic exercise, and at worst a serious waste of somebody's time and money. Sooner or later somebody's got to program the thing. I should end this section by just saying, "you have to program it," but I won't.

Usually, the problem is getting to this stage too soon. Too, often OOP is used as an excuse not to design: It's new, it's improved, it's the greatest thing since sliced bread. We can throw all the old stuff like design out the window (NOT !!!).

OOP is a style, not a language. It is possible, although often difficult, to write procedural code in even a "pure" object-oriented language. (I've seen it done in Actor; it's not pretty.) OOP can be accomplished in non-OOP languages like C [Brumbaugh, 1990]. OOP languages make implementing the OOP style easier.

To be object-oriented, the program must have "objects" with inheritance, encapsulation of code, and data and polymorphism.

If OOA and OOD are used in the system definition and design, the translation of design into OOP code should be intuitive. Note that I did not say "easy," but the translation should be easier to understand. I'll go into this more in a later chapter.

2.4.1.4   Make It Better

Your program isn't going to be perfect. Every model of development recognizes this. The waterfall model places maintenance at the bottom of the list. The iterative prototype model has improvement built into every step. This activity may include debugging, revising requirements, altering the design, creating a new version of the program with enhancements, or any combination of all of these things. Improvement can occur during any phase or as a phase by itself.

A popular form of improvement in OO development is prototype development. A prototype is built from "stock" objects. The object engineer analyzes weaknesses in the prototype and determines the need for change for one or more of the following: requirements, design, or code. A new prototype, better than the previous prototype, is constructed and the process continues.

2.5   SUMMARY

Object engineering is the application of software engineering principles to object-oriented development.

The fundamental components of object-oriented development include classes, objects, inheritance, and polymorphism.

A *class* describes what something is and what it does.
An *attribute* is the data in a class.
A *method* is the behavior of a class.
An *object* contains the information described by a class. It also performs the behaviors defined in a class. This is called the encapsulation of attributes and behaviors.
Polymorphism refers to functions that have the same name, but different behavior.
Inheritance is the means by which data and behavior are transferred from one class to another.

No matter what development model you use, you will perform the following activities:

1. Figure Out What You Want To Do—Analysis
2. Figure Out How You Want To Do It—Design
3. Do It—Write The Program
4. Make It Better—Debug, Enhance, Maintain, Support

In object engineering, analysis consists of identifying actual things the system needs to deal with. Design consists of mapping those things into a programmable form. Writing the program consists of translating the design into code. OO programs must have objects that have inheritance, encapsulation of code, and data and polymorphism. The object engineer often builds improvement into development by prototyping.

CHAPTER 3
Managing and Documenting OO Development

"Demonstrating respect for others is the cornerstone for improving communications among people."

Neal Whitten, *Managing Software Development Projects*, 1990,
John Wiley & Sons, New York.

3.1   INTRODUCTION

This chapter discusses the key issues involved in managing OO development: methodology selection, training and staffing, costs, planning and scheduling, and productivity. Issues involved in documenting this process are discussed, including how the tools in this book can help.

Management is about helping people do a good job. People can't do a good job if they don't know what they are supposed to be doing. Clear communication is the key to good management. The primary advantage of Object Engineering over traditional techniques is its clarity of expression. Since objects represent real things, there is less of an intuitive leap from the problem to the representation in analysis, design, and programming with Object Engineering than there is with traditional development. By "intuitive leap" I refer to the intense brain work that normally occurs between traditional programming phases.

3.2   CHOOSING A METHODOLOGY

A methodology is more than just a set of graphical notation standards or a set of rules for defining how those standards are used; it consists of philosophies, development models, strategies, and notation styles. One principle of software engineering is that any software development process should be defined and repeatable. A methodology is the set of rules and guidelines intended to make the development process defined and repeatable.

I'm not going to hand you a canned methodology that you can simply lift from the pages of this book and plug into your organization. Instead, I will describe the components of methodologies which will help you to assemble your own.

3.2.1   Philosophies

There are several philosophies permeating the OO field. For example:

1. Old problems should not need to be continually resolved. Therefore, designs should be reusable.
2. Programmers should not spend time rewriting the same programs. Therefore, code should be reusable.
3. Software should model the real world.
4. There should not be a large semantic gap between the domain experts and the software development team.

You may choose any or all of these philosophies or make up some of your own.

3.2.2   Development Models

A development model defines the steps or phases followed during the development process. It also defines the transitions between phases. When discussing development models, remember that they are only models, and all models have limits. When the model fails, it's time to use intuition.

Different development models have different strengths and weaknesses. Some models may be more appropriate than others, depending on the specific project. Below is a list of criteria to be used in selecting a development model. Not all criteria will apply to all projects. Additionally, other project-specific criteria are likely to surface.

Typical Criteria for Selecting a Development Model
- Development Team's Familiarity with Application
- Probability of Changes During Development
- Degree of Customer Involvement During Development
- The Need for Customer to Give and Receive Feedback
- Contractual Considerations

- Familiarity With Target Platform
- Familiarity With Development Platform

As I pointed out in Chapter 2, all development models have four components: *what, how, action* and *improvement*. You may look back at Figures 2-1, 2-2, and 2-3 to see the diagrams of these models. Here is a list of when some models are most appropriate:

Development Models and When They Are Most Appropriate

Traditional Waterfall (Figure 2-1)
Most likely valid when:
- Little or no change is expected in the requirements during the life of the project
- Application domain is very familiar, for example, enhancements to an existing system
- Low risk project, for example, target and development environments are familiar
- Customer involvement is to be low except in the early phases
- Procedural programming language is to be used

Spiral Model (Figure 2-2)
Most likely valid when:
- Using OOP language or fourth generation languages
- Changes early in the life of the project are probable
- Customer is to be somewhat involved through the life of the project
- Application domain is somewhat familiar
- Medium risk project, for example, target and development environments are somewhat familiar

Iterative Prototyping Model (Figure 2-3)
Most likely valid when:
- Using OOP language or fourth generation languages
- Changes through out the entire life of the project are probable
- Customer is to be very involved through the life of the project
- Application domain is unfamiliar
- High risk project

3.2.3   Strategy

Strategy is how you go about "attacking" your problem. The basic strategy of all software development is simple: "Divide and conquer." But how do you decide where to start dividing? The development model you choose will be the primary strategic decision. Other strategic decisions will be guided by your philosophies, goals, budget, and schedule. Here are some strategic decisions you'll need to make in OO development:

1. How tightly do you want your application to be bound to a specific user interface style, library or platform?
2. How tightly do you want your application to be bound to a particular DBMS?
3. Which programming language should you use?
4. In which order should you develop your system's classes?
5. How much time, energy and money do you put into making your classes reusable?
6. Which development model do you use? If you use an iterative model, how finely do you break up your iterations?
7. How much separation do you want between analysis, design, and programming?

3.2.4   Notation

3.2.4.1   Common Features of OO Notations

Graphical representations help designers, programmers, users and domain experts see how the components of a software system fit together. Any OO notation must contain symbols for the following:

- Classes—Should Include Data and Functionality
- Objects (Instances of Classes)
- Inheritance
- Communication and Relationships Between Objects and Classes

Since traditional structured notations are inadequate for representing OO ideas, several OO pioneers have proposed new notations. Figure 3-1 displays how some of the most common OO notations represent the concepts listed above. The *Booch* notation comes from Grady Booch's book on OOD [Booch]. The *Coad and Yourdon* notation comes from Peter Coad and Ed Yourdon's books on OOA and OOD [Coad, Yourdon, 1990,91] [Coad, Yourdon, 1991]. *OOSD* notation comes from several articles in various computer publications [Wasserman, Pircher, Muller].

In general, the Booch notation is the most complex, followed by OOSD. The Coad and Yourdon notation is the simplest. To date, the industry has not standardized notation, so you may encounter one or more of these notations during your work. There are other notations as well, but these are the three most practical for use in the analysis and design chapters.

OO diagrams are typically accompanied by templates (or forms) that describe the classes, attributes, and methods. These templates provide a level of necessary detail that would clutter a diagram.

Another thing these notations have in common is that they are model independent. Unlike structured analysis and design, different types of diagrams are not necessary for different phases of development. You can construct diagrams

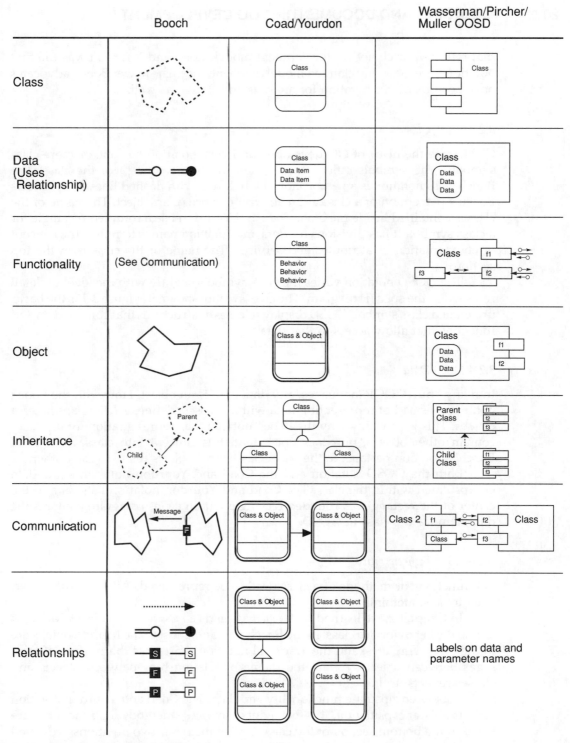

FIGURE 3-1 Common object oriented notations.

that reflect your choice of development model. Coad and Yourdon was the first notation I ever saw that claimed model independence. The newer Booch advocates have been using his notation for analysis and design as well.

3.2.4.1.1   *Classes*

Classes are the heart of OO development. Every notation has one or more class symbols. The symbols reflect the notation inventor's concept of the class. The Booch class notation is an amorphous blob drawn with dashed lines. This reflects Booch's perception of a class as an abstract essence of an object. The name of the class is contained inside the blob. Coad and Yourdon use a rounded rectangle for a class symbol. It has divisions for data and function names to reflect the concept of encapsulation of attributes and services. The name of the class is in the top section.

The OOSD notation varies the class symbols slightly with the level of detail reflected in the specific diagram. The class symbol shown in Figure 3-1 is the basic, undetailed class symbol. OOSD displays classes as structures that contain data and functions that allow access to that data.

3.2.4.1.2   *Data*

In many "pure" OOP languages, any data item is an object. However, the Booch notation, instead of representing data within classes, defines *relationships between* classes. This is probably why the Booch notation has representation for *objects* to contain other objects, but does not extend this concept into classes. Much of Booch's notation pertains to the ways classes and objects relate to each other.

Both the OOSD notation and the Coad and Yourdon notation show data encapsulated within the class. The Coad and Yourdon notation lists data in the center of the rectangle. A rounded rectangle within a class diagram contains the data item for the class in OOSD.

3.2.4.1.3   *Functionality*

The functions or methods of a class need to be represented. After all, the objects need to *do* something.

In Chapter 2, we learned that a *method* sends a *message* to an object. Methods define the behavior of a class. In the Booch notation, most of the method details are in the class templates, and the graphical notation represents the passing of messages between objects. Again, the theme of relationships between objects and classes repeats itself.

Classes encapsulate functionality and data. The Coad and Yourdon notation reflects this encapsulation. The behaviors (services, methods, or functions) are listed in the bottom section of the class. Unlike the other two notations presented here, there is no explicit differentiation between interface and implementation methods in the Coad and Yourdon notation. Since the notation originated with analysis rather than detailed design, the primary emphasis is on externally-observable behaviors, i.e. public methods.

Classes hide their data from the rest of the program. Methods provide an interface to the data within a class. The OOSD notation reflects this concept by depicting methods as boxes that overlap the inside and outside the class boundaries. Wasserman's OOSD notation reflects this as well. It uses small arrows as symbols for parameters, much like traditional structure charts.

A class usually has internal functions as well as interfaces. The OOSD notation depicts internal methods as boxes that are completely enclosed by the class boundary.

3.2.4.1.4   *Objects*

Objects are concrete instances of classes. The Booch notation reflects this concept. It represents objects as classes with solid lines instead of broken lines. The name of the object (as opposed to the name of the class) is contained in the object.

Some classes are never instantiated into objects. These classes exist for the sole purpose of providing ancestors for other classes. Coad and Yourdon differentiate between classes with objects and classes without objects by drawing a thick gray line around the class symbols with objects.

The OOSD notation does not have a specific symbol for an object that differentiates it from a class. OOSD, like the other notations described here, does not require all the information known about an object to be displayed with an object; you only need to show the data and functions of the objects relevant to the area being diagramed.

3.2.4.1.5   *Inheritance*

The Booch and OOSD notations both show inheritance relationships as arrows pointing from the child class to the parent class. The arrow is thick and solid in the former notation, while in the latter, the arrow is made of a broken line. The Coad and Yourdon notation shows inheritance as a line with a semicircle in it. The open end of the semicircle points toward the child class.

None of the notation requires a relative position on the diagram. It is traditional to place the parent classes above the child classes in inheritance diagrams. This is one of the few things everyone agrees on.

3.2.4.1.6   *Communication Between Objects*

Objects communicate with each other by passing messages to each other. All OO notations need to represent this communication. All of the notations discussed here use arrows pointed from the sender to the receiver.

Booch typically shows the messages being passed along relationship lines. The name of the message can be placed along the arrow for clarity. The next section will discuss relationships a little more.

Coad and Yourdon show message connections as thick gray arrows. The ends of the arrows connect at the object layer of the class and object diagram. Again, the message arrow can be labeled for clarity if necessary.

Passing messages between objects and object functionality are closely related enough to be perceived as the same thing. OOSD notation does just that. It uses function call symbols similar to those in traditional structure charts.

3.2.4.1.7   *Relationships Between Objects*

There are several ways of thinking about relationships between objects and classes. The most common type of relationship between classes is the "kind of" relationship. Inheritance relationships show this.

Common relationships between objects include "using" relationships, "part of" relationships and "containing" relationships. OO notations are as diverse on these relationships as any.

Booch specifies how objects are related by noting whether the object is a field, parameter or part of a shared scope. A square with the appropriate letter in the middle denotes how the objects relate to each other. If the square is not filled, it suggests that the two objects share the field, parameter or scope. The Booch notation also describes relationships between classes. Besides inheritance relationships, it shows that classes use other classes with a circle on the using class's edge and a double line connecting to the used class. The circle is open if the using relationship is for the class interface (protocol) and filled if for the implementation.

Coad and Yourdon show two types of relationships between objects; instance relationships and whole-part relationships. Instance relationships are part of the attribute specification in the Coad and Yourdon notation. An instance is a special kind of attribute represented as a single line connecting objects. Whole-part relationships represent objects that are inherently part of another object. A line with a triangle pointing toward the "whole" object represents this type of relationship.

The relationships in OOSD are represented as connections between the data and functions encapsulated within the class. Any additional detail is provided by labels for the arrows and other connections.

3.2.4.1.8   *Other Symbols*

All of the notations have more symbols than just the ones listed in the common list. Each of the notation inventors could perceive different needs to be addressed in OO development, so each of them added more symbols to address those needs. One important concept found in both the Booch and Coad and Yourdon notations is the grouping of related classes together. Booch calls this grouping a "category." Coad and Yourdon call a group of related classes a "subject."

For more details on these notations, see the original sources. These are listed in the recommended reading list at the back of this book.

3.2.5   Notation Summary

Each of the notations listed above has its own strengths and weaknesses. Those strengths and weaknesses are listed below. I also indicate which notation I've selected for use in this book and why.

All of the notations have the following strengths:

1. Each has been developed by a well respected leader in the industry
2. Each has enough symbols to represent OO analysis and design. OO programs can be written using any of these notations.
3. All of them are development model independent.
4. Any of these notations can be used for both analysis and design.

3.2.5.1   Booch Notation

Strengths:
1. The full Booch notation provides a way to graphically model all parts of the system: logical, physical, and temporal. It is a "rich" notation. Just about anything can be represented graphically.
2. The notation is well accepted in the OO community and is supported by several CASE vendors. It has a good chance of becoming a standard.
3. The extended notation supports new OO language features, such as templates.
4. It contains an explicit mechanism for managing large groups of classes: "categories."

Weaknesses:
1. The Booch symbols and notations are very complex. This makes it hard to sketch out an idea on the back of a piece of junk mail using the notation. (This specifically refers to the dotted, amorphous blob that represents a class.)
2. Because of the complexity, no single CASE vendor supports the whole notation.
3. The notation uses a lot of room on a piece of paper and on a screen.
4. Many generic drawing programs can't easily draw many of the essential symbols in the Booch notation.

3.2.5.2   Coad and Yourdon Notation

Strengths:
1. The notation is clear and concise. None of the other notations listed have the same economy of expression.
2. The notation is easy to draw manually. You can sketch ideas on the back of a piece of junk mail using this notation.
3. It contains an explicit mechanism for managing large groups of classes: "subjects."

TABLE 3-1. Types of Training Needed by People in OO Development

Role	Training Required
System Architects, Project Leaders	General OO Techniques, Reusability, OO Analysis (and usually Design), High-Level Case Tools, Overview of Compilers and Other Tools
Model Builders	OOP Languages and Compilers, Domain-Specific Training, Prototyping Tools, OO Analysis and Design
Interface Builders	Operating Systems, Hardware/Software Details, Interface Libraries, OOP Languages and Compilers, OO Design (and usually Analysis)
Component Builders	OOP Languages & Compilers, OO Design (and usually Analysis)

4.   The notation is well accepted in the OO community. It has a good chance of becoming a standard.
5.   All the symbols are available in most generic drawing programs.
Weaknesses:
1.   There are no mechanisms to represent certain language-specific features (such as templates and utility functions).
2.   The notation focuses primarily upon relationships between objects and classes. There are no specific mechanisms for diagraming internal class methods and their interactions with one another.

3.2.5.3   Wasserman, Pircher and Muller OOSD

Strengths:
1.   The notation allows concise diagraming of interaction of internal and external methods.
2.   It has ties to traditional structured design, so it is likely to gain acceptance within the entire industry.
3.   It provides extensions for language-specific features like templates.
4.   Most generic drawing tools have the symbols used in the notation.
5.   The notation is simple enough to be drawn manually.
6.   It is more concise than the Booch notation.
Weaknesses:
1.   It is less concise than the Coad and Yourdon notation.
2.   It has no explicit mechanism for categorizing classes into subject areas. (Although their definition of the notation recommends automated support to handle this type of complexity.) [Wasserman,Pircher,Muller]
3.   There is no clear distinction between objects and classes.

3.2.5.4   And the Winner is . . .

Although each of the notations is good in its own right, I've chosen the Coad and Youdon notation for the projects in this book.

I rejected the Booch notation for two reasons:

1. I don't like the amorphous blobs. They're hard to draw, and they look "messy."
2. I didn't want to generate reams of paper to describe the systems we're building.

That left OOSD and Coad and Yourdon. I almost selected the OOSD notation for its ability to represent internal class mechanisms, but I selected Coad and Yourdon for the following reasons:

1. I believe the concept of "subject" is important. OOSD has no clear "subject" notation.
2. It is the most concise notation with the best economy of expression.
3. Object International has a CASE Tool, OOATool, which costs less than $100 and supports the notation. I used OOATool for some of the early Coad and Yourdon diagrams in this book.

3.3   TRAINING AND STAFFING

If your organization is new to OO technology, you and your staff will need training. Here, we'll discuss the types and sources of training needed to shift into an object orientation.

3.3.1   Topics Covered During Training by Staff Position

There are certain concepts common to all OO development. General training will help you and your staff get an overview of the concepts of OO development. General training should include coverage of encapsulation, inheritance, polymorphism, and reusability. The topics covered in Chapter 2 are examples of the types of things that should be addressed in basic OO training.

Managers and senior technical staff should have general training in OO technology. Other technical staff should have general training as a precursor to more specific training. The biggest problem with general training is that it often emphasizes the advantages of OO without mentioning potential drawbacks. Managers are given unrealistic productivity expectations, and consequently they tend to place the blame for failure on "lazy" programmers. These unrealistic expectations are often the products of "Free Training Seminars" which are, in fact, sales pitches.

Specific training should include in-depth converge of the topics above. Common types of specific training are language classes, training on analysis, design, and management.

Table 3-1 shows the types of training required by people who play various roles in the organization. The roles listed are typical and will, of course, vary from organization to organization. Here's a short explanation of the roles listed.

3.3.1.1   System Architects and Project Managers

These are the people with the "whole picture" of the system. They envision the high-level classes and the important relationships between them. They often work with the users and clients to find out exactly what they want. This is not a job for the inexperienced or the cybernetically ignorant. If your organization is new to object orientation, this individual should be experienced in your organization's methodology. He or she should be open to new ideas and should look for ways to fit the new ideas into your organization. This category also covers the analysts and designers, if you choose to separate the roles or the individuals.

3.3.1.2   Model Builders

Ideally, model builders should make up the majority of your staff or, in the case of a small staff, model building should make up the majority of the work. These people work with the users and domain experts to model the problem domain with classes and objects. They work on "the real" application using existing libraries, utility functions, and classes.

3.3.1.3   Interface Builders

Even if you purchase libraries for user and database interfaces, you should have one or two experts able to create subclasses specific to your applications. In larger organizations these could be support positions, providing classes to model builders as necessary.

3.3.1.4   Component Builders

In smaller organizations, component builders may be the same people as the interface builders. The difference is that component builders create and maintain platform-independent utility classes. Again, you will probably want to purchase commercial components and specialize them to your needs via inheritance.

3.3.1.5   Staffing Summary

To sum up, you should have four basic roles in your OO organization: Component Builders, Model Builders, Interface Builders, and Designers and/or Managers. You can divide up these roles in whatever way best suits your organization. You should focus your attention and staffing on model building with class reuse.

3.3.2   Training Sources

Ok, we need training. Where do we get it?

3.3.2.1   Colleges and Universities

Check with nearby schools. Most colleges and universities have computer science departments. Most of them also have instructors who will provide training in continuing education programs. You should check the qualifications and experience of the instructor before making any commitments. Occasionally, state funding may be available for specific individuals or for your entire company.

For individuals, the major advantages of training from colleges and universities are cost and availability. Often, there will be state discounts, incentives, or money for instruction from local institutes of higher learning. Most of the time, instructors will be available during the summer and vacation times. You also may be able to enroll in regular classes.

3.3.2.2   Seminars and Special Classes

Many companies offer OO training. There is a list of some companies that provide seminar training along with some comments in Appendix A. Be certain that the material covered matches the needs of your organization. Sometimes special events and seminars are held. If you subscribe to magazines or journals that include OO articles, you're likely to be flooded with information about seminars.

A note about "free" seminars: Typically, companies will offer free seminars to get you to buy their product. This doesn't imply that the information you gain from these seminars is not valid, it simply means that certain claims made by the seminar sponsors should be considered with this in mind.

The major advantage of seminars and special classes comes from the people you meet there. Most seminars have opportunities for socialization, small groups, and questions. These are chances to meet people from all over and exchange ideas and information.

3.3.2.3   Consultants

Consultants are the most flexible, and often most expensive, option for training. If you have the budget for it, nothing is better for your organization than an expert who can teach you about OO development with a focus on your unique problems. There is also nothing worse than a poorly prepared so-called expert, who has no respect for the specific needs of your organization. Interestingly enough, I could be describing the same person consulting for different organizations. To get the most from a consultant, plan to spend the time and money to explain your wants and needs. A good consultant will be willing to spend the "up front" time to learn about you and your organization. The difference between a good consultant and a poor consultant is how well your needs are met. A consultant can meet your needs better if he or she understands them.

You should, of course, check the credentials and get the references of anyone you're considering hiring.

3.3.2.4   Self-Teaching Media

Of course, you don't have to go anywhere to learn about OO development. Plenty of material is available to help you teach yourself. Some of these media include:

- Video Tapes
- Books
- Software
- On-line Services

See the recommended reading list in Appendix C for more details.

3.4   OTHER COSTS

> "The costs of changing to an OO paradigm are quite correctly perceived as being very high—not necessarily in hardware or software, but rather in staff training, conversion of applications, and the impact on the organization." [Wasserman, 1991]

The costs of the types of training listed above vary from the trivial to the extreme, but the real cost is in the "down time," the time the people are not productive while they are learning. This "double hit" makes it the single most expensive part of moving to object orientation. This section discusses some other costs involved.

3.4.1   Case Tools

Since CASE stands for "Computer Aided Software Engineering," I define CASE as any software or hardware/software combination that aids in the specification, definition, or construction of software or simplifies communication among the parties involved in the development process.

When considering the costs of new development tools, the initial price tag is only a small part of the cost. It is an unfortunate myth that a high price is the assurance of high quality. The value of a tool includes its productivity bonus, ease of learning, ease of use, technical support, and the vendor's upgrade policy. Often an efficient company can provide the best of these at a low cost, while an inefficient company will charge more for less.

Booch lists some tools that he feels are helpful in OO development. [Booch] I'd like to discuss some of those tools in a little more detail here.

3.4.1.1 Graphic Tools

The graphic tools will be used mostly during analysis and design. The documents created by the tool will be used during programming, prototyping, and testing. This tool should allow the developer to represent classes, inheritance, data, and functionality in an OO graphic notation. The graphic tool should be more than a drawing program. (Although a good drawing program beats some of the CASE tools I've used.) It should tie to descriptions of objects, classes, and, ultimately, to their source code. Often, this is done through access to a browser. Personally, I don't like graphic tools that enforce rules of "good" design. The artificial enforcement interferes with creativity and company policy. If you choose a tool that enforces rules, make sure they are rules you can live with.

Ideally the tool should support more than one notation, and it should even support traditional structured notation. You never know when you may need to interface with a non-OO system.

If you have more than one person on your development team, you should seriously consider a multiuser system. PC-based systems should have LAN support, which is generally less expensive per station for smaller companies than a minicomputer-based, X-Windows solution.

Each notation listed above is supported by at least one company. Each of the CASE tools they support is more than just a drawing tool. Appendix B lists the sources of some of these tools.

3.4.1.2 Browsers

Browsers are multi-windowed programs that allow developers to navigate class hierarchies. They typically allow direct access to the source code of the class for editing. Most often, browsers are used during coding, however a browser with a good search function is beneficial for finding reusable codes during design. I'm aware of a couple of C++ browsers for MS-Windows and one for DOS. Most of the time, browsers are part of a development package; they don't usually come as stand-alone programs. There are several browsers available for UNIX X-Windows that are part of a more comprehensive CASE package. Some PC-based browsers come with compilers, editors, or class libraries. Appendix B lists some products and the companies that sell or provide C++ class browsers.

3.4.1.3 Librarian

Classes that are not used are not usually reusable. As class inventories grow, you need some way to find the ones you can use. The librarian is a tool that allows for the selection of classes, functions, and their descriptions by whatever criteria are necessary. It also allows for the addition, editing, and deletion of these class descriptions. Most often the librarian is used in design to enhance reuse.

3.4.2   Components

OO evangelists promised increased productivity due to a plethora of reliable off-the-shelf components that could be easily assembled into a complete system. Unfortunately at the time those claims were made, not too many components were available "off-the-shelf." Today, we have more components available. Since this book concentrates on C++, you can assume that unless otherwise noted, any specifics discussed below are for the C++ language.

If you plan to build all your own software, you're missing the OO boat. Most programs contain a significant amount of code that is not much different from the code found in many other programs. You can buy those common components, and concentrate on the code that makes your program unique. What if your program needs changes in the areas normally considered "common?" Unlike traditional function libraries, object-oriented class libraries allow customization via inheritance.

3.4.2.1   Which Types of Components?

I organize classes into six categories. Any given class can fall into several categories. For example, the C++ stream classes are both data transformers and device interfaces. Here are the categories:

- Primitives—Numbers, Characters, and Other "Atomic" Values
- Container Classes—Classes for Holding Groups of Objects
- Computer Interface—Data Base Managers, User Interfaces, Communications, Other Device Interfaces
- Data Transformers—Classes that take data, change it, and pass it on
- Models—Simulations of "Real World" Things
- Adapters—Classes that combine two or more previously unrelated classes

The first category of classes, the primitives, usually comes with the compiler. Although technically primitives are defined by only the language, any class that has a full scope of numeric operations like complex or binary coded decimals belong in this category. Math classes are fairly common. If your applications are mathematically intensive, I suggest you invest in one of them.

Container classes are probably the most commonly available types of classes. Most of them are based in some way on the Smalltalk container classes. Many C++ containers are based on the "template class" concepts. Every OO developer needs a good set of containers.

The next most commonly available classes are the device interface classes. These are classes that allow the program to interface to the rest of the system. They include user interface classes, data base interface classes, and serial port interface classes. These classes are usually the most costly in terms of the initial investment, but they provide the most opportunity for reuse. If you only invest in one category of classes, this is the category I recommend.

Data transformers include things like parsers that take streams of characters and transform them into meaningful tokens. Commercial data transformers are somewhat less common than commercial containers and device interface classes. This category of classes is often more closely connected to the application domain than the previously discussed classes. Therefore, you'll be more likely to be building these types of classes. It's always important to design classes for reuse, but this category is one that you'll be likely to need to reuse more.

Models are at the heart of OO development. This is where you should spend most of your application development time. This is not to imply that the other categories are unimportant, but rather that you can concentrate on the real-world problem you're trying to solve.

Adapters provide platform and library independence. Often, adapters use multiple inheritance to do their jobs. Usually adapters are built to help otherwise incompatible commercial classes to work together.

3.4.2.2   Selection Criteria

OK, you're convinced you need to invest in a couple of commercial libraries. You've got a catalog listing the latest and greatest class libraries. You look through the list at the most expensive ones only because they're the best, right? Wrong! Oh, then they must all be the same, so just get the least expensive one, right? Wrong again. Here is a list of features to look for when considering class libraries. (Many of these criteria apply to other types of software as well.)

1. *Sufficient Trial Period.* You won't know if a library suits your needs until you try it. Thirty days is the minimum acceptable trial period and sixty days is more appropriate.
2. *Upgrade Policy.* Look at the company's history of upgrades. Have they charged exorbitant prices for each minor enhancement fix, or have they provided free maintenance upgrades?
3. *Source Code.* You should have the source code for every part of your product. The company that publishes the library may go out of business. The code may have a bug that can't wait for the next maintenance release. If you need to create a child class, seeing how the parent class performs its duties can be a very valuable time saver. If the source code is unavailable or costs too much, consider a competing product.
4. *Technical Support.* If you plan to support your customers, then you should have the support of your vendors. Some vendors provide free support for a year or more after the purchase. Others begin charging immediately. Remember, count the cost of support when considering your investment.
5. *Licensing and Royalties.* Be sure the licence agreement allows you to use the classes for your intended purpose. Royalties will eat a small company alive, not only in direct costs but in the additional record keeping and administrative costs.

6. *Documentation.* Check this out during your trial period. Is it well in-dexed? Is it logically arranged? Are both on-line and paper documenta-tion provided? (This is important. You still can't take on-line documen-tation to the bathroom.)

7. *Completeness and Extensibility.* Is the class complete enough? Can you easily extend it through inheritance? Check this out during your evalu-ation period.

8. *Portability and Platform Specific Support.* This is especially important for device interface classes. Is the class library available for all the platforms you currently need? Will it be available for platforms you intend to support in the future?

9. *Does It Meet Your Needs?* It's almost too obvious to state, but, most importantly, if the class library doesn't meet your needs, it's pretty useless.

3.5   PLANNING AND SCHEDULING

As I said in a previous chapter, each software project is in some way unique, so no single model accurately represents "the best" way to develop software. It is possible, and sometimes desirable, to use the waterfall model for OO develop-ment. More often it seems that OO developers prefer the iterative prototype model. So this section will discuss planning and scheduling in general and focus on planning and scheduling OO development using the iterative prototype model.

3.5.1   Important OO Planning Tasks

3.5.1.1   Reuse

You have heard it said, I am sure, that OO software is reusable. That statement alone is not totally accurate. OO software lends itself more readily to reuse than does procedural programming. That reuse is not automatic, however. You have to plan for reuse in all phases of any development.

No matter what development model you use, you should plan for reuse in the *What* and *How* phases and be sure the plans are implemented in the *Action* and *Improvement* phases. In analysis, look to other programs in the same problem do-main, and try to define new classes so you can reuse them in future programs. In design you make more detailed choices that allow for practical as well as concep-tual reuse. By allowing time in the analysis and design schedules to plan for reuse, you can consistently improve productivity during programming and testing.

3.5.1.2   Class Reviews

Structured walk throughs don't go away during OO development, they change focus. This is obviously a good place to examine possibilities for reuse. Class names, data member names, and function names should combine to make classes self documenting. Early in analysis, some of these walk throughs should include users and domain experts. During design, programmers should be included in the walk throughs.

Allow time in the schedule to walk through each class hierarchy. Concentrate on the problem domain classes during analysis, and other classes during design.

3.5.2   Scheduling for the Iterative Prototype Model

An often-asked question of proponents of the iterative prototype model is, "How do you know when you'll be done?" That's a fair question. Frankly, in practice one can prototype forever if the process is not well planned.

The key to planning in this model is to treat each iteration as a miniature project. Each iteration builds on and improves the previous prototype. In your first iteration, during the analysis, identify as many key classes as possible. Divide the program into its major features. The first prototype will contain the base upon which to build subsequent features. Each subsequent prototype consists of the addition of features by implementing new key classes and modifying previous ones. Plan the total number of iterations by determining when each of the key classes and features will be implemented. Set target dates for the completion of each iteration. Your completion date is when you plan to complete the last iteration.

Allow time for analysis, design, coding, testing, and revision in each iteration. Plan which classes will be designed and coded, but be aware that your increased understanding of the problem will lead to the discovery of the need for new classes, or extreme modifications of existing classes. Allow buffer time for this in your project plan. Before beginning a new iteration, the analysis and design documents, source code for the prototype, executables, and planned revisions in the next prototype should be "frozen," preferably with some form of source code control system.

Figure 3-2 has a template for a project schedule using the iterative prototype model. The items enclosed in angle brackets, <>, are project, or class, specific items.

The initial requirements analysis helps clarify exactly what the users expect from the program. It helps you develop an initial understanding of what is expected. Note that there is an initial prototype created at the end of this phase. This should be a menu with a few major screens, it should reflect your current understanding of the requirements.

After the initial analysis, you can schedule the rest of the project. Schedule milestones based on features. A "focal" area can be a milestone with all the features and attendant classes. A "subject" makes a good focal area. The activities between milestones can shift around a bit, but try not to let the milestones slip.

The first round of analysis will probably be the longest. This is where you try to identify all the major classes in the system. In each subsequent iteration, you focus on a particular area so you can find the classes that have been left out. You review the current prototype for ideas at the beginning of the phase. At the end of each small analysis, you may want to revise the design plan. This may cause

Activity	Who	Hours	Planned Start	Planned End

Initial Requirements Analysis:
    User interviews
    Domain expert interviews
    Create initial requirements list
        Develop list of required features
        Develop list of constraints
        Modify list of requirements
        Identify optional and future features
    Create initial prototype
OO Analysis <First Iteration:Full System Overview, Successive Iterations: Focal Area>
    Review prototype
        Identify changes
        Revise requirements
    Brain storming session
        Identify potential classes & objects
        Identify attributes & behaviors
        Identify initial relationships
    Revise class list
        Remove unnecessary classes
        Identify and add new classes
        Expand/define attributes and behaviors
        Identify & revise relationships
    Wrap up OOA
        Identify potential problem areas
        Clarify any ambiguities
        Resolve outstanding issues
    Revise design plan
OO Design (Focus on <Feature or Class Group>)
    Identify classes in focal area
    Requirements and analysis review
    Refine focal classes
        Search for reusable classes
        Identify existing hierarchies
        Create new hierarchies
        Refine protocol
    <For Each Class...>
        Design the protocol
            <details>
        Design implementation
            <details>
        Class design review
    Review relationships
        Within focal area
        Outside focal area
Program <Focal Area>
    <For Each Class>
        <Build/Revise Class Definition>
        <Build/Revise Each Method>
    Integrate into current prototype & test
Milestone (Prototype with planned features)
<Choose New Focal Area and Repeat From Analysis Until All Features Added>

FIGURE 3-2 Template for scheduling iterative prototype development.

scheduling problems. If features are more difficult than originally planned, you may want to remove them or defer them to a later prototype. The analysis and design chapters have more details on these activities.

3.6   PRODUCTIVITY

If you've been in this business for any significant period of time, you know of the enormous backlog of software development projects. Object orientation is, among other things, an attempt to reduce this backlog by increasing productivity.

3.6.1   Sources of Productivity

Where does productivity come from? The first productivity gain is in analysis, where the analysis team can relate to the information providers in their own language (see the next chapter). During design and programming, the productivity gains come from reuse.

To get this productivity boost from reuse you need a catalog or library of classes ready for reuse. If you avoid the "not invented here" syndrome and make wise purchases of commercial components, you can focus on your product instead of constantly "reinventing the . . . ," well, you know.

Don't expect productivity gains on your first OO project; there will be learning curves and mistakes. Take this into account when choosing and planning your first project. (Despite the learning curve, I was surprised at the high productivity on my first OO project.)

3.6.2   OO Quality

One of the keys to productivity is quality. The key to OO quality is the assertion that a high-quality system can be built only from high-quality parts.

A Software Quality Assurance (SQA) plan for OO systems differs little from SQA plans for traditional systems. You should still do inspections, tests, and defect tracking. Instead of inspecting functions and sub-systems, you would inspect classes and subjects. Defects, their causes and their resolutions should be cataloged for each class.

3.7   DOCUMENTATION

3.7.1   Types of Documentation

Your choice of development model and notation will affect the details, but your OO project should have the following types of documentation:

1. *Schedule/Workplan*—Instead of planning the production of functions and modules, as in traditional development, you plan the production and modification of classes and objects.

2. *System Overview Diagrams*—You need some kind of high-level view of the system. This will be notation dependent. You need to have a single page diagram that gives a clear picture of what the system is supposed to do. You may also have overviews of subsystems.

3. *Class Hierarchies*—There will be several of these in your project documentation. You will have one or more for each of the major features in your program. The details will be notation dependent.

4. *Class and Object Definition Diagrams*—These diagrams show the internals of objects and classes. They may also show non-inheritance relationships with other classes and objects.

5. *Object Communication Diagrams*—Objects communicate with each other by passing messages. These diagrams represent the specific communication necessary to accomplish the tasks you require.

6. *Diagram Narratives*—Some diagrams listed above may require additional textual descriptions. Include them with each diagram as necessary.

7. *Class Descriptions*—These are textual descriptions of the classes. They should include the name, ancestors, purpose, data items, and functionality of each class in the system. The descriptions should also include details on the data items, including data type, common i/o format, purpose, and source.

8. *Method and Function Descriptions*—These should include name, parameters, purpose, and maybe logic tables or pseudo-code. In methods, they should also include the name of the class that owns them.

9. *Traditional Diagrams*—You may choose not to use "pure" OO techniques and notations. You may want or need to add entity-relationship diagrams, data flow diagrams, or structure charts. You should use these to supplement your OO development, and take care not to "fall back" to using only the old techniques.

3.7.2   How the Tools in This Book Can Help

The tools developed in the latter two-thirds of this book will allow you to produce OO project documentation. These tools are:

1. *Librarian*—The librarian will be able to store and access class, function, and method descriptions. You will be able to print these descriptions to store with your project documentation.

2. *Graphic Design Tool*—This tool will allow you develop and produce the diagrams listed above. There will also be connections to the library through the browser.

3.8   SUMMARY

This chapter discusses the key issues involved in managing OO development: methodology selection, training and staffing, costs, planning and scheduling, and productivity. Issues involved in documenting this process are discussed, including how the tools in this book can help.

Methodologies consist of notations, development models, philosophies, and strategies. Three notation styles (Coad and Yourdon, Booch, and OOSD) are discussed. Several philosophies, models, and strategies are also discussed.

Types and sources of training are discussed, along with the roles of the various staff members in an OO development organization. Your programming staff should be divided into a few component builders and many class reusers.

Training and staffing are the most costly part of OO development. Other costs include new development tools and libraries. We review the types of CASE tools required in OO development: Graphic tools, librarians, and browsers. Classes are divided into six categories: Primitives, containers, interface, transformers, models, and adapters. The selection criteria and availability of these types of classes is then discussed.

Object orientation lends itself well to reuse. But, that reuse is not automatic. It is important to plan and schedule for that reuse. It is also important to schedule class walk throughs to insure clarity and reusability.

Productivity gains in object orientation are realized in two major ways. The first is from the reduction in the semantic gap between users and developers. The second is from reuse. The productivity gains from reuse are not likely to manifest themselves in your first OO project because of mistakes and the learning curve. To get a productivity boost from reuse you need a library of classes ready for reuse, and avoidance of the "not invented here" syndrome is essential.

Your choice of development model and notation will affect the details, but your OO project should have the following types of documentation: Schedule/Workplan, System Overview Diagrams, Class Hierarchies, Class and Object Definition Diagrams, Object Communication Diagrams, Diagram Narratives, Class Descriptions, Method and Function Descriptions, and Traditional Diagrams. Some tools in this book can help produce and maintain several of these documents.

CHAPTER 4
Analysis: Object-Oriented vs. Traditional

"Just *what* do you think you're doing?"

Everybody's Mom.

4.1 INTRODUCTION

4.1.1 Purposes of Analysis

4.1.1.1 Understanding the Problem

We have already seen the first law of initial requirements:

Users generally start out with only a vague notion of what they want.

We also know that the users will probably change their minds. This brings the software engineer into direct conflict with yet another law of software engineering, The Law of Problem Comprehension:

Before you can solve a problem, you must understand it.

And its four corollaries:

1. The more you understand about a problem, the easier it is to solve.
2. When a problem is fully understood, it is solved.
3. A problem is never fully understood until it has been solved.

4. Work must begin on a solution to a problem before the problem is fully understood.

Analysis is the process of understanding a problem in order to solve it. In the process of understanding, you will begin to discover solutions to those problems.

4.1.1.2   Building Relationships

Analysis has another purpose which is at least as important as the process of understanding the problem: Analysis is where the development team begins to develop relationships with the users, clients, and domain experts. Each of these people has information the analysts need to develop a good understanding of the problem. The way you relate to each of them will determine how willing and able they are to give you what you need.

4.1.1.3   Putting it Together

Sometimes you can understand requirements and build relationships with customers by writing usage scenarios. A usage scenario is like a small story describing what the user is likely to do and how the system should respond. In these scenarios, don't try to account for every possible eventuality. Write scenarios for the most typical situations. Include scenarios for the most common exceptions and user errors.

You should have some idea about what the user wants to do from your initial conversations. Write the most typical scenarios during your user meetings. Look through them after the meetings, and try to identify common mistakes the user may make or logical extensions to what the user might want to do. Write these up and show them to the users at your next meetings. In subsequent meetings, refine the scenarios with the users and domain experts. You can see an example of usage scenarios in Chapter 11.

4.1.2   The Structured Point of View

In structured analysis, the job of the analyst is to separate the problem into tasks that must be performed. Each task consists of taking a flow of data, transforming it, and passing it along. A process transforms the data. A process can expand into several more processes, which in turn may expand into several more, etc. Data stores hold data between processes. Data stores contain records. Records contain elements. The analysts describe the records and elements. The data flows, processes, and data stores are recorded on a data flow diagram.

Analysts have a second, separate job: the modeling of the data. Sometimes this job is performed by a separate team. This team describes records (sometimes called "entities") and the relationships between them. This description is recorded on an "Entity Relationship diagram." The entities should match the data stores in the data flow.

The results of structured analysis, data flow diagrams, and entity relationship diagrams reflect a view of the problem from the computer's point of view. These diagrams reflect how the computer will process the information, especially if procedural programming techniques are used.

4.1.3   The OO Point of View

In object-oriented analysis (OOA), the analyst must find the "real world" objects which the system will model and define the attributes of the objects. The analyst also defines the services required of an object. Relationships between the objects are discovered and recorded. In the Coad and Yourdon method of OOA, these elements of analysis are recorded in layers. Any given diagram can focus on any layers necessary to give a clear view of the system.

OOA views the problem as a human would see it, not necessarily as the computer would see it. If OO design and programming are also used, this view is maintained through out the development process.

4.2   THE SCORE CARD

It's been said that you can't tell the players without a score card. Well, this section gives you a score card. These are the people involved in the process of analysis along with their typical roles and concerns. For any given project, these roles may overlap. For example, the client may also be the user and the domain expert. In other cases, the client may be a large corporate entity. The users may be employees of the client. The domain experts may be consultants hired by the corporation for the project.

4.2.1   The Analysts

4.2.1.1   Role

Analysts are part of the development team. They are the people who discover what the system is supposed to do, and record their discoveries. The analysis team may be employees of the client or consultants. Depending on the size of the project, the analysis team may have one or many people. I've seen some large projects successfully developed with only two or three people on the analysis team. The analysis team typically coordinates communication with the other people involved in the analysis process. They interview users to learn their needs. They report progress to the client. Analysts work with information providers (users and domain experts) to assure the correctness of their perceptions of the problem.

The problem definitions developed by the analysis team will be the starting point for design. I believe very strongly that at least one member of the analysis team should be on the design team. If only one person from the design team is on the analysis team, it should be the leader of the design team. It has been my experience that if most of the analysis team is also on the design team, the transition from analysis to design is much smoother.

4.2.1.2   Concerns

Typically, the analysis team is primarily concerned with "getting the job done." They are concerned with obtaining the information necessary to understand what the system is supposed to do. They should also be concerned with communicating their current understanding clearly to all interested parties and receiving corrections to any misconceptions.

4.2.1.3   Points of Contention

Usually one of two problems interferes with the goals of the analyst: either not getting enough information, or getting too much information.

There are times that the analysts are not able get the information they need from the people that have it. The reasons may be practical or political. Sometimes the system in question is perceived as a threat to the job of the person who has the information the analysts need. The analysts are suddenly thrown into the middle of a political hot bed. The best you can do in those situations is to honestly assess the concerns of the individual and try to put to rest any misconceptions they may have. If their concerns are well-founded, you must find a way to address these concerns, but you don't want to be perceived as a snoop or busybody.

The best you can do is treat all persons involved with honesty and respect, no matter how frustrated you become. Recognize the things that are out of your hands, deal with the things you can influence, and hope for the best.

Another reason that the analysis team may not be able to get information is simply a physical limitation. They may be separated from the potential information providers by time and space. Information providers typically have their own schedules or concerns and may not perceive the need for meeting with members of the analysis team as a priority, especially if they are expected to originate communication or travel long distances. The analysis team members must recognize the validity of these priorities and try to schedule meetings and phone conversations that are not perceived as interfering with "real work." Typically, if you treat people with honesty and respect, some compromise can be worked out. Again, if you are in this situation, don't let your frustration control your actions.

The other problem, getting too much information, is usually not as frustrating. The analysts must sift through the information they receive, separate the relevant from the irrelevant, and defer some decisions until they have a more unambiguous view of the problem.

4.2.2   Client

4.2.2.1   Role

The client is the person or entity paying for the project. Often, but not always, the client is also the user.

4.2.2.2   Concerns

The client typically has two concerns: "How long is this going to take?" and "How much is it going to cost?".

Typically the client also will be concerned with the value of the product. The system is an investment for the client. Clients have every right to expect the system to produce more than it costs to develop. This expectation encompasses the quality of the system and the productivity gained by using the system.

4.2.2.3   Points of Contention

The points of contention with a client will rise from the client's primary concerns. If the client perceives the system as taking too long to develop, or costing more than it produces, he or she will not be happy. Problems occur most often when the client does not understand the development process. "What do you mean you haven't started programming yet? You've been in analysis for two hours!"

The analyst should help the client understand the development process before a commitment is made between the client and the development team. The analyst should help the client to understand that if the analysis is not done well, the client will not receive a high quality system, and starting to program without sufficient analysis and design will cause the entire project to fall behind schedule.

If the information providers work for the client, the client may be concerned with the time required of the information providers during analysis and design. The best way to address this concern is to let the client know, as far in advance as possible, who will be needed, when they will be needed, and how long they will be needed. Try to arrange this at the client's convenience. (Don't ask for the stock manager at inventory time.) If you can't have access to the information providers, it's best to know as soon as possible, so you can make other arrangements.

4.2.3   The Users

4.2.3.1   Role

The users are the ones who utilize the system. It is ultimately their satisfaction with the system that will determine its success or failure. The system in question should make the users' lives easier. That's why the analysis team should consult with users and potential users throughout the analysis process.

Users play an important role as information providers. Often users are also the domain experts. They might not know what they want until they hear it, but they generally know what they need to do their jobs.

4.2.3.2   Concerns

Users will probably have more concerns with the specifics of the system than almost anyone else involved in the project. They want a system that is easy to learn, easy to use and one that helps them do their job more effectively and pleasantly. Some users may be intimidated by the new system. Often they will be concerned that their wants or needs will not be met.

4.2.3.3   Points of Contention

If someone is intimidated by the system, getting information from them is going to be difficult. People tend to fear what they don't understand. Many people still don't have a good understanding of computer-related issues. Nobody likes to feel stupid. The best way to address this concern is to show respect for the person and accept the validity of their feelings. Explain the things they don't understand without being condescending.

Not surprisingly, the user interface is a major point of contention between users and developers. Get as much feed back as possible from the user about the interface. The interface should be intuitive, easy to learn, and fast. Once the user has learned it, the interface should not interfere with the rapid completion of the user's tasks.

4.2.4   Domain Experts

4.2.4.1   Role

Domain experts are the people who know about the "real world" issues involved in the system under development. For an accounting package, the domain expert will probably be an accountant; engineers and draftsmen would be called in to consult about CAD systems. If a domain expert is not the user, he or she may be the user's supervisor or subordinate. Domain experts are the primary information providers during analysis. Often their participation continues through design and testing. Complex systems may cover several domains and therefore need many different domain experts.

4.2.4.2   Concerns

Domain experts are concerned with the accuracy of the system. They provide information about how to turn input into reliable output. They should also be concerned with any legal, ethical, or professional implications of the system.

4.2.4.3   Points of Contention

If the domain expert is not also a user, his or her primary concerns may have little to do with the system under development. An engineer may be too busy at the drafting table to talk about a CAD system he or she may never use. This can cause a great deal of frustration when the development team needs access to this expertise.

A personal touch may be needed here. Most professionals will be intrigued by an interesting problem in their field of expertise. Find a point of common interest to exploit and respect the fact that they also have a job to do.

4.2.5   Relationships Between the Parties Involved in Development

4.2.5.1   The Ideal World

Figure 4-1 shows the ideal relationships between parties involved in software development. The client hires the development team and receives reports on the status of the project as it progresses. The users communicate their needs to the development team, which in turn provides software to the user. The development team asks domain experts to provide problem specific information. The domain experts communicate this information to the development team.

The figure also shows that there are usually other relationships among the clients, users and domain experts. These relationships will determine how easily required information flows. Before and during analysis the individuals filling these roles are identified and the lines of communication are established. If the analysis team has any choice in the matter, they should try to establish the lines of communication based on the ideal model. The diagram shows the client, domain experts, and users as separate entities. If these roles are assumed by the same people, the model is still valid.

4.2.5.2   The Real World

Figure 4-2 shows a common deviation from the ideal. The client acts as a conduit between the information providers and the development team. There may be any number of reasons for this arrangement. The development team may be subcontracting for the client; the client's organizational hierarchy may dictate the lines of communication; a client may wish to control the flow of information; the information providers may be unable to interact directly with the development team because of physical distance. No matter what the reasons, this arrangement is far less efficient than the ideal. Opportunities for misunderstandings abound. The time lapse between the request for information and the receipt of the information increases.

Since relationships and lines of communication are established during analysis, this is the time to actively seek the ideal relationship model if possible.

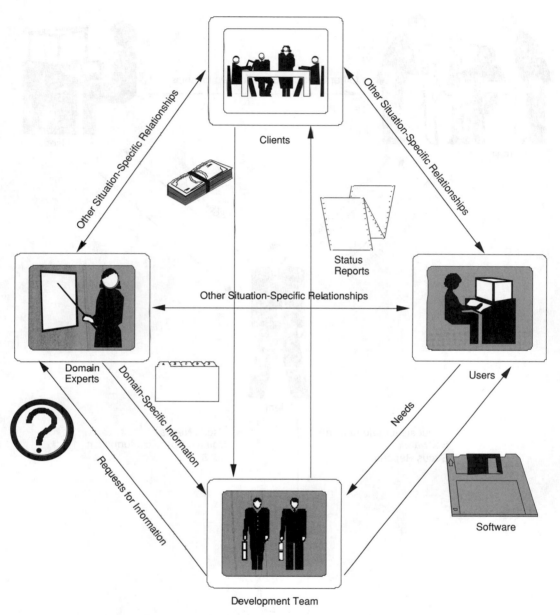

FIGURE 4-1 Ideal relationships between parties involved in software development projects.

4.2.6   Now That You Know the Players . . .

Now we know who's involved in the process, and we have a better understanding of their concerns. By understanding and addressing those concerns, you should be able to minimize the points of contention.

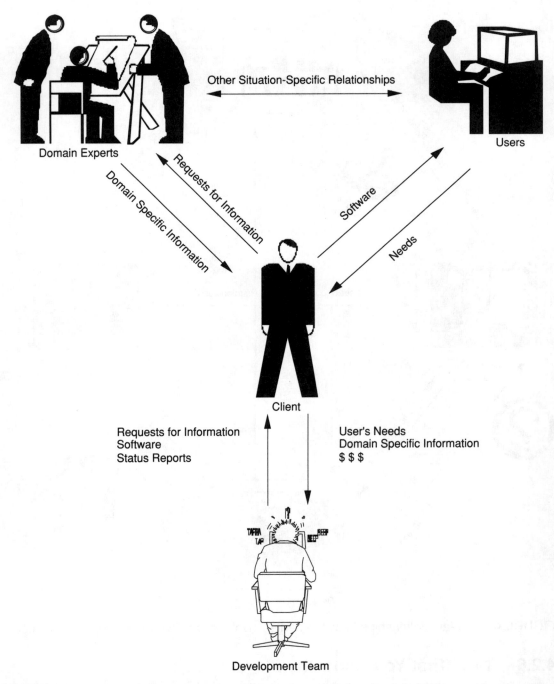

FIGURE 4-2 Common relationships between parties involved in software development projects.

Next, we'll compare traditional structured analysis with OOA and see how each method attempts to address the concerns of the people involved in the analysis.

4.3   THE STRUCTURED POINT OF VIEW

In traditional development, the line between analysis and design is supposed to be pretty clear. There is a specific point at which analysis is supposedly terminated and design begins. There are formal rules for translating the products of analysis into a program design. I say "supposedly" because my experience has been that additional requirements become clear as design progresses. These requirements are things that "should have" been specified in analysis, but weren't because the development team did not yet have a full understanding of the subtleties and nuances of the users' requirements. They didn't have enough information to ask the right questions.

Since the first CASE tool we're going to build is a class librarian, I thought about how real librarians do their jobs, and in this section, and in the OOA, I'll be using examples from an imaginary automated card catalog system for a public library.

4.3.1   Data Flow Diagrams

The key to structured analysis is breaking the problem into smaller sub-problems. Each sub-problem is then broken into even smaller problems. The solutions to the problems become a kind of "to do" list. Each item in the "to do" list is called a process. A process takes data, transforms it, and passes it along. The flow of data from one process to another is recorded in a picture called a data flow diagram. Figure 4-3 shows an example of a simple data flow diagram.

A circle represents a process. *Data flows*, represented by the lines between the other symbols, consist of data elements to be transformed. If data needs to be retained between transformations, this is represented by an open box called a *data store*. An *external entity*, represented by square, is a person or other entity that provides data from outside the system or receives data from the system.

Two other types of documents accompany the data flow diagram: a *data dictionary* and *process descriptions*. Process descriptions explain what happens inside the circles. A data dictionary describes the *data elements* in the data flows and data stores. For more details on these topics, see the recommended reading list.

Data Flow Diagrams focus on what happens to the data (the "algorithm" part), and how the data moves from process to process. They have nothing to do with the relationships among the data. Relationships among data entities are described in Entity Relationship Diagrams.

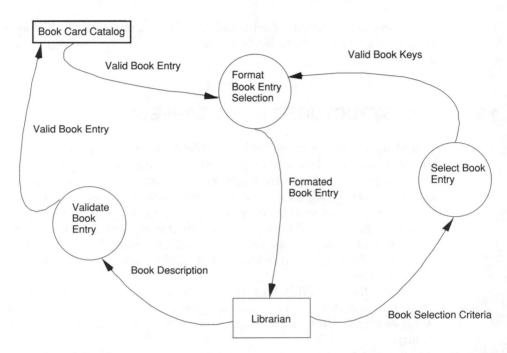

FIGURE 4-3 Example of a data flow diagram (Librarian Card Catalog Entry and Retrieval System).

4.3.2   Entity Relationship Diagrams

A second type of diagram, an entity relationship diagram, describes how persistent data entities relate to each other. The entities in the entity relationship diagrams are tied to the data stores in the data flow diagrams through the data dictionary. An entity has attributes. These attributes are usually data elements in the data dictionary.

An entity can be associate with other entities. These associations are called relationships. There are several kinds of relationships between entities: optional, mandatory, one-to-one, one-to-many, to name a few. Entity relationship diagrams are often used to design application-independent databases. This technique is especially popular with the development of relational databases. In these cases, the entities are mapped to tables.

The creation of entity relationship diagrams is called data modeling. This is the "data structure" part of Wirth's Law. Figure 4-4 shows an example of an entity relationship diagram.

4.3.3   Creating Structured Analysis Diagrams

In structured analysis, the creation of the data flow diagrams and entity relationship diagrams takes place in two separate steps. In some organizations, two

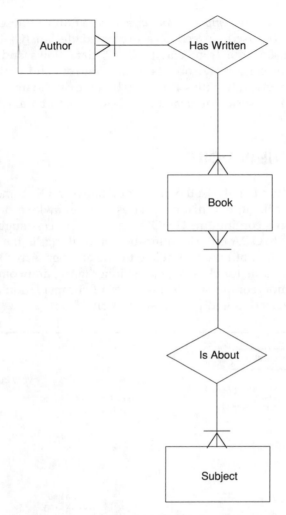

FIGURE 4-4   Example of book entry entity relationship diagram.

different teams create the two types of diagrams, at others, the analysis team first creates the data model and then the same team creates the data flow diagram.

4.3.4   Moving to Design

Originally, structured analysis was intended to serve as a starting place for structured design. There are formal rules for translating data flow diagrams into structure charts. Even so, transition from structured analysis to structured design is widely acknowledged as the most difficult part of structured software development.

In an article in *Computer Language*, David Bullman describes how traditional analysis can be used to feed object-oriented design (OOD). When structured analysis is used as a front end to OOD, data flows and data stores become candidates for classes and objects. Data elements and entity attributes become candidates for class attributes. Processes become candidates for methods [Bullman, 1989]. Figure 4-5 shows an example of how structured analysis can be used as a front end to OOD.

4.4   THE OO VIEW POINT

Unlike structured analysis, the distinction between OOA and OOD is not clear at all. Instead of being two distinct phases with an awkward transition, OOA and OOD exist on a continuum. The OO discovery process suggests a solution.

The key to OOA is the identification of the things in the problem domain and the determination of how they relate to one another. Any OOA notation must at least have symbols for classes, objects, inheritance, and communication between objects. The notation must reflect the idea of encapsulation of data structure and functionality, as opposed to their separation.

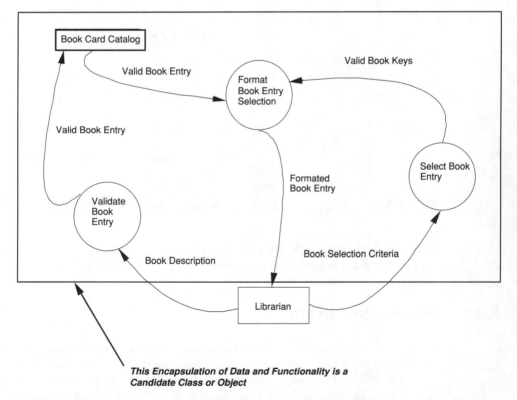

FIGURE 4-5 Example of how a data flow diagram can be used to identify candidate objects.

This section is based on the book *Object-Oriented Analysis* by Peter Coad and Ed Yourdon [Coad, Yourdon 1990, 91]. Chapter 3 has an overview of the Coad and Yourdon notation. The Coad and Yourdon technique describes how to identify objects in the problem domain, their contents, and the relationships between them. The activities of the Coad and Yourdon OOA include:

1. Identifying Classes and Objects—Real world things the system needs to deal with.
2. Defining Attributes—Data elements in objects and certain structures.
3. Defining Services—Processing performed by an object.
4. Identifying Structures—Relationships between real world objects.
5. Identifying Subjects—Grouping of Structures or Objects to control how much of the system the reader sees at once.

4.4.1   Layered Approach

Coad and Yourdon use a layered approach in their OOA techniques. They show one layer for each activity listed above.

The advantage of this layered approach is that it hides complexity until it is needed. The key to successful analysis and design is proper management of complexity. In the Coad and Yourdon approach, you work on the layer that corresponds to your current activity.

4.4.2   The Class and Object Layer

Working on the Class and Object Layer reveals persons, places, events, and other things the system has to deal with. The most important part of this activity is naming the classes and objects. Let the information providers direct the naming of the classes and objects. Resist the urge to change the names to make them "more accurate." Use real words or reasonable abbreviations. The information providers can communicate more clearly in terms they are familiar with.

In OOA, the Class and Object Layer describes the "things" you discover. A class is represented by a rounded rectangle divided horizontally into three parts. The name of the class is in the upper portion. When a lighter rectangle is drawn around the class rectangle, it represents objects that are instances of the class. A class without the object notation is an abstract class. Figure 4-6 has an example of the Class and Object layer for some of our classes in the library system.

4.4.3   The Structure Layer

There are two types of structures described in the Structure Layer. The first is what Coad and Yourdon call a Generalization-Specialization or Gen-Spec Structure. The other is called a Whole-Part Structure.

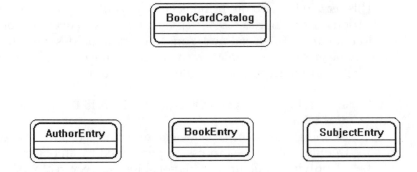

FIGURE 4-6   Class and object layer for a card catalog system.

4.4.3.1   "Part of" Structure

A Whole-Part structure shows how classes relate when an object is a "part of" another object. A line with a triangle in the middle connects the classes. The triangle points to the "whole" class. The ends of the lines touch the "object" part of the Object and Class diagram.

Near the ends of the lines are notations showing the nature of the relationships between the objects. For example, "0,M" means that there can be anywhere from 0, to an arbitrarily large number of objects as part of another object. The notation "1" indicates one and only one object. Figure 4-7 shows how several "BookEntries" are part of a "BookCardCatalog." Each "BookCardCatalog" must contain at least one, and could contain many books. A "BookEntry" is part of one and only one "BookCardCatalog."

4.4.3.2   "Kind of" Structure

The Gen-Spec structure shows inheritance relationships when a class "is a kind of" another class. A line with a semicircle in the middle connects the classes. The "open" end of the semicircle points to the specialization class. Figure 4-8 shows how BookEntry is a "kind of" Entry. There are also "MusicEntries" and

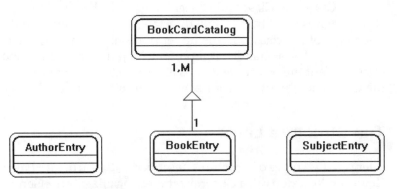

FIGURE 4-7   "Whole Part" structure for library system.

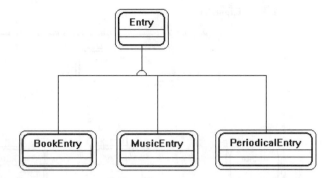

FIGURE 4-8   Generalization-specialization structure for library system.

"PeriodicalEntries." Gen-Spec structures are typically used to show inheritance relationships between classes. That is why the lines touch the class part of the Object and Class diagram.

4.4.4   Subject Layer

A Subject Layer is a way of managing complexity in large system. Several related Classes and Objects are "collapsed" into a rectangle representing the entire subject. This lets you get a feel for how all the major parts of the problem domain fit together.

A subject has a number and a name. Frequently, a subject consists of a single Gen-Spec structure so the name of the subject is the name of the top level class. A subject can contain other subjects, if that helps to manage complexity. A class or structure can be in more than one subject if that will help people's understanding.

A subject can be shown in one of three states: collapsed, partially collapsed, or fully expanded. A collapsed subject shows only its name and number. Partially collapsed subjects shows their names, numbers, and lists of items in the subject. A fully expanded subject shows everything.

Figure 4-9 shows how a set of related structures become a subject. Other subjects in our imaginary library program might include a "MusicCatalog" subject and a "PeriodicalCatalog."

4.4.5   Attribute Layer

Attributes are the data items that describe objects. Sometimes they are called "things the object needs to remember." The attributes of the objects in a class are listed in the center portion of the Class and Object diagram. Attributes common to all of the classes in an inheritance structure are placed in the "general" class.

An attribute can be another object. Lines between the objects define these instance connections. The multiplicity and participation notation is the same as in the Whole-Part structure layer.

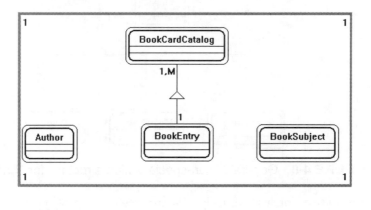

A. Fully Expanded

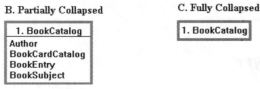

B. Partially Collapsed

1. BookCatalog
Author
BookCardCatalog
BookEntry
BookSubject

C. Fully Collapsed

1. BookCatalog

FIGURE 4-9   Subject layer.

During the discovery of attributes, you may need to add more objects and classes by specializing or generalizing existing classes. You may also find the opportunity to remove objects and classes.

Accompanying the attribute layer is a document with attribute specifications. The specification should have at least the name and description of each attribute. I don't use the Coad and Yourdon specification template exactly. During analysis, I fill in as much detail on the template as I can, but I don't actively pursue any missing information beyond the name and description until I get into design a little more.

Figure 4-10 shows an example of the attribute layer. Form 4-1 shows an example of the type of template I prefer to use. The underlined fields are the ones I usually fill in during analysis. Most of the fields are self explanatory. However, some may require a little more explanation. The version field helps keep track of changes. The classification field is for your own organizational purposes. I usually use it to show abstract classes. You may also choose to put the subject name in this field. Table 4-1 contains a summary of the fields in the class definition form.

4.4.6   Service Layer

The services, or behaviors, of an object are represented in the service layer. The services are "what the objects need to do." Services are listed in the bottom portion of the Class and Object diagram.

In analysis, only those services providing externally-visible behavior should

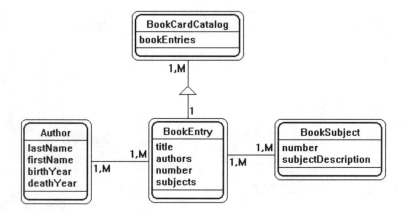

FIGURE 4-10 Attribute layer for library system.

be defined. While developing externally-visible services, some possibilities for internal services (i.e. *HOW* to implement behaviors) may present themselves. Depending on your development model, you may defer internal services until your design phase or perform a small bit of design during analysis and make an initial recommendation about internal services.

The service layer also shows message connections between objects. A message connection is shown with a thick, gray arrow between objects. Arrows point from a sender of the message to the receiver. If there is a double headed arrow, it shows that the objects send messages to each other. Sometimes adding a name to an arrow clarifies its purpose. (Other times it clutters the diagram without providing any useful information.)

The services listed in the diagram are specified in an accompanying document just as the attributes are. The specification should contain at least the name and a description listing the responsibilities of the service. I use a different template than the Coad and Yourdon template. When specifying services, I fill out the bottom of the template in Form 4-1, and then I specify the details a little more in another form (Form 4-2).

Figure 4-11 shows an example of a service layer, and Form 4-2 has a template for specifying services. Again, I use the same template for design, so the fields I usually fill out during analysis are underlined. Besides the service templates, other specifications such as data flow diagrams, data communication diagrams, and state transition diagrams are sometimes necessary to clarify the services developed in this activity.

4.4.7 Moving to Design

Not surprisingly, Coad and Yourdon OOA fits nicely into the Coad and Yourdon OOD technique. The activities, diagrams, and layers of the Coad and Yourdon OOA are the same as in the Coad and Yourdon OOD; the Coad and Yourdon Design starts where Coad and Yourdon Analysis leaves off. You may need to

<u>Class Name:</u>   <u>Version:</u>

Classifications:

Ancestors: Defined:

<u>Description/Purpose:</u>

Data Attributes:

Visibility	Type	<u>Name</u>	<u>Purpose/Comment</u>

Methods/Functions

Visibility	<u>Name</u>	<u>Purpose</u>	Coded	Tested

FORM 4–1   Template for class design.

modify analysis results in design to reflect pragmatic considerations. The major advantage to using Coad and Yourdon OOD notation after using Coad and Yourdon OOA is the consistency of notation and activities.

The Coad and Yourdon design notation is not your only option, however. You may choose to use Coad and Yourdon Analysis with other notations and techniques. If you prefer other notions, you can still adopt the Coad and Yourdon philosophy of using the same notation for analysis and design. I'll discuss OOD notation and other details of design in Chapter 5.

4.4.8   Deliverables

For those who choose to use the waterfall model or other development model requiring formal deliverables at the end of a phase, I'll list my recommendations for OOA deliverables.

TABLE 4–1   Explanation of fields class definition form.

The underlined fields are those typically filled in during analysis.

Field	Explanation
Class Name	Name of the class being defined.
Version	Keeps track of changes to class design.
Classifications	A class could be abstract or concrete. Other classifications may be appropriate depending upon the application.
Ancestors	The parent class or, in case of multiple inheritance, parent classes.
Defined	This is marked if the class has been defined in code. In C++, this would mean, for example, that the class header has been created.
Description/Purpose	Reason the class exists, what it is supposed to do.
Data Attributes	List of data items defined in the class.
Visibility	How this data item can be seen by "the outside" world. In C++ this would be: Public—Access by all classes and functions. Protected—Access only by class, descendants, and friends. Private—Access only by class and frients.
Type	Data type for item.
Name	Name of data item.
Purpose/Comment	Description of data item.

Upon completion of formal OOA I recommend the following deliverables:

- Usage Scenarios
- Refined Candidate Class List
- Coad and Yourdon Diagrams showing:
  - Inheritance Relationships Between Classes
  - Whole-Part and Attribute Relationships Between Objects
  - Subject Groupings of Classes
- Class Definition Templates

4.5   THE PLAYER'S PERSPECTIVE

4.5.1   Users, Domain Experts, Clients

4.5.1.1   Structured Analysis

Let's look at structured analysis from a "non-computer" person's point of view. The analysis team needs to verify its perceptions of what the system is supposed to do. The team presents the data flow diagram to the information providers and clients.

The analysis team first has to explain things like "data flows," "processes"

Owning Class:

Name: Version:

Purpose:

Return Value:

Parameters:

Type   Name   Purpose   Default Value

Description/Logic

Form 4-2   Template for method specification.

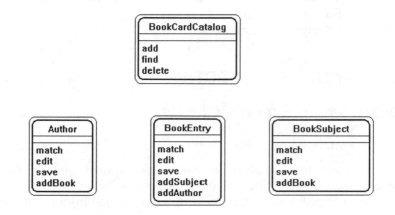

FIGURE 4-11   The service layer.

and "data stores." While the information providers are still grappling with these new ideas, the analysis team asks them to verify that their analysis is correct. This semantic gap between the analysis team and the information providers is a potential barrier to accurate understanding.

4.5.1.2   OOA

Now we'll look at OOA from a "non-computer" person's point of view. We have the same situation. The analysis team needs to verify its perceptions of what the system is supposed to do. The team presents the OOA diagrams to the information providers and clients.

Instead of first explaining the meaning of new terms, the analysis team says, "These rounded rectangles are the things in your system. These lines show how they relate to one another." Since the information providers are immediately discussing things they are familiar with, there is less of a semantic gap. This is probably the single biggest argument in favor of OOA.

4.5.2   The Analysis Team

4.5.2.1   Structured Analysis

The analysis team is probably quite comfortable with structured analysis; it has been around since the 1970s, so it is familiar, well understood, and widely accepted. It is also possible that this is the only kind of analysis allowed in the organization.

Early in the relationship with information providers, time is spent filling the semantic gaps between the information providers' vocabulary and the analysts' vocabulary. We'll assume that all problems with semantic gaps between the information provider and the analysis team have been satisfactorily resolved. The processes, data flows, external entities, and data stores have been identified and verified. To move to OOD or OOP takes an extra step: mapping the analysis into objects and classes. This seems to impede the goal of increased productivity.

4.5.2.2   OOA

If this is something new to the analysis team, there could be a certain amount of insecurity among the team members. They may be having trouble thinking in terms of "things" instead of "processes." There also may be resistance in the organization to this kind of change. Most of these issues can be overcome with training and experience.

Once past the inevitable learning curve, the analysis team continues with OOA. The transition from OOA to OOD and OOP is smoother and has fewer superfluous steps than with structured development. Since the team spends more time discussing "real world" things, they should develop a better understanding of the problem domain. This better understanding should lead to a higher quality product, developed in less time than a comparable traditional system.

4.6   ANOTHER KIND OF ANALYSIS

Booch brings up another form of analysis, informal analysis based on the English description of the problem. The nouns become candidates for objects and classes. Adjectives become clues to attributes. Verbs become candidates for methods. Design begins from these candidates.

Going directly from the English problem description to OOD is probably OK for small projects where the problem domain is well understood by the developer. For larger systems, the informal analysis is a good starting place for more detailed, formal OOA.

Jeff Duntemann, in his March 1992 *Dr. Dobb's Journal* column, "Structured Programming," presents a "Plain English" analysis methodology. I'll summarize it here:

1. Write an overview to orient the outsider. Put any jargon in a glossary. Enumerate major processing tasks. Explain these items briefly.
2. Write a structured description. This would be the body of the document. Separate each of the enumerated items into smaller hierarchies of elements. Deal with input, output, and processing of each element. Be sure to include the reasons that processing needs to be done in a certain way. (Duntemann recommends using an outline processor to organize the structured description.)
3. Write a recommendations summary. Put any design suggestions in this section.
4. Write a warnings summary. Include any constraints or caveats.
5. Include a glossary describing any acronyms and insider jargon.

4.7   PRACTICAL TIPS ON ANALYSIS

4.7.1   Keys to Successful Analysis

This section contains some miscellaneous tips on analysis in general. It's based on experiences I've had during various development projects. The tips are valid for both OO and structured analysis.

4.7.1.1   Develop Relationships with Clients, Users, and Domain Experts

The most important reason for developing good relationships with your clients and information providers is that good relationships make working more pleasant for everyone involved; we are in a *service* industry. Our job is to help people solve their problems, not impress them with our knowledge of things cybernetic and arcane.

4.7.1.1.1   *Listen to Their Concerns*

The concerns I mentioned earlier are only examples. Each person and project is unique, so each set of concerns will be unique. People need to tell you their concerns. You need to listen. Address the concerns as honestly and directly as you can. If you don't know whether you can address the concerns, *tell them*. **Don't** try to substitute cattle excrement for real knowledge.

4.7.1.1.2   *Minimize the Use of "Computerese"*

Save the technical jargon for your colleagues. The clients and information providers will not be impressed with your knowledge of words with which they are not familiar. If you must use "computerese" to explain something, be certain to be sure to explain what you mean without being condescending. If they have a sufficient understanding of a term or phrase, resist the urge to correct insignificant details.

One of my favorite things about this profession is the opportunity to experience a multitude of various fields from high finance to high technology to games and entertainment. Since the goal of analysis is to come to an understanding of the problem to be solved, try to learn and use the correct or common terminology of the problem domain instead of "computerese."

4.7.1.2   **Make the Most of Your Meetings**

Meetings are probably the most common method of exchanging information during analysis. Avoid unnecessary meetings. Repeating meetings to get the same information is generally a frustrating waste of time. Meetings are intended to accomplish something, to come a little closer to solving a problem, or at least to develop a better understanding of the problem.

4.7.1.2.1   *The Agenda*

Before the meeting starts, everyone involved should have a copy of the agenda and know what you expect to accomplish.

You don't have to stick to the agenda religiously. If a subject leads to a relevant discussion of something not on the agenda, make a judgment call; sometimes the divergent discussion is more important than the original agenda. Other times, the discussion will need to be deferred until another meeting.

Often during analysis meetings the clients begin to discuss policies and procedures among themselves. Again, your judgment must come into play. Sometimes, these discussions are among the most valuable products of the analysis process. If the clients seem to be making progress among themselves, just hang on and try to keep up. If the discussion gets too far out of hand, try to reschedule it and get back to the original agenda.

4.7.1.2.2   Record the Meeting and the Decisions Made

At the very least, someone should be taking minutes during the meetings. The minutes, or a summary of the meeting, should be distributed to the meeting participants.

If all the participants of the meeting agree, you can tape record the meeting. If you're taping the meeting, be sure to state each decision clearly after it has been made. This will give people a final chance to clear up any misunderstandings before moving on to the next topic. I've found that taping the meetings helps to keep track of what decisions were made, and it also helps to keep track of why they were made. Summaries of the meeting should be distributed, and copies of the meeting tapes should be made available to any participants who want them.

4.7.2   When to Use Traditional Structured Analysis

Although OOA is generally superior to the older, structured analysis, there are reasons to use structured analysis. This is true even if you intend to use OOD and OOP.

4.7.2.1   Organizational Inertia

This is probably the single best reason for continuing with traditional analysis. Even if the upper management agrees in principle to the concepts of object orientation, time is required to adjust to new ideas. There is usually a resistance to change in any organization. Even if you know that OOA is a "better" alternative, sometimes it's best to go ahead and perform traditional analysis rather than face delays in changing policy.

4.7.2.2   The OO Model Doesn't Apply

Sometimes, the OO model just doesn't make sense. There is a certain amount of overhead involved in OOP. In device drivers, embedded systems, or other application areas where memory and processing power are at a premium, the overhead is not acceptable. Since the OOP overhead is not acceptable, you may not want to use OOA or OOD.

If the project involves enhancing an existing non-OO system, or if you truly can't find "things" in the problem domain to model, it may be better to use traditional functional decomposition and structured analysis.

4.7.3   When to Use Informal English Analysis

If the problem you want to solve is small and well understood by the development team, you can often go straight into design from a textual description by inheriting from existing classes. This works best if you *have* a rich set of existing classes.

Depending on your development model, this may be a moot point. In some models, analysis and initial design are so intertwined, a distinct analysis activity can't be identified. In that case, the initial "English analysis" is the first step in design.

4.7.4 When to Use OOA

4.7.4.1 When Time is at a Premium

Having a tight schedule is not an excuse to skimp on analysis and design. Failure to understand a problem well inevitably leads to failure to design a proper solution to the problem. A poorly designed system will be a poorly programmed system, although time and again development teams start "as soon as possible" to expedite an aggressive schedule. There is an attitude of, "Don't waste time talking in meetings. *Do something!*." A poorly designed system will take longer to develop because you will be constantly fixing the "Oh, I forgot to tell you about . . . " problems.

Since there is a smaller semantic gap during OOA, time is saved by talking about the problem instead of explaining mysterious symbols and concepts. If there is a need for clients or others to see progress quickly, I recommend using an iterative prototyping development model. OO techniques work quite well for iterative prototyping.

4.7.4.2 As Part of a Complete OO Strategy

You don't want your notations and techniques interfering with your software development. If you want the advantages of OOD and OOP, it only makes sense to use some form of OOA. Taking an extra step to "objectify" a functional diagram seems like an unnecessary obstacle.

4.7.5 An OOA Strategy

Every problem is different, so at some point the generic "by the book" strategy fails. You have to start somewhere, though. This section describes some general strategies I often use when I start an OO project.

4.7.5.1 Low-Tech Brain Storming

After a few initial meetings or phone calls, I generally have some idea of what the client wants. Maybe we've written up a few usage scenarios. I try to set up a brain storming meeting with the key domain experts and users. The plan is to come up with a list of candidate classes and objects.

The standard "brain storming" rules apply: Nobody should evaluate the candidates during the session; some candidates will be similar, some will be irrelevant, and some will be just right. The bad ones have value because they could spark a good idea.

I usually start out by asking something like, "What kinds of things do you want the system to deal with?" I then start the list by naming something I've picked up from the initial discussions or usage scenarios and write it on the white board or paper. This usually gets the ball rolling. I just write down the ideas as quickly as I can. After about a half an hour or so, the flow of ideas starts to slow. Then we usually start crossing off the "bad" candidates.

The next step is usually to brain storm for ideas on data and services for each class. For each class left on the candidate list, we list the potential data and services.

4.7.5.2   Refine Results

After the initial brain storming, we start the normal OOA activities. These activities include, but are not necessarily limited to:

1. Correction of candidate class list by both addition and deletion.
2. Further expansion and definition of data, and functionality.
3. Identification of inheritance, message, and containing relationships.

You need to record and communicate the results of these activities. I'm not dogmatic about "the best" notation. I like the Coad and Yourdon notation because it's the same for both analysis and design.

4.7.5.3   Run With the Idea or Postpone the Decision?

In traditional analysis fairly strict rules apply to what issues you can address in analysis and what issues you can address in design. You're not to address issues of performance or memory requirements, for example, until analysis has been completed.

In most of the OO work I do, the distinction between analysis and design is small. If I have a concern about performance or size, even if it occurs "during analysis," I often deal with it right away; I don't automatically "wait until design," but if I don't think the decision will affect the view of the object, I may wait.

4.7.5.4   Move to Design

At some point we move from high level specification to detailed design. You decide when to do this based on your development model. At some point in the development process, you finally gain a pretty clear understanding of the requirements. At that point, you go back to analysis only to deal with changes in those requirements.

4.7.5.5.   Strategic Overview

So, where does this analysis strategy fit into the overall strategy presented in this book? Here is the list from Chapter 2 with expansion of the first item to reflect the analysis strategy listed in this section.

1. Figure Out What to Do.
    A. Develop Usage Scenarios
    B. Brain Storm
        a. Develop List of Candidate Classes and Objects
        b. List Initial Data and Functionality
    C. Refine Results of Storming
        a. Correct candidate class list by both addition and deletion.
        b. Expand and define data and functionality.
        c. Identify inheritance, messaging, and containing relationships.
    D. Resolve Concerns
        a. Address concerns that may affect the view of objects.
        b. Postpone addressing concerns that don't affect the view of objects.
    E. Move on to Design
        a. Have a clear understanding of requirements.
        b. Come back to analysis when requirements change.
2. Figure Out How to Do It.
3. Do It.
4. Make It Better.

4.8 SUMMARY

This chapter discusses both traditional and OO analysis. Here are the key points of this chapter.

The purpose of analysis is to learn *what* the system is supposed to do. A secondary part of analysis, which is almost as important, is the development of relationships with the clients, users, and domain experts.

Structured analysis reflects a view of the problem from the computer's view point; OOA views the problem from a human's view point.

There are several players in the analysis process. Each has a distinct role and set of concerns that can lead to several points of contention. The analyst discovers what the system is and what it is supposed to do, the client pays for the development of the system, and the user actually utilizes the system. Domain experts know about the problem space and provide the needed information to the analysts.

In structured analysis, the analyst develops data flow diagrams to develop an understanding of the algorithmic part of the problem space and entity relationship diagrams to model the data structure relationships.

The key to OOA is the identification of the things in the problem domain and the determination of how they relate to one another. OOA reflects the encapsulation of functionality and data structures. The Coad and Yourdon technique describes how to identify objects in the problem domain, their contents, and the relationships between them. The activities of the Coad and Yourdon OOA include:

1. Identifying Classes and Objects—Real world things the system needs to deal with.
2. Identifying Structures—Relationships between real world objects.
3. Identifying Subjects—Grouping of Structures or Objects to control how much of the system the reader sees at once.
4. Defining Attributes—Data elements in objects and certain structures.
5. Defining Services—Processing performed by an object.

The Coad and Yourdon notation reflects these activities.

While traditional analysis techniques may be more comfortable for software engineers, OOA allows for a smaller semantic gap between the technical and non-technical people. Sometimes, a more informal English analysis is a possible front end to OOD. More often, the informal English analysis makes a good starting place for OOA.

There were several guidelines for making analysis presentation easier and more pleasant. We are in a service industry. We need to be sure we know the concerns of the people involved and address them as honestly, directly, and clearly as possible. Meetings should have a clear, but somewhat flexible, agenda. They should be recorded, and a summary should be distributed to all participants.

No one type of analysis is always the best. Structured, OO, and informal English analyses all have certain conditions under which they are valid.

An example starting OOA strategy has been presented in this chapter, in the context of the entire strategy presented earlier, but remember that every problem is different, so at some point the generic "by the book" strategy fails which will require that you improvise as the situation requires.

CHAPTER 5
A Closer Look at Object-Oriented Design

"Is there truly a general method for designing software? There is, indeed. It is in fact, summarized in just one word: Think!"

Jeff Duntemann, "Structured Programming: Pondering the Imponderable"
Dr. Dobb's Journal, February, 1991.

5.1   WHERE DESIGN FITS INTO DEVELOPMENT

Analysis can and should be implementation independent. Design, on the other hand is very implementation dependent. You should know the language, the libraries and the skill of the programmers before you begin design (or at least before you finish it). Since we will be using C++ to build the projects in the latter part of this book, I will address C++ specific design issues in this chapter.

Design, as most of us know, is figuring out *how* the system under development is supposed to work. There have been, are, and will continue to be, debates within our industry has to exactly when to design and how to design.

5.1.1   Various Models

Long ago there was one model for developing software, and it was called, "The Waterfall." In that model there was always an isolated phase. It was bounded at the top by analysis and at the bottom by design. And when the design phase was completed, it was finished.

But, like many things, "The Waterfall" was rigid, and when the winds of change blew, "The Waterfall" broke and became only one model among many.

Now we can choose among many models: "The Spiral," "The Iterative Prototype," and more. We are free to choose, and design is no longer bound as it was in the old model.

Or is it? If you take a good look at any development model you will observe one thing about design. It is still bound by analysis on top, and programming on the bottom.

5.1.2   Before Programming

I admit that in school, I would occasionally design my programs *after* they had been written. Back then, it was called "cheating." Today it is called reverse engineering. Seriously, though, before you write any nontrivial code, *Think it Through*. Know exactly how you're going to build the code. If you think it through, you'll spend less time debugging and more time creating new code.

5.1.3   After Analysis

In some models, analysis happens only once, in others it occurs several times. No matter what model you use or what design method you use, you should figure out *what* you want to know before trying to figure out how to do it. Again, *think it through*. If you're clear on what needs to happen, half your design battle is over.

5.1.4   Before and After Prototyping

When using the iterative prototype model, design still occurs before programming. It also occurs after programming, which is, in fact, before programming again. Use what you learn from the prototype in the next design. The advantage of this is that each successive design should be more accurate.

5.2   THE PURPOSES OF DESIGN

Sections 5-2, 5-3 and 5-4 are based on an article I wrote that appeared in the October/November 1992 issue of *PC Techniques* called "Seven Sizzling Design Tips." The article was about design in general. Here I focus more on OOD. These sections expound on some ideas that were just touched on in that article.

Have you ever heard (or made) any of the following statements?

"Design is a waste of time."

"I can program, compile, and link in less time than it takes to write all that stuff out."

"Design? Why bother?"

There are three reasons to "bother:"

1. You need to experience the process of figuring out how the system is supposed to work. It is a learning experience.
2. You need to record this understanding.
3. Others will need this understanding as well.

5.2.1   To Develop an Understanding of How the System Works

The main purpose of software design is to develop an understanding of how the system you're building is going to work. In OOD you find the proper data structures and algorithms and encapsulate them into classes for programming. This is crucial to quality and to productivity.

Productivity? How can spending time drawing diagrams increase productivity? It only makes sense that you will create fewer bugs if you understand how your software works. It should also be obvious that a clear understanding of how your software does its job will help find and eliminate bugs that do creep in more quickly. We all know that bugs compromise quality and waste time. If you have fewer bugs, you spend less time debugging, and you have a higher quality product.

There is one productivity myth regarding design that I must dispel. You cannot, under any circumstances, design "buggless" programs. You can, however, design programs that are easier to debug.

5.2.2   To Record This Understanding

The activities of design record your understanding as it develops and changes. OO developers use class hierarchies, class specifications, and object communication diagrams. The chapter on management contains examples of popular OO notations. The creation of these diagrams is not design. Design occurs in the mind of the designer.

In addition to the diagrams, most OO designers use class and method templates to record specification details. The templates I prefer to use are described in the management chapter. Any fields not filled out during analysis are filled out in design.

5.2.3   To Communicate Understanding

The design documents communicate the understanding developed by the designer to others. You may say, "I'm a one person shop. There are no others." Then the design documents are a record so you can remember in six months what you understand now. If you're not a one person shop, you need to communicate this understanding to other developers (programmers, designers, etc.). If you're not the owner of the company, your superiors may need to see how the system works.

5.3   THE PRINCIPLES OF HUMAN-FRIENDLY DESIGN

Here are a few, simple, practical principles that can help make design a little friendlier to the designer and the programmer:

1. Have Clear Requirements.
2. Use a Methodology, but Avoid Dogma.
3. Know Your Audience.
4. Maintain Perspective.
5. Match Design to Requirements.
6. Know and Use the Elements of Good Design.
7. Make the Design Testable.

5.3.1   Have Clear Requirements

In the previous chapter we talked about requirements and analysis. We talked about it again earlier in this chapter, and now we're returning to it again. You absolutely must have a clear idea of what you want to do before you have any chance of succeeding at it. Requirements include not only the list of what the program must do, but also what it must not do. Clear constraints are as important as clear expectations.

Please note that the title of this section is "CLEAR Requirements," not firm requirements. The requirements will change. Why is this? As the project progresses, you will gain a greater understanding of the requirements. This understanding will inevitably lead to changes from initial requirements. Business conditions change. Clients and users could simply change their minds. If your requirements are clear, you will be able to track these changes and know the effects of the changes on your design.

How do you handle changing requirements? It's less expensive and less time consuming to change the design than to change the program. If the change is mandated by business conditions or governmental regulations, you'll probably just have to bite the bullet and make the change, no matter how far along you are in development. If a change will have a major impact on existing code, or have major ramifications on completed design, you may want to put the change on a list for the next version of the software.

When a user or your client requests a change, don't respond immediately. Examine the ramifications of the change. How will it affect existing work? What kind of impact will it have on the delivery date or final cost of the program? You may decide that there is no problem with the change and just say yes. If the change will cause major disruption to development, you may find that you need to strongly recommend that the change be delayed until the next version.

Sometimes you can disclose your findings on time and cost and let the clients or users make the decision. Even if you're in a position that doesn't give you much choice in the matter, be certain to explain the ramifications of the change to those who will make the decision.

5.3.2   Know Your Methodology but Avoid Dogma

I think the best summary of methodology came from a colleague of mine at AIS, Doug Horton: "It's the way we do things." Earlier in the book, we discussed the various components of methodologies: philosophies, notations, strategies, development models, etc. While researching this book, I originally planned to find the best methodology and recommend it. I found, however, that the inventors of methodologies come from diverse backgrounds. The methodologies they developed were valid for them, the differences reflected a difference in experience. You should find a methodology that fits your needs and learn it well.

You have two choices when it comes to finding a methodology: choose one that is established, or create your own. Your methodology search should start with a philosophy, a set of principles upon which you or your organization bases its thinking. If you can find an established methodology that comes close to fitting your philosophies, use it, modify it, and build on it until you mold it to your needs.

If you can't find an established methodology that's suitable for you, start making your own. Find a development model or two that you're comfortable with. Choose a notation that fits into that model. Decide how you're going to annotate your diagrams. What rules will you enforce? What guidelines will you follow to assure consistency? What forms and templates will you use to supplement your diagrams? The availability of automated tools may affect your thinking.

Understanding the strengths and weaknesses of any methodology you use is important. You should also be aware of alternative methodologies. The one you use most of the time may not be adequate for all projects.

Each software development project is in some way unique. No methodology can cover all the possible situations a designer may encounter. When the cookbook doesn't have the answer, you have to rely on your own experience, knowledge, and intuition. That means you need to avoid dogmatically sticking to a methodology.

5.3.3   Know Your Audience

When designing software, it helps to know who you're creating the documents for. One audience will always be the programmers. Another likely audience is the people who will maintain the software after it has been released. What about your boss or client?

Here is a list of questions you should ask yourself about your audience:

1.   Who are you creating design documents for?
2.   How will they use the documents?
3.   How much technical expertise do they have?
4.   What do they want to know?
5.   What do they need to know?
6.   How much time can they spend looking at the design documents?

The answers to these questions will guide you in deciding how much detail to put into your documents. You can focus your efforts on the creation of a few useful documents instead of reams of diagrams and specifications that someone may or may not need to see.

5.3.4   Maintain Perspective

For each document you create, you need to keep your perspective. If you have a high level overview, don't delve into the details of the underlying algorithms. This goes along with knowing your audience. It's easy to get so caught up in the process of creating the design documents that you loose track of the purpose of design. It's just as easy to be so anxious to move on to programming that you gloss over something that requires detailed consideration.

So, how much detail do you put into your design documents? You need to be as complete as necessary. You should put all the information your audience needs into your design documents, but you should also avoid unnecessary details. This may seem like a contradiction and sometimes it is. There is no safe extreme. Too much detail will bog you down; if you don't have enough, someone may not be able to do his or her job. A general rule for diagram details is "seven plus or minus two." That is, you should have from five to nine major symbols on a chart. If a section logically contains three or eleven parts, you're probably OK. The point is, if you need more detail than that, create another diagram.

The one audience you should concentrate on while considering details is the programmers. You should have a good idea about the programmers' project familiarity and technical expertise. This is especially true if you're the programmer. If you don't know exactly who will be programming from your design, you need to provide more detail than if you were designing for a specific person. You also need to consider how much access the programmers will have to the design team while programming. Sometimes it's OK to say, "If this isn't clear, see me."

5.3.5   Match Design to Requirements

There are two types of requirements: explicit and implicit. The explicit requirements come from the analysis or the early part of design. Each explicit requirement carries a multitude of implicit requirements. For example, if you have a requirement that states: "The user interface will be CUA compliant," it implies a windowed environment with certain types of menus and controls. Each class in an OOD, each method, each attribute should exist to meet one or more requirements. These can be implicit or explicit requirements.

Once you get into design it's easy to find nice features that wouldn't be all that hard to program. "While I'm at it," you might say, "I'll just add this nice feature." Of course, this feature isn't required, but it sure is clever. Clever new features, however small, take time and energy away from required features. If you really think this clever new feature will add value to your program, change the requirements to include the new feature. Treat any requirement change as something significant, even if it seems small. Each change could have repercussions that are not obvious at first glance.

5.3.6 Know and Use the Elements of Good Design

We'll discuss more details of the elements of good design in section 5.4. Some of these elements are applicable to all software design, but I'm going to focus on the principles of good OOD.

Here is a summary of the elements of good OOD:

1. Classes and class hierarchies should be highly cohesive.
2. Classes should be loosely coupled with other classes. The exception to this is that since class hierarchies should be cohesive, classes will be tightly coupled with their ancestors.
3. The data implementation details of a class should be hidden from other classes.
4. Design for optimum reusability.
5. Keep class and method definitions small.
6. When designing classes and families of classes, keep the protocol, or class interface, stable.

5.3.7 Make the Design Testable

You need to be certain that you can tell when you've successfully completed each requirement. Successful completion means that the program performs as required, within the stated constraints, without errors.

Your design should include testable completion criteria. For each requirement, make a list of conditions that, when met, will assure that the requirement is satisfactorily completed. For example, you may design a program to test one branch of a class hierarchy. If the test program provides certain output for specific input, the test is successful. That is called "black box" testing.

You should also design for "white box" testing. This is when you test to be sure that the program is doing what you think it should be doing. Debuggers are great for white box testing. You can be certain data within classes have the correct values and follow the execution of a method to be certain it does what it's supposed to do. Try to put criteria for white box testing into your design where possible.

5.4   ELEMENTS OF GOOD DESIGN

In this section, we'll discuss the elements of good design in a little more detail. Although the discussion focuses on OO-specific implementation, the elements in this section are valid for all software design: cohesion, coupling, reuse of code, and design, and for keeping program elements small. In section 5.5, we'll discuss issues specific to good OOD.

5.4.1   Cohesion—Do One Thing, and Do It Right

Classes and class hierarchies should have singularity of purpose. If a class has more than one purpose, it should be broken down into specialized classes. Suppose, for example, you want an analog clock that draws a circle on the screen and draws hands representing the current time. It would be inappropriate to create a "Circle" class with a "draw" method and a "getTime" method. Instead, perhaps you should create a "Clock" class that inherits from a "Circle" class and from a "TimeOfDay" class.

Each class in a hierarchy should be a specialization of all the classes above it. If you decide to add a class to a class hierarchy, be sure it fits. There is a song on *Sesame Street* that goes something like "One of these things is not like the others. . . ." I'm sure you remember it. Play that game with the classes in your hierarchy. If you find anything, your class hierarchy is not very cohesive.

5.4.2   Coupling—Paddle Your Own Canoe

Coupling refers to the interdependence of program elements. Interdependent program elements are tightly coupled. Usually, tight coupling is undesirable. Program elements, such as methods and classes, should be designed to be as independent as possible. If a class depends on too many other classes to do its job, reusability and portability are sacrificed. This class interdependency is called tight coupling. Tight coupling between classes is usually not very good.

Obviously, classes in a system need to be able to depend upon one another for the system to work. Classes should depend upon the behaviors of other classes and their protocols, not in the implementation details. Suppose, for example, that a method in a "Circle" class depends on a directly global variable "screenType" which is set by a class "Display." This is bad coupling. Instead, the "Circle" should be able to ask "Display" for the screen type with a method "getScreenType." The coupling is through the protocol, and therefore looser. The "Circle" can use any class at all with a valid "getScreenType" method.

One set of classes which a class can be tightly coupled with is its ancestors. A class should use as much of its parent class as possible, changing only those things necessary to its particular specialty.

5.4.3   Information Hiding

Information hiding is related to coupling. I know "Information Hiding" sounds like a course in spy school, but you're not keeping information a secret. Encapsulating the implementation of a solution helps improve maintainability and portability. The example above is not just an example of tight coupling. The tight coupling is a result of poor information hiding.

When designing C++ classes you know you have poor information hiding if any of the following is true:

1. You have a large number of public data elements in a class.
2. You depend on global variables.
3. Your classes have a large number of "friend" functions.

5.4.4   Reuse of Existing Code and Design

Code reuse begins in design. When examining the analysis results, look for ways to use existing classes. If new classes need to be created, the protocols for the new classes should be designed with reusability in mind.

5.4.4.1   Reuse of Non-C++ Code

Contrary to the opinions of some OO evangelists, code reuse existed before most of use ever heard of OOP. You can, and should, try to reuse code, even if you don't use OO techniques.

The singular advantage of C++ over all other OOP languages is that it is a superset of ANSI C. If you are a C programmer with a lot of C libraries, you can take advantage of this property of C++ by using a technique known as "wrapping." The details of this are discussed more in Chapter 6. In design, you should identify opportunities for wrapping existing C functions with Class wrappers.

5.4.4.2   Reuse Existing Classes

When you first begin OO development, finding existing classes should be easy because you won't have many of them. As time goes on, and the number of projects and classes grow, finding classes for possible reuse will become more difficult. The volume of classes will make it hard to remember exactly what's available. If you develop in an organization with more than two or three people, or have any kind of personnel turn over, some developers may not know what the others have done.

Let's face it, if designers can't find an existing class quickly, they're likely to design an entirely new class. This is true even if they would save more time in the long run by spending a little more time looking for the right class. A class isn't reusable unless it's reused. That's why the first tool built in this book is a class librarian. It will encourage reuse by making classes easier to find. Reuse is vital to quality and productivity.

5.4.4.3   Inherit as Necessary

Often you won't be able to find exactly the class you're looking for, but one or two will be close. This is where inheritance comes in. Find the class that comes closest to what you want, and specialize through inheritance. By using inheritance, you make controlled, specific changes, and you leave the rest of the class alone.

5.4.4.4   Go from Specific to General to Specific

When designing classes hierarchies, you seldom use a top-down approach, although class hierarchies are usually explained that way. More often, you develop classes for a specific purpose, and then find a way to generalize them. Then, once you have some general classes, you can specialize them as needed. The discussion on inheritance will go into this further.

5.4.4.5   Reuse of Design

Pieces of code aren't the only thing that can be reused. OO technology lends itself well to design reuse. Borland's Application Framework is a good example of design reuse. Elements of the program are built around the same event handling concepts in the application classes. I'll show you an example of design reuse in the chapters on the graphic design tool. I should note here that design reuse will often lead to code reuse. Look for opportunities to reuse design as well as code.

5.4.5   Byte Sized Chunks

I think we've all heard the joke, "How do you eat an elephant?"; "One bite at a time." Try to keep your classes small and manageable. If classes get too big, it's harder to remember all their methods. Ideally, I've found that classes are easier to work with if their definitions don't take up more than two screens, or one page. I use the same rule for functions and methods. There are plenty of exceptions to this, but it's a good goal to keep in mind during design.

One problem that occurs during large system development is that you end up with a large number of small classes. This can lead to complexity. One way of handling complexity during design is to group classes together logically. In the

Booch method, this is accomplished with "categories." Coad and Yourdon use "subjects" for the same purpose.

5.5   ISSUES SPECIFIC TO OBJECT-ORIENTED DESIGN

You should pay attention to certain things in order to have a good OOD, and good designs of C++ programming in particular. The first is class protocols, also called interfaces. You should also concentrate on developing good class hierarchies, internal functions, friend functions, and class implementation details.

There was a time when certain data processing professionals championed the notion that designers should not be programmers. If there ever was a place for this attitude, object engineering is not it. Those who design should be intimately familiar with the programming language and environment in which the system will be developed. Furthermore they should participate in writing code from their own designs and work with the other programmers who are implementing design.

5.5.1   Developing Class Protocols

A class can be thought of as being divided into two logical parts. The first is the implementation, consisting of data and functions not available to most other classes. The second is the protocol, sometimes called the class interface.

There is absolutely nothing more important in OOD than class protocol. A class protocol defines how the class interacts with the rest of the world. It is a pledge to the rest of the world that the class will accept requests to do its job in a certain way, and that it will provide information in a certain way.

5.5.1.1   Be VERY VERY Careful

Since class protocol is so important, you must be very careful about how you define it. Carefully think through what you want the class to say to the rest of the world. Once you make up your mind and make the class available, you're pretty much stuck with it, for better or worse.

If the class keeps its protocol stable, existing code will continue to work. Remember, you can always add to a class protocol without breaking existing code. Elimination or change of protocol methods and data is a violation of the pledge it has made to the rest of the world. This will require rewrites of existing code.

5.5.1.2   Keep It as Small and Simple as Possible

Since you can add to the protocol in the future, keep the initial protocol as small as possible. Use consistent and logical names for your public member functions. Keep the names generic, and use overloading to handle different needs.

5.5.1.3   Public Methods

In C++ public methods of a class and public data members define the protocol of the class. A public method is the member function of a class that any other class or function can use. It is possible to allow other functions and classes to have direct access to the data of a class, but this is considered bad form by most OO advocates.

5.5.1.3.1   *What to Do?*

One of the first questions you need to ask of yourself while defining public methods is, "What should these methods do?" Although the answers to this question will vary greatly from class to class, some typical answers include, "Set some data values" and "Get some data values." Other methods instruct an object to "start doing this job" or "stop doing that job."

5.5.1.3.2   *What Information to Do It With?*

An object's data members contain most of the information a method needs to do a job. However, sometimes an object needs additional information in order to accomplish its task. This information should be contained in the parameters of the member functions.

Since the order and types of parameters define unique functions in C++, defining them well is key to good protocol design. Parameter lists can get long. In order to minimize this, use default data values whenever possible. You should put the parameters most likely to change at the front of the list and those most likely to keep their default values at the end.

While developing protocol method parameters, take advantage of C++'s tight type checking. If you have flags or other data that aren't really numbers, don't use integers or unsigned integers to represent them. User defined data types are more appropriate, and they will clarify your meaning to programmers using your classes later. They will also give you more opportunities to take advantage of function overloading if you need the same method in a different context.

5.5.1.4   Public Data

Any data item you make public becomes part of your protocol, whether you intend it to or not. An object's public data can be seen by any other object or function. That part's not so bad. Any other object or function can change an object's public data, which is not necessarily desirable. Because of the possibility of having an object's data changed in a way not controlled by the object, public data is not usually the best way to provide access to that data.

5.5.1.4.1   *Using const*

You can make any data item "read only" by using the **const** key word. This is one way to assure that no other object changes the data. It also assures that the owning object won't change the data. Once a **const** variable is initialized, it can't be changed.

5.5.1.4.2 Who Can Change the Data?

The question you need to ask yourself while defining data items is exactly who you want to be able to change the data in any objects of that class. Then you need to ask yourself "Why ?" Most of the time you will not want many people to be able to change the data.

5.5.1.4.3 Reasons for Public Data

Although this is heresy to OO purists, there are times when using public data is the best solution to a particular problem. Sometimes the primary purpose of a class is to contain application data. If a class consists of nothing but data members and functions to set and get the values of the data members and one or two other functions, perhaps the data should be public. In this case, it may even be better to make the **class** a **struct.** If a class is defined more by its data than by its operations and it is unlikely that the structure of the data or the data types will change, public data may be acceptable.

5.5.1.4.4 Reasons Against Public Data

Quite often an object contains information that can be considered application independent. It may contain data about the state of the object, intermediate calculations results, or information about the way the object was initialized. Your program may need to take certain actions when the value of a field within an object changes. Arbitrary changes to data by functions outside a class jeopardize the integrity of your objects.

Making data public limits your ability to change the implementation of the class. If you want to provide access to a class's data, it is usually better to allow access through public methods. For example, suppose you choose to store a month, day, and year as integers in a "date" class, using the Gregorian style. Then, at some latter time, you discover some good algorithms that use Julian dates instead of Gregorian. If you started by allowing direct access to the year, month, and day variables, you must either choose not to change your implementation or change a lot of code.

5.5.1.5 Protected Methods and Data

Protected methods and protected data form a special type of protocol. Instead of being an interface to the rest of the world, protected methods and data are interfaces to the descendants of a class. In order to encourage reuse through inheritance, any non-public functions and methods should be **protected.** Even though C++ class members are private by default, you should only use private class members sparingly. In fact, I have never seen a good reason for using private class members instead of protected.

There is one thing you should remember when making these decisions: You can always loosen access restrictions without breaking existing code. If you tighten access restrictions, you are likely to break existing code. If you're in doubt during the initial class specifications, tend toward tight restrictions, you can always loosen them later.

5.5.1.6   Changes to Existing Classes

Change is inevitable. At times this seems more true in this profession than elsewhere. If our class protocols are designed well, we should be able to change our implementations almost at will. However, each change should be designed at least as carefully as the original class.

Change to the internals of the class can become almost routine. There may be times when we need to change the class protocols, however. Here are some guidelines to making changes to existing classes that will help you keep your pledge to the outside world.

5.5.1.6.1   *Don't Mess with Protocol Parameters*

If you change the order or data types of existing protocol functions, you break every piece of code that uses that function. This squelches any productivity gains you may have had otherwise.

Adding parameters to protocol methods isn't bad. If you must add to the parameters on protocol methods, add the new parameters to the end of the parameter lists with default values that won't break existing code.

If you must delete or change the order of parameters in protocol methods of classes in use (and this should be an emergency last resort action), publish the changes needed to keep existing code working when you release the new version of the class.

5.5.1.6.2   *Add to Protocol*

Whenever an inevitable change in requirements mandates a mutation of your protocol, try to add methods instead of changing existing ones. Changes by addition won't break existing code.

5.5.1.6.3   *Inherit and Change*

Often requests for change reflect a special condition for a more general case. Instead of changing a class and affecting every piece of code that uses that class, create a specialized version of the class using inheritance. Then change only the code that needs to be changed.

5.5.1.6.4   Use Version Control

Finally, if you must make a change to an existing class, provide some way to get back to the previous version of the code. Think about how this will be done during design or make a policy before design begins. A good way to do this is to use a version control system.

5.5.2   Developing Class Hierarchies

Inheritance is a key feature in OO development. It allows you to specify "is a kind of " relationships between classes. Inheritance allows you to define a protocol for a family of classes, implement common code between classes, and reduce redundant code. A base class and its descendants are known collectively as a class hierarchy. In OO design, the importance of building good class hierarchies is second only to development of that protocol. Class hierarchies allow you to organize your classes into a logical structure.

5.5.2.1   Specific, General, Specific . . .

It would be nice if class hierarchies simply fell together they way they're supposed to, but it doesn't work that way in real life. Usually, you discover class hierarchies by designing several "stand-alone" classes. You then look for classes with the following things in common:

- Similar purposes
- Common attributes
- Common behaviors

When you have grouped similar classes together, you can generalize them into a cohesive hierarchy. Remember that you can usually generalize a class without breaking code that depends upon it. When generalizing existing classes, you need to be certain that you're still keeping the contract you made to the rest of the world when you defined the class protocol.

One way of generalizing classes is to define an abstract class from which to derive all similar classes. An abstract class defines the attributes, internal implementations, and protocols common to all the classes in a hierarchy, just like any base class. Abstract classes, however, are used only as base classes. They don't have instantiated objects. In C++, abstract classes can assure that derived classes define certain required services. Figure 5-1 shows how specific classes can be generalized.

As time goes on, you are likely to discover needs that were not addressed by your original classes and hierarchies. You may need to modify existing classes. You will probably need to add specific derivations of the abstract class. Figure 5-2 shows how the hierarchy could have evolved over time.

A. Before Generalization

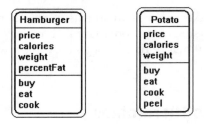

B. After Generalization

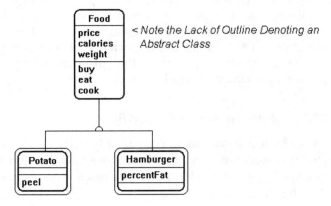

FIGURE 5-1 Generalization during inheritance.

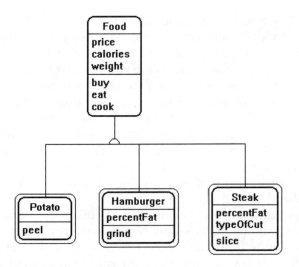

FIGURE 5-2 After further specialization.

This is a continuous process for certain class hierarchies. After a few special-izations, it may be time to generalize again. Figure 5-3 shows a further set of modifications to the example hierarchy. Note that a general "Meat" class has been added as a generalization of "Steak" and "Hamburger." You can see how in an evolving project this could go on for almost ever.

5.5.2.2   Multiple Inheritance

Remember, a key goal to OO development is the accurate modeling of the appli-cation domain. If a class is more than one kind of thing, then we need to be able to represent that in our program and in our designs. This is where multiple inheritance comes in. Multiple inheritance is a powerful tool, and it can be easily abused. Used carefully, it is a valuable aid to OO development.

5.5.2.2.1   *Purpose*

Sometimes a class is not just one kind of thing. It can be accurately stated that a potato is a kind of food and that a potato is a kind of plant. Frequently a program needs to deal with a class that can accurately fit into several different base classes. Multiple inheritance fills that need.

5.5.2.2.2   *Multiple Inheritance is Good*

Multiple inheritance is useful in many situations. It can help you to accurately model objects in your problem domain. That's the situation in the food example

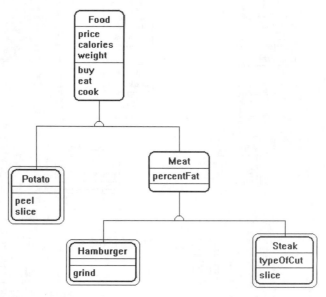

FIGURE 5-3   Yet another generalization.

cited above. Figure 5-4 shows an example of how multiple inheritance can be used to model our food example.

Multiple inheritance can allow a new class to conveniently implement the behavior of two or more other classes, even if those two classes were developed independently of one another. One common use for this behavior is to add persistence to objects. I will demonstrate this in the class librarian chapters.

5.5.2.2.3   *Multiple Inheritance is Bad*

There are a couple of problems associated with multiple inheritance. Sometimes confusion and unpredicted behavior are caused by inheriting from classes with methods that have the same names but have different meanings. In Figure 5-5, the "pick" method for "Plant" means to "harvest" and "pick" for "Food" means to "choose." Potato must resolve the ambiguity. Each language that supports multiple inheritance has its own rules for dealing with this ambiguity. We'll pursue this matter further in the C++ chapter.

Multiple inheritance also adds overhead to your programs. Some of this overhead is there even if you never create any classes using multiple inheritance. (Frankly I consider this to be a problem for the compiler vendors to solve, not a problem with multiple inheritance.)

5.5.3   Defer Internals Until Understand Full Scope of Class Duties

You don't have to be as careful with the private and protected members of a class as you do its public members. You have to be more careful with protected mem-

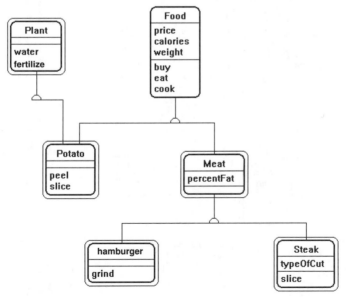

FIGURE 5-4   Multiple inheritance.

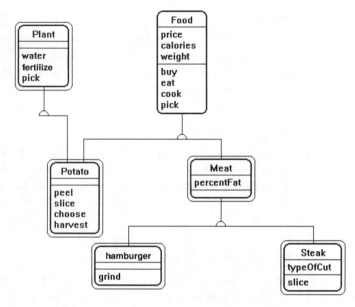

FIGURE 5-5 Problems with multiple inheritance.

bers than you do with private ones, because descendants can depend on protected members. You don't need to specify their details until the latter part of design. By first focusing on how you want a class to provide and receive data and instructions, you can defer the decisions on the implementation of the class until you have enough information to make a good decision.

5.5.4 Choose Your Friends Carefully

In C++, as in life, you must choose your friends carefully. A friend is a class or function that has full access to protected and private members. I once heard it put like this, "In C++, it's ok to let your friends touch your private parts." Because friends have full access to a class, it's best to treat them as an extension of the protocol of that class, rather than part of the class's implementation.

5.5.5 Identifying How Objects and Classes Perform Their Duties

No man is an island, and the same can be said about objects and classes. (I've been making a lot of anthropomorphisms in this chapter.) Classes need to relate to one another to form a program. In design, we identify exactly how they're going to do that.

5.5.5.1   Class Purposes

One way to help identify the way objects relate to each other is to identify the purposes of their classes. Any given class can have several purposes. Some purposes are very context-specific. Others are more general. The following are the categories I often divide classes into:

5.5.5.1.1   *Model—Real World*

Applications often model some aspect of the real world. Model classes represent objects in the real world, focusing on the attributes and behaviors required for the system under development. Model classes are less likely to be reused than almost any other type of class. This is not as true if the systems you develop typically are all in the same problem domain.

5.5.5.1.2   *Collection—Holds Other Objects*

A collection or container class exists to hold objects. These classes are some of the most widely available commercial C++ classes. Typically there are two types of container class libraries: the "tree" and the "forest."

A "tree" collection hierarchy requires that all objects to be contained are of types descended from one root class, often called "Object" in deference to SmallTalk's built-in collection classes. The entire class hierarchy forms a single tree. If your class isn't on that tree, the objects of that class can't be held in the collection classes. Often, an entire application is built from objects of classes that descend from "Object." Thus, the entire application forms a single "tree."

A "forest" collection hierarchy allows objects from any class into its containers. The application consists of objects from several class hierarchies, or "trees." If your application has a lot of "trees" it is a "forest."

5.5.5.1.3   *Computer Device Interface*

These classes work with the hardware, operating systems, database management systems, and other "computerish" stuff. Two commonly available class library types in this category are database interface libraries and user interface libraries. Ideally, the concrete classes should descend from abstract classes that define protocols for accessing the system in question. Platform dependencies should be isolated from other classes. Porting a program to another platform should be as "easy" as creating a class with new platform dependent internals. One commercial class library that does an exceptionally good job of this is the Zinc User Interface Library. I'll discuss Zinc a little more in chapter 7.

5.5.5.1.4   *Adapters*

Adapters are classes that help incompatible classes work together. An adapter may translate the protocol of one class into another. Suppose you're using two different commercial class libraries. One class library has a "List" class and another has a "Queue" class. Classes in the first library expect a "List" and the ones in the second expect a "Queue." An adapter could make a "List" look like a "Queue" and a "Queue" look like a "List." Adapters often use multiple inheritance to accomplish their tasks.

5.5.5.1.5   *Transformers—Rearrange Data For Other Classes*

A transformer is a class that takes data in, manipulates it, and puts it back out. A "Tokenizer" is a good example of a transformer. It takes a stream of characters in and sends a stream of tokens out. The C++ iostreams make use of transformers.

Remember, a class can fall into more than one of these categories. A "FileCabinet" class, for example, may be both a model and a collection.

5.5.5.2   "The Guts" of The Object

Before you start writing code, you should have a good idea of how you want your objects to work. The "guts" of an object should be planned as well as the interface. In the latter part of design, you solidify these plans. If you've done your "up front" work well, this won't be nearly as complicated as planning the details of a procedural system.

5.5.5.2.1   *Protected and Private Members*

In C++, the protected and private members make up the implementation or "guts" of a class. Just like the public protocol functions, each internal function should have a clearly stated purpose. Its responsibilities, constraints, performance criteria, and available resources should be clearly defined.

5.5.5.2.2   *Specific Algorithms and Logic*

Sometimes, you need to specify exactly how you want a member function to work. In these cases, you may want to use pseudo-code, flow charts or logic tables to specify the details of the underlying algorithms and logic of the functions. Other times, you may want to depend on the programmer to come up with an acceptable algorithm.

5.6   A GENERAL DESIGN STRATEGY

How does all this fit into our overall plan of *What, How, Action,* and *Improvement?* Here's how design fits our overall development strategy:

1.   Figure Out What You Want to Do. (See Analysis Chapter for Details)
2.   Figure Out How You Want to Do It.

    A. Clarify Requirements from Analysis
       a. Identify High Level Protocol For Candidate Classes
       b. Identify Major Relationships Between Objects
       c. Gather Classes Into Subject Areas or Categories
       d. Record the Results Using Your Selected Notation and Specification Technique
    B. Select an Area Upon Which To Focus
    C. Refine List of Candidate Classes, Applying the Elements of "Good" Design
       a. Look for Existing Classes to Reuse
       b. Look for Existing Hierarchies to Inherit From
       c. Gather What's Left Into New Hierarchies
       d. Complete the Protocol
       e. Record the Results Using Your Selected Notation and Specification Technique
    D. Design the Implementation
       a. Clarify the Responsibilities, Constraints, and Available Resources of Internals
       b. Specify Underlying Algorithms and Logic or Defer to Programmer
       c. Record the Results Using Your Selected Notation and Specification Technique
    E. Reaffirm Object Relationships Within Focal Area
    F. Reaffirm Object Relationships Outside Focal Area
    G. Move on To Programming or Next Focal Area
  3. Do It.
  4. Make It Better.

5.6.1   Clarify Requirements from Analysis

The details of this activity will depend on how and when you did analysis. If you did not do an OO analysis, you will need to examine the results of analysis and create a list of candidate classes. If you used structured analysis, data stores and external entities are candidates for classes. Processes are good starts for protocol methods. If you developed an English analysis, start by identifying important nouns as class candidates and verbs as potential methods.

If you did OOA, this activity will overlap with the strategy presented in the previous chapter. That's not a coincidence. The transition from analysis to design is really both analysis and design.

You will also need to specify (or confirm) the way these objects relate to one another. (See the discussion on protocol earlier in this chapter.) In design, you want to focus on the details of how this can be accomplished. You ask questions like, "What parameters do these functions need?"

If you're using a notation that supports the concept of categories or subjects (like Booch or Coad and Yourdon), and you haven't done so in analysis, gather your classes into related subject areas early. You can change them later if you need to. Note that each major strategic section has the step "Record Results." See the discussions on notations and methodologies for details.

5.6.2   Select an Area Upon Which to Focus

Again, some of this selection will depend on your development model. If you're using an iterative model, you may want to focus on an area that implements certain features. At any rate, you need to narrow your focus to concentrate on the design details. In their OOD book, Coad and Yourdon identify four major components that could serve as focal areas: the Problem Domain Component, the User Interface Component, the Data Management Component, and the Task Management Component [Coad, Yourdon 1991]. In large systems, these components may be separated into finer focal areas. Other organizational divisions are possible. It depends on how you perceive the system.

5.6.3   Refine the List of Candidate Classes

Now we get down to the finer details of design. Until now, we've been working with candidate classes, classes that would probably be included in the program. Now we need to decide whether the candidates really can do the job.

Before deciding to create a new class, see if you have any old ones that can do the job. The class librarian we develop in this book can make that job easier. You may have a "Car" class in your candidate list. Before creating a detailed specification for a "Car," search your class catalog and find an "Automobile" class that accomplishes the same tasks. Obviously, you need to replace your "Car" candidate with "Automobile."

Usually, you will have candidates that are, in fact, simply specializations of existing classes. Again, inheriting from an existing class is preferable to creating a new hierarchy. You may have to modify your ideas about your initial protocol to fit it into the hierarchy.

After you've identified reusable classes and specialized other classes, probably some candidates will be left over. If you haven't done so already, gather these classes into hierarchies. (See the discussion on inheritance.)

By now, you've probably got a much better idea about how your focal classes relate to other classes. You should have a better understanding of what the classes need to do and what information will enable them to do it. You've probably discovered some holes in your protocol. Fill in these holes while you're refining your candidate list. David Bullman has some good ideas on object completion [Bullman, 1991]. He has the following suggestions:

1.   Look for inverse operations. If you have an "add" method, perhaps you also need a "delete."

2. Perhaps you need an "undo" type of operation for error handling.
3. Look for complementary operations. If you have an "add" and a "delete," perhaps you need a "modify" as well.
4. Look for other logical extensions. (He admits this is rather open ended, but necessary.)

5.6.4   Design the Implementation

We discussed most of the issues regarding implementation in sections 5.5.3. Be certain you're clear on what needs to be done in the implementation, specifically the algorithms and logic.

5.6.5   Reaffirm Object Relationships in the Focal Area

When you think you're done changing the protocols of your classes, take another look at the objects in the area you're working on. Do the relationships you established earlier still work? Have you broken anything that needs to be fixed? Walk through the design documents looking for inconsistencies in your protocols.

5.6.6   Reaffirm Object Relationships Outside the Focal Area

Some objects will have relationships with objects not in your area of focus. After you've checked for internal inconsistencies, be certain to check for external inconsistencies. Are the objects that relate to other objects outside the area still able to get and provide the required data?

5.6.7   Move on to Programming or the Next Focal Area

This activity will vary with the development model you use. If you're using a waterfall model, you may complete designing before moving on to begin programming. If you're using the iterative model, you may want to code the area you've just designed.

5.7   SUMMARY

Design is figuring out how the system under development is supposed to work. Design is implementation dependent. You should know the language, the libraries, and the skill of the programmers before you begin design. No matter what development model you use, design comes after analysis and before programming.

Design has a three fold purpose:

1. You need to experience the process of figuring out how the system is supposed to work. It is a learning experience.
2. You need to record this understanding.
3. Others will need this understanding as well.

The seven principles for making design and the process of design "human friendly" are:

1. Have Clear Requirements.
2. Use a Methodology, But Avoid Dogma.
3. Know Your Audience.
4. Maintain Perspective.
5. Match Design to Requirements.
6. Know and Use the Elements of Good Design.
7. Make the Design Testable.

Here is a summary of the elements of good OO design:

1. Classes and class hierarchies should be highly cohesive.
2. Classes should be loosely coupled with other classes. The exception to this is that since class hierarchies should be cohesive, classes will be tightly coupled with their ancestors.
3. The data implementation details of a class should be hidden from other classes.
4. Design to optimize reuse.
5. Keep class and method definitions small.
6. When designing classes and families of classes, keep the protocol, or class interface, stable.

CHAPTER 6
OOP in C++

"C++ is, as at least one wit observed, a classy programming language."

Al Stevens, *Teach Yourself . . . C++*, 1990, MIS: Press.

6.1   RECOMMENDATIONS FOR C++ NOVICES

This chapter is not intended to be a tutorial on the C++ programming language. It is intended to be an overview of how to use C++ to implement the concepts presented in the previous chapters and a preview of the upcoming chapters. If you are not at least somewhat familiar with C++, I recommend that you find an introductory book on the subject. The recommended reading list in the appendix has a list of some good C++ books.

Whether you've only seen a little C++, or you are very familiar with C, you will probably find this chapter useful. It will highlight many of the C++ features that make it a good choice for OO development. The examples in this chapter will give you a taste of things to come in future chapters. If you have trouble with these examples and want to fully understand the code in upcoming chapters, see the recommended reading list. If you have a good introductory book on C++ and a good C++ reference, you'll do OK.

6.2   Support for OOP in C++

6.2.1   Why C++?

One does not require an OO language to use an OO programming style. If you use a programming language designed to support OOP, you don't necessarily get an OO program. If you want to use the OOP style, it's usually easier to use a language that has explicit support for OOP. I've chosen C++ as my primary OOP development language for the following reasons:

1.   C++ is a superset of C. I've been programming in C since 1985. I won't lose my existing code.

2. Most other OOP languages have slower execution speeds and end up using more memory.
3. C++ is more flexible because it is a hybrid language. There are still times when the object model does not apply.
4. It is likely that C++ will become the industry's language of choice within the next few years. I don't want to play catch-up.

6.2.2   What Features This Chapter will Cover

In rest of this chapter we'll discuss the following OO C++ features:

1. Classes and Objects
2. Polymorphism Using Overloaded Functions and Operators
3. Inheritance and Other Forms of Abstraction and Specialization
4. C++ I/O Streams

C++ has other important features. Some just make it a better C. Others are more subtle OOP support features. The features I'm presenting in this chapter are those which I believe to be the most important for OO development.

6.2.3   How This Chapter will Cover Them

As this chapter progresses we'll begin building the tools we've been talking about in the past five chapters. As we discuss C++, we'll build the core classes for the Librarian, Browser, and Graphic Tool. You may want to put a bookmark at Figure 6-1 and Listings 6-1 through 6-5. I will refer to these extensively through the chapter. These listings can be found in Appendix D.

6.2.3.1   The Problem Domain Model

6.2.3.1.1   *Modeling OO Components*

To build the OO CASE tools in later chapters, we want to model the components of OO development. The core of that model will consist of the following classes:

ClassDefinition: This class models the class definition. It encapsulates data and function definitions. It serves as the focus for everything we're going to do with automated OOA and OOD.

ClassMemberDefinition: This abstract class models the class members. There are two types of members: data members and member functions. This models their common attributes and behaviors.

DataMemberDefinition: This concrete descendant of ClassMemberDefinition models the data members of each class.

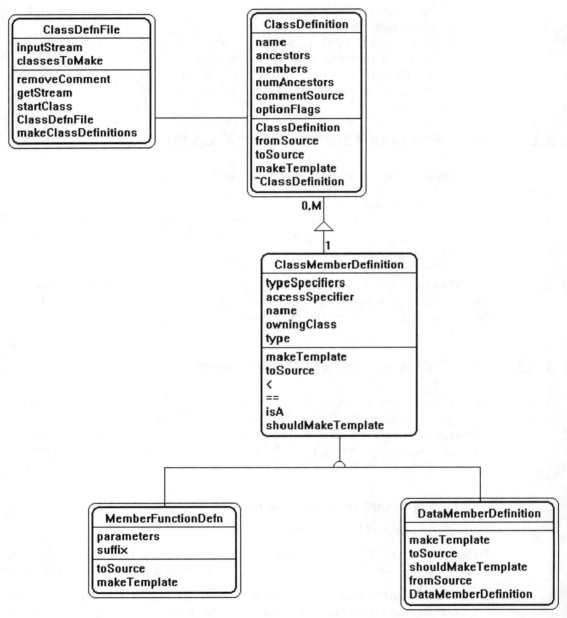

FIGURE 6-1   Initial analysis/design diagram for ClassDefinition model.

MemberFunctionDefinition: This class models the member functions of each class.

ClassDefnFile: This class provides access to a header file containing the source code for one or more classes.

Figure 6-1 has a Coad and Yourdon diagram of OOP components. A ClassDefinitionFile contains several ClassDefinitions. A ClassDefinition consists of a list of ClassMemberDefinitions. Each ClassMemberDefinition can be either a MemberFunctionDefinition or a DataMemberDefinition. Let's look at some basic requirements for classes that model OO development.

1. Each class, member, or function knows all of its vital statistics. (Name, data type, ancestors, etc.)
2. Given syntactically correct source code, each component can build an object of itself.
3. Each component can generate its own definition in source code form.
4. Class function members can generate empty templates of themselves.

These classes and their relationships form the foundations upon which all of the tools in this book are built. The analysis, design, and coding of this particular model took about three iterations. The source code here is the result of those iterations. Since the focus of this chapter is C++ programming, I haven't gone into the complete analysis and design here, nor have I detailed each iteration. The essential information usually found in the templates for these diagrams is found in the source code comments.

6.2.3.1.2   Prototypes

Often in a new project, the OO developer will prototype vital parts of the system to develop an understanding of unfamiliar parts of the problem domain. It also allows him or her to become familiar with the features and limitations of any classes he or she plans to reuse. The ClassDefinition family of classes used in this chapter is just such a prototype. Before building these classes, my experience with C++ streams was limited to simple input and output. One of my goals in the construction of these classes was to learn how to use streams more efficiently.

6.2.3.1.3   A Small Sample Application, the Template Builder

The computer is a great tool for automating repetitive tasks. One of the tasks I find myself repeating often is the creation of empty functions within a ".CPP" file after I've just typed a class definition into a ".H" file. There are just enough differences between a function declaration within a class specification and the function definition that "cut and paste" operations are only slightly faster than typing the entire definition into the editor. The application we'll be building will read class specifications from a header file and write empty function definitions and static data member definitions into a source file.

We'll need the following commands in the application:

Command	Meaning	Modifer(s)	Description
H	Header File	File Name	Header file with class declarations
O	CPP File	File Name	Output file for templates
C	Class Spec	Names or ALL	Specific classes in file for which to make templates
M	coMment	File Name	Use comments in templates. If a file name is specified, include its contents in the comments.
I	Inline	NONE	Expand the inline functions in the template file

These commands will be specified on the command line of the application.

6.3   CLASSES AND OBJECTS

In C++, a **class** is a special user defined data type. It encapsulates attributes and behaviors. An object, being an instance of a class, is considered to be a variable of that type. For those of you who are familiar with C, a **class** is similar to a **struct.** The difference is that while a struct usually allows full access to its members, a class does not. Note the ClassOffset struct in listing 6-3. It is both like and unlike a C struct. In C, structs do not contain function members.

Objects are instances of classes. A function can instantiate a class in one of two ways. It can use the new operator to allocate the object from the heap, or it can simply declare an object on the stack like a normal variable (examine Listings 6-2 and 6-4). Stack objects have a local scope, heap objects exist until the delete operator is used.

By convention, classes are defined in header files to be included by any file that requires the class definition. Also by convention, these files have either a " .H" or ".HPP" extension. The source code that implements the behavior of a class is usually placed in a file with the same base name as the header, but with a ".CPP" extension.

6.3.1   Class Members

6.3.1.1   C++ Class Members from Design Diagrams

Figure 6-1 shows the members of the various classes which are built in this chapter. The diagram shows the attributes in the center sections and the behaviors in the bottom sections. These will translate to C++ data members and member functions respectively.

The center of Figure 6-1 shows the design notation for the "ClassDefinition" class. The last class listed in Listing 6-1, found in Appendix D, shows how the diagram translates into a C++ class definition. Form 6-1 shows the design template for this class. I added the comments in parentheses after the classes were coded. We'll find that these templates evolve over the course of the book. The comments in parentheses will guide us in modification of future versions of the class.

Other things you may want to take note of while examining the ClassDefinition class in Listing 6-1 and Figure 6-1:

1. Only the public methods are displayed in the design diagram. I deferred internal details on all of these classes intentionally because I'm using these classes to learn about the problem domain.
2. The header is enclosed with a **#ifndef CLSDFN_H, #endif** pair. This prevents multiple inclusion of the file.
3. Not all the data items listed in the class definition are listed in Figure 6-1. Some of the variables are "working" variables shared by several of the internal methods, I don't usually list all these in the design because they can change so frequently. The need for others were discovered in the course of writing the code. These will be added in the next version of the design diagram.

6.3.1.2   Special Member Functions: Constructors and Destructors

C++ has two special kinds of member functions. One is called a constructor. A constructor is invoked whenever an object is created. You use a constructor to initialize the members of a class and to perform any other processing necessary before the object can be valid. A constructor is a member function with the same name as its class. Each of the classes defined in Listings 6-1 and 6-3 has a constructor. For example, the class ClassDefnFile has two constructors. If a class member does not have a default constructor (a constructor with no arguments), the constructor for that class must be called before the body of the function. See the constructor for "ClassDefinition" Listing 6-2 which initializes its data members, "members" and "numAncestors."

The other type of function is called a destructor. It performs any necessary cleanup before the object is destroyed. A destructor is a member function with the same name as its class with a tilde (~) in front of it. The destructor is automatically called when a stack object goes out of scope or when the delete operator is used.

6.3.1.3   A Special Data Member, "this"

Each instance of an object has an "invisible" pointer to itself called "this." Member functions that need to refer to the owning object can use "this." In Listing 6-2, **ClassMemberDefinition::operator ==** has a reference to this.

Class Name: ClassDefinition   **Version:** Chapter 6

Classifications: Model, Concrete

Ancestors: Defined: 7/10/92

Description/Purpose:

Defines a C++ class. This model will be used for a series of OO Case Tools. This class model can be created by reading a syntactically correct header file. Future versions or descendants of this class will allow other forms of model creation. It will have the ability to declare itself in a source file and make empty templates for its functions.

Keep your eye on this space for future enhancements to this class.

Data Attributes:

Visibility	Type	Name	Purpose/Comment
private	int	forwardDeclaration	Sometimes in a header file, a class is not fully defined but is a forward declaration. If that's true, we want to know about it. This variable is set to a non-zero value if this is in that case.
protected	IdString	name	Name of the class
	AncestorSpec	ancestors	List of this class's base class. (This name may be misleading, this is really a list of base classes, not ancestors. We may change this in future versions of the class.)
	int	numAncestors	Number of base classes in the array. (Again, note the misleading name, we may want to remove this particular member altogether and change the ancestors to a BIDS list.)
	MemberList	members	List of class members. These may be data members or member functions.
	istream	commentSource	Source for comment template for the class.

FORM 6-1   Template for class design.

	bitfield	expandInline	TRUE if the user wants inline functions to be included in the function templates.
	bitfield	useComments	TRUE if the user wants comments in the source files and templates.

Methods/Functions

Visibility	Name	Purpose	Coded	Tested
public	int getClassName(istream &in)	Return the class name from the input stream "in" Returns non-0 if there is a list of base classes after the name.	Yes	Yes
	void getAncestors(istream &in)	Fills ancestors (base class) list from input stream.	Yes	Yes
	void getMembers(istream &in)	Fills the member list from the input stream.	Yes	Yes
	void putComment(ostream &out, char *what, char *id)	Places the comments into the output stream.	Yes	Yes

FORM 6-1 *(continued).*

6.3.2 Private Members

There are three access specifiers in C++: private, protected, and public. Each access specifier indicates the visibility of the data members.

In C++, class members are private by default. Class members are private until a different access specifier is encountered. The private keyword is redundant for the "forwardDeclaration" data member of ClassDefinition class in Listing 6-1. But, by placing the keyword there, we clarify our intention. *258521*

Class members designated as private can be accessed in three ways. They can be accessed by members of the class to which they belong. They can be accessed by any class designated as friend. And they can be accessed by any function designated as friend. They cannot be accessed by descendant classes unless those descendants are also friends.

I try to limit the number of private members in my classes. If a member function using that private variable needs to be overloaded in a descendant classes, the task is often more complicated. If you make a member private, be certain you will have no need of it in a descendant class. Since I don't expect to need "ClassDefinition" descendants that have to access the "forwardDeclaration" variable, and since I needed an example of a private variable, I made it private.

6.3.3   Protected Members

Most data members should be protected. That means that only the functions in the owning class, the functions in descendant classes, and friend classes and functions have access to the members. Direct access to data members by the "outside" world is considered bad form in OO development. This helps enforce coupling and cohesion design decisions.

Protected member functions are used in the class implementation. These are the functions that do the detail work. The private functions are also used in the implementation, but protected functions are also available to descendant classes.

The classes in listings 6-1 and 6-3 have plenty of protected members. All of the data members after the protected keyword are protected until the next access specifier is encountered.

6.3.4   Public Members and Friends

Any class member, data, or function specified as public is accessible to any other class or function. These members form the class interface. The public keyword specifies which members form this interface.

6.3.5   Static Members

Static class members do not belong to specific objects, but rather to the entire class. Static member functions do not have access to non-static data members. Non-static data members have different values for each object. Static data members have one value to be shared by all instances of the class. Listings 6-1 and 6-2 show the static data members of "ClassMemberDefinition": "lastTypeSpec" and "numInstances."

They also show the static member function "showCount." The "showCount" function is a debugging function that I left in for this example. It is not part of the original design, nor will it be included in later versions of this class.

6.4   POLYMORPHISM AND FUNCTION OVERLOADING

Function and operator overloading provide polymorphism in C++. In C++, unlike most other existing computer languages (especially procedural languages), a function name is not a unique identifier. A function is identified by its name and its parameter type list. For example: **foo(int x),** is a different function than **foo(float x).** In the current version of C++, the return type of a function does not have any bearing on its uniqueness. This is called function overloading. In listing 6-3, the constructors and "makeClassTemplates" functions are overloaded. Each function with the same name should have the same purpose, so I don't duplicate function names on the design diagrams. Functions can be overloaded from base classes to derived classes. Section 6.5 discusses this further.

Although a function name alone does not normally identify a unique function, the function name alone does overload the function in a derived class. Listing 6-6 will not compile properly.

Operators (=,==,<,etc.) can also be overloaded. This is a very powerful C++ feature that is easily abused. The "==" operator and "<" operator are overloaded in several places in Listings 6-1, 6-2, and 6-3.

6.5   INHERITANCE, ABSTRACTION, AND SPECIALIZATION

In C++ classes can be derived from other classes using inheritance. Note the Generalization/Specialization structure of the "ClassMember" family in Figure 6-1. Examine Listing 6-1 to see how C++ implements these relationships.

6.5.1   Virtual Members

In C++ a pointer to a base class can point to an object in a derived class. **Virtual** member functions "expect" to be overloaded in derived classes. Consider the class "ClassMemberDefinition" in Listing 6-1. The functions "isA," "getName," "getTypeSpec," etc. do not have the virtual key word in front of them. If "MemberFunctionDefinition" decides to overload them, that overload will not be recognized in a pointer to "ClassMemberDefinition" that points to a "MemberFunctionDefinition" object . The classes with the virtual keyword will not have that problem. Virtual functions have slightly more overhead than non-**virtual** functions.

6.5.2   Purely Virtual Members and Abstract Data Types

Normally the **virtual** keyword is simply an invitation to descendants to overload a function. However, sometimes a function MUST be overloaded by its descendants. In that case, an "=0" is placed after the function declaration. This is called a "purely virtual function."

Any class with one or more purely virtual functions is called an abstract class and it cannot be instantiated. Note the lack of outline around the "Class MemberDefinition" in Figure 6-1 indicating an abstract class. Also note the number of purely virtual functions in its implementation in Listing 6-1.

6.5.3   Inheritance

C++ directly supports the OO concept of inheritance. The base classes for a derived class are listed between the class name and the beginning of the class declaration.

The access specifiers for class members also apply to base classes. Classes are private by default. In Listing 6-1 "DataMemberDefinition" and "MemberFunctionDefinition" classes have the "ClassMemberDefinition" class as a base class.

A public base class is fully visible to all subsequently derived classes (given the restrictions of the accesses specifiers within the base class), if a base class is specified as protected, inherited public and protected members are considered to be protected members of the derived class. If a class is specified as private, public and protected members are considered to be private.

6.5.3.1   Single Inheritance

In Section 5.2, we explored the basic concepts of inheritance and class hierarchies. Figure 6-1 and Listing 6-1 show examples of single inheritance in the "ClassMemberDefinition" family. As you can see it's fairly simple.

6.5.3.1.1   *Constructors and Destructors with Single Inheritance*

Objects of derived classes contain all the members of their base classes. Therefore, the constructor of the derived class must call the constructor of the base class. If the base class has a default constructor, this happens automatically. See Listing 6-7.

If a class does not have a default constructor, the derived class must initialize the base class just like other members. See Listing 6-8.

Note in the output of Listing 6-7 that the destructors are called in reverse order. If you ever intend to use a pointer to a base class to access a derived class (read almost always) you should use a virtual destructor. Look at the results of Listing 6-7 when there is no virtual destructor.

Let me explain the significance of Listing 6-7 in regard to virtual destructors. A base class pointer will often point to a derived class, just as *c1 points to a C3 class. Although C1::C1, C2::C2, and C3::C3 were called when the object *c1 was instantiated, only C1::~C1 was called during destruction. That is because C1::~C1 was not declared as virtual. This is, in fact, a programming error. If C3::C3 is ever called, there should always be a corresponding call to C3::~C3. C++ programmers count on it. In a non-trivial class, this could cause problems ranging from unfreed memory to unclosed files. These problems could be very hard to find.

6.5.3.1.2   *Scope Resolution Operator*

Since you may not always want to use the overloaded function in a class, C++ provides a scope resolution operator, "::",to bypass the overload. See Listing 6-9 for a sample of the scope resolution operator.

6.5.3.2   Multiple Inheritance

In Section 5.5.2.2.3, we briefly discussed the problems with multiple inheritance. The specifics of these problems vary from language to language. Examine Listing

6-10 for the ambiguity problems associated with multiple inheritance. This listing generates the errors listed below each line at compile time.

Listing 6-11 shows one way to resolve the ambiguities with the first problem using the scope resolution operator. Note that direct access to "C1" is still not possible from "c4."

Note in the output of Listing 6-11 that the constructor for "C1" is called twice. "C4" does in fact contain two copies of "C1." Although OO designers do not often show this type of multiple inheritance this way, Figure 6-2 shows how it really works. Sometimes you may want multiple copies of common ancestors, more often however, this is just a waste of your system's memory.

6.5.3.3   Virtual Base Classes

Suppose you *don't* want multiple copies of the common ancestor in your derived class. Most of the time you would like reality to reflect Figure 6-3. The C++ mechanism for accomplishing this is the virtual base class. When specifying a base class as virtual you are planning for the future, just as when you specify a function as virtual. If you plan to use a class in conjunction with another class that has the same base class, specify the base class as virtual, in both classes.

See Listing 6-12 for an example of the use of a virtual base class. Note the order of the constructor calls in the output. Note also that the default constructor for "C1" was called. The constructor was *not* called for each base class as it was in the previous examples.

Listing 6-13 shows that the constructor for "C1" can be called in the constructor of "C4." Examine the output. If you're not comfortable with what's happening in these examples, get the examples from the disk that comes with this book, and play with them for awhile.

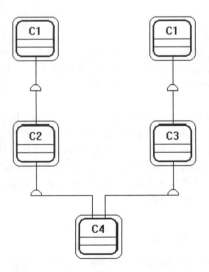

FIGURE 6-2   Multiple inheritance using base classes with a common ancestor.

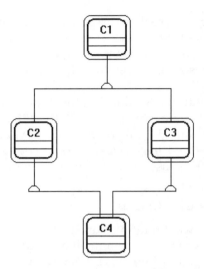

FIGURE 6-3 Normal notation of base classes with common ancestor (also the way virtual base classes work).

6.5.3.4   What Does All This Mean?

If you use multiple inheritance in your design, you need to be aware of the caveats listed above. You should decide how to resolve potential ambiguities as soon as you see a structure like the one in Figure 6-3 in your design. This could be a matter of policy "Always use virtual base classes in these circumstances," or you could make this decision on a case-by-case basis. Whatever decision you make should be noted on the class design templates.

6.5.4   Templates

Recent implementations of C++ have included the concept of "templates." At the time of this writing, the only PC-based C+ compiler that supports this is Borland's. By the time you see this book, Microsoft may also support templates in its C++ compiler.

Templates are C++'s ultimate form of data abstraction. They allow you to define a general solution to a problem and then apply it to several types of classes. The most common use of templates is the formation of container classes. Template functions are also supported in C++. Since these aren't as important to OOP concepts, I've decided not to cover them here. Some of books in the recommended reading list on C++ will have details.

6.5.4.1   Using Templates

Templates allow the substitution of the identifier specified in the angle brackets, "<>," within the rest of the class. Listing 6-14 shows the how to use templates to create a simple "Stack" class.

Borland uses templates in its BIDS container library. The BIDS container class library comes with the Borland C++ compiler. BIDS uses class templates to define the underlying container mechanisms. It also uses templates to define what the containers will hold.

I use the BIDS library extensively when I need to use containers in Listings 6-1 through 6-4. (This is a good example of code reuse.) If you aren't using Borland's C++ compiler and you want to modify and compile these listings, you have several options:

1. If you have a compiler that supports templates, you can create your own container class that supports the protocol used in these classes.
2. If your compiler does not yet support templates, you can create a container class for each of the classes that needs to be contained. Again, examine the use of the BIDS containers in these classes and use the same protocol.
3. You can purchase a container class library and substitute it for the BIDS containers. You will probably need to rewrite those listings for the new protocol. As a variant on this, you can inherit from the commercial class and create an adapter class by defining a new protocol so you don't have to change Listings 6-1 through 6-4.
4. You can rewrite the classes using arrays like I did for the ancestor list.

There is one thing you should try to do for the users of your templates. If the template expects to use any operators or functions that all classes everywhere don't have, let the user (that is, other programmers) know about it in your comments or in the class's documentation. You will notice that the operators, "==" and "<" have comments to the effect that "BIDS needs this." Nowhere in Borland's documentation could I find that fact. I discovered it at compile time.

6.5.4.2   Using Templates with Inheritance

There are three ways to use template classes in inheritance. Listing 6-15 shows the two I use most often. The first way, "FloatStack," shows how to use a specific instance of a template class as a base class. The second way, "SafeStack," uses a template class as the base class for a template class. The third way is to use a normal class as a base class. Listing 6-16 shows how this works.

6.6   C++ STREAMS

As you've been examining the various example listings, you've no doubt noticed things like **"in >> c"** and **"cout << x"**. These are examples of the use of C++ streams. A stream is simply a series of bytes. This series can exist in a file, go to a screen, or come from the keyboard. The C++ stream hierarchy uses multiple inheritance with common ancestors. Figure 6-4 shows some of the most influential members of the C++ I/O stream family.

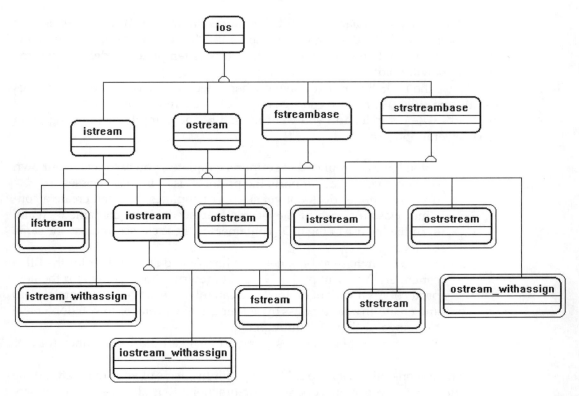

FIGURE 6-4   The C++ I/O stream family portrait.

6.6.1   Input, Output, and I/O Streams

The granddaddy of the iostream family is "ios." This class provides all the basic information and functionality needed by the rest of the family. It provides error checking and data formatting.

Any streams that provide input descend from "istream." They normally provide data to the rest of the world by using an overloaded **">>"** operator. Each data type has its own version of that operator. I would like to make a point about using this operator on strings. By default, all the white space before any input is skipped. White space always delimits an input string; the stream stops flowing into a string when white space is encountered. If the "ios::skipws" flag is turned off, before another string may be read the white space must be skipped by using the "ws" manipulator. The reason I'm mentioning this little detail, is that I didn't do it originally in the "MemberFunctionDefinition::makeSuffix" function. This created an infinite loop which took me a *very* long time to find.

Input streams have a "get" pointer that keeps track of the current location in the stream. The member functions "seekg" and "tellg" move and report on that pointer.

Any stream that accepts output descends from "ostream." The "ostream" uses an overloaded "<<" operator to transfer the data into the stream. Again, format flags and manipulators control the flow of data out of the stream. Output streams have a "put" pointer. The member functions "seekp" and "tellp" move and report on that pointer.

The "iostream" class (and its progeny) allows both input and output. It uses both the "<<" and ">>" overloaded operators. As a descendant of both istream and ostream it has both a "get" and a "put" pointer and uses "seekg," "seekp," "tellg," and "tellp" to manipulate those pointers.

6.6.2   Human Interface Streams

There are four standard global objects in C++, "cin," "cout," "cerr," and "clog." These correspond to "standard in," "standard out," buffered "standard error," and unbuffered "standard error," respectively.

The "cin" object is of the type istream_withassign, a descendant of istream. This means that "cin" could be assigned to something besides your keyboard if you want. The other objects are of the "ostream_withassign" type. These also can be reassigned. Note the use of "cout" in most of the examples in Listings 6-7 and beyond.

6.6.3   String Streams

A stream can provide input to and output from a string. Streams that do this descend from "strstreambase." In Listing 6-2, "MemberFunctionDefinition::make TypeAndName" and "MemberFunctionDefinition::makeParamList" use "istrstream" to take stream input from a string. Note that "istrstream" also descends from "istream."

The class "ostrstream" provides a stream to transfer characters out of a string. It decends from "strstreambase" and "ostream."

Listing 6-4 shows the use of the "strstream" class in the function "ClassDefnFile::getClassName." This class is not only an "iostream," providing input and output services, but a "strstreambase" descendant as well. One interesting feature of the "strsteam" class is that the "get" and "put" pointers are identical.

6.6.4   File Streams

By now, you've probably got a good feel for how this stuff works. The classes "ifstream," "ofstream," and "fstream" provide for input, output and both "to" and "from" files. If you examine Listings 6-2 and 6-4 you will see the repeated use of these file streams in various contexts.

6.6.5   Deferred Functionality

The beauty of this hierarchy is that you don't have to know where the data is coming from in order to use it. In most cases in Listings 6-2 and 6-4, especially in the class protocols, I use the abstract "iostream," "istream," and "ostream." That means I can use a temporary file or a string buffer without changing the interface to the class.

6.7   PUTTING IT ALL TOGETHER

The class and class member models can be assembled in any number of ways. (At least that's the intent.) The first application, the function template generator, has three purposes:

1. It is a prototype with which to learn the most critical classes of more complicated tools.
2. It is a test of some of the key methods in the classes.
3. It is a useful tool in its own right, not a "throw away" test program. Because we will use the program in our regular work, purpose number one is fulfilled.

6.7.1   Using the "ClassDefinition" and "ClassMemberDefinition" Classes

If you look at the application in Listings 6-1 through 6-5, you'll see that the application really has two tasks: read the header file and write the source template. The two methods used for these tasks are "fromSource" and "makeTemplate." The "ClassDefinition" class and the descendants of "ClassMemberDefinition" all have instances of these methods.

6.7.1.1   The "fromSource" Methods

Notice that the "fromSource" method is called in the constructor of each of the classes. The data members of the classes that define the model are filled with the "fromSource" methods. The methods read the header file in which a class is declared and fill the data in the class. Notice that the "fromSource" method of each class only knows how to deal with the source code of its own class.

Originally I had intended to buy or download some sort of "Parser" class. I really couldn't find an acceptable, affordable parser class. Rather than going immediately into a "build my own parser" mode, I decided to see what I could find in the procedural world. Most of the parsers I found were based on YACC and LEX. If I were to follow that path, I would have ended up defining the whole C++ grammar and having a HUGE procedural program. This program would be almost a full C++ compiler. This was much bigger than I had intended and not consistent with the theme of this book.

After the first OO maxim, "try to reuse rather than make" failed, I tried another OO maxim: "Every object, given the proper data should be able to do its own job." Rather than build an entire parser, I decided to build a pseudo-parser for each class. In order to simplify the task I decided to make a couple of assumptions:

1. Assume there are no comments in the source stream.
2. The pseudo-parser source stream's get pointer for the class will start at the beginning of the specific source code declaration of each class. The pseudo-parser will do no more than it needs to do.
3. Assume the source code is syntactically correct.

I used the *Borland C++ Programmer's Guide* to learn the formal C++ syntax, and I used it to design the pseudo-parser. The results can be seen in the "fromSource" methods in Listing 6-2.

6.7.1.2   The "makeTemplate" Methods

The second part of the application, writing the source template is almost trivial. The data stored in the class is written to the output stream using the standard "<< " operator. The "makeTemplate" methods use various flags to implement the user's preferences. One of the preferences, whether or not to use comments, will trigger the use of the "putComment" methods. These methods are also a fairly straight-forward use of streams.

6.7.1.3   The "toSource" Methods

The "toSource" methods generate a class declaration like the one that would be contained in a header file. The methods are not needed in the sample application, since the application starts with a header as input, and they provide a service you would expect from a complete model of a class and its members.

6.7.2   Using the "ClassDefnFile" Class

The class "ClassDefnFile" is a model of a header file that contains class definitions. It performs file specific "pre-processing" such as comment removal and class identification. In effect it "owns" the classes contained in the file.

The constructor builds the class from the source file. It helps assure the correctness of many of the assumptions made for the other classes. It removes the comments and finds the start of each class declaration so the stream's get pointer can be positioned properly. It's also the "controlling" class of the application. The class remembers the user's options and from which classes the user wants templates.

6.7.3   The Program

The main program is almost trivial. It interprets the user's options. Next, it instantiates an object of the class "ClassDefnFile." Then it asks that object to make the templates.

The "main" function is procedural and not object-oriented. It works, it's easy to understand, and it was easy to write. Are we sacrificing anything by using a procedural function to drive our application? In this case, no. There's not much of a chance that this particular function will be used again. That's not much of a sacrifice; it's a small function.

Listing 6-17 shows the input, output, and comment files to demonstrate how the program works. The source Listings 6-1 through 6-17 and the executable program generated from them are in the CHAP6 subdirectory on the accompanying disk.

6.7.4   A "Post-mortem" on the Project

Every development model has an improvement activity. This is where we look back over the classes and the program and make some observations on how we could improve them. This activity is more important in OO development than it is in traditional development because we intend to reuse the components.

If most of the code were for a single-use program, "good enough" would be good enough. In OO development, however, the quality of your program is tied directly to the quality of your components. Even if we don't have the time to make the improvements right now, we should identify places the classes could be improved for the benefit of future users of the class. In a prototyping application such as this one, this is not an optional activity.

For the benefit of work in future chapters, I've made the following observations:

1. There is no way to recognize templates in the "fromSource" methods.
2. There "ClassDefnFile" class is not a complete model of a typical C++ header file. It lacks the ability to recognize the existence of the following:
   a. Function Prototypes.
   b. **#define** Values and Other Macros.
   c. Files **#include**d in the Header File.
   d. Variables Declared as **const.**
   e. Variables Used as **extern.**
3. There is no way other than "fromSource" to fill some of the data members in several classes.
4. The term "ancestors" refers to *all* classes that a class descends from: Its parents, its parents' parents, etc. What I really mean when I use this term is "base class" or "parent class." This error is included in the class design templates.

5. Design flaws and omissions were found during programming. The design diagram is not up to date with the code.
6. There is an inconsistent use of BIDS lists and arrays.
7. The use of the "IdString" type is inconsistent. It may be redundant with the use of the "String" class.
8. The classes rely heavily on a "non-standard" class library, BIDS. This could effect portability and their use by programmers non-Borland compilers.
9. The "ClassDefinition" class is only used for class constructs. C++ treats class, struct and union constructs as variations on the same construct. We need a way to deal with struct and union constructs.

6.7.5   Action Items on the "Post-mortem"

Before we try to use these classes in the "real" tools, I need to take some actions based on the observations in the previous section. I'll need to take the following steps to improve the classes:

1. Since templates are not a completely standardized part of C++, this action will be deferred indefinitely.
2. Change the "ClassDefnFile" into "HeaderFileDefn." Include data members and functions to implement the missing features. Again, there will be a design which will be evaluated before coding on this new class begins.
3. Add more "get" and "set" methods to classes where they're missing.
4. Change the word "Ancestor" to "Parent" or "BaseClass" in variable names and forms where it is inappropriately used. If this class were more mature, this action might not be taken because of the ramifications in other classes. That's why we do the post-mortem at the end of the initial prototype.
5. Figure 6-5 has design diagram that reflects the current code.
6. The arrays will be changed to appropriate containers. Therefore variables like "numAncestors" can be removed.
7. The use of "IdString" will be limited to those places where an identifier is used. Any other use of the type will be replaced with a char array or "String."
8. In cases where portability is important, it pays to create an "adapter" class that shields the programmer from non-portable code. The "D_List" class is such a class. Its design will be reviewed in Chapter 9. The source code for this class is in the CHAP10 subdirectory.
9. During the design and construction of the next tool, "Librarian," we'll add struct and union functionality to "ClassDefinition."

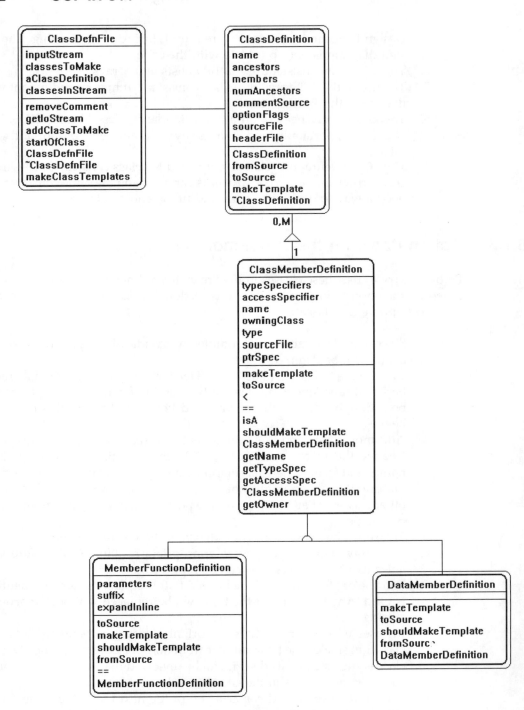

FIGURE 6-5 Current model of ClassDefinition classes.

6.8   SUMMARY

This chapter is not for C++ novices. If you need more C++ background, see the recommended reading list at the back of this book. C++ has several features that make it a good language for OOP. The OOP features covered here include: classes and objects, inheritance via derived classes, polymorphism via operator, and function overloading and data abstraction via templates.

Streams are some of the most useful C++ classes. They form a reusable core of very flexible classes. This chapter explains in a general way how to use streams to control the flow of data through classes.

In order to explain the important OO features of C++, we've built a set of classes that model the components of C++ programs. We built a program that reads a C++ header file and generates empty functions. These functions serve as templates for C++ programs.

In OO development, the quality of a program is directly tied to the quality of its components. Therefore, once the program was built, we made a list of things that could be improved. Then we made a list of things that could be done in response to the first list.

C++ has other important features. Some just make it a better C. Others are more subtle OOP support features. The features I've presented in this chapter are those I feel are the most important for OO development.

CHAPTER 7
The Overview—
SSOOT CASE

"CASE can be viewed in a much larger context than the hotly publicized drawing tools of the present."

Peter Coad and Ed Yourdon, *Object-Oriented Design*, 1991, Prentice-Hall.

7.1   INTRODUCTION

7.1.1   We Have a Vague Notion

Ideas don't often come out in a nice organized fashion. I thought it would be interesting to watch a vague notion become a clearer set of initial requirements and a work plan. This chapter explores how to take a vague notion and solidify it. After I had about a third of this chapter written, I realized it should probably be laid out in a slightly different order. I decided to leave the order alone because it reflects how people really think when they start building a system.

7.1.2   Why CASE Tools?

There were several reasons why I chose CASE as the primary application domain for this book.

1.   Although this is changing even as I write this, CASE tools are some of the most expensive programs on the market. This may be fine for large companies, but the American software industry owes much of its success to small consortium of one or two developers.
2.   Programmer's tools are low risk. A significant factor in considering the risks associated with a project is the development team's familiarity with the problem domain. Software development is a problem domain with which you and I are intimately familiar.

3. These tools are needed. Most CASE tools still assume a structured analysis, design, and programming methodology. Again, as OO technology moves into the main stream, this will change. (Frankly, this book is part of that change.)

7.1.3 Puns, Acronyms, and Misspelled Words

Now that we know what we're going to build and why we're going to build it, we need to name it. I have observed two factors that go into naming most software: acronyms that form misspelled words, and puns. I've decided that the CASE tools we'll be building will be called "SSOOT CASE." It stands for "Some Simple Object-Oriented Tools for Computer Aided Software Engineering." In the rest of this chapter, we'll start the project. We'll look at the people involved, some of the issues we may have to deal with, and some of the initial requirements.

7.2   "PLAYERS" IDENTIFIED

In Chapter 4, we talked about the importance of knowing the players for any project we're going to work on. This project is no exception. In this section we'll identify the key players in this project. This isn't something you'd necessarily do formally in your projects, but you should probably do it informally for your own benefit.

7.2.1 Development Team

This one's easy. It's me. The publisher will have the product reviewed technically before he or she releases it, and I'll have some friends look it over and give me their opinions. But other than that, I'm the development team.

7.2.2 Users

This one's easy, too. It's you. The intended audience for this book includes software engineers, programmers and development managers. Ultimately, you will decide the success or failure of the programs developed here.

7.2.3 Client

This is a little more difficult, but not much. Remember, the client is the one who pays for the project. My client is the publisher. I'll get my money from it; you're its client. Since I'll be paid based on how many books are sold, indirectly you're also my client.

7.2.4 Domain Experts

The domain experts are the ones who know about the problem. In this case, there are several.

1. The development team. I'm a team of one, but this is an area I've been working in since 1989, so I consider myself an expert in this field.
2. Publications. I've gone through journals, magazines, books, and on-line services researching this book, looking for experiences and ideas which pertain to the current problem. I've cited the relevant sources. (See the bibliography.)
3. Colleagues. I don't always work alone. I learn from my co-workers, ask advice of friends in the field, and get tips from mentors. Most of this didn't come as advice on this project specifically. When you work with people, you learn from them. Every time someone says "I wish we had a program that would . . ." or "It works better if we . . ." it contributes to your personal knowledge base.

7.3 NOTATIONS TO SUPPORT?

One of the tools we're going to build is a graphic tool. A constant of our industry is change. If I choose to build a tool that supports only one of the notations listed here, it'll be obsolete before this book hits the shelves. We'll need to decide which notation to support.

What follows is a discussion of which notations we want to consider. At this point, we're still developing requirements. This is kind of a brain storming session for the graphic tool. We'll revisit some of these issues in more detail in Chapter 14.

7.3.1 Coad and Yourdon

Since the Coad and Yourdon notation is the one I've chosen to use for the purposes of this book, I should probably support it in the graphic tool.

7.3.2 Booch

The Booch notation seems to be taking a small lead in the notation-standards race. To not support it would be a gross "sin of omission." It probably has more symbols than any other. Even Rational, the company with which Booch is associated, doesn't support all the symbols in the Booch Notation. Booch has published an essential subset of the Booch Notation. At the very least, we should try to support that subset.

7.3.3   OOSD

The OOSD notation has the capability to show more detail than Coad and Yourdon without the sheer size of the Booch notation. This level of detail should be available if designers want it.

7.3.4   Structured A/D

I am philosophically opposed to dogmatic software engineering. There will be times when structured analysis and design (A/D) still make sense. We don't want to trash the progress of the past in order to make way for the future. We should seriously consider supporting structured notation.

7.3.5   Advances in Technology and Methods

What about the next generation of software methods and methodologies? One of the great failings of this generation of CASE tools was that they weren't able to adapt when OOA/D came on the scene. On my first OO project, I spent too much time trying to make Excelerator (a questionable value in CASE tools anyway) work for any kind of OO design specification. I don't want that to happen with this tool. We need to find some way to support new, currently unknown notation when it makes its appearance.

7.3.6   An AfterThought

This section is this chapter's first substantial look at what we want SSOOT CASE to be like. When I laid out the initial outline for this chapter, I fell into the very trap I've been trying to warn people about. As soon as I saw the word CASE, I thought of drawing tools, and my first concern was about notation. I thought about rewriting this chapter and putting the notation at the end, but that would be cheating. As I said in the introduction, this is the thought process I really went through.

7.4   PLATFORMS?

Most new CASE tools seem to be targeted at high power UNIX and VAX based X-Windows work stations. What is the small company or lone programmer to do? I'd like to focus on small systems. The most common and affordable system available today is MS-DOS 5.0, on a '386 SX with a VGA color monitor. If the current trend continues, however, by the time this book is in your hand, hardware prices will be so low that '486s are the standard.), a 40-60 megabyte hard drive, and approximately 2 megabytes of RAM. This will be the target platform for SSOOT CASE.

Again, this section is a kind of brain storming session. These decisions, however, can't be deferred until later. We need to have a clear operating environment requirement before we continue.

7.4.1   Windows

Microsoft Windows is an ideal environment for CASE. The multi-window environment is great for simultaneously viewing drawings, specifications, and source code. At the time of this writing, it is also the fastest growing platform for small computers. Microsoft is announcing plans for Windows versions for larger systems that are compatible with current versions of Windows. We can't ignore this platform. SSOOT CASE will be available for Windows.

7.4.2   DOS

As nice as Windows is, not everybody has it, wants it, or likes it. We don't want to require Windows for SSOOT case. We don't even want to require graphics for the Librarian and Browser. Graphics require memory and CPU power that the developer may not want to "waste" on pretty displays. Graphics mode should be available but not required.

7.4.3   X-Windows, MAC, OS/2 PM?

What about other platforms? Should we exclude X-Windows, the Macintosh, and IBM's OS/2 Presentation manager? Ideally, we should be able to take advantage of the portability of C++ and find some way to shield ourselves from the details of specific platforms. While we're shopping for program components, these platforms won't be a high priority, but we want the possibility of easy migration to these and other platforms.

7.5   OVERALL REQUIREMENTS

What about the general requirements for this tool? We've looked at the users, the developer, the OO notations, and the operating platform upon which the tools will run.

Maybe this section should have come first, but I'm presenting the topics in this chapter in the order I thought of them. Users start out with a vague notion of what they want. It's up to us, the development team, to capture these ideas and impose order on them as quickly as possible. This section is where we say, "Slow down a minute. What exactly do we want to do?"

What follows in the rest of this section is an imaginary conversation between some users and a development team. This is the type of dialog that happens between software developers and users all the time. We have an advantage here because the users are technically sophisticated, and we speak the same language. The semantic gap starts out small.

7.5.1   Easy to Use

Users: "We've got to have some programs that are easy to use."
Developers: "Well, what about making the programs CUA compliant? The industry seems to be moving toward that standard. It's supported in Windows, and we can also support it in DOS."
Users: "OK, but we don't want to be muddling through a hundred layers of menus to get to the good stuff."
Developers: "So you'd like hot keys for the most common services?"
Users: "Right, and they better be responsive. I don't want to wait for 20 minutes after I've hit a key to find out that I made a mistake."
Developers: "Anything else?"

7.5.2   "Seamless"

Users: "Yeah, we want the programs to be seamless. We want seamless access to all of our other programming tools and project management tools."

At this point, the developer has to realize that the user has just made a very large, though seemingly reasonable, request. This "seamless" concept sounds great on the surface, but it involves working with other tools which we currently know nothing about. This sounds like the scope of the project is about to take a quantum leap. We've got to get this under control without losing the users. It's compromise time.

7.5.2.1   What are Seams?

Developers: "Exactly what do you mean by 'seamless'? Can you tell me what you mean by 'seams'?"
Users: "You know, seams. Like when you have to get out of one program to run another and then get back in. Then you have to find your place again in the first program."
Developers: (Still trying to narrow the requirement without saying "no") : "Is this a problem in Windows, too?"

Users: "No, in Windows we don't usually have problems; it's DOS that gives us the problem with seams. But you've got to support the clipboard in Windows so we can transfer data between programs."

7.5.2.2   Types of Seams

Developers: "What kind seams do you see in DOS? Specifically, what DOS programs do you run that you need to be 'seamless' with SSOOT CASE?"

Users: "Well, we should be able to get from the editor to the Browser and Librarian and back again pretty easily. And if we've got a file selected in the Librarian or Browser, we want to get it into editor without having to type in the whole file name. We don't want to be searching all over to find the function or class that we want, either."

Developers: "What editor do you use most?"

Users: "Mostly Borland's IDE, but some of us use other things. Really, we use all kinds."

Developers: (Still trying to narrow this requirement): "How important is this feature?"

           Now, the users huddle. The developers can tell there's severe disagreement. An argument is brewing over whose editor is best. Suddenly, the huddle breaks.

Users: "Well, its pretty important, but not absolutely necessary. We can't really agree on the details."

Developers: "How about if we research it a bit more and come back to this?"

Users: "Sure, OK."

           (Note that if you're using a pure waterfall model, this solution really isn't a good idea.)

7.5.3   Multiuser

Developers: "OK, what else?"

Users: "We need to be able to work together. This has to be a multiuser program."

7.5.3.1   Check Documents In and Out

Developers: (Expecting the worst): "You don't want to have two people working on the same document at the same time do you?"

Users: "No, were we're thinking of being able to check documents and drawings in and out. You know, like a source code control system."

Developers: "Are you asking for version control of the Library entries and Graphic Documents?"

Users: "Yeah, and we need to have the Browser able to use our code management system so that we can check out a file when we find what we're looking for."

Developers: "How much time do we have to get SSOOT CASE completed?" The users look at one another, then look rather sheepish.

Users: "OK, maybe we can defer the interface to the code management system."

7.5.3.2   Allow Inquiry on Checked Out Items

Developers: "So, if something is checked out, no one can change it."

Users: "But, we want to be able to see things that are checked out."

7.5.3.3   Reserve Identifiers

Users: "What about letting us reserve identifiers so we don't both begin creating the same entries at the same time?"

Developers: "Could you clarify that?"

Users: "Suppose one of us is creating an entry, like a new class definition for the Librarian. Someone else shouldn't be able to create an entry with the same name."

Developers: "So an entry should be given a unique identifier upon creation. This identifier should be immediately 'checked out'."

Users: "Right."

7.5.4   General Requirements Summary

Before the meeting concludes, the developers should summarize what they think has been said. They should be sure the users agree with their conclusions.

Developers: "Before we go, we want to be sure we're clear on what you want." Now, one of the developers begins writing on the board. After a couple of reminders and digressions the following list is compiled:

1. All the tools should be easy to use. The user interface will be CUA compliant.
2. You would like seamless access to other programming tools. Because of the sketchy nature of this request, the details will be explored and clarified for each specific tool later.
3. This should be a multi-user system. Documents and entries should be accessible through a "check in/ check out" mechanism similar to most source code control systems. Documents and entries that are "checked out" should be available for browsing.
4. Users should be able to reserve identifiers to prevent other users from creating identical entries.

Users: "OK, that's a good start. Next time we meet, we'll go into more detail about the requirements for each of the tools."

7.6   TOOLS IN SSOOT CASE

The developers know from previous discussions with the users the general nature of the types of tools in SSOOT CASE. Here, our imaginary development team begins to explore the specifics of each tool with the imaginary users. Instead of recreating the entire dialog I'll list the initial requirements summary for each tool. Obviously, these requirements are in addition to the general requirements listed above.

These requirements will be refined in the appropriate analysis chapters.

7.6.1   Class Librarian

1. The Class Librarian will act like an automated catalog to keep track of all classes available for reuse. It should have standard add/change/delete capabilities for its entries.
2. Because in C++, classes aren't the only thing to be reused, the Librarian will also keep track of stand-alone functions.
3. The catalog should be searchable on any combination of name, description, entry type, and file name. Output should be directable to the screen, printer, or file.
4. Entries should be added into the catalog in any one of the following ways:
   a. *Data Entry.* The user should be able to enter information into a dialog box similar to the class design forms discussed in previous chapters.
   b. *Source Code.* The Librarian should be able to read header files for class declarations and function prototypes to create entries.
5. The Librarian should provide the following types of output (all directable as in # 3):
   a. Search results from # 3.
   b. Documentation templates (filled out for specific classes), functions, and groups thereof.
   c. Source code (written into header files for specific classes) and functions.
   d. Empty function templates for classes and function prototypes.

7.6.2   Class Browser

The Class Browser will be a program that allows us to peruse the classes stored in the library catalog. Where the Librarian will allow us to identify classes and functions that meet certain criteria, the Browser will allow us to examine the details of the classes and functions and their relationship to one another. If we think of our collection of classes as a library, the SSOOT CASE Librarian can be thought of as an automated "card catalog" and the Browsers as an automated way to look through the contents of the library. Our imaginary user group has given our imaginary development team these requirements.

1. The Browser will coexist with the Librarian. Any class found by the librarian should be easily accessed by the Browser.
2. The Browser will have its own text editor for modifying class and function source code, however, since editors are such a personal thing, the browser will provide access to any other editor that will accept command line search directions.
3. We will look into the possibility of making the Browser a "Transfer" option in Borland's IDE.
4. The Browser will provide cross reference capability. For example, the Browser should be able to list the ancestors and descendants for a given class. The number of generations listed should be user definable at run time.

7.6.3   Graphic Design Tool

This one is the hard one. We had a discussion earlier about which notation to support. I have my own preferences, but to include one and not include the others is a violation of the spirit of my own analysis and design philosophy. Also, keep in mind that these are some *simple* OO tools. In order to keep the tool simple, there will be no rule checking or methodology critiques. The other general requirements follow.

1. The tool will use kinds of graphic classes: Shapes and Connectors.
2. The tool will explicitly recognize classes, objects, functions, and inheritance. The information in the library will be accessible to these symbols.
3. Users can define their own symbols for classes, objects, functions, and their own connection symbol for inheritance.
4. Users can define their own symbols for use in any diagram, and they must explicitly make any connections into the library.
5. Users can define their own connections. They may name the connections, but they will have no input from or output to the library.
6. In DOS, the tool will support the entire range of industry standard printers: Epson 9 and 24 pin, HP, and Postscript. In Windows, the tool will support any installed printer.
7. The Librarian reports will be accessible for all classes and functions in an entire diagram.
8. The Librarian and Browser will be accessible from the Graphic Tool.

7.7   SOFTWARE COMPONENTS—MAKE OR BUY?

This question is central to the philosophy of your application development organization. Obviously if you're in an organization that specializes in component building, you'll be making components. Most of us, however, are application developers and therefore component users. As our users become more demanding, we cannot afford to maintain application specific code and general purpose components. If, however, we buy the general purpose components we need from a good company with a good support and upgrade policy, we have not only quite affordably enhanced the quality of our application, we've freed ourselves to work on the application itself. Therefore, I have adopted this philosophy: Buy components whenever possible, providing that they can meet the following criteria (this is a reproduction of the criteria in Section 3.4.2.2):

1. Sufficient Trial Period.
2. Upgrade Policy.
3. Source Code.
4. Technical Support.
5. Licensing and Royalties.
6. Documentation.
7. Completeness and Extendibility.
8. Portability and Platform Specific Support.
9. Does It Meet Your Needs?

7.7.1   Components Needed

As I look over the requirements for the SSOOT CASE tools, I see two needs immediately. We need a user interface library and a database library. We will probably need some general purpose classes like strings and dates.

7.7.2   User Interface

As we examine the requirements, we can find several that affect our user interface library decision. We need to have support DOS in text mode, DOS in graphics mode, and MS-Windows. We need support for CUA compliance.

7.7.2.1   Possibilities

Building an interface library like the one we're discussing can be a daunting task. In keeping with my "Don't make if you can buy" philosophy, I've decided to take a look at some choices.

7.7.2.1.1   OWL

I considered using Borland's Object Window Library for MS-Windows for this project. It has several advantages:

1. The price is right. The combination of Borland's Application Framework and their C++ compiler was an incredible bargain.
2. Borland provides online help for the library in their integrated development environment. This would make it easier to user than many alternatives.
3. A lot of people have it. Borland has shipped lots and lots and lots of their Application Framework packages. This wide spread availability would make it a good candidate for inclusion in a book.

Borland's Object Window Library also has several features that may make it less than ideal for this project.

1. It is compiler specific. There are at least two other groups of major compiler users who should be able to get the most out of this book with a small amount of conversion, the Microsoft users and the Zortech users. In many projects this is not a consideration, but for this one it has to be. (Note that this is different than using templates. Templates are a language feature. Most compiler vendors plan to support them in one or two more releases.)
2. It is platform specific. Current implementations of OWL are specific to Windows. This is only one of our target platforms. If we choose this library, we will need to choose some other library for our project for DOS.

Borland's OWL has a lot going for it. I don't think I can use it for this project, though. The bottom line on OWL is that its scope is just too narrow for what we need.

7.7.2.1.2   TurboVision

TurboVision, also part of Borland's application framework, could be used for the DOS version of the SSOOT CASE Librarian and the Browser. However, it has all the disadvantages of OWL with one more: It doesn't support graphics in DOS, so we couldn't write the graphic tool with it. I considered writing some of SSOOT CASE in Turbo Vision again in OWL, but I didn't want to rewrite functionally identical code.

7.7.2.1.3   Others

After rejecting the two user interface libraries that came with my compiler I started look for others. I looked at shareware, where there are some good values, but nothing that would give me access to all three initial platforms. I found a lot of text window libraries, and a few DOS graphic libraries in shareware. I would have liked to find one that met all the criteria so I could include it with the disk that accompanies the book but I was unable to do so.

Things were a little better in the commercial arena. I found two libraries that met all three criteria. One is called XVT and the other, Zinc. The source code and object libraries for XVT for all three platforms cost considerably more than the same Zinc product. After reviewing the XVT sales material and the needs of this project, I decided that there was nothing in XVT that justified the additional expense, so I rejected it. (By the time you're reading this, I'm sure each of the products I've mentioned will have been upgraded and new products will be on the market. I encourage you to go through your own evaluation process.)

7.7.2.1.4   *Zinc*

Zinc was one of the first OO Libraries on the market. I've been using it since version 1.0. I'd like to share my reasons for using it and highlight some of my favorite features.

Zinc is the epitome of OO development. Its classes are well-defined and highly cohesive. They are coupled at the abstract class level. The display device specific code is well-encapsulated in classes derived from UI_DISPLAY. This class defines a protocol that other classes, like windows and menus, use to write to the screen. By changing the specific UI_DISPLAY descendant you can change which platform you use. Currently Zinc supports Windows, DOS text, and DOS graphics, X-Windows Motif, and OS/2 for all major PC C++ compilers. No application source code needs to be changed to use any of these platforms. DOS and Windows hold much of the market, so these are the two platforms for which I'll buy the Zinc libraries.

7.7.3   DBMS

Now that we've decided on the user interface, what about the data base manager? There are several possibilities.

7.7.3.1   Possibilities

The users want a multi-user system. That eliminates most of the shareware data-base managers I might have chosen. The call for OO Data Base Management System from the OO purists was so loud, I almost rejected the relational model entirely. My research shows that neither OODBMS or Relational DMBS is inherently superior. The relational model is good for program-independent (usually), text-based data. The Librarian and perhaps the Browser could use a relational DBMS. The Graphics Tool could probably use an OODBMS.

What a dilemma! Most OODBMS schemes for making objects persistent aren't yet multi-user. I considered force fitting everything into an xBase data base. The data files are an industry standard and many inexpensive libraries are available for it.

I looked into some others, too. ORACLE would require an incredibly expensive hardware and software investment for me and for potential users. I rejected several because their vendors had a bad reputation. I rejected others for various technical reasons. Finally, I found a good, reliable relational DBMS that could easily be made to behave like an OODBMS when necessary.

7.7.3.2   Criteria

These are the criteria, in addition to the standard criteria (Section 3.4.2.2) I used in making my selection:

1. *Speed.* Nobody likes waiting for a program to spin the disk for a half hour looking for data.
2. Reliability.
3. *Ease of use.* The product must easily and logically fit into a C++ program *without a preprocessor to slow down development time.* Running your source code through an extra compile step to accommodate your DBMS is not a good idea.
4. *Localized impact of change.* One DBMS I considered briefly required that all source code using the database at all be recompiled every time there was a schema change. Development time should not be wasted constantly recompiling all the code every time the user has a change request.

7.7.3.3   Pinnacle

I chose Pinnacle Relational Engine from Vermont Database Corporation as the database management system for this project. It is written in portable C so it works well on any platform we might need. It was written using OO principles before object orientation was a big thing. It has a set of C++ classes wrapped around the C code so we can easily specialize the classes with inheritance.

Pinnacle meets the general and specific criteria listed above. It provides good solid functionality without a lot of frills. Its online documentation is a simple text file, not a hypertext system or anything, but it's complete and clear with good examples.

You may know that relational databases are founded on a mathematical model developed by E.F. Codd. There is a strict set of rules governing tables, columns, and rows that make up relational databases. Many RDBMS products strictly enforce these rules. OO databases are not founded on mathematical models, but on intuitive experiences and classification theory. The OODBMS is not yet well-defined. In order to truly store an object, you would need to store code and data. Most OO systems still concentrate on the data aspect.

Some features of Pinnacle make it nice for building a hybrid OO and relational DBMS. It supports the relational model without strongly enforcing it. That means we can break some of the relational rules without feeling the wrath of Codd. Its columns can be typed or untyped. It has support for user defined columns and arbitrarily large binary columns (Binary Large Objects, or BLOBS); my plan is to use tables for abstract classes and use BLOBS for holding data of derived classes. We'll see how well this works as the book unfolds.

7.7.4 "Parts"

We'll probably need some additional classes, like a good date class, a string class, some containers, and some other "parts." We really need a standard set of C++ classes which should include times, dates, and strings. Zinc provides a string class and a date class. Pinnacle provides a good string class. Borland also has a decent string class.

If I were building this project for myself only, I would consider using Zinc's date class for all date representations, even those that had nothing to do with user interfaces. I want to keep the core model, found in Chapter 6, independent of the user interface library. That way if you decide not to use Zinc and build this project yourself with another library, you can port the core code without being concerned about proprietary classes.

The Borland "String" class has the minimal set of operations one would expect from a string class. It allows assignment to and from char *s, it can be cast to a char *, and it provides equality and inequality operators. Since any viable string class can be expected to have this minimal set of features, I'll use Borland's String class in the problem domain model. If you find a different class to replace it, it should have at least this set of features.

Borland's Date class provides fewer features than a fully functional Date class should. Notably missing is the ability to assign and receive Julian values. Storing a date as a long number in Julian format is terribly convenient. I found a better, public domain Date class on CompuServe. I'll use that one to represent dates in the problem domain classes.

To avoid container conflicts if you decide to use a different DBMS and a different compiler, I'll provide a project-specific protocol in the abstract class, D_List. This gives you two advantages, consistency and portability. Zinc, Pinnacle, and Borland all have container classes of some sort. By providing D_List as a front end, you can change list implementations to your heart's content without touching the application-specific code.

7.8 WORK PLAN

Figure 7-1 shows the overall work plan for this project. It kind of looks like a cross between the waterfall model and the iterative prototype model. Really, the only difference is the size and scope of each iteration. Each tool will have its own

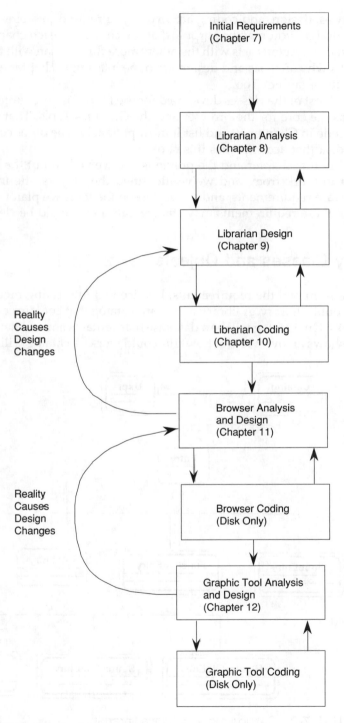

FIGURE 7-1 Work plan.

analysis, design, and coding activity. If you're used to seeing structured analysis and design, you may be surprised at the content of each chapter. Each activity is distinct, but it interacts with the others more fluidly than with traditional methods. That's why analysis and design are done in a single chapter each for the Browser and the Graphics Tool.

Most of the classes developed for the Librarian in Chapters 8 through 10 will act as the core for the Browser and the Graphics Tools. That's why we'll discuss the code in Chapter 10 and list it in Appendix D. The other code is found only on the disk that accompanies this book.

In this chapter and the previous one we've laid out the basic OO model we plan to work from, and we've identified the players, the initial hardware and software requirements, and we've chosen the tools we plan to work with. Any or all of these requirements may change, but they should be clear, if general.

7.8.1   Key Classes and Objects

As I examined the requirements, I noticed an interesting model developing, that of a public library. A library has a card catalog that contains entries which refer to works. Our catalog will be a database that contains entries that refer to files. Figure 7-2 shows an overview of how this could work. A catalog will contain any kind of

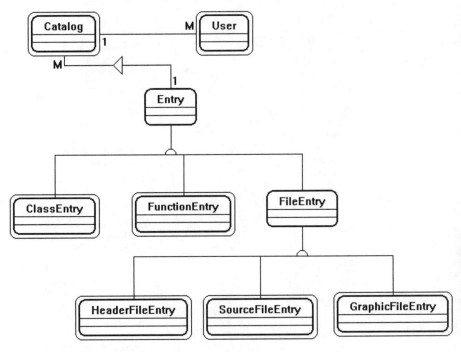

FIGURE 7-2   Catalog model of class librarian.

entry. Entries can be class entries, function entries, or file entries. Users can find entries in the catalog. Users can create and delete entries. They can browse through them, check them out, change them, and check them in.

A graphic document is an entity with a corresponding entry in the catalog. Graphic documents contain symbols. They can be created, destroyed, modified, and printed.

7.8.2   Key Relationships

As we examine Figure 7-2, we can observe several key relationships between the classes. Most of the classes are derived from Entry. Several Entries make part of a Catalog. Entries have several potential Users. Entries and Users can be part of a Project.

7.8.3   More Details Later

Our imaginary user group has agreed to this basic model of SSOOT CASE. In Chapter 8 we'll begin filling in the details of the Catalog and Entry class protocols and important data. In subsequent chapters we will change this model as we fill in more details. For major message traffic, we'll show Coad and Yourdon message arrows between specific objects. I'll use any combination of five different techniques to specify design details for specific member functions. I won't specify all of the functions, I'll only use those I feel are the most important. The others I'll defer until programming.

Listed below are the function specification techniques and, generally, when they are applicable: All of these specification methods come from non-OO backgrounds. Since member functions should be small (ideally less than 20 lines [Plum, Saks]), any specification should be small and clear. I'll try to keep that in mind as I select individual specification techniques.

Specification Technique	Conditions For Use
Pseudo Code	Simple step-wise algorithm with few loops or decisions.
Structure Charts	Method acts as "manager" function with details delegated to other functions.
Logic Table	Method must make a series of complex interrelated decisions.
Flow Chart	Method must make a few simple decisions, perhaps within one or two simple loops.
Defer to Programmer	Method is simple or routine without significant behavioral constraints. These include get/set methods for assigning and retrieving values from data members.

7.9   SUMMARY

This chapter contains the hardware and software requirements for SSOOT CASE. SSOOT CASE stands for "Some Simple Object-Oriented Tools for Computer Aided Software Engineering."

The target platform for SSOOT CASE will be MS-DOS 5.0, on a '386 SX with a VGA color monitor, a 40 megabyte hard drive and about 2 megabytes of RAM. The system will initially operate in DOS text mode, DOS graphics mode, and in MS-Windows. We will consider other platforms in our planning, but these are our initial targets.

SSOOT CASE has the following general requirements:

1. All the tools should be easy to use. The user interface will be CUA compliant.
2. The users would like seamless access to other programming tools. The details will be explored and clarified for each specific tool later.
3. This should be a multi-user system. Documents and entries should be accessible through a "check in/ check out" mechanism similar to most source code control systems. Documents and entries that are "checked out" should be available for browsing.
4. Users should be able to reserve identifiers to prevent other users from creating identical entries.

Each tool in SSOOT CASE has its own initial requirements: The details are listed in section 7.6.

For this project we have chosen Zinc Application Framework and Pinnacle Relational Engine. Next, we've decided on some general components: Borland's String Class and a public domain Date Class. We'll use a custom container class protocol D_List to isolate the application from compiler or library dependent container classes.

Finally, we identified key classes and objects and the important relationships between them: Our catalog will be a database that contains entries that refer to files.

Now, on to the Librarian.

CHAPTER 8
The First CASE Tool—
A Class Librarian

"With 1000 or more components, there is no hope that the average software engineer will *ever* remember what's in the library."

Ed Yourdon, *The Decline and Fall of the American Programmer*,
1992, Prentice Hall.

8.1 WHO IS THIS FOR?

Remember, analysis is where we decide *what* we want to do. In this chapter we'll do an OOA of the SSOOT CASE Librarian. Let's begin by clarifying the initial analysis. Before we get into what the Librarian is supposed to do, we should remind ourselves who is going to be using this.

Our imaginary user group is made up of managers, analysts, designers, and programmers. Your organization may call them by the collective name "Software Engineers" or "Object Engineers."

OOD is actually two distinct activities: component building and component using. The component designers and builders provide input into the catalog with the Librarian. The component users use the Librarian to find those components. OO managers can use the tool to determine things such as the number and the types of components available for reuse, the degree of reuse, etc.

8.2 FUNCTIONAL REQUIREMENTS

8.2.1 Expansion and Clarification of Initial Requirements

Since we are going into more analytical detail for the librarian, we'll start with the known requirements and expand them. First, we'll assemble the initial requirements, then we'll discuss them with the users one by one. Returning to the notes we made at the end of Chapter 7, we prepare the following list for presentation to the users:

1. All the tools should be easy to use. The user interface will be CUA compliant.
2. The tools should be seamless. We need to clarify exactly what that means for this tool in this chapter.
3. This should be a multi-user system. Documents and entries should be accessible through a "check in/check out" mechanism similar to most source code control systems. Documents and entries that are "checked out" should be available for browsing.
4. Users should be able to reserve identifiers to prevent other users from creating identical entries.
5. The Class Librarian will act like an automated catalog to keep track of all classes available for reuse. It should have standard add/change/delete capabilities for its entries.
6. Because in C++ classes aren't the only thing to be reused, the Librarian will also keep track of stand-alone functions.
7. The catalog should be searchable on any combination of name, description, entry type, and file name. Output should be directable to the screen, printer, or file.
8. Entries should be added into the catalog in any one of the following ways:
    a. Data Entry. The user should be able to enter information into a dialog box similar to the class design forms discussed in previous chapters.
    b. Source Code. The Librarian should be able to read header files for class declarations and function prototypes to create entries.
9. The Librarian should provide the following types of output (all directable as in # 7):
    a. Search results from # 7.
    b. Documentation templates (filled out for specific classes) functions, and groups thereof.
    c. Source code (written into header files for specific-classes) and functions.
    d. Empty function templates for classes and function prototypes.

Let's address each requirement to see if we need to clarify it.

Requirement 1. All the tools should be easy to use: This one has to do with the user interface. I decided to prototype some screens to show to our "users." (In reality I wanted to see some progress for myself. The users are figments of my imagination.) Figure 8-1a and 8-1b show a picture of a screen I put together with Zinc Designer. (Zinc Designer is a program to draw windows, dialog boxes, menus, etc. The resulting objects can be used in a program.)

We'll show it to the users and see what they think.

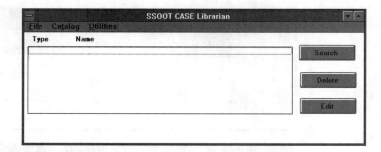

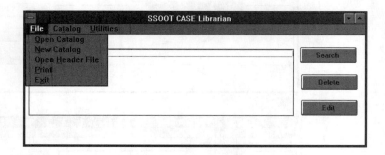

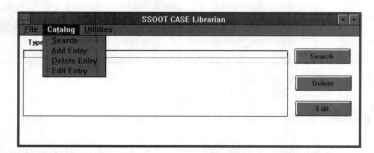

FIGURE 8-1a   Prototype for SSOOT CASE librarian.

Developers: "So, What do you think, is it what you had in mind?"
Users: "Well, mostly. What's that big square in the middle?"
Developers: "That's the list box where the selected entries are displayed."
Users: "Will we have online help to explain what the list box is and what the buttons and menu items do?"

This is a reasonable request. It may even be implied in the requirements. The initial prototype lets us find this requirement early. Since we found it early we avoid the agony caused by discovering requirements late in the project. We add online help to our general requirement list. After some additional discussion we make a few other changes to the prototype. The resultant prototype is in the CHAP8 subdirectory on the disk that accompanies this book.

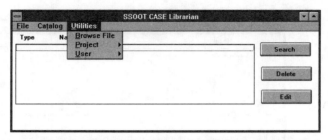

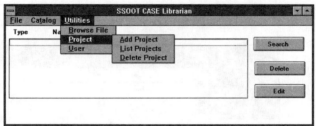

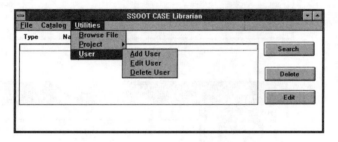

FIGURE 8-1b   SSOOT CASE librarian prototype screens.

Requirement 2. The tools should be seamless: Here is an obscure requirement which must be dealt with.

Developers:	"Let's examine this seamless requirement a little more closely. How do you imagine this working together with other programming tools."
Users:	"We're really not sure."
Developers:	"How about if we suspend this requirement for this version of the program."
	The users protest and argue among themselves then they come to a consensus.
Users:	"Very well."

Requirement 3: This should be a multiuser system: At this point, a functional requirement really becomes a system requirement. We'll defer discussion of this requirement to Section 8.3.

Requirement 4: Users should be able to reserve identifiers: This one is pretty clear.

Requirements 5 and 6: The Librarian will keep track of all classes available for reuse, and it will keep track of stand-alone functions: We need to clarify exactly what entries we'll be keeping track of with the librarian. After some discussion with the users using Figure 8-1a and 8-1b, we've decided to keep track of the following types of entries:

A. Classes: We will differentiate between class, struct and union entries.
B. Functions: We will keep track of C and C++ stand-alone functions. Class member functions will not be accessible as separate entries.
C. Files: We'll keep track of source code files (.C and .CPP), and header files (.H and .HPP) if they can be related to class or function entries. We'll keep track of graphic file entries when we have graphic files to keep track of. We'll defer this functionality until then.

Requirements 7, 8, and 9 are clear enough. We don't need to go into more detail.

8.2.2   Librarian Functional Requirements Recap

When you've had a lot of discussions with users and clients it's usually a good idea to present a summary of your conclusions for final examination. Here's our clarified and modified requirement list. The additions and changes from the list at the beginning of the chapter are listed in italics.

1. All the tools should be easy to use. The user interface will be CUA compliant. *This will include an online help system.*
2. This needs to be a multi-user system. Details will be listed in the system requirements section.
3. Users should be able to reserve identifiers to prevent other users from creating identical entries.
4. The Class Librarian will act like an automated catalog to keep track of all classes available for reuse. It should have standard add/change/delete capabilities for its entries. *We will differentiate between class, struct, and union entries.*
5. Because in C++ classes aren't the only thing to be reused, the Librarian will also keep track of stand-alone functions. *Class member functions will not be accessible as separate entries.*
6. *We will keep track of source (.CPP and C) and header files (.H and .HPP) for class and function entries.*
7. The catalog should be searchable on any combination of name, description, entry type, and file name. Output should be directable to the screen, printer, or file.
8. Entries should be added into the catalog in any one of the following ways:

    a.   Data Entry. The user should be able to enter information into a dialog box similar to the class design forms discussed in previous chapters.

    b.   Source Code. The Librarian should be able to read header files for class declarations and function prototypes to create entries.

9. The Librarian should provide the following types of output (all directable as in # 7):

    a.   Search results from # 7.

    b.   Documentation templates (filled out for specific classes) functions, and groups thereof.

    c.   Source code (written into header files for specific classes) and functions.

    d.   Empty function templates for classes and function prototypes.

We deferred the ability to keep track of graphic file entries until we have a graphic capability.

8.3   SYSTEM REQUIREMENTS

There are no special system requirements for the librarian not covered in Section 7.4. We should specify a limit on the amount of hard drive space the Librarian and its data files can use initially. Software should not take up all the space on the hard drive. There really is no way to accurately judge the size at this point except by setting a limit and trying not to exceed it. For now we'll set an arbitrary limit of 3 megabytes for the program and data files for each version of the librarian.

We need to clarify the "multi-user" requirement. Since we've chosen Pinnacle as the target DBMS, we'll use its multi-user requirements (the following is taken from the Pinnacle Documentation):

Since Pinnacle is a relational database management system (RDBMS) with full commit and rollback, multi-user operations must be handled by a Server that maintains concurrency and data integrity. This Server is a program that:

- receives request messages from client programs
- performs the requested actions
- sends a message that returns results to the requesting client program

In addition, the server is responsible for handling row and table locking.

Pinnacle client programs have a C API identical to the Pinnacle single-user C API, with the addition of several calls to connect to the server and to lock rows and tables. Certain single-user Pinnacle functions are missing in the multi-user library. This is because they perform actions that are reserved for the server. Client programs are linked with an alternate library (pfmc.lib in DOS, pfmc.olb in VMS, pfmc.a in UNIX) that encodes function calls into messages that are sent to the server via NETBIOS, VMS mailboxes, or UNIX named pipes (TCP/IP is expected to be available shortly).

In summary our system requirements are:

- Stand-alone DOS version:
  386SX or better CPU
  2 Megabytes RAM
  Hard drive with about 3 megabytes free. (Librarian only)
  MS-DOS 5.0 or higher.
  Mouse supported but not required.
- Add the following for the stand-alone Windows version:
  Windows 3.0 or higher
  4 Megabytes RAM recommended
- Add the following for the multiuser version:
  Dedicated Server
  Netbios Compatible Network

8.4 OOA

In Chapter 4 I presented an analysis strategy. Here it is again for your convenience.

1. Figure Out What to Do
   A. Brain Storm
      a. Develop List of Candidate Classes and Objects
      b. List Initial Data and Functionality
   B. Refine Results of Storming
      a. Correct candidate class list by both addition and deletion
      b. Expand and define data and functionality
      c. Identify inheritance, messaging and containing relationships
   C. Resolve Concerns
      a. Address concerns that may affect the view of objects
      b. Postpone addressing concerns that don't have to
   D. Move on to Design
      a. Have a clear understanding of requirements
      b. Come back to analysis when requirements change

8.4.1 Candidate Classes and Objects

8.4.1.1 Finding the Classes and Objects

During the brain storming session we look for candidate classes and objects. Chapter 7 has an initial overview of some candidate classes. If we examine the requirements list in the previous section, we can find some more. The search of these sources for SSOOT CASE Librarian classes yields the following candidates: Entry, Catalog, ClassEntry, FileEntry, FunctionEntry, User, ClassDefinition, SourceEntry, HeaderEntry.

We've already decided to defer the graphic file information. What about the other types of FileEntries? Since we really don't need FileEntry, SourceEntry and HeaderEntry until we get to the Browser, we'll drop them for now.

    The ClassDefinition class was defined and coded in Chapter 6. Since we have its diagram in Chapter 6, and it already exists in C++, we won't repeat its analysis here.

8.4.1.2   Attributes and Services

Once we've made our list, we need to list the initial data and functionality. Forms 8-1 through 8-5 show the analysis templates where we've defined the initial services and attributes of the Entry, Catalog, ClassEntry, FunctionEntry, and User classes.

8.4.2   Define Relationships

8.4.2.1   Catalogs and Entries

Figure 8-2 shows the relationships among the Catalog and a generic Entry. A Catalog is defined as a descriptive list. We have a list in our component inventory, the D_List. I presented the first incarnation of D_list in C, in the *C User's Journal* in July of 1990 in an article showing how to do OOP in C [Brumbaugh 90]. In the January, 1992, *C User's Journal*, I presented a C++ version of the class [Brumbaugh 92].

    Let's say a catalog is a kind of D_List. 8-6 has the analysis template for the D_List class. Its source code is in the CHAP10 subdirectory on this book's disk. Figure 8-2 shows that a Catalog is a "kind of" D_List. Specifically, it is a kind D_List that contains Entry objects.

    An Entry is an integral part of a Catalog. Figure 8-2 also shows that many Entry objects can be part of a Catalog object.

    The thick, gray arrow shows that a Catalog object can interact with an Entry object. Labeling the arrow with the names of the Entry services helps define exactly what the Catalog expects from its Entries. The Catalog expects an Entry to know how to store itself in the catalog with "put," and it can retrieve itself from the catalog with "get". Since we know we'll be searching for Entries, we know that the Catalog will need to know if it found the right entry. Therefore, we'll probably need the equality operator.

8.4.2.2   The Entry Class Family

A ClassEntry is a special kind of Entry. It is also a description of a Class. Figure 8-3 illustrates that a ClassEntry is both an Entry and a ClassDefinition.

    A ClassEntry will need to put more information into and get more information from the catalog than the abstract Entry. It is likely that it will have different equality conditions than an abstract Entry. I've shown in Figure 8-3 that we need to overload those functions in the ClassEntry class.

Class Name: Entry

Version: 1.0

Base Classes:

Categories: Abstract, Model

Class Purpose/Description:

An Entry is a descriptive item. It is an abstract class. It exists primarily to be contained in a Catalog. Specific types of Entries include ClassEntries and FunctionEntries.

Data Members (Attributes)

Visibility	Type	Name	Description
Protected	String	Identity	Name or code by which the entry is identified.
		Version	Identifies which Entry varient this is. (Identity+Version = unique Entry).
		AddedBy	Identity of User that added this Entry to the Catalog.
		ChangedBy	Identity of the last user to check this entry out.
	Boolean	CheckedOut	Set to True if this Entry has been checked out for modification.
	Date	DateChecked	Date upon which this Entry was last checked in our out.
		DateAdded	Date upon which this Entry was added to the catalog.
	String	Description	Textual description of Entries.
	String	EntryType	Entry indicating the exact type of this Entry.

Member Functions (Services)

Visibility	Name	Description
Public	Entry	Constructor
	CheckIn	Check an Entry into a Catalog
	CheckOut	Check Entry out from a Catalog
	operator ==	Compare Entries for Equality
	operator <	Compare two Entries for Sorting
	operator >	Compare two Entries for Sorting
	get	Get the data items for this Entry from the Catalog
	put	Put this Entry into the Catalog

FORM 8-1 Entry class definition.

Class Name: Catalog

Version: 1.0

Base Classes: D_List<Entry *>

Categories:

Class Purpose/Description:
A Catalog contains descriptive Entries of reusable program components.

Data Members (Attributes)

Visibility   Type   Name   Description

(No new catalog infomation needs to be remembered.)

Member Functions (Services)

Visibility   Name   Description

Public   at_end   Return TRUE if current Entry is last member.
             find   Search the list for an Entry. If not found don't change currency.
             prev   Make the Entry previous to this one current. If current member
                          is top, do nothing.
             next   Make the Entry after this one current. If current member is last,
                          do nothing.
             seek   Search to a position in the list.
             add   Add a new Entry into the catalog.
             replace   Replace the current Entry in the catalog.
             top   Make the top member current.
             end   Make the last member current.
             current   Return a pointer to the current Entry
             total   Return the total number of Entries in the catalog.
             tell   Return the position of the current Entry in the catalog.

FORM 8-2   Catalog class definition.

Figure 8-4 shows a "family portrait" of the FunctionEntry class. Since we had a ClassDefinition class, it seems logical to have a FunctionDefinition class. It's a consistent approach to the problem. Since we've identified a new class, we need to identify its services and attributes. Figure 8-7 shows the template for the FunctionDefinition class.

```
Class Name:       ClassEntry

Version:          1.0

Base Classes:     Entry, ClassDefinition

Categories:       Model

Class Purpose/Description:

The ClassEntry is a Catalog Entry responsible for tracking classes in the reuse library. It
helps software engineers identify classes for potential reuse.

Data Members (Attributes)

Visibility      Type    Name    Description

(All data members in this class are inherited, it has none of its own.)

Member Functions (Services)

Visibility    Name          Description
Public        get           Gets a ClassEntry from the catalog.
              put           Puts a ClassEntry into the catalog.
              operator ==   Matches Entries to one another.
```

FORM 8-3   ClassEntry class definition.

8.4.3   Resolve Concerns

8.4.3.1   FunctionDefinition vs. MemberFunctionDefinition

Users   (some of whom are Object Engineers): "That new class, FunctionDefinition, is a lot like a class we've already got. Remember MemberFunctionDefinition? We used it in the ClassDefinition class."

Developers: "Well, we've got MemberFunctionDefinition defined already. But, you're right, it is more correct to say that a MemberFunction Definition is a kind of FunctionDefinition. Should we go with what's right or with what's convenient?"

A short debate follows. The group finally comes to a consensus. The relationships will be defined during analysis; during design we'll decide whether or not to implement the change. Figure 8-5 shows the inheritance diagram for our change.

Class Name: User   Date: 9/26/92

Version: 1.0

Base Classes:

Categories: Model

Class Purpose/Description:

The User class allows the system to identify users.

Visibility	Type	Name	Description
Protected	String	name	Name of user.
		password	Encrypted password assures user is properly identifed.
	Bit fields	security	List of flags indicating what the user is allowed to do in the system.

Member Functions (Services)

Visibility	Name	Description
Public	User	Constructor.
	logOn	Allows a user to identify him or herself to the system.
	logOff	Allows user to leave the system.
	getName	Returns the name of the user.
	setSecurity	Assigns security flags for user.
	getSecurity	Returns one or more security flags.
	setPassword	Assigns password to user.
	checkPassword	Validates user password.

FORM 8-4   User class definition.

8.4.3.2   Implementation of D_List and Catalog

Users: "D_List is an abstract class. The catalog is only lightly specified. How are we going to tie the catalog to the database we've chosen?"

Developers: "That's one of the first details we were planning to take care of in design. "

Sometimes details need to be addressed before larger issues can be addressed. Usually, however, deferring implementation details until design lets

Class Name: FunctionEntry   Date: 9/26/92

Version: 1.0

Base Classes: Entry, FunctionDefn

Categories: Model

Class Purpose/Description:

This is an Entry in the Catalog to describe stand-alone functions.

Data Members (Attributes)

Visibility   Type   Name   Description

(All data members are inherited.)

Member Functions (Services)

Visibility   Name   Description

Public   FunctionEntry   Constructor.
         operator ==   Compare FunctionEntries and return TRUE if they match.
         put   Puts FunctionEntry in to the Catalog.
         get   Gets FunctionEntry from the Catalog.

FORM 8-5   FunctionEntry class definition.

users and developers get a good general overview of the proposed system. Too many details makes focusing difficult. That's why only the relevant methods and attributes are shown in each diagram.

8.4.3.3   Did We Implement D_List Too Soon?

If we look at our overall strategy, we don't try to reuse existing classes until design. D_List is a specific class already in our component collection. If we were maintaining a strict distinction between analysis and design, this would be true. However, if we see analysis, design, and programming as a continuum of activity rather than a set of distinct phases, we can make certain allowances for our own convenience. In this case, it was convenient to select a specific type list so the necessary services were already defined.

ClassName: D_List<T>

Version: 1.0

Base Classes:

Classification: Container, Template, Abstract

Class Purpose/Description:

A D_List contains members of type T.

Data Members (Attributes)

Visibility	Type	Name	Description
Protected	T	buffer	Working buffer for list

Member Functions (Services)

Visibility	Name	Description
Public	at_top	Return TRUE if current member is first member.
	at_end	Return TRUE if current member is last member.
	is_empty	Return TRUE if there are no members in the list.
	find	Search the list for a specific member. If not found, don't change currency.
	prev	Make the member previous to this one current. If current member is top, do nothing.
	next	Make the member after this one current. If current member is last, do nothing.
	seek	Search to a position in the list.
	add	Add a new member into the D_List.
	replace	Replace the current member in the D_List.
	top	Make the top member current.
	end	Make the last member current.
	current	Return a copy of the current member.
	total	Return the total number of Entries in the catalog.
	tell	Return the position of the current Entry in the catalog.

FORM 8-6   D_List class definition.

Class Name: FunctionDefn   Date: 9/26/92

Version: 1.0

Base Classes:

Categories: Model

Class Purpose/Description:

A FunctionDefinition contains the essential information for handling C++ function declarations. (Not Member Functions)

Data Members (Attributes)

Visibility	Type	Name	Description
Protected	String	name	Name of function
		returnValue	Type and purpose of the return value.
	D_List	parameters	List of parameters and their definitions.

Member Functions (Services)

Visibility	Name	Description
Public	FunctionDefn	Constructor
	toSource	Creates a function prototype and writes it to a source file.
	fromSource	Fills data member from source code file.

FORM 8-7 FunctionDefn class definition.

8.4.4   Prepare For Design

8.4.4.1   "Completing" Analysis for the Librarian

Our analysis activity isn't really complete. During design, it is likely that we'll find it necessary to address some analysis issues. Although in reality we have a nearly seamless transition from analysis to design, sometimes, for project tracking purposes, a phase must be officially completed. So, we "complete" the analysis for the Librarian here.

If we had to specify deliverables for this phase they would be:

- The requirements listed in Section 8.2.2
- The diagrams Figures 6-1, 7-1, and 8-1 through 8-5
- Forms 8-1 through 8-7

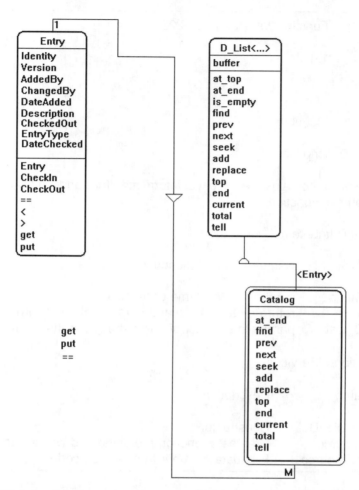

FIGURE 8-2 Catalog and entry clases.

- The Design Plan we're getting ready to make
- The prototype started with Figure 8-1

As you examine these diagrams and documents again, notice a couple of things: There is no one "all encompassing" diagram or set of diagrams for every aspect of the system, the diagrams focus on specific important relationships and interactions. Also the class templates are small. I've tried to be sure there's no more than one page per template. I've found that it helps "keep me honest" in my coupling and cohesion issues.

8.4.4.2   The Design Plan

In design, we'll follow the strategy laid out in Chapter 5. As we look over our analysis we can see some things we want to be sure to address in design.

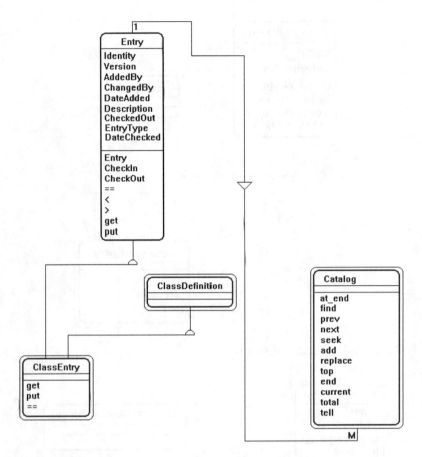

FIGURE 8-3 ClassEntry and parents.

In the class templates, I deliberately kept the member descriptions small. If you can't write a valid one or two sentence statement of what is expected of each service, the service is not cohesive enough. In their OOA book, Coad and Yourdon create a more detailed service specification [Coad, Yourdon 1990,91]. Obviously, since our development effort is a continuum, there's nothing wrong with this. But, as a matter of personal style, I think that should be deferred to design. Therefore, one of the things we know we need to do in design is specify each service.

We assured the users that we'd address the issue of making Catalog work with the DBMS. We'll also need to be certain our user interface classes work with the problem domain classes we've defined here.

Here's what we need to do in the design activities for the Librarian:

Figure Out How You Want to Do It

A. Clarify Requirements from Analysis
    a.   *Identify High Level Protocol For Candidate Classes*

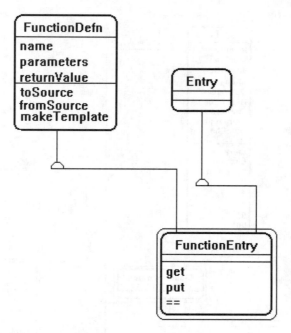

FIGURE 8-4   FunctionEntry.

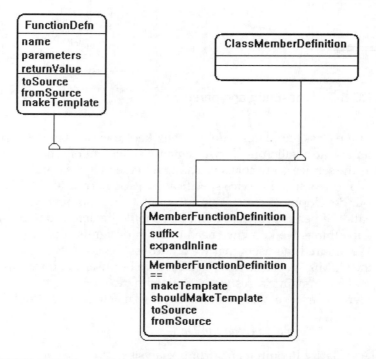

FIGURE 8-5   Possible generalization of MemberFunction class.

Write the specifications for the protocols we've begun to establish in this chapter.

b. *Identify Major Relationships Between Objects*

Look into message connections and "part of" relationships between classes and objects. Also look more into the types of classes and objects that make up the attributes of the classes identified here.

c. *Gather Classes Into Subject Areas or Categories*

This hasn't been done yet. Perhaps the D_List Catalog hierarchy would make a good subject area and the Entry hierarchy would make another. We'll no doubt encounter more classes in design. Those may need their own subjects as well.

d. *Record the Results Using Your Selected Notation and Specification Technique*

We've done that so far. We'll make any necessary additions and changes to the diagrams and templates to reflect our clarifications.

B. Select an Area Upon Which To Focus

We've already selected the Librarian as our focal area. In this case, the focal areas, analysis design and programming activities, were selected to fit nicely into a chapter format. In your own cases you'll want to select focal areas based on your specific needs.

C. Refine List of Candidate Classes, Applying the Elements of "Good" Design

We'll be adding classes for databases and user interfaces. We'll be looking for classes to reuse, and we'll be sure the protocol of the classes defined so far fits with our new classes.

D. Design the Implementation

E. Reaffirm Object Relationships Within Focal Area

F. Reaffirm Object Relationships Outside Focal Area

G. Move on To Programming

Note that these strategic activities are not necessarily "steps." We won't take all these actions in the sequence they're listed. For example, specific activities within A can be embedded in some of these other activities.

8.5 PROTOTYPE REVIEW

As part of the analysis activity, I created a prototype. It's a small application that shows seven major screens in the user interface. Most of the buttons and menu selections don't do anything. It shows potential users the types of data we'll be recording and our "look and feel" concept. It starts with a modification of the main screen we showed you earlier in Figure 8-1a and 8-1b. There are a few fake entries in the catalog list.

The CHAP8 subdirectory has a DOS application called SSOOTLIB.EXE. If you don't have a graphics adapter, or if you start it with the /t option on the command line, the program will run in text mode. A Windows application named WSOOTLIB.EXE runs the prototype in Microsoft Windows version 3.0 or higher.

If you haven't yet, I'd recommend that you run the prototype. The next couple of paragraphs explain what you can expect from the prototype. If you don't run the prototype, you may be confused by the rest of this section and the beginning of the next chapter.

The following selections are active within the prototype (if you select anything else, nothing will happen):

Main Window:

> File | Print Setup,
>
> File | Exit,
>
> Catalog | Search,
>
> Catalog | Add Class Entry,
>
> Catalog | Add Function Entry,
>
> Catalog | Add Class Entry,
>
> Catalog | Edit Entry (although this calls up a class entry window, in the real program the currently selected entry would be edited),
>
> Search and Edit buttons.

Class Entry Window:

> The Add and Edit buttons for class members are active.

If this were a formal development process with real clients and real users, we would go over the forms, diagrams, and the prototype to be sure we were on the right track. Instead, I've gone over it a few times. We'll use the prototype as a guide in our design activities.

8.6   SUMMARY

OO development can be considered two distinct activities: component building and component using. The component designers and builders will provide input into the catalog with the Librarian. The component users will use the Librarian to find those components.

We discussed specific requirements in Section 8.2 and 8.3. We've selected Entry, Catalog, ClassEntry, FunctionEntry, and User classes as candidate classes. Forms 8-1 through 8-5 show the analysis templates which define the initial services and attributes for these classes.

The two primary classes for the Librarian are the Catalog class, a descendant of D_List and the Entry class and its descendants.

The following items make up the "completed" analysis activity:

- The requirements listed in Section 8.2.2
- The diagrams Figures 6-1, 7-1, and 8-1 through 8-5
- Forms 8-1 through 8-7
- The Design Plan described in 8.4.4.2
- The prototype started with Figure 8-1

The prototype is a small application that shows seven major screens in the user interface. Most of the buttons and menu selections don't do anything. It shows potential users, the types of data we'll be recording, and our "look and feel" concept. It's in the CHAP8 subdirectory as a DOS application called SSOOTLIB.EXE. A Windows application named WSOOTLIB.EXE runs the prototype in Microsoft Windows version 3.0 or higher.

Now, let's figure out *HOW* we're going to build this thing.

CHAPTER 9
Designing the Librarian

"The process of object-oriented design is the antithesis of cookbook approaches."

Grady Booch, *Object-Oriented Design with Applications*, 1991,
The Benjamin/Cummings Publishing Co., Inc.

9.1   THE DESIGN PLAN

9.1.1   Review Plan

Let's look at our design strategy and the initial plan we made in the last chapter.

1. Clarify Requirements from Analysis
2. Select an Area Upon Which to Focus
3. Refine List of Candidate Classes, Applying the Elements of "Good" Design
4. Design the Implementation
5. Reaffirm Object Relationships Within Focal Area
6. Reaffirm Object Relationships Outside Focal Area
7. Move on to Programming

9.1.2   Requirements Clarification

If you haven't done so yet, you'll probably want to run through the prototype. Section 8.5 explains where to find the prototype and its basic operation. If you haven't looked over the prototype, you may be confused by the user feedback.

9.1.2.1   User Feedback

Users: "We've looked at the prototype, and we've made a list of questions and concerns."

The users hand the developers a list:

1. How exactly do we reserve identifiers?
2. Does it make sense to have the report setup under a menu item called "Print Setup . . .?" Usually, that sets up specific printer options. Could you put that under "Utilities?"
3. The icons look like garbage when we minimize the main window and class window.
4. How do you plan to keep track of source and header files for stand-alone functions?
5. Do you really want to assume that a class will only have one source file? Member functions could be in different files (don't force us to adopt your coding style). What about static data members (don't force us to use only one source file for a class)?
6. What is a "Summary" in the report detail group of the report setup? How does it relate to Requirement 7 (in Section 8.2.1)?
7. Let's wait to work on the project specific things in the "Utilities" menu. We want this librarian to cross project boundaries.
8. The only place the class records line up right is in the Windows version of the program. They've got to look better than that in the real thing.
9. The "Exit Box" at the end of the program is unnecessary. If you want to remind us about a record that needs to be saved, that's fine. Don't make us hit that extra button to exit normally.

The developers look over the list, discuss among themselves, and then they respond to the users in a few days:

Developers: "We may have overlooked requirement number one. We could add a 'Reserve' Entry under the 'File' Menu in the Class Entry and Function Entry windows. We'll only make it active if the entry is being added. If the identifier already exists, you'll get a warning box.

"There's no problem with number two. We'll put a 'Report Setup' option under the 'Utilities' menu.

"Number three was caused by a bug in the Zinc designer. We didn't notice it until you had the prototype. We reported the bug, and we'll fix the icons.

"Number four was an oversight; we'll put source and header fields in the window.

"Are you sure about number five?"

Users: "Yes, we have some class member functions spread out over three or four files. We know it's probably not good style, but we need you to support it."

Developers: "How about if we put source file fields in the data member and member function windows? They can default to the same source file that's in the class. If you want to change it you can."

Users: "That'll work."

Developers: "Regarding number six: The 'Summary' report is like those forms
we filled out in analysis. The full report includes everything, function descriptions and all. We'll show you more details later (Section
9.4.2)."

9.1.2.2   How the Changes Affect Our Model so Far

Any change in concept, even the supposedly small ones, could have potentially
major ramifications on our project. The sooner we identify the changes, the smaller
the impact is likely to be. That's why we began by showing the users prototypes
as soon as possible. Let's see how we can work the latest changes into our
development effort.

Figure 9-1 shows the classes we've built or identified since Chapter 6. I've
divided them into subjects. I put all the classes we defined in Chapter 6 into the
first subject. They directly model the problem space. The FunctionDefn class
wasn't discovered until Chapter 8, but it logically goes in the first subject. In the
second subject, I made up some initial class names to match the windows in the

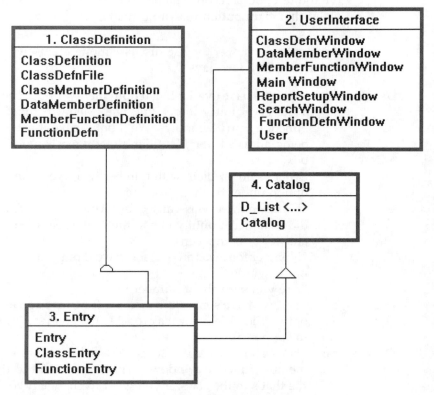

FIGURE 9-1 Initial subjects for SSOOT CASE librarian.

demo. We briefly glanced at a User class in Chapter 7; I also put it in Subject 2. I don't know if it really goes there, but the User seems to go with the User Interface. You should recognize the Entry and Catalog subjects' classes from the previous chapter.

Many of the changes and clarifications (Requirements 1, 2, 3, 7, 8, and 9) the users have requested affect the user interface. We'll address them specifically in Section 9.4.

The other changes (Requirements 4 and 5) will affect the problem space model, and Requirement 6 is really a clarification. We should probably mock up a full set of reports to be sure the users understand what we plan to give them. We'll address these issues more fully in Section 9.4.2.

9.1.3   Focal Areas

There will be three focal areas in this chapter: the problem space, the user interface and the database. We've got most of the class interfaces identified for subject Numbers 1, 3, and 4. Zinc has defined the interfaces for the classes in subject Number 2. As we address each focal area, we'll specify the details of each interface method and design the implementation of each class.

Two of the three focal areas deal with commercial libraries. Object Engineering allows us to keep the problem space classes independent of commercial libraries. The secret? *Use adapter classes.* By using data abstraction to isolate library dependent functionality, you can change user interface or database libraries and keep your essential model intact. If it is necessary for a problem space class to be dependent upon user interface or database classes, we'll make it dependent upon the adapters instead.

I learned this trick by examining the Zinc interface library. They use the UI_DISPLAY class as an adapter to isolate platform dependent video functions. If you examine the code in SSOOTLIB.CPP in the CHAP8 subdirectory, you can see how this is implemented.

9.2   DESIGNING THE PROBLEM SPACE

Requirements 1 and 2 define the classes in the problem space. We've had several suggested modifications to the original class concepts. We'll revise our class list using the elements of "good" design:

1.   Look for Existing Classes to Reuse

I found a good Date class and a good string class on CompuServe. I'm also going to use some classes that came with my compiler, the Zinc library, and the Pinnacle library.

2.   Look for Existing Hierarchies to Inherit From

I used Borland's BIDS classes, my own D_List class, and classes defined in Pinnacle.

3.   Gather What's Left Into New Hierarchies
4.   Complete the Protocol
5.   Record the Results Using the Coad and Yourdon Notation and the Class Specification Forms we used in Chapter 8.

You'll see the results of c, d, and e in the figures and forms throughout this chapter.

Then we'll design the class implementations:

1.   Clarify the Responsibilities, Constraints, and Available Resources of Internals
2.   Specify Underlying Algorithms and Logic or Defer to Programmer Using and combinations of the Following Techniques:
      a.   Pseudo Code
      b.   Structure Charts
      c.   Logic Tables
      d.   Flow Charts
      e.   Simple Narration
3.   Record the Results Using the Coad and Yourdon Notation, the Class Specification Forms, and the techniques listed above.

9.2.1   Class Design Subject

9.2.1.1   "Corrections" from Chapter 6

At the end of Chapter 6, we listed some things we could do to make the core class model better. Here I'm listing what I actually did.

9.2.1.1.1   *Lists and Strings*

Let's start with the lists and strings in the classes we built in Chapter 6. We'll replace the arrays with specific lists derived from D_List. We first specified D_List in our analysis in Chapter 8 with Figure 8-2 and Form 8-6. Since D_List is nothing more than a protocol, we don't need to delve into more design detail.

Figure 9-2 shows my first plan to implement a BIDS doubly linked list with a D_List to create a D_ListImp. I wasn't sure about how to describe this in the templates. Since I'd never used an iterator, I decided to build a small prototype. If you turn to Chapter 10 and examine Listing 10-1, you'll see that I decided not to do it that way. Instead, it looks more like Figure 9-3.

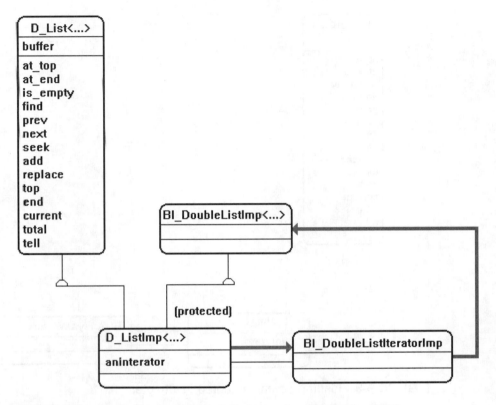

FIGURE 9-2 An implementation of D_List using Borland's BIDS.

When I wrote Chapter 7, I really thought Borland's String class would be adequate. Then I began making the changes we discussed at the end of Chapter 6, and I found that Borland's String class features were insufficient. My old instincts said, "Build one the way you want it." That, however, is not reuse, so I decided to search for a better string class. I found one that did almost everything I wanted, "for free," on CompuServe. It's in the CHAP10 subdirectory. The files STR.CPP and STR.H have the code to that class.

9.2.1.1.2 *Refining the Class List*

Our initial model classes were incomplete and, in some cases, incorrect. Figure 9-4 shows how I've changed and added to the class definition model. Form 9-1 has the specifications of the new class definition. Most of the code already exists for this classes, so we will consider the member function specifications to be "deferred to the programmer."

Figure 9-5 shows some new and changed classes. I've changed the ClsDefnFile to HeaderDefnFile to reflect the types of things typically found in a C++ header file. It can keep track of template classes, template functions, and stand-alone

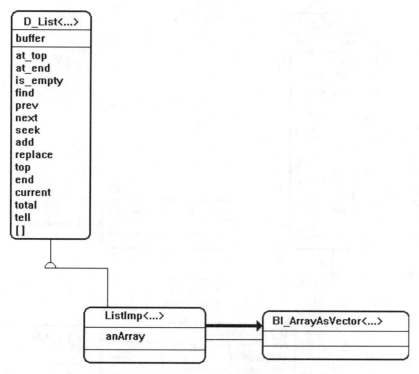

FIGURE 9-3 ListImp as implemented in Chapter 10.

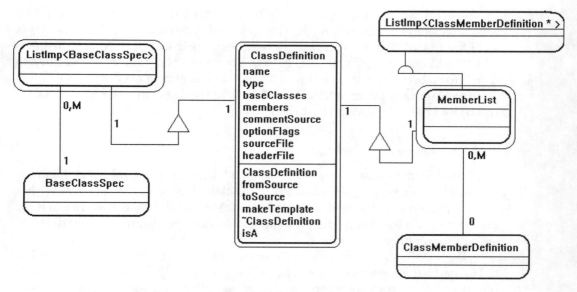

Figure 9-4 Further refinement of ClassDefinition.

Class Name: ClassDefinition   **Date:**   10/10/92

Version: 2.0 (Chapter 10)

Base Classes: None

Categories: Model

Class Purpose/Description:

This class models a C++ class definition. It serves as an interface between SSOOT CASE and source code.

Data Members (Attributes)

Visibility	Type	Name	Description
protected	int	forwardDeclaration	Set to TRUE if this class is a forward declaration.
	IdString	name	Name of Class.
	ListImp	baseClasses	List of base classes.
	MemberList	Members	List of Member functions and data members.
	istream*	commentSource	Stream with a comment template.
	bitfield	expandline	If set to TRUE, the inline functions will be included in the source file.
		useComments	If set to TRUE, comment templates will be included in source.
	ListImp	nestedClasses	List of class definitions nested within this class definition.
	classType	type	Indicates whether this is a class, union or structure.

Member Functions (Services)

Visibility	Name	Description
protected	getClassName	Gets the name of the class from the input stream.
	getParents	Reads the base class list from the input stream.
	getMembers	Reads the members from the input stream.
	getNested	Reads nested members from the input stream.
	putComment	Writes comments to source file or template.
public	fromSource	Reads input stream and builds class from source file.
	toSource	Writes the class declaration to a header file stream.
	makeTemplate	Creates empty function templates on a source stream.

FORM 9-1   Class definition template.

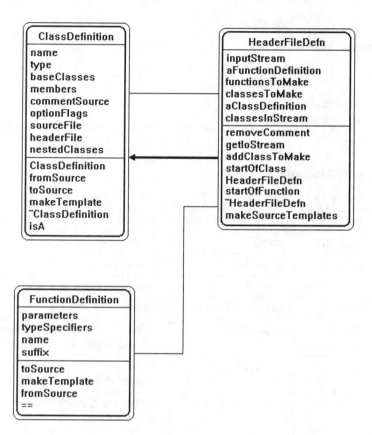

FIGURE 9-5   Latest model of the class definition classes.

functions, as well as the classes we kept track of before. Forms 9-2 and 9-3 give the general class specifications of HeaderFileDefn and FunctionDefinition.

I'd like to explain the reasons for some of the design decisions reflected in the forms and figures mentioned above. I decided not to make FunctionDefinition parent of MemberFunctionDefinition because of the rework involved, although I may do it in a future version of the software. The data members and member functions listed in Form 9-2 are similar to the ones already in ClsDefnFile, so all the methods are deferred to the programmer. See Listing 10-4 and 10-5 and the discussion in Section 10.1.2 for the details.

While developing the FunctionDefinition and MemberFunctionDefinition classes and the FunctOffset structure (see Listings 10-4 and 10-5), I found myself copying a lot of code. This is what OOP is supposed to prevent! Maybe FunctionDefiniton and MemberFunctionDefinition belonged in the same family tree, but not FunctOffset. I did find one thing they had in common: They all needed a list of parameters that could be read from or written to a stream. (This section was added to the design *after* programming started.)

Figure 9-6 shows the relationships a ParamList has with other classes. Form

Class Name:	HeaderFileDefin	Date:	10/12/92

Version: 2.0 (Formerly ClsDefnFile)

Base Classes: None

Categories: Model

Class Purpose/Description:

Models a typical C++ Header file. Does not currently deal with constants, #defines or #included files. Instead, it deals primarily with declarations: classes, functions, and templates.

Data Members (Attributes)

Visibility	Type	Name	Description
protected	iostream*	anIoStream	A working stream for a copy of the header file.
	FunctionDefinition	aFunction	Working variable that contains the FunctionDefinition being read.
	ListImp	fnctnsToMk	List of functions to be processed by makeSourceTemplates.
	ListImp	classesToMk	List of classes to be processed by makeSourceTemplates.
	ClassDefinition	aClsDfntn	A working variable for the ClassDefinition.
	ListImp	clsssInStrm	List of the names, types, and offsets of the classes in the stream.
	ListImp	fnctnsInStrm	List of names, types, and offsets of the functions in the stream.
	char []	tmpFileName	Name of temporary file associated with iostream.
	unsigned	options	Flags for specific options associated with the file.

Member Functions (Services)

Visibility	Name	Description
protected	init	Initializes the class. Called by the constructor.
	removeComments	Removes the comments from the file before processing the rest of the file.
	findClasses	Locate the start of each class in the iostream.

FORM 9-2 Class definition template.

	findFunctions	Locate the start of each function in the iostream.
Visibility	**Name**	**Description**
	getClassName	Retrieve the name of the class from the iostream.
	getFunctionName	Retrieve the name of the function from the iostream.
public	getioStream	Returns the "anIoStream" variable.
	startOfClass	Finds the start of a named class in the iostream.
	addClassToMake	Adds a class name to the classesToMake list.
	addFctnToMake	Adds a function name to the functions ToMake list.
	mkSrcTmplts	Makes the source code templates of the functions and classes in the lists.

FORM 9-2   *(continued).*

9-4 has a class specification for the ParamList. Forms 9-5 and 9-6 define the two major functions, toSource and fromSource. The toString and fromString functions are similar and therefore deferred to the programmer.

9.2.1.2   The Entry Classes

Figures 8-2 through 8-4 show the analysis diagrams of the other part of the domain model, the Entry class family. If you remember, we first saw the Entry class family in Figure 7-2. We further refined the analysis in Forms 8-1 through 8-6.

Many of the changes to the Entry class and Catalog class reflect design decisions on database interface, so I'll discuss them in the database section.

9.3   DATA BASE CLASS DESIGN

9.3.1   D_Record and Entry

The "Entry" class has a few changes from the analysis. For example, if we look at the analysis prototype, we see that we need some sort of summary string to put in the list box.

As I examined the "Entry" class analysis, I noticed the "get" and "put" methods. As I began to design these methods, I found that they would require knowledge of whatever database the Catalog would use. This violates the concept of database independence I wanted. I needed some way to transfer class data to and from any database, object-oriented, or relational. With this in mind, during

| **Class Name:** | FunctionDefinition | **Date:** | 10/12/92 |

Version: 1.0

Base Classes: None

Categories: Model

Class Purpose/Description:

Models the definition of a stand-alone function.

Maybe this should be a base class for MemberFunctionDefinition in the future.

Data Members (Attributes)

Visibility	Type	Name	Description
protected	ListImp	parameters	List of parameters for the function.
	string	type Specifiers	Function return type and value.
	string	name	Name of this function.
	string	suffix	Things like 'const.'

Member Functions (Services)

Visibility	Name	Description
public	toSource	Creates a prototype in a header file.
	makeTemplate	Creates an empty function in a .CPP file.
	fromSource	Reads the source file and builds this function definition.
	operator ==	Compares FunctionDefinitions for equality.
protected	mkTypAndNm	MakeTypeAndName fills the type specifier and name variables from an input stream.
	makeParamList	Makes the list of parameters from an input stream.
	makeSuffix	Determines if there is a 'const' before the end of the function prototype.

FORM 9-3 Class definition template.

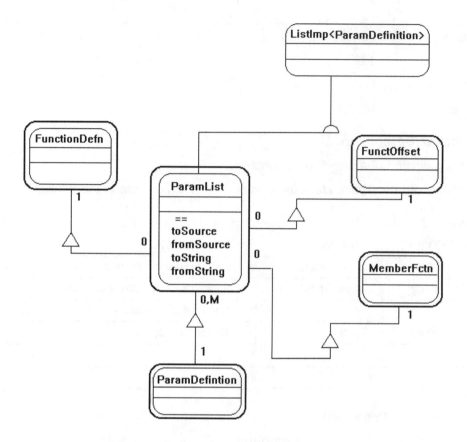

FIGURE 9-6 ParamList and its relationships.

design, I changed the methods "put" and "get" to "toRecord" and "fromRecord." Figure 9-7 illustrates the changes to the Entry class and the classes Class DefinitionEntry and FunctionDefinitionEntry.

The Entry class and each of its descendants has a toRecord and fromRecord function. Every important data member in each Entry object (and its descendants), including inherited data members, can be placed into or retrieved from a special adapter class called a D_Record.

The D_Record class acts as a "universal database adapter." Most databases have some concept of "records" and "fields." A record is, in fact, a list of fields. D_Field has the data members to keep track of the field's name, its type, and its value. It also has the member functions to allow assignment to and from those values. Most database libraries allow access to and from named fields in a record. To support a new DBMS, write a set of methods or functions to translate the D_Record into a record that DBMS can understand. See Figure 9-8 for an illustration of D_Record and D_Field. Forms 9-7 and 9-8 specify these classes. Each of the methods is really quite trivial so they're deferred to the programmer.

There is a cost associated with using this technique that I might not pay if I

Class Name:	ParamList	Date:	10/92
Version	1		
Base Classes:	ListImp<ParamDefinition>		
Categories:	Container, Model		

Class Purpose/Description:

List of parameters. Could be for member functions, stand-alone functions, or other function specifications.

Data Members (Attributes)

(None, all members are inherited)

Member Functions (Services)

Visibility	Name	Description
public	operator ==	True if the list's parameters are all the same type.
	toSource	Converts parameter list to C++ source code stream.
	from Source	Creates parameter list from source code stream.
	toString	Converts parameter list to C++ source code string.
	fromString	Creates parameter list from source code string.

FORM 9-4   Class definition template.

didn't need database independence. Allowing an Entry to interact directly with a database library would take less time and memory. The resulting code, however, would be far less portable.

Remember *design occurs in the brain, not in a notation*. Although Figure 9-8 appears in a nicely finished form for publication, I originally sketched it out on the back of a printout while compiling another program. I wrote listings 10-11 and 10-12 straight from the scrap paper. I will therefore "defer the specification to the programmer."

9.3.2   Relational vs. OO

We have two choices for mapping our data to records: OO mapping or relational mapping. An OO record contains all the state information for a single object, including any sub-objects. Relational rules would require each type of class to have its own table.

As I write this, there aren't very many truly OODBMS systems commercially available, and those that are available are still quite expensive. An OODBMS is

Owning Class:	ParamList			
Function Name:	fromSource			
Purpose:	Converts source stream into a parameters list.			
Parameters:	**Type**	**Name**	**Default**	**Purpose**
	istream &	in	None	Parameter source code stream.

Description/Specification:

Using the io stream operations, this function creates a series of ParamDefinition structures and adds them to "this" ParamList object.

1. Read the stream up to the closing parenthesis into a buffer. Keep track of the level of nesting.
2. Separate the buffer into different parameters by finding commas.
3. Separate each parameter into ParamDefinition structures using the following rules for each "word":
    a. Anything after an '=' sign is a default value;
    b. The last word is a variable name, unless it's the only word, then it's a type;
    c. Everything in front of the name is a type specification;
    d. Any pointer or reference characters are part of the type specification.
4. Add the parameter definition to the list.

FORM 9-5   Member function template.

more like a hierarchical or network DBMS than a relational DBMS. I need aspects of both types to make this librarian work.

9.3.3   "Bottom Up" Design

9.3.3.1   Examine the Components—Taking Advantage of the Database While Maintaining Independence

Since this book is for general publication it would be irresponsible of me to force you to use a particular database management system. Too often, however, good

Owning Class: ParamList

Function Name: toSource

Purpose: Puts ParamList into a source stream.

Parameters:

Type	Name	Default	Purpose
ostream &	out	None	Parameter source code stream.
Boolean	withNames	true	Include name in source?
	withDefaults	false	Include default values in source?

Description/Specification:

Put the '(' to Out.

For each ParamDefinition member in the list:

    Put the type specifier to Out;

    if withName is true put the name to Out;

    If withDefault is true put '=' and the default value to Out;

    If this isn't the last parameter put a ',' to Out.

Put the ')' to Out.

FORM 9-6   Member function template.

library specific features are lost in the name of portability, because everything is distilled into the least common denominator.

Figure 9-9 shows a PFM_List—a D_List derivative that uses the Pinnacle File Manger DBMS from Vermont Database corporation by also inheriting from Pinnacle's "table" class. (A variation of this class first appeared in an article I wrote for the January 1992 *C Users Journal*.) Pinnacle is a C library that takes full advantage of C++ by wrapping C++ classes around the C functions. I chose Pinnacle for the following reasons:

1. It was designed around OO concepts before most people knew what that meant.

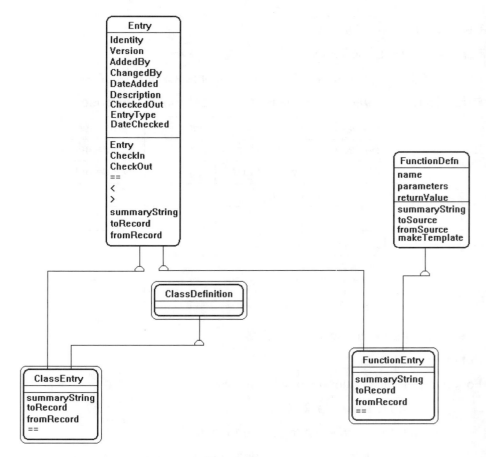

FIGURE 9-7 Entry and its child classes.

2. It has very powerful search capabilities. The searches have a very "C-like" syntax. This makes programming for this DBMS very natural.
3. It supports, but does not enforce, relational rules.
4. It has one of the most flexible database interfaces I've ever seen.
5. You can get a free sample library limited to 100 records per table by calling Vermont Database Corporation.

See Appendix A for details on Pinnacle Data Manager and Vermont Database Corporation. If you want to make SSOOT CASE multi-user without changing any source code, or if you want to make any small changes to the code in this book, you can purchase the Pinnacle DBMS Library.

The PFM_List adds two concepts to a standard D_List—selection and order. The member function "select" limits the members of the PFM_List to those that meet the criteria specified in the criteria parameter. Since it works by passing its criteria on to the Pinnacle table, I won't specify it specifically in a form. However

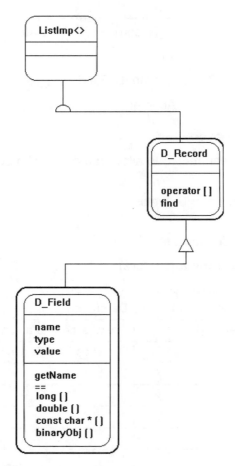

FIGURE 9-8 AD_Record is a list of D_Fields.

I will list, with the permission of Vermont Database Corporation, the selection syntax in Form 9-9.

The syntax listed in Form 9-9 also works for the "find" method of PFM_List. The user won't have to learn this syntax. We'll build the strings based on the user's input from the dialog boxes, and we will allow the user to use it in the advanced query dialog box.

The "set_order" method assigns a column by which the "first," "last," "next," and "prev" methods will navigate the list. The "clear_order" and "clear_select" methods remove the criteria from the list.

9.3.3.2   Mapping Classes To DBMS

At this point we can use the D_List protocol to access the catalog without worrying about database specific issues. The D_List protocol also gives us consistent access to our lists. If we want to know how many rows in the table, we use the same method as we do to find the number of elements in an array - total.

Class Name:	D_Record	**Date:**	
Version:	1.0		
Base Classes:	ListImp<D_Field>		
Categories:	Adapter		

Class Purpose/Description:

Acts as a "universal" record to allow transfer of data between a database record and the application.

A D_Record is a list of D_Fields.

Data Members (Attributes)

(None, inherited from ancestors)

Member Functions (Services)

Visibility	Name	Description
public	operator[]	Allows access to a particular field by name or number.
	find	Searches for a field in the record.

FORM 9-7   Class definition template.

With Figure 9-9, a Catalog is no longer merely a D_List, it is a RecList. The RecList class is a PFM_List instantiated with a D_Record. A Catalog is a list of D_Records. In addition to list navigation, we need the following services from a Catalog:

1. We need a summary string for each entry displayed in the selection window.
2. We need to get the FunctionEntry or a ClassEntry selected by the user for display, edit, or reporting.
3. We need to put a created or edited Entry into the Catalog.

Class Name:	D_Field	**Date**	10/12/92
Version:	1.0		
Base Classes:	None		
Categories:	Adapter		

Class Purpose/Description

Contains a named data value of a particular type.

The semantics of a D_Field allow it to be treated like any standard data value. A binary object is a struct with a byte count and a void * to point to any data you need.

Data Members (Attributes)

Visibility	Type	Name	Description
protected	Char *	name	Field name.
	fieldType	type	Indicates whether field is a long, double, string, or binary object.
	union	value	Contains the fields data; can be a long, double, string, binary object

Member Functions (Services)

Visibility	Name	Description
public	getName	Returns the name of the field.
	operator ==	Compares the value in the D_Field to some other value (long, double, string ...)
	long()	Casts the field value into a long.
	double()	Casts the field value into a double.
	const char * ()	Casts the field value into a char pointer.
	binaryObj()	Casts the field value into a binary object.

FORM 9-8   Class definition template.

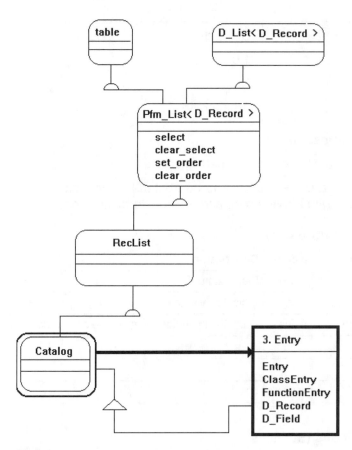

FIGURE 9-9   Lists, catalogs, and database tables.

Therefore, we add the following methods to the Catalog definition: getEntry, setEntry, getSummary. Form 9-10 has the class specification for Catalog.

The D_Records can be converted to and from ClassEntries or FunctionEntries. The Entry class and its descendants each have a toRecord and fromRecord method. These member functions load the data in the class to and from a record. Figure 9-10 shows more detail regarding communication to and from the Catalog.

9.3.4   Record Descriptions

Since we're using a relational DBMS, I decided to use an ER Diagram (Figure 9-11) to describe the records in the SSOOT CASE Librarian. Listing 9-1 (in Appendix D) is a Pinnacle DBMS database definition language file to create the SSOOT CASE Librarian database. Vermont Database corporation has graciously allowed me to include the PINNACLE.H file and an abbreviated manual, PINNACLE.TXT (both

Filters have a syntax that is similar to C expressions. Here is a description of the filter syntax:

Blanks have no significance outside strings

Strings are enclosed in ' quotes

expr:	expr6 END
string:	quoted characters; embedded quote (or anything) preceeded by backslash (\) (single quotes ' be used)
number	usual rules for formation of C numeric constants
constant:	number | string
name:	string of alphanums or underscore (_) not starting with a digit
parameter:	% followed by R, r, I, i, S, s, N, n, B, or b.
expr0:	name | constant | (expr6)
op1:	"−" | "!"
expr1:	op1 expr1 | expr0
op2:	"*" | "/" | "%"
expr1:	op1 expr1 | expr0
op2:	"*" | "/" | "%"
expr2:	expr1 op2 expr2 | expr1
op3:	"+" | "−"
expr3:	expr2 op3 expr3 | expr2
op4:	"<" | ">" | "<=" | ">=" | "==" | "!=" | "?" | "??"
expr4:	expr3 op4 expr4 | expr3
expr5:	expr4 "&&" expr5 | expr4
expr6:	expr5 "||" expr6 | expr5

A filter expression, when applied to a row in a table, produces a TRUE or FALSE value. Here are the semantic rules:

o   There are binary expressions and unary expressions; binary expressions have the form

term1 operator term2

Unary expressions have the form

operator term1

o   Parentheses cause the evaluation of the expression inside parentheses as a term
o   term1 + term2: add term1 to term2
o   term1 − term2: subtract term2 from term1
o   term1 * term2: multiply term1 by term2
o   term1 / term2: divide term1 by term2
o   term1 % term2: moduls of term1, term2

FORM 9-9   Selection filter syntax—from Pinnacle Relational Engine.

o   term1 > term2: 1 if term1 is greater than term2, otherwise 0
o   term1 < term2: 1 if term1 is less than term2, otherwise 0
o   term1 == term2: 1 if term1 is equal to term2, otherwise 0
o   term1 >= term2: 1 if term1 is greater than or equal to term2,
    otherwise 0
o   term1 <= term2: 1 if term1 is less than or equal to term2,
    otherwise 0
o   term1 != term2: 1 if term1 is not equal to term2, otherwise 0
o   term1 ? term2: 1 if term1 matches the wildcard expression term2
    (see below), otherwise 0
o   term1 ??= term2: 1 if term1 satisfies the wordsearch string,term2
    (see below), otherwise 0
o   !term1: 1 if term1 is zero; 0 if term1 is nonzero
o   -term1: the negative value of term1
o   after evaluation of the filter expression, a non-zero value is
    considered TRUE, a zero value is considered FALSE

Wildcard Patterns
A wildcard pattern is comprised of a sequence of wildcard phrases. A
wildcard phrase is one of:

o   Any non-null character except asterisk (*), question mark (?), left
    brace ([), left bracket ({), or circumflex (^). These ordinary
    characters are matched literally.
o   An asterisk to match an arbitrary string.
o   A question mark to match any signal character.
o   A list of wildcard patterns enclosed within braces and separated by
    commas. This matches any of those wildcard patterns.
o   A list of characters or ranges of characters (like "a-z" for "a"
    to "z") enclosed within square brackets and with no separators
    except a hyphen between the two characters of a range. The list
    may be preceeded with a circumflex (^) to match any character BUT
    the specified ones.

Wildcard Examples:
"*"   matches anything.
"a*z" matches "a" followed by 0 or more characters followed by "z".
"a?c" matches "aac", "abc", "acc", "adc", and so forth.
"{if, and, but}" matches any of "if", "and", or "but"
"[a-f,z]*" matches any string that starts with "a", "b", "c", "d",
"e", "f", or "z".
"[^x]*" matches any string that doesn't start with an "x".
"\[*]" matches anything within square brackets. The \ means the next
character is quoted. Use the \ just like you would in C.

FORM 9-9   *(continued).*

Wordsearch (Lexical) Operations

The operator "??" indicates a wordsearch operation. The wordsearch operation permits the scanning of text fields for the presence or absence of words. The wordsearch operator is much more convenient than the wildcard operator for this sort of application.

A **word** is defined as a sequence of characters comprised entirely of digits, upper or lower case letters, underscores, apostrophes, and dashes. Words do not include whitespace or punctuation.

A **phrase** is defined as a sequence of words.

Wordsearch Operators comprise the following: && (and), || (or), ! (not), () (parentheses), [] (phrase brackets].

The wordsearch operator takes as an operand a string that contains a wordsearch expression. The wordsearch expression consists of words and operators.

```
'Kentucky && racing'
'Kentucky || racing'
'!Kentucky && racing'
'Senate && (welfare || education)'
'[Abraham Lincoln] && abolition'
'O\'Bryan || O\'Malley'
```

Precedence from highest to lowest: [], (), !, &&, ||.

FORM 9-9   *(continued)*.

found in the CHAP9 subdirectory) so you can fully understand how I've implemented their library.

9.3.4.1   Entry

An Entry record is the record in the database that "owns" most of the other records. Any data common to all entries is found in the Entry record. Additionally, there are keys and indexes so the DBMS can help us to maintain data integrity and to access data quickly. The names of the columns match (or nearly match) the names of the data members.

9.3.4.2   Class and Function Entry

The FunctionEntry and ClassEntry records will each have data in an Entry record. There will be one and only one Entry record for each ClassEntry or FunctionEntry. Relational rules would dictate that the BaseClasses and Parameters be in their own tables. We'll store them as strings, similar to their source code counterparts, since we can translate them to and from source code.

Class Name:	Catalog
Version:	2.0
Base Classes:	RecList

Class Purpose/Description:
A Catalog contains descriptive entries of reusable program components.
It acts as a bridge between the database and the user interface. It models a library's card catalog.

Data Members (Attributes)

Visibility	Type	Name	Description
public	RecList	theClassTbl	Allows access to the database table with the ClassEntry records.
	RecList	theFctnTbl	Allows access to the database table with the FunctionEntry records.
	RecList	theMemTbl	Allows access to the database table that contains class members.

Member Functions (Services)

(Previously specified methods are inherited)

Visibility	Name	Description
public	getEntry	Gets a ClassEntry or Function Entry (based on parameter) from current catalog record.
	setEntry	Writes data from ClassEntry or FunctionEntry into the database.
	getSummary	Returns a summary string for display for current record from catalog.
	Catalog	Constructor.

FORM 9-10   Class definition template.

9.3.4.3   Class Member

Since we have two types of class members, originally I thought we would have two tables, one for data and one for functions. There were a few more fields in the function record, so I kept the two records together. This will also keep the programming overhead down because one table will translate into one internal list.

9.4   DESIGNING THE USER INTERFACE

We got some general ideas about the user interface from Chapter 8. The users gave us some feedback at the beginning of this chapter. Now we'll get the details.

I used the Zinc Interface Library to develop the user interface. I used adapter

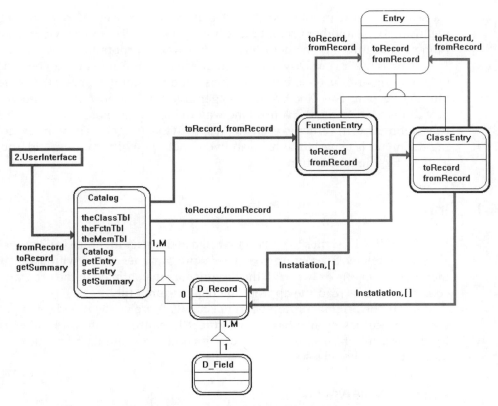

FIGURE 9-10. Catalog and entry message activity.

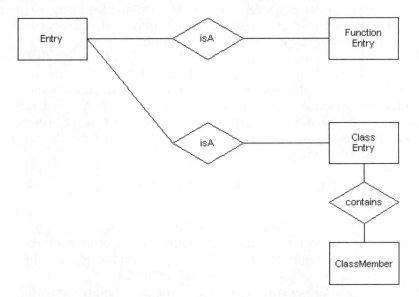

FIGURE 9-11 Entity relationship diagram for SSOOT CASE librarian.

classes to keep the problem space independent of the user interface classes, so if you want to use another user interface library you can. There's a review of the Zinc Library and information about the Zinc Software Corporation in Appendix A.

Zinc is an "Event Driven" user interface library. An Event can be generated by any number of user activities, such as a mouse action, a keystroke, a menu or button selection. The Zinc Event Manager gives the window objects the opportunity to respond to those Events. One way to handle menu selections is to assign user-defined event values to each menu item in the designer. The window containing the menu is expected to have an Event method which can respond appropriately to the menu selection.

9.4.1   Input

I used the Zinc Designer to make a first stab at our user interface in Chapter 8. The Zinc Designer is a program that lets a programmer draw windows, dialogs, menus, etc. Objects drawn with the designer are instantiated in the program using constructors that read the appropriate object from a file.

From the original prototype from Chapter 8, we've identified some potential user interface classes in Subject 2 in Figure 9-1. Figure 9-12 shows a full expansion for the user interface subject. We'll discuss each class and its interaction with the user and the other classes.

9.4.1.1   MainWindow

Figure 9-13 shows the main window after some revision from Chapter 8. The main window has three major features: the Main Menu, the Entry list, and the buttons. The Entry list is a special special child window that knows how to access the catalog and display the selected Entries in it.

The following outline describes the main menu. I built the screen and menu with the Zinc Designer. If you have the Zinc Designer you can see the Event value is the numeric value sent to the event manager when the menu is selected. The Member Function called is the name of the function called when the event is triggered. The file SOOTLIB.DAT in the CHAP10 subdirectory has the main window in the resource SOOT_LIB_1. If you have the Zinc designer you can examine and change the menu.

SSOOT CASE LIBRARIAN MAIN MENU

A. File
1. Open Catalog—Event Value: 10001
Opens a database file containing the catalog information.
Member Function Called by Event: Catalog::Catalog
2. New Catalog—Event Value: 10002
Closes current database, creates an empty database.

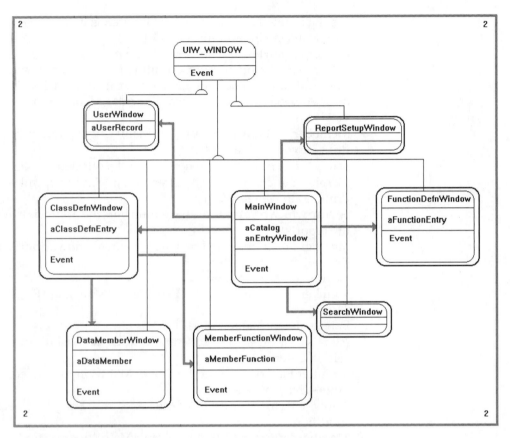

FIGURE 9-12　The user interface classes, derived from Zinc Interface Library.

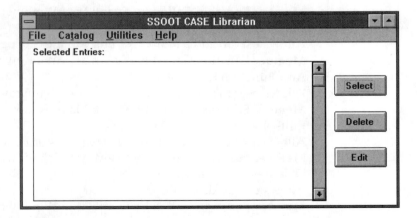

FIGURE 9-13　SSOOT CASE librarian main window.

Member Function Called by Event: Catalog::create
(Not available in multi-user mode)

3. Import From Header File—Event Value: 10003
Allows a user to open a syntactically correct header file and import its class and function definitions into the catalog. Entries are "Checked out." Any classes that match a particular identifier are given a new version.
Member Function Called by Event: MainWindow::importFromHeader

4. Print—Event Value: 10004
Sends the currently selected report to the selected printer.
Member Function Called by Event: MainWindow::print

5. Print Setup—Event Value: 10005
Sets up which printer and what parameters the printer is to use to print the reports.
Member Function Called by Event: MainWindow::printSetup

6. Exit—Event Value: 10006
Terminates the program.
Member Function Called by Event: eventManager->Put(L_EXIT);

B. Catalog

1. **Select**—Event Value: 20001
Allows user to narrow the scope of the current list to entries meeting certain criteria.
Member Function Called by Event: MainWindow::select

2. **Find**—Event Value: 20002
Allows user to locate the first occurrence of an Entry that meets a given condition.
Member Function Called by Event: MainWindow::find

3. **Order By**—Event Value: 20003
Allows user to determine the order in which the Entries are listed in the entry window.
Member Function Called by Event: MainWindow::orderBy

4. **Add Class**—Event Value: 20004
Allows user to add a new Class Entry to the catalog.
Member Function Called by Event: MainWindow::addClass

5. **Add Function Entry**—Event Value: 20005
Allows user to add a new Function Entry to the catalog.
Member Function Called by Event: MainWindow::addFunction

6. **Edit**—Event Value: 20006
Allows user to edit the current Entry (Class or Function)
Member Function Called by Event: MainWindow::editEntry

7. **Delete**—Event Value: 20007
Allows user to delete the current Entry.
Member Function Called by Event: MainWindow::deleteEntry

C. Utilities

1. **Browse File**—Event Value: 30001

Brings up a window for the user to browse through text files.
Member Function Called by Event: MainWindow::browseFile

2. **User**

   a. **Add**—Event Value: 31001
   Allows user to add another user.
   Member Function Called by Event: MainWindow::addUser

   b. **Edit**—Event Value: 31002
   Allows user to change a user's id or password.
   Member Function Called by Event: MainWindow::editUser

   c. **Delete**—Event Value: 31003
   Allows user to delete another user, but not itself.
   Member Function Called by Event: MainWindow::deleteUser

D. **Help**—Event Value : L_HELP
   Brings up Zinc's Context Sensitive help system.

The buttons correspond to the menu entries, Catalog-Edit, Catalog-Delete, and Catalog-Select for speedy access to the most common functions. Form 9-11 has the specification for the main window class. Figure 9-14 shows the major relationships around the main window. One of the main components of the MainWindow is the CatalogWindow. The CatalogWindow has a Catalog attached to it. The CatalogWindow and the MainWindow share a single Catalog object. The CatalogWindow is based on Zinc's VLIST example and acts as a window into the catalog. The CatalogWindow is a very interesting class, but it's Zinc specific and not exactly my design, so I'm not putting any design detail for it into this chapter. Examine the CATWIN.CPP and CATWIN.HPP files in the CHAP10 subdirectory for details. If you get Zinc, you can study its workings in more detail. If you get other user interface libraries, this code might be of some help.

9.4.1.2   ClassDefnWindow

A ClassDefnWindow allows the user to add or edit a ClassEntry. Figure 9-15 shows a picture of the window. Most of the data items in the menu are obvious. They correspond to the data in the ClassEntry class.

The following outline explains the menu:

Class Definition Menu

A. **File**

   1. **To Source**—Event Value: 11001
   Generates a class definition for a header file.

   2. **Make Template**—Event Value: 11002
   Generates a series of empty functions and static data members.

   3. **From Source**—Event Value: 11003
   Generates a class entry from a source file.

   4. **Reserve Item**—Event Value: 11004

Class Name	MainWindow		Date:	11/92

Version: 1.0

Base Classes: UIW_WINDOW

Categories: User Interface

Class Purpose/Description:

Primary means of access to the SSOOT CASE Librarian.

Data Members (Attributes)

Visibility	Type	Name	Description
protected	CatalogWin	theCatalogWin	The scrolling window for access to the catalog entries.
	Catalog	theCatalog	The currently open catalog.
	string	theSelection	Working variable. Current selection or find string.
	HeaderFileDefn	theFileDefn	Header file from which imports occur.

Member Functions (Services)

Visibility	Name	Description
public	ImportFromHeader	Adds to catalog by importing class and function definitions.
	print	Prints report selected in utility menu.
	printSetup	Sets up the printer and the options.
	select	Determines which entries are displayed in CatalogWindow.
	find	Locates a catalog entry.
	orderBy	Determines the order of the displayed entries.
	addClass	Adds a class to the catalog.
	addFunction	Adds a function to the catalog.
	editEntry	Edits the current entry.
	deleteEntry	Removes an entry from the catalog.
	browseFile	Permits browsing through a text file.
	addUser	Adds a user allowed to access the library.
	editUser	Changes a user id or password.
	deleteUser	Removes the user.
	Event	Handles the events called by buttons and menus. Calls these other functions.

FORM 9-11   Class definition template.

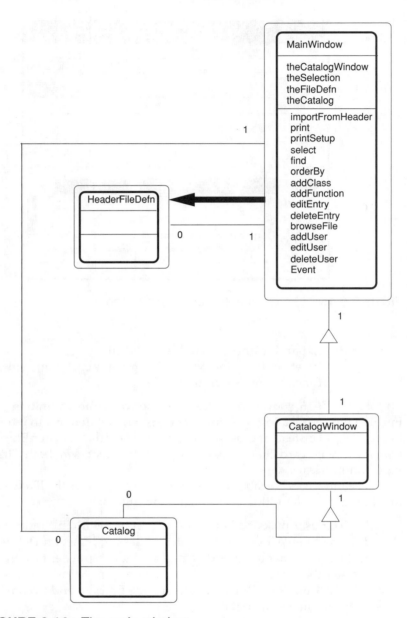

FIGURE 9-14 The main window.

Reserves the class name in the database so someone else doesn't accidentally add a class with the same name. (Multi-user version only)

B. **Options**

1. **Use Comments**—Event Value: 11005

If set to True, the **Make Template** and **To Source** menu item output will include comment templates.

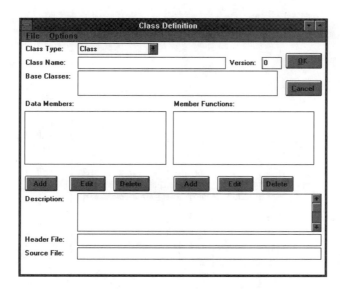

FIGURE 9-15   The class definition editing window.

2.   **Expand Inline**—Event Value: 11006
     If set to True, the **Make Template** menu item will include inline functions in its output.

Figure 9-16 shows the interaction between the Definition Windows, the Entries, and the Catalog. This interaction is largely identical to the FunctionEntry interaction, so instead of repeating the diagram for the FunctionEntry, I labeled the items with wild card characters so the figure can represent both Class Entries and Function Entries.

The messages are labeled from 1 to 6. This indicates the likely series of events in either a class definition or a function definition:

1.   The user picks add or edit Entry from the MainWindow menu.
2.   The MainWindow instantiates a Class or Function Definition Window.
3.   The user manipulates data in the window, presses buttons, makes menu selection, etc.
4.   The Definition Window converts the Entry to and from records so it can manipulate the data.
5.   When the user needs to put the Entry into the Catalog, or update the Catalog, it gets the Catalog from the MainWindow.
6.   The user locates and updates or adds the Entry to the Catalog.

9.4.1.2.1   *DataMemberWindow*

Figure 9-17 shows the DataMemberWindow. The Owning Class is filled in automatically when it is instantiated. The user can't change it. Other than that, it's generally a straight forward data entry window.

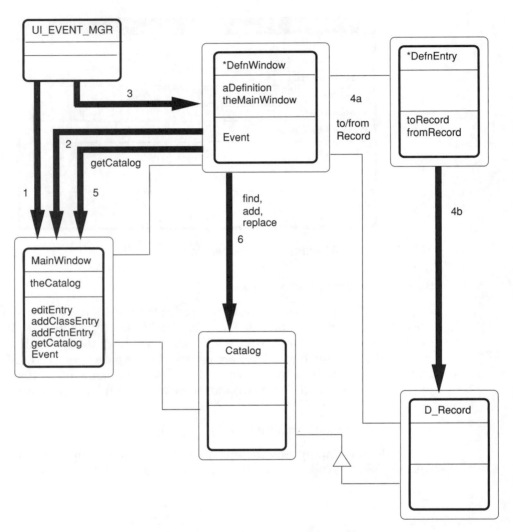

FIGURE 9-16   Class/function definition window object interaction.

Figure 9-18 shows the interaction between the ClassDefinitionWindow and its member windows. The figure is valid for both data members and member functions. The message connections are labeled in the likely order of their occurrence.

1. The ClassDefintionWindow instantiates the MemberWindow in response to a user's button push.
2. Data is transferred to and from the appropriate ClassMember when the window is opened or closed.
3. The ClassMember is added to or replaces the member in the class member list in the ClassDefinition.

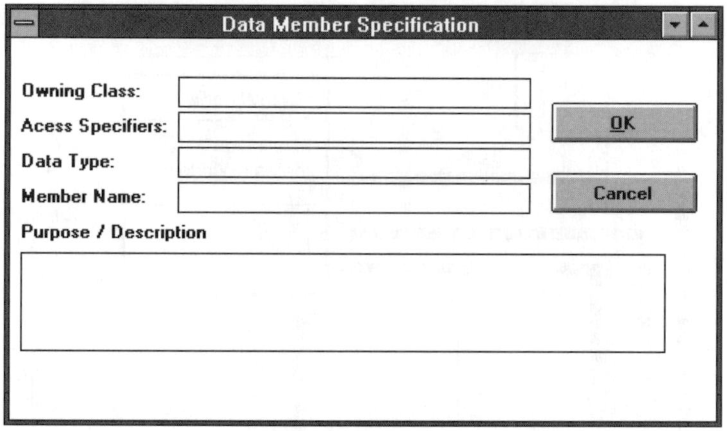

Data Member Specification

Owning Class:

Acess Specifiers:

Data Type:

Member Name:

OK

Cancel

Purpose / Description

FIGURE 9-17 The data member window.

9.4.1.2.2 MemberFunctionWindow

Figure 9-19 shows the MemberFunctionWindow. It interacts with the ClassDefinitionWindow the same way the DataMemberWindow does. Figure 9-20 shows the support windows for the FunctionWindows (both member functions and stand-alone functions). They are invoked by the parameter Add/Edit buttons and the Specify button, respectively. They follow the same interaction pattern as the ClassWindow and FunctionWindow follow with the MainWindow.

9.4.1.3   FunctionDefnWindow

The FunctionWindow is very much like the MemberFunctionWindow but it has no Owner field and it has a menu similar to the ClassMemberWindow.

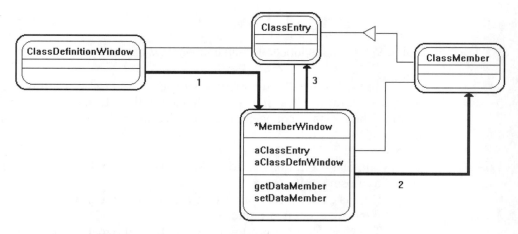

FIGURE 9-18 Class member windows.

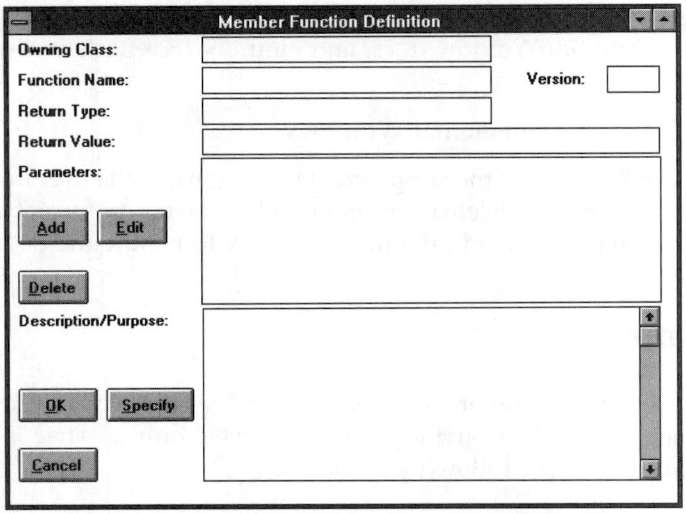

FIGURE 9-19 Member function window.

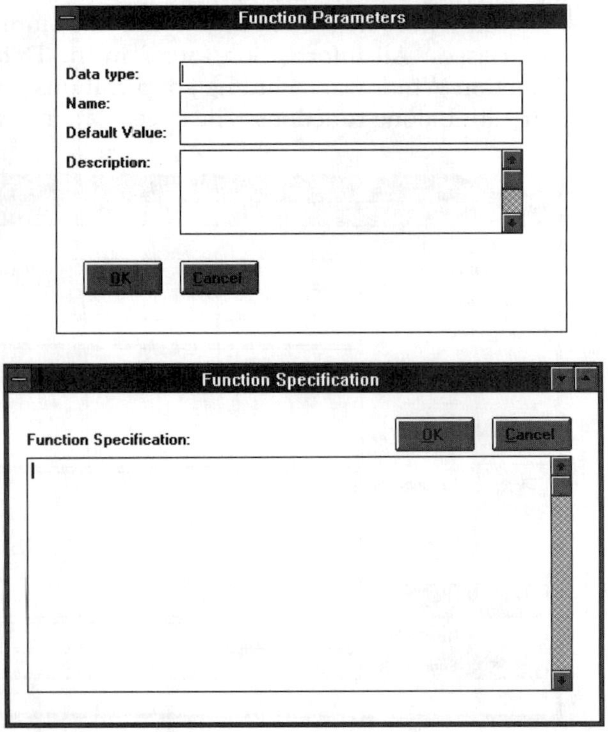

FIGURE 9-20 Function support windows.

Figure 9-21 illustrates this. It interacts with the MainWindow the same way the ClassDefintionWindow does, and Figure 9-16 reflects its behavior.

9.4.1.4   Supplemental Windows

Figure 9-22 shows the supplemental windows in the user interface. They allow us to add, edit, and delete users and to select the report format and destination. We'll need data members in the main window to handle the data in these windows.

9.4.2   Output

There are three report formats listed in the supplemental windows. Any reports generated will be from the currently selected Entries. The reports will be generated according to the following guidelines:

1. The List will be the summary list as found in the central window.
2. The Summary will be similar in format and content to the Class Definition Templates we've listed in the various forms in this chapter and in Chapter 8. Function summaries will contain the information found in the FunctionDefinitionWindow.
3. The full report will list in addition to the summary information:
   For classes: All information found in the Data Member and Member Function Windows, including specifications.
   For stand-alone functions: The specification.

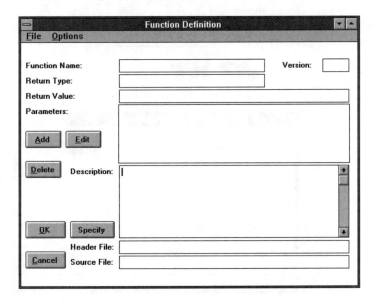

FIGURE 9-21   Function definition window.

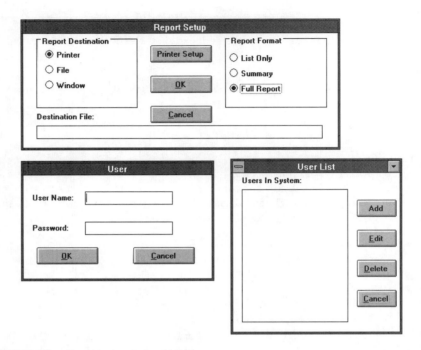

FIGURE 9-22 Supplemental windows.

Rather than describe each report in detail here, I'll simply state that I will model them after the forms and windows listed here.

The major difference between Form 9-12 and many of the forms you've seen in much of the book is that we won't have any special fonts in the librarian reports. (Remember, the second S in SSOOT case stands for SIMPLE.) They will be text only. We'll create a new class, independent of any other classes, that helps programmers build text-based reports. I designed the TextReport class after I'd built most of the librarian, so this is the first "real" class I designed with SSOOT CASE. Form 9-12 was generated using the TextReport class. Fittingly, it defines the TextReport class.

9.5 SUMMARY

We covered three major focal areas in this chapter: the problem model, the database, and the user interface.

The problem model was designed to be independent of database and user interface. It consists of the Catalog, FunctionEntry, ClassEntry classes, their ancestors, and supporting classes such as ClassMembers and ParamDefinitions.

The database is built on classes from Pinnacle File Manager from Vermont Database Corporation and the D_List class. The abstract D_List class defines an independent protocol. It allows uniform access to the various internal lists and the

```
         Class  Definition  Report  Wednesday,  March  3,  1993

Class  Name:  TextReport

Version:  1

Base  Classes:

Description:
Class  to  build  a  report.  The  height  and  width  is  specified,  as  well  as
the  margins,  header  and  footer.  You  then  put  the  text  of  the  report
out  to  an  object  of  this  class.  The  object  formats  the  report.  You  can
also  use  it  to  build  fixed  column  reports.

Data  Members:

Member  Name                          Description
protected  ostream  *  out            Output  stream  that  will  hold  the
                                      report.

protected  int  leftMargin            Number  of  spaces  on  the  left  of  the
                                      report  before  the  text  begins.

protected  int  width                 Total  number  of  characters  from  the
                                      left  margin  before  a  new  line  needs  to
                                      be  generated.

protected  int  topMargin             Number  of  lines  from  the  top  of  the
                                      page,  (not  including  the  title)  at
                                      which  to  begin  printing.

protected  int  bottom  margin        Number  of  lines  from  the  bottom  to
                                      stop  printing.  Does  not  include
                                      footer.

protected  int  height                Total  number  of  lines  before  form  feed
                                      is  generated.

protected  string  header             The  string  to  print  at  the  top  line  of
                                      each  page.  A  %P%  will  put  the  page
                                      number  into  the  header.  A  %D%  will  put
                                      in  today's  date.
```

FORM 9-12 Text report class definition.

protected string footer	The string to put at the bottom of each page. A %P% will insert the current page number. A %D% will put in today's date.
protected int currentLine	Working line number.
protected int currentPage	Current page number.
protected int	Widths of the columns in a multi-column colWidths[MAXCOLS] report.
protected int	Offsets from margins of columns. colOffsets[MAXCOLS]
Member Functions: Member Name public TextReport(ostream * out,char * _header,char * _footer,int _leftMargin,int _topMargin,int _bottomMargin,int _height,int _width)	Description. Constructor.
public void put(char * outString,Boolean newLine,int _leftMargin,int _rightMargin)	Puts the string to the output stream. Performs formatting as defined in the class and the parameters.
public void setMargins(int left,int top,int right,int bottom)	Redefines the margins for the report.
public void incLine()	Increments the line, handling page breaks, headers, and footers if necessary.
public void newPage()	Generates a new page on the report generator.
public void doHeader()	Puts header to out.

FORM 9-12   *(continued).*

`public void doFooter()`	Puts footer to out.
`public void defineColumns (int`	When this is used, subsequent column puts can be used.
`firstWidth, ...)`	The parameter list should be 0 terminated.
`public void put(char *`	Puts a series of fixed column values out
`col1, char * col2, ...)`	on one or more lines. The columns must first have been defined with defineColumn.
`public void setFooter (char * footerString)`	Assigns footer to the report.
`public void setHeader(char * aHeader)`	Assigns header to report.
`public void setHW (int_height,int _width)`	Sets a new height and width, in characters, of the current report.

FORM 9-12   *(continued).*

database. The D_Record class provides an adapter between the database and the problem space. The D_Record is built on the D_List protocol. The adapter classes provide database independence.

The user interface classes are built from the Zinc User Interface Library and Zinc Designer. The problem space classes do not depend on the user interface. (The user interface classes depend on the problem space classes, though.) You can get information on Zinc and the Pinnacle File Manager from Appendix A.

CHAPTER 10
Coding the Class Librarian

"Object-oriented programming's effectiveness will be determined largely by the software developer's acceptance of the value of reusable code, even code written by someone else."

J.D. Hildebrand, "You Asked for It,"*Computer Language*, August, 1989.

The substance of this chapter is found in its listings, not in its text. The text acts as a guide through those listings, pointing out those features I consider noteworthy. The actual source code is in Appendix D. It is also on the accompanying disk.

10.1   REUSING EXISTING CODE

10.1.1   Fixing up Containers with an Adapter Class

At the end of Chapter 6 we listed some changes we needed to make to the core classes we built. Some of the changes included making use of the D_List In Chapter 9. Figure 9-2 showed a diagram for using a Borland doubly linked list and a list iterator to implement the D_List protocol. This diagram is a typical example of a design by someone who really didn't have enough knowledge of the problem area to make good design choices. It happens all the time.

In this case, I knew I didn't have enough information, so as soon as I drew the diagram, I tried it. Two problems were immediately apparent: First, there was no easy way to insert a node into the middle of Borland's list, and, second, there was no easy way to keep track of the index of the current node. I could have kept searching, but I found a better way. In a strict waterfall model I would have had to take the time to force the code to fit into the design. Instead, I chose to use the BI_ArrayAsVector class to implement the D_List protocol. (See Figure 9-2 for a picture of this design decision.) Listing 10-2 shows its implementation. The file D_List.H is in the CHAP10 subdirectory and listed here as Listing 10-1.

10.1.2   Reusing Class Models

Many of the member functions and services listed in Chapter 9 are "deferred to the programmer." *That does not mean that they are not designed ! ! !* It simply means that the scopes of the member functions are limited enough and their purposes are clear enough that an experienced programmer can design the functions and record the results in the source code. When a programmer makes design decisions, the results are recorded in the source code in one or more of the following ways:

1. Comments: A standard comment template should be used whenever possible so the reader always knows where to find certain information.
2. Logical variable names: Counters in *for* loops can be simple, one letter variables, but in other contexts don't use *x* if you can use *theTotal* instead.
3. Complex Conditions: Explain non-obvious *if* and loop conditions. A simple comment will usually do.
4. Logical Function Names: Use logical names for utility functions and member functions.
5. Clarity of Purpose: If you use call a function with a non-obvious purpose, include a comment.
6. Simple Functions: Keep the functions small and simple. If a function gets too big, use new *protected* or *private* member functions to delegate details that may have been overlooked by the designer. Use these principles in designing the new functions as well.
7. Sketch Diagrams: It's OK for the programmer to sketch out any diagram necessary to clarify what should be happening.

I deferred the design of the member functions to the programmer because much of the "ClassDefinition" code has already been written. In this case, since I deferred the design to myself, I didn't have the communication problem a separate programmer and designer might have.

10.1.2.1   The ClassDefinition

Examine Listings 10-3 and 10-4. Compare them to their counterparts in Chapter 6. You should notice the "ListImp<>" for lists and "string" class for strings. I've also changed any reference from "ancestor" to "base class" or "parent." Notice that the implementations have changed a lot, but the protocol has remained virtually untouched.

10.1.2.2   The HeaderFileDefinition

In Listings 10-5 and 10-6 (DEFNFILE.H and DEFNFILE.CPP) we made most of the changes we talked about in previous chapters.

The most significant change to this class, aside from its name, is the addition of support for stand-alone functions. Listings 10-7 and 10-8 (FUNCDEF.H and

FUNCDEF.CPP) show the implementation of the FunctionDefinition class. Remember that some of the member functions were deferred until programming. Figure 10-1 shows one of the sketches I made before programming the findFunctions method of HeaderFileDefinition.

Frankly, much of the code in 10-7 and 10-8 is similar to the MemberFunctionDefinition class in 10-3 and 10-4. Repeating this code was faster than generalizing the MemberFunctionDefinition class. In a future version of the software, we may want to allow the consolidation of MemberFunctionDefinition and FunctionDefinition.

Instead of a full merger, I separated out the parameter specific code and created the ParamList class. This put some of the most complex, common code in one class. In order to support the Librarian's requirement, I added description

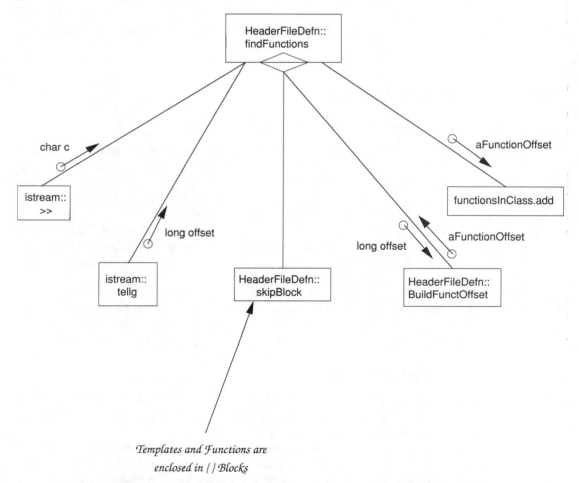

FIGURE 10-1 Programmer's sketch of a "Deferred to Programmer" method design.

handling code. Since the data was more important than the functionality, I made the ParamDefinition a structure, not a class. ParamDefinition is in the CLSDEFN.H and CLSDEFN.CPP.

10.2   NEW MODEL CODE

10.2.1   Entry Classes

Listings 10-9 and 10-10 show the Entry class family. You can look back at Chapter 9 at Figure 9-1 and 9-7, as well as Forms 8-1, 8-3, and 8-6. As we began to clarify how we are going to interact with a database, we added the toRecord and fromRecord methods in place of the put and get methods. I added some routine get/set routines that allow access to data members. As I looked over the user interface windows, I noticed that the return value needed an explanation, so I added it to FunctionEntry.

10.2.2   The Adapter Classes

10.2.2.1   D_Record and D_Field

I explained in Section 9.3 why we needed a "universal database adapter." Listings 10-11 and 10-12 show exactly how I've implemented the D_Record and D_Field. Note that it uses no "special" classes. Instead of using something like the string class, which would make the D_Record easier to implement, I only used primitive constructs like char *. I did this to enhance portability.

You also probably noticed in Listings 10-3 and 10-4 that the ClassMember family has some new methods I didn't put in the design documents in Chapter 9 because I didn't notice the need until I started coding. Those methods are the toRecord and fromRecord.

A D_Record is simply a list of D_Fields. A D_Field can hold "anything," thanks to the binary object. The binary object concept is based on the blob in the Pinnacle Relational Engine. I included it specifically to be sure I could interface with Pinnacle. This flexibility should work with just about anything, however.

10.2.2.2   The Catalog Class

Listings 10-13 and 10-14 show the implementation of the Catalog, the heart of the Librarian. Basically the Catalog is a database table implemented as a list of D_Records. Logically, the Catalog is a list of Entries.

FunctionEntries and ClassEntries are specializations of Entries that use the Entry table to hold common data and have their own tables for the special data of the child classes. ClassMembers' data values are kept in their own table, and physically, the Catalog is a list of Entry D_Records with direct access to FunctionEntry D_Records, ClassEntry D_Records, and ClassMember D_Records.

10.3   THE DATA BASE CODE

The RecList class defined and implemented in Listings 10-15 and 10-16 is the last portable class in this program. It is an implementation of a D_Record list. All problem domain classes count on the RecList to have a particular protocol and to isolate all database specific code. If you change database systems, this is the only class you should have to rewrite.

I've been using the Pinnacle database system for longer than I've been programming in C++. One of the first things I did when I started programming in C++ was to wrap C++ code around the C functions. (This was first published in the January 1992 issue of the *C User's Journal*.) The programmers at Vermont Database corporation had been doing the same thing, so, when I rewrote the Pfm_List for my next project, I used the Pinnacle table class as a base class for Pfm_List. You can see the result in Listing 10-17. (Vermont Database has let me include PINNACLE.H and PINNACLE.HPP in the disk accompanying this book so you can understand what I've done. It's in the CHAP9 subdirectory.)

In the original design, there was no database dependence within the Catalog interface. Now, the Catalog class does have a dependence on the Pinnacle database. This was a compromise for memory and performance.

10.4   THE USER INTERFACE

Some of the first types of classes established when OOP became popular were user interface classes or "application frameworks." This section describes the classes I've derived from the Zinc application framework classes to build the user interface for the SSOOT CASE Librarian.

10.4.1   LibMainWindow and CATALOG_LIST

Listings 10-18 and 10-19 (files LIBMWIN.HPP and LIBMWIN.CPP) define the main librarian window class, LibMainWindow. Most of the class was defined with Zinc Designer, but Listings 10-20 and 10-21 (CATLIST.HPP and CATLIST.CPP) show the CATALOG_LIST and ENTRY_ELEMENT classes. The CATALOG_LIST class is a special scrolling list to browse through the database. (If you have the Zinc library, you may notice that it is a variation of the VIRTUAL_LIST used in their examples.) The LibMainWindow constructor adds an object of the class CATALOG_LIST to itself.

Figures 9-12, 9-14, 9-16, and others clearly show that LibMainWindow is supposed to be called MainWindow and CATALOG_LIST is supposed to be called CatalogWindow. During the coding of these classes, these labels were changed. The changes were not arbitrary. "MainWindow" was too generic. The "Lib" was placed at the beginning of the label to specify which "MainWindow" we were discussing.

The name of CATALOG_LIST was chosen because of the way it was built. Instead of being a new class, I modified an existing class called VIRTUAL_LIST that came with Zinc. I decided that the similarity in names would make the code more readable. I could refer to Zinc's documentation more readily.

10.4.2 The ClassDefinitionWindow

Listings 10-22 and 10-23 show the files CLSDFWIN.H and CLSDFWIN.CPP. This is one of the "busiest" windows in the system. ClassEntry performs much of the "real" work. The ClassDefinition part holds the data, and it interfaces to source code. The Entry part interfaces to the database.

As I was building the ClassDefinition I found that I needed several small data entry dialog boxes. I didn't need much data from any given box. There were so many that it didn't really seem like a good idea to create a new class for each dialog I needed. So, I drew the dialogs I wanted into Zinc Designer and created the DataEntryDialog class, Listings 10-24 and 10-25.

Listings 10-26 and 10-27 show the TextReport class. The ClassDefinitionWindow uses it to generate the class description report. You can examine the print method of ClassDefinitionWindow to see how it's used.

The member functions are fairly complex objects. Listings 10-28 and 10-29 have the implementation of the windows to define member functions of the class, MemFunctionDefnWindow.

10.4.3 FunctionDefinitionWindow

The FunctionDefinitionWindow, Listings 10-30 and 10-31, contain much of the same type of data and functionality as the ClassDefinition window. In retrospect, too much of the code in FunctionDefinitionWindow is like the MemFunctionDefnWindow. A lot of it was copied and then modified. I should have come up with some kind of inheritance structure. We learn from our mistakes.

10.5   OTHER LISTINGS

Listings 10-32 and 10-33 explicate the EntrySearchWindow class. This code helps users to find specific entries or to narrow the list to those entries meeting specific criteria.

Listing 10-34 shows the startup code for the class librarian.

10.6   SUMMARY

The code listed here is on the disk that accompanies this book in the CHAP10 subdirectory. This code is not necessarily the final code that winds up on the disk.

I'll continue to review and test the programs after the book has gone to press. Any additions or changes to the code on the disk from the code here in the book will be in the file named README.10.

This chapter has acted as a guide to the source code listings in Appendix D. Most of the classes we designed in Chapter 9 are listed. This chapter explains the deviation from the design that occurred during programming.

CHAPTER 11
Analysis and Design of the Class Browser

"Class hierarchies can become so complex that it is difficult even to find all of the abstractions that are part of the design or are candidates for reuse."

Grady Booch, *Object-Oriented Design with Applications*, 1991,
The Benjamin/Cummings Publishing Company, Inc.

11.1 USER SCENARIOS

First, we'll talk with the users about what they want to do with the browser. As we discuss the users' needs (Purpose), we come up with the following scenarios (User Actions/System Response).

11.1.1 Hierarchy Exploration

Scenario 11.1

Title: Exploring The Hierarchy

Purpose: The users have an idea for a class. They suspect that they have a pre-existing hierarchy into which they can place the class. The users find a class or classes that meet a specific criteria (like in the librarian). They then need to check its ancestors, and its descendants, to determine the exact nature of the class hierarchy.

User Actions	System Response
User selects View	Find from the menu.	Displays a SearchWindow like the librarians.

User Actions	System Response
User enters name of class known to be in the hierarchy. Hits OK.	Displays a list of classes meeting criteria OR Dialog box indicating failure.
User selects a class from list.	The main window displays the class name, the class members, the base classes, and child classes.
User selects a base class.	This class becomes the current class. Displays as above.
User selects a child class.	The child class becomes the current class. Response as above.

11.1.2 Examination of Source Code

Scenario 11.2

Title: Examination of Source Code

Purpose: Once the users have found a class that may fit their needs, they wish to examine the source code.

User Actions	System Response
User locates class as above.	Main window is showing the class.
User selects view source.	System brings up a file browser window for the currently selected function OR displays a dialog box indicating failure.

11.1.3 Source Editing

Scenario 11.3

Title: Examination of Source Code

Purpose: The users have found a class that may fit their needs. As they examine the source code, they discover an error and then wish to edit the source code.

User Actions	System Response
User locates class as above.	Main window is showing the class.
User selects view source.	System brings up a text editor of the user's choice for the currently selected function OR displays a dialog box indicating failure.

11.2   BROWSER REQUIREMENTS

Chapter 7 and Chapter 8 give the general requirements of SSOOT CASE. Let's examine the Browser in the light of our user scenarios, and what we want from it. We also want to examine the possible constraints imposed by our environment.

As we go over the scenarios with the users, they remember a few more things they'd like to do.

Users: "We may want to use the browser to find classes for reuse, so why don't you let us just see the public members sometimes. Also, sometimes we want to see which members are available from a class's ancestors, so we can use them, too."

11.2.1   User Interface Requirements

The SSOOT CASE Browser is defined by its user interface. As we talk to the users and examine the scenarios, we gather the following requirements:

1. The Browser should allow the user to view the parents, children, data, and functions for a selected class.
2. The user should be able to browse through a parent or child class quickly by selecting it in the browser window.
3. The user should be able to edit or view the source code of selected member functions. In the Windows version, where there are fewer memory constraints, the user should be able to use any editor that accepts the file name (and line number?) from the command line. The development team should research the possibility of making this feature available in DOS as well.
4. The user should be able to search for a class from the browser using the same criteria as from the librarian.
5. The user should be able to select how the class members are to be viewed, based on the following criteria:
    a. Access Specifier—The user should be able to select any and all combinations of public, private, or protected members.
    b. Inherited Members—The user should be able to decide whether or not the members inherited from its ancestors are to be viewed.

Some browsers let you see an entire graphical hierarchy, and then select a class to view. The SSOOT CASE Browser will not have this feature. Any graphic features will be saved for the SSOOT CASE Graphic Tool.

11.2.2   Database Requirements

We can use the same basic data model for the Librarian, we just need some extra pieces of information. Since different versions of each class can exist, we need to have some way to know which version of a particular class is the appropriate child or parent. Without some sort of field in the database to indicate which version of the class is "active," our searches could find too many classes. If we add the field to the database to mark a class as active, we need to make that information available to the librarian and allow the librarian to change it. This change is reflected in the final version of the librarian; we'll note the change to the database and cover the details in design.

11.2.3 Overall Model

Figure 11-1 shows the general model for the browser. It looks very much like the librarian. This is the type of design reuse OO advocates constantly tout. Note that the only significant difference between the browser and the librarian is in the user interface.

We need to make some changes in the problem domain model. We need to know the file and the offset each member function so we can view or edit them. Depending on the editor we plan to invoke, we may also need the line number.

11.3   THE USER INTERFACE MODEL

11.3.1 The Browser's Main Window

Figure 11-2 shows a picture of the browser's main window. In the CHAP11 subdirectory, you can find a couple of executables, SOOTBRW.EXE and

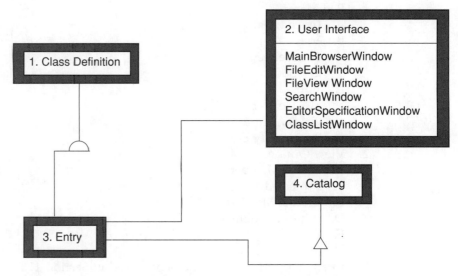

FIGURE 11-1 Subject model of SSOOT CASE browser.

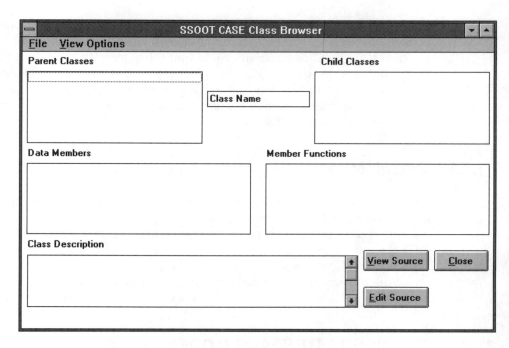

FIGURE 11-2   SSOOT CASE browser main window.

WSOOTBRW.EXE, that contain the browser. WSOOTBRW.EXE is the Windows application. If we examine the main menu, we see the following options:

1. File Menu
   A. Open Catalog
   B. View
      1. Header
      2. Source
   C. Edit
      1. Header
      2. Source
      3. Specify Editor
2. View Options
   A. Public Members
   B. Protected Members
   C. Private Members
   D. Inherited Members
   E. Find

Each item supports the requirements listed in Section 11.2.1. We'll get into the details of how the menu maps to specific member functions in another section.

11.3.2 The Main Window Class

Figure 11-3 shows the diagram for the class MainBrowserWindow. Forms 11-1 through 11-3 specify the class details and details of member classes. The basic design is the same as the main window for the librarian. We have an event-handling function called Event, and member functions to handle specific events.

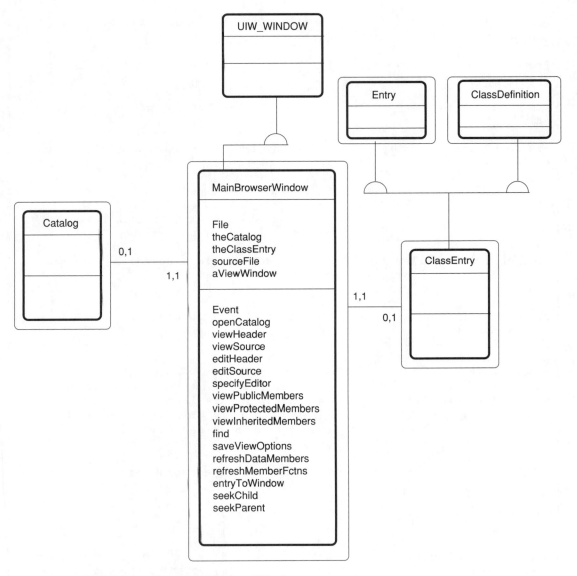

FIGURE 11-3 MainBrowserWindow.

```
Class Name:        MainBrowserWindow
Version:           1
Base Classes: public UIW_WINDOW


Description:
The main window for the SSOOT Case class browser.

Data Members:
Member Name                    Description
protected HeaderFileDefn       Working variable to deal with the header.
* File file for the class being browsed.

protected Catalog *            Catalog of classes being browsed.
theCatalog

Protected ClassEntry *         The entry for the main class.
theClassEntry

protected string               Contains the editor invocation string.
editorSpec

protected unsigned int         Holds the options selected by the user.
optionFlags                    The following flags are used:
                               0x01 - Use Public
                               0x02 - Use Protected
                               0x04 - Use Inherited
                               These values are ANDED together when
                               selected from the option menu.

protected SourceFileDefn       Keeps track of class header and source
                               code.
sourceFile

protected FileViewWindow       For browsing the source file.
* aViewWindow

Member Functions:
Member Name                    Description
public virtual                 This function allows the main window to
EVENT_TYPE Event(const         respond to events like user's buttons and
UI_EVENT & event)              menu selections. Additionally, handles
                               events sent by other windows or pro-
                               cesses.

public virtual void            Lets the user open a different catalog to
openCatalog()                  browse.

public virtual void            Lets the user see the header file
viewHeader()                   associated with the current class.

public virtual void            Lets the user look at the source code of
viewSource()                   the currently selected class and member
                               function.
```

FORM 11-1 MainBrowserWindow class definition.

public virtual void editHeader()	Lets the user change the header file associated with the class being viewed in the browser.
public virtual void editSource()	Allows the user to change the source code associated with a member function of the current class.
public virtual void specifyEditor()	Lets the user specify which editor to use in the previous two functions.
public virtual void viewPublicMembers()	When selected, this makes the public members of the class the user is browsing visible.
public virtual void viewProtectedMembers()	When selected, allows the user to see the protected members of the current class.
public virtual void viewInheritedMembers()	When this is selected, all the class members inherited from base classes in the catalog are visible to the user.
public find()	Invokes the EntrySearchWindow so the user can find a specific entry in the catalog.
public virtual void saveViewOptions()	Allows the favorite view options of the user to be saved from above to the configuration file.
protected virtual void refreshDataMembers()	Relists the data members in the window.
protected virtual void refreshMemberFctns()	Relists the member functions in the window.
protected virtual void entryToWindow()	Moves the entry data to the window from the ClassEntry.
protected virtual void refreshParentList()	Refills the parent list with the current entries base classes.
protected virtual void refreshChildList()	Refills the windows child list.
protected virtual void completeSpedifyEditor()	Completes the editor specification.

FORM 11-1   *(continued).*

```
Member Function: public virtual EVENT_TYPE
MainBrowserWindow::Event(const UI_EVENT & event)

Description:
This function allows the main window to respond to events like user's
buttons and menu selections. Additionally, it handles events sent by
other windows or processes.

Parameter Definition:
    Parameter                    Definition.

    const UI_EVENT & event     Event to process.

Function Specification:
The Event function is a large switch that handles the following menu
items and buttons by calling the member function specified after the
event item.

For the menu:
File
    Open - openCatalog
    View
        Header - viewHeader
        Source - viewSource
    Edit
        Header - editHeader
        Source - editSource
        Specify Editor - specifyEditor
    Save Options - saveViewOptions
    Exit - Terminates the program
View Options
    Public Members - viewPublicMembers
    Protected Members - viewProtectedMembers
    Inherited Members - viewInheritedMembers
    Find - find

For the buttons:
    View Source - viewSource
    Edit Source - editSource
    Close - Terminates the program

Other Events:
    GET_ENTRY - Gets the current entry from the catalog and loads it
    COMPLETE_QUERY - Instantiates a ClassListWindow

Otherwise:
    Calls UIW_WINDOW::Event
========================================================================
```

FORM 11-2   Menu/Button interface member functions.

```
Member Function: public virtual void MainBrowserWindow::openCatalog()

Description:
Lets the user open a different catalog to browse.

Parameter Definition:

(No parameters)

Function Specification:
Commits and closes the current catalog.

Then presents a file selection dialog box that allows the user to find
and select a database file.
=======================================================================
Member Function: public virtual void MainBrowserWindow::viewHeader()

Description:
Lets the user see the header file associated with the current class.

Parameter Definition:
(No parameters)

Function Specification:
    1. Assures the FileDefinition pointer File is pointing at the right
       file.
    2. Seeks to start of class in header file.
    3. Invokes FileViewWindow
=======================================================================
Member Function: public virtual void MainBrowserWindow::viewSource()

Description:
Lets the user look at the source code of the currently selected class
and member function.

Parameter Definition:
(No parameters)

Function Specification:
Searches to start of implementation of code instead of beginning of
class. See viewHeader for most details.
=======================================================================
Member Function: public virtual void MainBrowserWindow::editHeader()

Description:
Lets the user change the header file associated with the class being
viewed in the browser.
```

FORM 11-2 *(continued).*

```
Parameter Definition:
(No parameters)

Function Specification:
If the user hasn't selected an editor, it seeks to the start of the
class in the header and invokes FileEditWindow.
======================================================================
Member Function: public virtual void MainBrowserWindow::editSource()

Description:
Allows the user to change the source code associated with a member
function of the current class.

Parameter Definition:
(No parameters)

Function Specification:
Similar to edit header, but for member functions. Basic logic is like
viewSource.
======================================================================
Member Function: public virtual void
MainBrowserWindow::specifyEditor()

Description:
Lets the user specify which editor to use in the previous two functions.

Parameter Definition:
(No parameters)

Function Specification:
Invokes EditorSpecificationWindow. Uses DataEntryDialog class instead
of a special class. Uses completeEditSpec to move the resulting data
into editorSpec string.
======================================================================
Member Function: public virtual void
MainBrowserWindow::viewPublicMembers()

Description:
When selected, this makes the public members of the class you're
browsing visible.

Parameter Definition:
(No parameters)

Function Specification:
Toggles the menu item and the optionsFlag. Then it invokes
refreshDataMembers and refreshMemberFctns.
======================================================================
Member Function: public virtual void
MainBrowserWindow::viewProtectedMembers()
```

FORM 11-2 *(continued).*

```
Description:
When selected, allows the user to see the protected members of the
current class.

Parameter Definition:
(No parameters)

Function Specification:
Identical to viewProtected members, except that it uses different flag.
=========================================================================
Member Function: public virtual void
MainBrowserWindow::viewInheritedMembers()

Description:
When this is selected, all the class members inherited from base
classes in the catalog are visible to the user.

Parameter Definition:
(No parameters)

Function Specification:
Identical to viewPublicMembers and viewProtectedMembers, except it has
a different flag.
=========================================================================
Member Function: public MainBrowserWindow::find()

Description:
Invokes the EntrySearchWindow so the user can find a specific entry
in the catalog.

Parameter Definition:
(No parameters)

Function Specification:
Instantiates a SearchWindow and adds it to the window manager.
=========================================================================
Member Function: public virtual void
MainBrowserWindow::saveViewOptions()

Description:
Allows the user to save most-used view options from above to the
configuration file.

Parameter Definition:
(No parameters)

Function Specification:
Writes the optionsFlags and the editorSpec string to the file
ssootbrw.cfg. (Details deferred to programmer.)
=========================================================================
```

FORM 11-2   *(continued).*

```
Member Function: protected virtual void
MainBrowserWindow::refreshDataMembers()

Description:
Relists the data members in the window.

Parameter Definition:
(No parameters)

Function Specification:
If the View Inherited option is selected, calls
theClassEntry->findInheritedMembers.

Gets the list DATA_MEM_LIST from this.
Clears it.

Moves the data members (and possibly inherited data member) from
theClassEntry into DATA_MEM_LIST using the same logic as the data
member list in the ClassDefinitionWindow.

=======================================================================
Member Function: protected virtual void
MainBrowserWindow::refreshMemberFctns()

Description:
Relists the member functions in the window.

Parameter Definition:
(No parameters)

Function Specification:
If the View Inherited option is selected, calls
theClassEntry->findInheritedMembers.

Gets the list MEM_FCTN_LST from this.
Clears it.

Moves the member functions (and possibly inherited member functions)
from theClassEntry into MEM_FCTN_LST using the same logic as the
member function list in the ClassDefinitionWindow.

=======================================================================
Member Function: protected virtual void
MainBrowserWindow::entryToWindow()

Description:
Moves the entry data to the window from the ClassEntry.

Parameter Definition:
(No parameters)
```

FORM 11-3 Main window support functions.

```
Function  Specification:
Details  deferred  to  programmer.

=======================================================================
Member  Function:  protected  virtual  void
MainBrowserWindow::refreshParentList()

Description:
Refills  the  parent  list  with  the  current  entries  base  classes.

Parameter  Definition:
 (No  parameters)

Function  Specification:
Gets  the  list  CLASS_PARENTS  from  this.
Clears  it.

Copies  the  base  classes  from  theClassEntry  into  CLASS_PARENTS  using
the  same  type  of  logic  as  the  data  member  list  in  the
ClassDefinitionWindow.

=======================================================================
Member  Function:  protected  virtual  void
MainBrowserWindow::refreshChildList()

Description:
Refills  the  windows  child  list.

Parameter  Definition:
 (No  parameters)

Function  Specification:
Gets  the  CLASS_CHILD  from  this.
Clears  it.

Calls  theClassEntry->findChildren.

Uses  the  resulting  child  list  to  fill  the  CLASS_CHILD.

=======================================================================
```

FORM 11-3   *(continued).*

As an aside, the class definition and member specification forms for this chapter and subsequent chapters were imported from text files generated by the class librarian.

11.3.3   The FileEditWindow and FileViewWindow Class

Although we have a requirement to allow the users to access their own editor, we should probably provide a default editor. In DOS, it may be the only editor we have the memory for. As we examine the needs for the viewer and the needs for the editor, we discover that an editor is a kind of viewer. So we make the editor a specialization of viewer.

Figure 11-4 shows a diagram for the editor and the viewer. Forms 11-4 through 11-6 detail the workings of the classes.

11.3.4   SearchWindow and ClassListWindow

Here we have an example of OO code and design reuse. We can use basically the same search window in the browser as we use in the librarian. We'll need to take away the function and union choices. Since the main window doesn't have an entry list like the librarian, we'll need a window that lists the classes we find, so we have ClassListWindow. Figure 11-5 and Forms 11-7 and 11-8 specify these classes. Form 11-9 is a narration of the event activity noted in Figure 11-5.

The script notations on Figure 11-5 illustrate the probable order of events that occur when the user selects View Options Find. Form 11-9 explains it textually.

11.3.5   EditorSpecificationWindow

If the user wants to specify a specific editor, we'll need some way to allow it. Figure 11-6 shows a picture of the editor specification window. This window was built in the Zinc designer. Instead of using a special class for this window, we'll use a data entry dialog as illustrated in Figure 11-7. The completeSpecifyEditor function fills the editorSpecification string.

11.4   CHANGES AND ADDITIONS TO THE PROBLEM DOMAIN MODEL

Most of the changes to the problem domain model are in the details of the relationships. The model is more tightly coupled to the database than the librarian is.

We need more services from the ClassEntry so it can provide the user

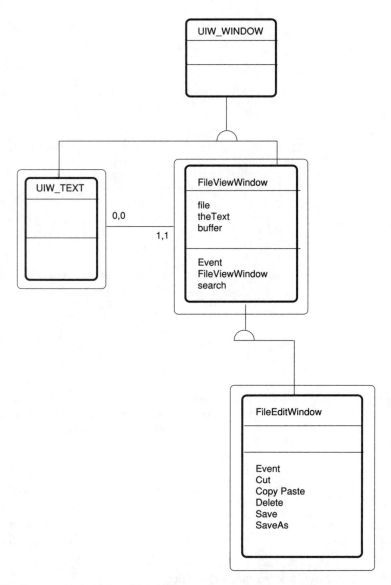

FIGURE 11-4   FileViewWindow and FileEditWindow.

interface with the proper information: findParents, findChildern, getInheritedMembers.

Figure 11-8 shows the addition of a few new attributes and methods to the ClassDefinition class family. Note that the ClassEntry must interact with the Catalog. Figure 11-9 shows more interaction with the database and interaction with the user interface functions. Form 11-10 specifies the new member functions.

When we choose to view or edit a function, we need to know where to search

```
Class  Name:          FileViewWindow
Version:          1
Base  Classes:
public  UIW_WINDOW


Description:
This class displays the contents of a text file, up to a maximum of 54K.

Data  Members:
    Member  Name                   Description
    protected  UIW_TEXT            This  is  where  the  viewing  takes  place.
    theText                            It's  attributes  are:
                                   WOF_NO_ALLOCATE_DATA
                                   WOF_NON_FIELD_REGION
                                   WOF_VIEW_ONLY
                                   Since  this  is  set  up  in  the  designer,
                                   we'll  put  the  Vertical  and  Horizontal
                                   Scroll  Bars  with  it.

    protected  char  *  buffer     This  is  the  buffer  that  holds  the  con-
                                   tents  of  the  file  being  viewed.  It  will
                                   be  the  size  of  the  file  or  50K,  whichever
                                   is  smaller.

    protected  int  file           The  file  handle  of  the  file  being  viewed.


Member  Functions:
    Member  Name                   Description
public  virtual                    This  function  processes  events  as  usual
        EVENT_TYPE                 for  Event  handlers.
    Event(UI_EVENT  event)

    public                         Constructor
    FileViewWindow(char  *
    fileName,int  offset)

    public  virtual  void          Searches  the  buffer  for  the  target  string
    search(const  char  *          and  positions  the  cursor  accordingly.
    targetString)
```

FORM 11-4 FileViewWindow class definition

```
Member  Function:  public  virtual  EVENT_TYPE
FileViewWindow::Event(UI_EVENT  event)

Description:
This  function  processes  events  as  usual  for  Event  handlers.

Parameter  Definition:
Parameter                          Definition.
```

FORM 11-5 FileViewWindow member function specifications.

```
UI_EVENT  event                      Event  to  process.

Function  Specification:
Handles  the  following  events:

    S_CLOSE
        Frees  the  buffer
        Closes  the  file

    STRING_SEARCH
        Searches  for  a  string  in  the  buffer,  if  found,  positions  the
        cursor  in  the  window  at  the  location  of  the  target  string.
========================================================================
Member  Function:  public  FileViewWindow::FileViewWindow(char  *
fileName,int  offset)

Description:
Constructor.

Parameter  Definition:
    Parameter                      Definition

    char  *  fileName              Name  of  file  to  view.
    int  offset                    Offset  to  search  to  in  the  file  to  begin
                                   viewing.

Function  Specification:
    Loads  the  window  resource  "FILE_VIEW_WIN".
    Assigns  theText  to  the  UIW_TEXT  member,  "THE_TEXT".

Allocates  a  buffer  the  size  of  the  file.  If  the  allocation  succeeds,
opens  the  specified  file  for  read.

    Reads  the  file  into  that  buffer.

    Invokes  L_RIGHT  until  the  offset  is  reached.
========================================================================
Member  Function:  public  virtual  void  FileViewWindow::search(const
char  *  targetString)

Description:
Searches  the  buffer  for  the  target  string  and  positions  the  cursor
accordingly.

Parameter  Definition:
    Parameter                      Definition

    const  char  *  targetString Target  to  search  for.

    (No  Specification)
========================================================================
```

FORM 11-5 *(continued)*.

```
Class Name:          FileEditWindow
Version:        1
Base Classes:
public FileViewWindow


Description:
This class is like its ancestor except that its menu is more exten
sive. The UIW_TEXT member is not view only, so the user can change the
information in the buffer.

Data Members:
   Member Name                        Description

   Member Functions:

   Member Name                        Description

   public virtual                     This handles the cut, paste, copy and

   EVENT_TYPE                         delete, save and save as events from

   Event(UI_EVENT event)              the menu and key board. Details

                                      deferred to the programmer.

   public virtual void Cut()          Sends the L_CUT event to theText.

   public virtual void Copy()         Sends the L_CUT message to theText.

   public virtual void Paste()        Sends the L_CUT_PASTE event to theText.

   public virtual void Delete()       Sends the L_DELETE to theText.

   public virtual void Save()         Saves the buffer text to a file.

   public virtual void SaveAs()       Saves the text buffer to a new file.
```

FORM 11-6   FileEditWindow class.

to, so we need a way to locate the start of the class in the header file and the start of each method in the source file. We did something like this in HeaderFileDefn. I've reworked the HeaderFileDefn class in Figure 11-10. This is a case of specific to general to specific (remember from Chapter 5?). We'll rewrite the removeComments function so we maintain the offset and line integrity in the temporary file. Figure 11-11 shows the message flow of a browse command. The new functions are listed on the figure. They'll use the same type of logic as the "find" functions of HeaderFileDefn.

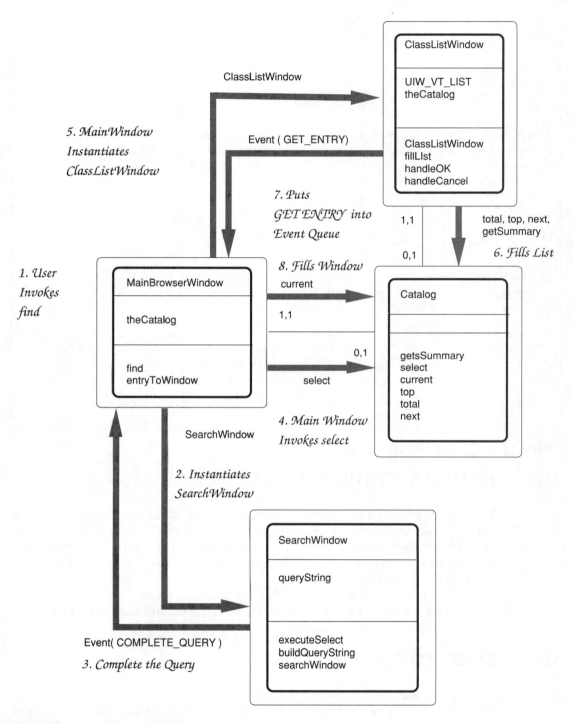

FIGURE 11-5 SearchWindow and ClassListWindow.

```
Class Name:          SearchWindow
Version:        1
Base Classes:
public EntrySearchWindow


Description:
This child of EntrySearchWindow is a SearchWindow that is not specific
to the Library main window. The member function executeSelect is over-
ridden.

Data Members:
    Member Name                  Description
    protected string             Holds the string that will be used to
    queryString                  search catalog.


Member Functions:
    Member Name                  Description
    public SearchWindow()        Constructor

    public virtual void          Sends the COMPLETE_QUERY event message to
    executeSelect()              the MainBrowserWindow. The data member of
                                 the event structure points to the query
                                 string.

                                 Further specification deferred to
                                 programmer.
```

FORM 11-7   SearchWindow class.

11.5   CHANGES TO THE DATABASE MODEL

The basic database model hasn't changed much from the Entry–Catalog model we built in Chapter 9. If you look back at Figure 9-10, you'll see that the database model covers our most of our needs quite sufficiently. The only real difference is that we won't need to deal with function entries in the browser. Figure 11-12 shows the modified database model.

We'll add the fields to the database to note the "active " class mentioned in section 11.2.2. Listing 11-1 shows the new Pinnacle database definition code.

11.6   GUIDE TO SOURCE CODE

The source code and executable for the browser is in the CHAP11 subdirectory on the disk that comes with this book. It is possible that I'll need to make changes to the code on the disk after this book has gone to press. Any changes to the directory will be noted in a file called README.11.

```
Class Name:          ClassListWindow
Version:        1
Base Classes:
public UIW_WINDOW

Description:
List of classes selected with the search window.

Data Members:
    Member Name                Description
    protected VirtualList      This list holds the names of the classes
    classList                  found in the search.

    protected Catalog *        The catalog being listed.
    theCatalog

    Member Functions:
    Member Name                Description
    public                     Constructor - Assigns the variable and
    ClassListWindow(Catalog    calls fillList.
    * _theCatalog)

    public virtual             Handles the OK and Cancel buttons.
    EVENT_TYPE
    Event(UI_EVENT event)

    public virtual void        Loads the list with the selected items in
    fillList()                 the catalog.

    public virtual void        Puts the GET_ENTRY event into the event.
    handleOK()                 queue and closes the window.

    public virtual void        Closes the window.
    handleCancel()
```

FORM 11-8 ClassListWindow.

```
1. User selects View Options|Find from main menu.
2. MainBrowserWindow instantiates SearchWindow and adds it to the
   window manager.
3. SearchWindow puts the COMPLETE_QUERY Event on the queue.
4. MainBrowserWindow sends the "select" message to the Catalog.
5. MainBrowserWindow instantiates the ClassListWindow.
6. ClassListWindow fills itself from the catalog.
7. When the user selects "OK" from the ClassListWindow,
   ClassListWindow puts GET_ENTRY event on the event queue.
8. When MainBrowserWindow reads the GET_ENTRY event, it gets the cur-
   rent member from Catalog and calls entryToWindow to fill itself.
```

FORM 11-9 Searching for a class.

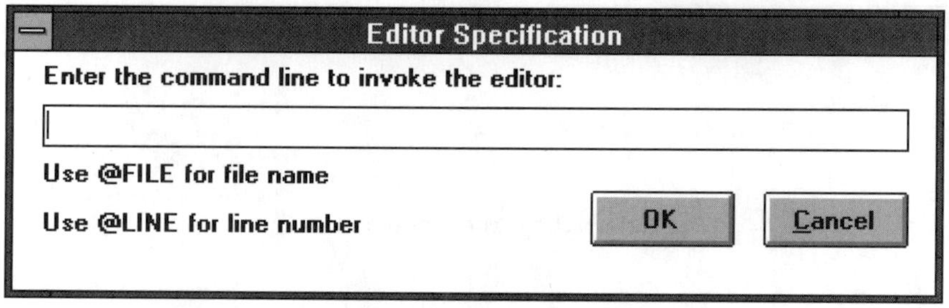

Editor Specification

Enter the command line to invoke the editor:

Use @FILE for file name

Use @LINE for line number   OK   Cancel

FIGURE 11-6   Editor specification window.

There were changes to the basic problem model, and those changes are reflected in the source code. The files CLSDFN.CPP and CLSDFN.H have the new files for the ClassDefinition class and its supporting classes.

The database model is basically unchanged from Chapters 8, 9, and 10. We just don't use FunctionEntry. Since I didn't change Catalog and Entry, their files are in the CHAP10 subdirectory. I didn't copy them to the CHAP11 directory.

The user interface classes represent the largest part of the class browser. The files BRMWIN.CPP and BRMWIN.H have the main window code. The FileEditWindow and FileViewWindow classes are in FILEWIN.CPP and FILEWIN.HPP. The SearchWindow code isn't here, since it hasn't changed much from Chapter 10. The ClassListWindow has its code in CLSLSTWN.CPP and CLSLSTWN.H. Finally, the EditorSpecificationWindow is in EDSPCWIN.CPP and EDSPCWIN.H.

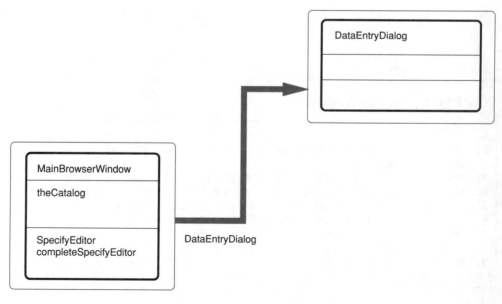

FIGURE 11-7   Editor specification window using data entry dialog.

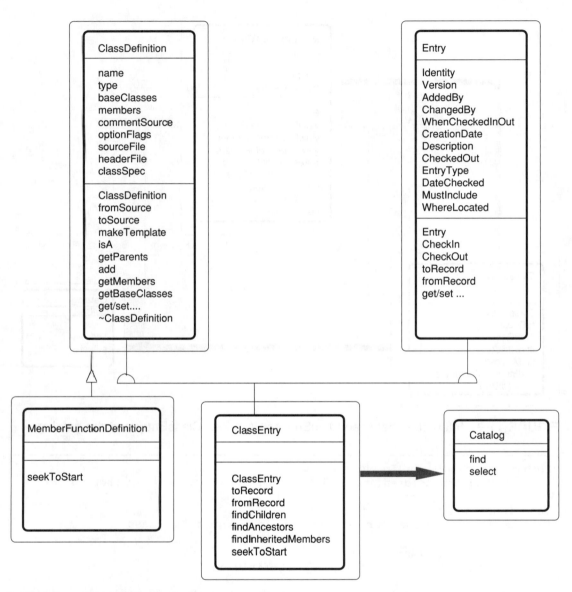

FIGURE 11-8 Additions to the ClassEntry class.

11.7   SUMMARY

The SSOOT CASE Class Browser is the second SSOOT CASE tool. The users will need the Browser to explore the classes in the library at several levels of detail. These levels may include hierarchy exploration and source code examination.

The user interface will allow the user to view the parents, children, member functions, and data items for any class in the database. The user will be able to

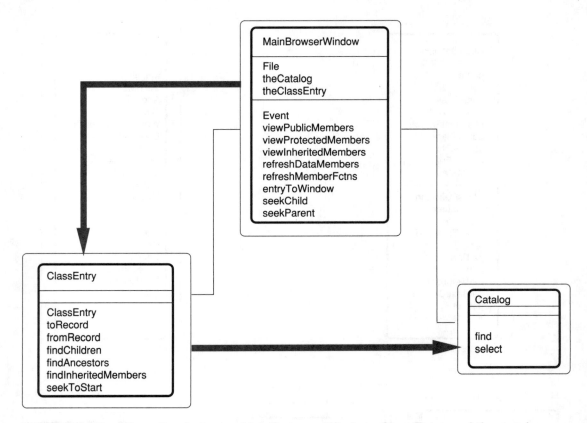

FIGURE 11-9   Interaction between MainBrowser Window, ClassEntry and the catalog.

```
Member  Function:  public  virtual  void
ClassEntry::findChildren(stringList  &  childList,Catalog  &  theCatalog)

Description:
Searches  the  database  for  all  the  children  of  this  class.

Parameter  Definition:
    Parameter                         Definition

    stringList  and  childList         List  of  children  returned  by  the
                                       function.
    Catalog  and  theCatalog          Catalog  to  search.

Function  Specification:
    1. Builds  the  search  string.
    2. Calls  theCatalog.select()  to  locate  all  the  children.
    3. Loops  through  the  resultant  list  to  fill  childList.
    4. Clears  the  selection.
```

FORM 11-10   New function in ClassEntry.

```
=========================================================================
Member Function: public virtual void
ClassEntry::findAncestors(stringList & ancestorList)

Description:
This functions finds ALL of the ancestors of this class (not just the
parents).

Parameter Definition:
   Parameter                        Definition

   stringList and ancestorList      List of all ancestors of this class.

Function Specification:
Starting with the classes in the base class, searches for the parents
of each class until there are no more classes to search for.

   For each parent:
        puts the class spec into ancestorList;
        makes the class the object of the search;
        builds the search string;
        finds the entry in the catalog;
        calls findAncestors for the built entry.

Note: The recursion could get kind of hairy on classes with deep
inheritance structures.


=========================================================================
Member Function: public virtual void
ClassEntry::findInheritedMembers(memberList & inheritedMembers)

Description:
The function finds the members inherited from ancestors.

Parameter Definition:
   Parameter                        Definition

   memberList and inheritedMembers  List of members inherited from
                                    ancestors (includes ancestor).

Function Specification:
Calls findAncestors. Gets the public or protected members from each
ancestor. Details deferred to programmer.

=========================================================================
```

FORM 11-10 *(continued).*

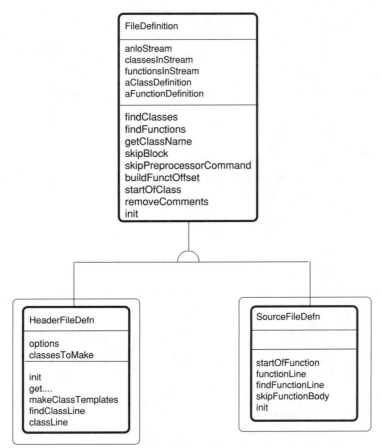

FIGURE 11-10   Reworking of HeaderDefnFile to accommodate browser.

view these items using access specifier and inheritance criteria. The Browser will also allow the user to search for a class on criteria similar to the search criteria in the librarian. It will not provide a graphical view of the hierarchy.

Most of the Browser's operation takes place in the main window, specified by the class MainBrowserWindow. In Section 11.3.1, we explored the main window's menu. In 11.3.2, we explored the details of the class. Other classes include the FileViewWindow that will allow browsing of a source file and a SearchWindow and ClassListWindow that allow the user to specify search criteria and see the results.

The problem domain and database model are essentially unchanged from the librarian. Most of the new classes in the Browser are in the user interface subject. In this chapter, we explored the requirements and design details of the classes that make up the Browser and their relationships with one another. The source code for these classes is found in the CHAP11 subdirectory on the disk that comes with this book.

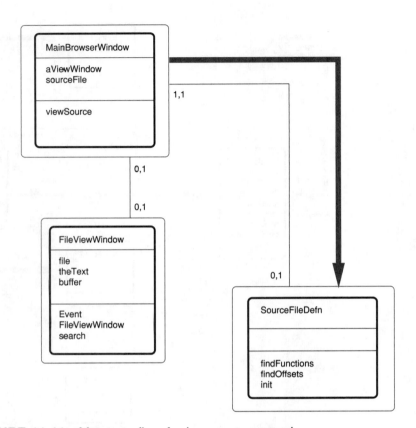

FIGURE 11-11   Message flow for browse command.

The forms in Chapter 11 were created by the librarian developed in Chapter 10. Each of these forms describes some aspect of the class design or the specification of member functions. Form 11-1 defines the MainBrowserWindow class. Form 11-2 defines the member functions that handle the menu and button events. The other BrowserMainWindow member functions are defined in Form 11-3. The FileViewWindow class is defined in Form 11-4. Form 11-5 defines the member functions of the FileViewWindow. Other forms define other classes and the interactions between them.

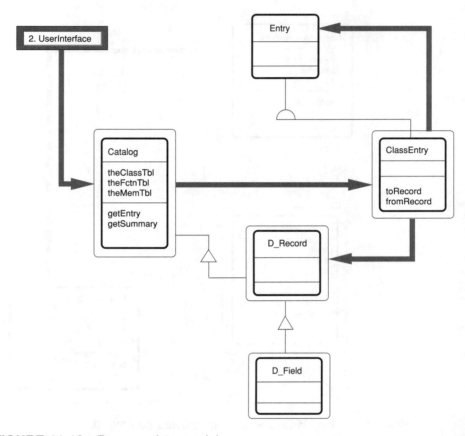

FIGURE 11-12   Browser data model.

CHAPTER 12

Analysis and Design of the SOOT CASE Graphics Tool

"One thing is already apparent: CASE vendors are getting carried away and beginning to deluge the software engineer with too many different types of diagrams."

Ed Yourdon, *The Decline and Fall of the American Programmer*,
Prentice Hall, 1992.

12.1 WHAT USERS WANT FROM A GRAPHIC TOOL

For this chapter the developers finally sit down to discuss the last CASE tool with the users, the graphic design tool.

Developers: "What kind of diagrams would you like to see from SSOOT CASE?" Suddenly, all the users begin to speak at once: "Booch!" "Coad and Yourdon!" "E/R Diagrams!" "Structure Charts!" "Flow Charts!" "Data Flow Diagrams!" . . .

Users: "STOP! Please. Slow down."

The developers and users begin a long discussion on what is needed and what is not. The discussion becomes quite frustrating because individual users insist that their favorite notation must be supported. Ed Yourdon may complain that vendors provide too many types of diagrams [Yourdon, 92]. The fault does not necessarily lie with the CASE vendor, but with the myriad of notations available. The fear of losing sales because of lack of notational support leads many vendors to err, perhaps, on the side of excess.

The second S in SSOOT CASE is supposed to stand for SIMPLE. We can't support every notation available, and we risk obsolescence if we support only a few. So, we fall back on the OO concept of "specific to general to specific." We begin to sample the types of things one finds in software development diagrams. We quickly find that there are two kinds of things common to diagrams: symbols and connectors. Figure 12-1 shows many of the specific symbols and connectors found in software diagrams.

12.2   FUNCTIONAL REQUIREMENTS

Many CASE tools enforce diagraming rules specific to one or more formal methodologies. Diagram enforcement isn't supported for three reasons:

1. It increases the complexity of the program.
2. It would be impossible to satisfy all possible rules because most organizations use a variant of a standard methodology.
3. Enforcing fixed rules would make improvements in methods or methodologies impossible.

Since we won't enforce a methodology, we can use any symbol with impunity. However, if we only allow the drawing of symbols, we don't really have a CASE tool, but a simple drawing tool. (By the way, I prefer simple drawing tools over some of the CASE tools I've used.)

Since the CASE tool focuses on OO techniques, we will need to directly support the following concepts:

- Classes (Should Include Data and Functionality)
- Objects (Instances of Classes)
- Inheritance
- Communication and Relationships Between Objects and Classes

Since we have class and function information available in the catalog, we need to be able to link symbols in the diagram to the entities in the catalog. Users should be able to browse the catalog to find the symbols to which they can link.

As we can see from the users' comments, they use many different notations and diagrams. The concepts listed above need to be independent of specific notations. We need to provide a way for users to define additional symbols and connectors for any methodologies they may choose.

Our functional requirements for the SSOOT CASE graphics tool are that it must:

1. Provide support for symbols for classes, objects, inheritance, and relationships;
2. Allow the user to browse the catalog;
3. Allow symbols to link with classes and functions in the catalog; and
4. Allow users to define their own symbols.

Stand-Alone Shapes

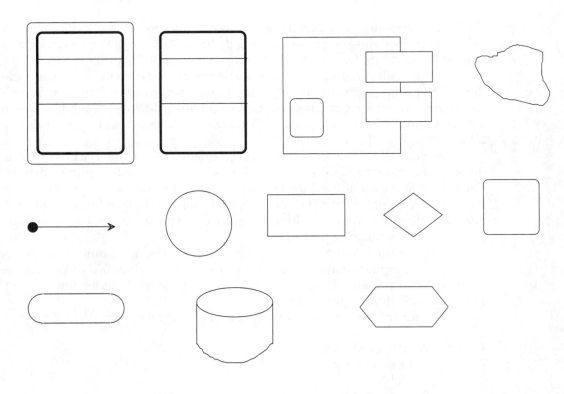

Connectors

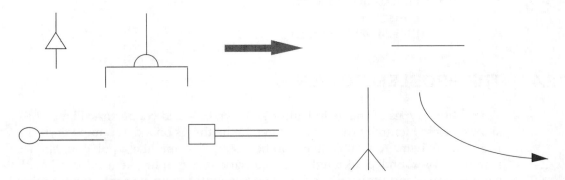

FIGURE 12-1   Types of images in software diagrams.

12.3   SYSTEM REQUIREMENTS

We'll need the standard minimal graphics capabilities for SSOOT CASE: an EGA or better screen, mouse or similar pointing device, a 386SX or better processor, and at least 4 megabytes free on the hard drive. What about the printer?

Traditionally, graphics are tied more tightly to hardware than other applications. The printers, screens, and plotters upon which diagrams are drawn each have their own features and properties. Zinc provides device-independent screen graphics, but has no printer output. Windows provides access to printer device information, but what about DOS?

The Borland version of Zinc uses BGI (Borland Graphic Interface) to provide device-independent graphics. Ryle Design sells a family of BGI printer drivers. The BGI printer interface and the Windows printer interface are very different, so the DOS version of the SSOOT CASE Graphics Tool and the Windows version will need slightly different printer driver interfaces. The printer control portion of the program will be the least portable.

Since we don't want to write new printer drivers, we'll build our system requirements around what we know is available. Ryle provides BGI drivers for the most common printers: Epson 24 and 9 pin printers, HP LaserJet and DeskJet, Postscript and IBM 24 pin Proprinter.

In summary, we have the following system requirements:

1. An EGA or better screen
2. Mouse or similar pointing device
3. A 386SX or better processor
4. 4 megabytes free on the hard drive
5. The Windows version:
   MS-Windows 3.0 or higher
   A graphic printer with a Windows driver
6. For the DOS version, a printer compatible with one of the following:
   - Epson 9 or 24 Pin
   - HP DeskJet or LaserJet
   - Postscript
   - IBM 24 pin Proprinter

12.4   THE PROBLEM DOMAIN

We find two types of things in Figure 12-1: symbols and connectors. Figure 12-2 shows a class hierarchy that helps us define the things on a diagram. Everything is a graphic item. A graphic item can be a simple shape like a polygon, ellipse, rectangle, or rounded rectangle. A connector is a graphic item adorned with simple shapes and perhaps a fork or two to split the connector into two or more parts. Lines and curves are kinds of connectors. A complex shape is, in fact, simply a collection of simple shapes and connectors.

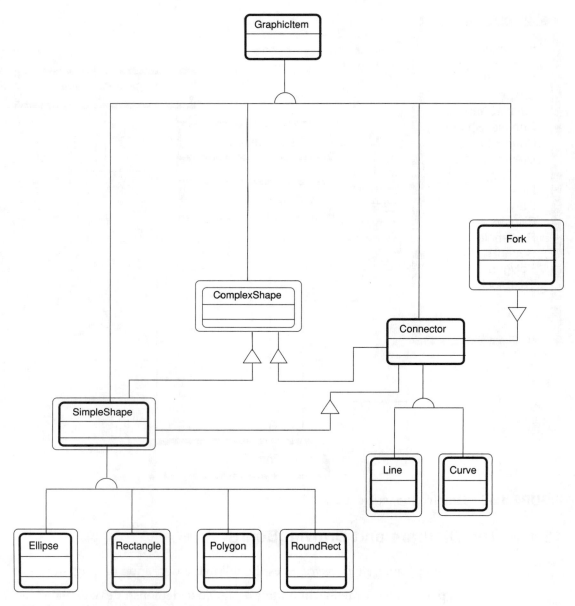

FIGURE 12-2 Types of things in a diagram.

The problem domain for this tool consists primarily of the graphic classes. Figure 12-3 shows the Graphics subject which contains the graphic classes. Note the relationships with the other subjects.

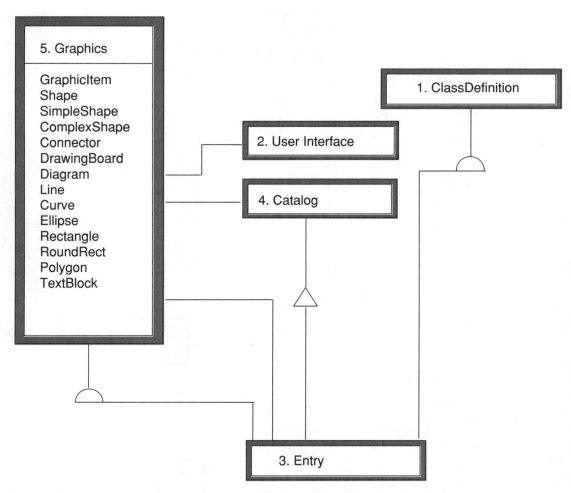

FIGURE 12-3   Graphic tool subjects.

12.4.1 The Diagram and DrawingBoard

The *American Heritage Dictionary* gives the following definition of diagram:

> "A plan, sketch, drawing, or outline designed to demonstrate or explain how something works or to clarify the relationship between the parts of a whole."

We'll define a Diagram as the entire document. It will include the drawing area, the margins, and the diagram title.

12.4.1.1 The DrawingBoard

Figure 12-4 shows that a DrawingBoard is inherently part of a Diagram. The drawing area is a grid upon which the user can place graphic items like symbols

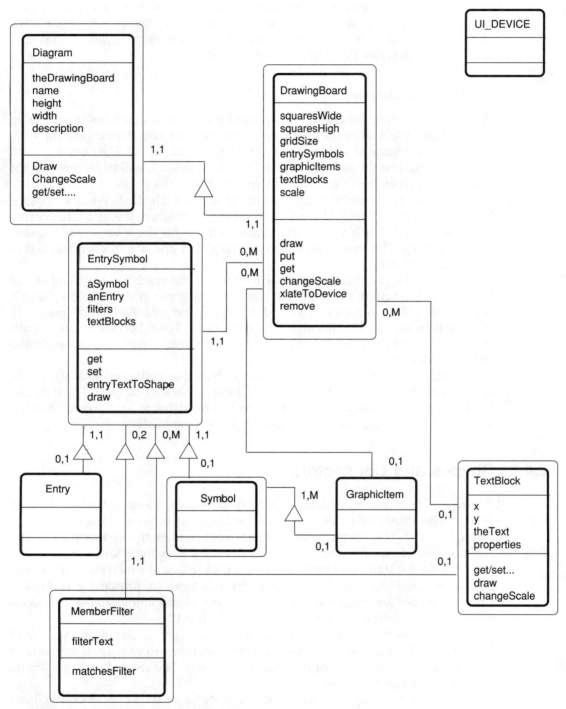

FIGURE 12-4 The DrawingBoard is the central object for the graphics tool.

and connectors. Some of these items can be associated with entries in the catalog like classes and functions. The user can also place text on the drawing board. The DrawingBoard class is really the central class of the graphic tool. Forms 12-1 through 12-5 describe the classes in Figure 12-4.

12.4.1.2   The Diagram

We'll build the diagram around the piece of paper. Most diagrams should fit on a single page. We'll allow the user to use more than one page if necessary, but we'll default to one. Figure 12-5 shows the way a diagram will be built. The DrawingBoard will be centered on the page (or pages). The diagram's title will be centered on the first page between the DrawingBoard and the top of the page.

We'll use two coordinate systems in the diagram. The first system will be the larger grid system. Our grid coordinate system will start in the upper left corner of the page at 0,0. The X value will increase to the right. The Y value will increase down the page. The maximum width and height in grid squares is contained in DrawingBoard data.

The second coordinate system will help us build symbols. Any symbol will begin with its origin in the upper left corner of any given grid square. Its X and Y coordinates will increase the right and down, like the grid. Each grid square will be 10 units wide and 10 units high. The symbols in Figure 12-5 are about 19 units by 19 units. The actual number of pixels in each unit varies with diagram scale and the target device.

Connectors are built relative to the symbols they connect. Usually the connectors will make a straight line between the symbols they connect. The user will be able to define points at which the connectors bend, however. If a connector has a midline symbol, the user will be able to place it explicitly.

12.4.2 Shapes and Connectors

Figure 12-6 goes into more detail about the relationships among the GraphicItem family. The PrinterInfo class helps define the ratio between logical units and physical units. The abstract class GraphicItem defines the common data and functionality of all items that can be placed on the drawing board.

The values startX and startY define the grid square in which the graphic item begins. SimpleShapes and Connectors have logical an physical coordinates. ComplexShapes are simply collections of connectors and simple shapes. Forms 12-6 through 12-8 define some of the classes in Figure 12-6.

The classes that descend from SimpleShape, Ellipse, Rectangle, Polygon, and RoundRect all overload the draw member function to draw specific kinds of simple shapes. Since much of the descriptions would be redundant there are no class design forms for them.

Connectors are special graphic items made up of lines or curves. We'll use

```
Class Name:          DrawingBoard
Version:         1
Base Classes:
Description:
The DrawingBoard is inherently part of a Diagram.  The drawing area
is a grid upon which the user can place graphic items like symbols

and connectors. This class contains the graphic items the user draws.

Data Members:
 Member Name                     Description
 protected int squaresWide       Number of grid squares across.

 protected int squaresHigh       Height of the drawing board, in grid
                                 squares.

 protected double gridSize       Size of grid in inches. This will default
                                 to 0.5, but it can be larger or smaller
                                 if the user desires. There will always be
                                 10 logical units on the grid. The
                                 physical size of the drawing in pixels
                                 will be calculated with this value.

                                 The drawing board will always be centered
                                 on the diagram, so this value combined
                                 with squaresWide and squaresHigh will
                                 determine the border size.

 protected                       List of symbols that correspond to Catlog
 EntrySymbolList                 entries.
 entrySymbols

 protected                       List of connections between symbols on
 GraphicItemList                 the drawing board and shapes that do not
 graphicItems                    correspond to Catalog entries.

 protected TextBlockList         This is a list of text not tied to
 textBlocks                      specific graphic items.

 protected double scale          This is the display scale. This value
                                 will be used to  determine physical size
                                 of the items on the screen or on the
                                 printer. The scale units are pixels per
                                 logical unit.

 protected int                   The absolute value of the left most
 leftVisibleX                    visible grid square.

 protected int topVisibleY       This is the value of the top visible
                                 grid.
```

FORM 12-1   The drawing board class.

Member Functions: Member Name	Description
public virtual void draw(UI_DISPLAY * theDevice,int startX,int startY,int width,int height)	This function draws the content of the drawing board on the device pointed to by UI_DISPLAY. (If you want to port this to a library besides Zinc, you need to change the device parameter.)
public virtual void put(EntrySymbol * theEntrySymbol,int gridX,int gridY)	Each "put" places an object on the drawing board by placing it in the appropriate list then calling draw. This particular put places an EntrySymbol on the drawing board.
public virtual void put(GraphicItem * theGrahicItem,int gridX,int gridY)	Each "put" places an object on the drawing board by placing it in the appropriate list then calling draw. This particular put places an GraphicItem on the drawing board.
public virtual void put(TextBlock * theTextBlock,int gridX,int gridY)	Each "put" places an object on the drawing board by placing it in the appropriate list then calling draw. This particular put places a TextBlock on the drawing board.
public virtual void get(int gridX,int gridY,GraphicItemList & theGraphicItems,EntrySymb bolList & symbols,TextBlockList & theTextBlocks)	This function gets the lists of the items that touch the point gridX,gridY.
public virtual void changeScale(double factor)	Changes the scale of the drawing board, calculates the new physical points int the items contained on the drawing board.
public virtual void xlateToDevice(GridLocatio on & logicalPoint,point physicalPoint,int physicalX0,int physicalY0)	This function translates a logical point (a point relative to a specific grid square) to a physical point.
public Boolean remove(int gridX,int gridY,string itemName)	Removes an item at gridX,gridY if there is only one item. If there is more than one, removes named item.

FORM 12-1   *(continued).*

```
Class Name:        Diagram
Version:        1
Base Classes:
Description:
The diagram is a model of any type of software design diagram. It
holds drawing board and other features of the Diagram.

Data Members:
 Member Name                    Description
 protected DrawingBoard *       The drawing board is the part of the
 theDrawingBoard                diagram that contains the symbols.

 protected string  name         The name of the diagram.

 protected double height        Height of the diagram in inches.

 protected double width         Width of diagram in inches.

 protected double scale         Number by which to multiply the points in
                                the drawing by. This determines "how big"
                                the diagram appears to be.


Member Functions:
 Member Name                    Description
 public  Diagram()              Constructor

 public virtual void            This is called whenever the value of scale
 ChangeScale()                  is changed so all the items on the draw-
                                ing board can change scale too.

 public virtual void            Assigns value to height.
 setHeight(double _height)

 public virtual void            Assigns a value to the diagram width.
 setWidth(double _width)

 public virtual void            Assigns a value to scale and then calls
 setScale(double _scale)        ChangeScale.

 public double getHeight()      Returns height member variable.

 public double getWidth()       Returns width.

 public double getScale()       Returns scale.
```

FORM 12-2   Diagram class.

```
Class Name:        EntrySymbol
Version:       1
Base Classes:

Description:

Data Members:
 Member Name                  Description
 protected Symbol *           Symbol associated with this object.
 aSymbol

 protected Entry * anEntry    The entry associated with this object.

 protected textBlockList      The text blocks associated with things
 textBlocks                   like member lists.


Member Functions:
 Member Name                  Description
 public virtual void          Creates text block from Entry text based
 entryTextToSymbol()          on the filters and symbol data. For
                              example, puts the Class Name, Data Mem-
                              bers and Member functions on the symbol
                              for a class.

 public virtual void          Draws the shapes and text for this symbol
 draw(UI_DISPLAY * device)    on the device passes as a parameter.

 public const char *          Puts the data in the entry symbol into a
 toString(string &            string so it can be saved to the data base.
 targetString)

 public virtual void          Reads the source string and converts it to
 fromString(string &          entry symbol data.
 sourceString)
```

FORM 12-3 EntrySymbol class.

them to show inheritance and communications relationships between classes as well as other types of relationships. A connector can have forks (for connecting multiple symbols) and shaped ends. Some connectors have special adornments in the middle. The top of Figure 12-7 shows the details of the connector class. The bottom of the figure shows the components of a connector. Forms 12-9 and 12-10 describe the classes related to connectors.

```
Class Name:        MemberFilter
Version:      1
Base Classes:

Description:
The member filter assures that only the class members the user wants
to see are displayed on the diagram.

Data Members:
 Member Name                Description
 public string filterText   The string holds the text which defines the
                            class members that should be displayed on the
                            diagram. This is a string containing the
                            following types words:
                            all, public, protected, private, <name>
                            The symbols & and | are used to indicate
                            AND and OR conditions.
                            The <name> is the name of a class member.


Member Functions:
 Member Name                Description
 public Boolean             Checks to see if the member matches the
 matchesFilter(ClassMember  filter string. If so, it returns true.
 rDefinition * mem)
```

FORM 12-4 MemberFilter class.

12.5 THE INTERFACE CLASSES

12.5.1 User Interface Classes

Figure 12-8 shows a partial expansion of the User Interface subject. Most are window classes with the same basic design, children of UIW_WINDOW with overloaded Event functions and member functions to handle menu or button selections.

12.5.1.1 The GraphicMainWindow Class

Figure 12-9 shows the main window and two of its supporting windows. The main window of the graphic tool, GraphMainWindow, is very much like our other main windows. Most of the window contains the diagram. The other parts of the main window include the scroll bars that allow the user to change which part of the diagram being viewed and the main menu. The following items can be found in the main menu:

243

```
Class Name:        TextBlock
Version:        1
Base Classes:

Description:
The text block is a block of text that is placed on the drawing board.

Data Members:
 Member Name                  Description
 protected int x              Logical X coordinate from top of symbol
                              this is attached to. If not attached to a
                              symbol, it's the logical X coordinate
                              from Grid 0,0.

 protected int y              Same as x but for rows not columns.

 protected string theText     The text within the text block.

 protected string            String of properties. It is a comma
 properties                   delimited string with the following
                              information:
                              Font, size, color.


Member Functions:
 Member Name                  Description
 public virtual void          Draws the text in the text block on the
 draw(UI_DISPLAY * device)    device.

 public virtual void          Changes the physical size of the text on
 changeScale(double           the device.
 factor)
```

FORM 12-5 TextBlock class.

File

    New—Creates a new diagram.

    Open—Opens an existing catalog.

    Load—Loads a diagram from the catalog.

    Save—Saves a diagram into the catalog.

    Save As—Saves the diagram with a new name.

    Print Setup—Sets up the printer.

    Print—Sends the diagram to the editor.

Edit

    Cut—Removes and saves one or more symbols.

    Copy—Copies one or more symbols for later pasting.

    Paste—Puts one or more symbols on the drawing board.

    Delete—Removes one or more symbols from the drawing board.

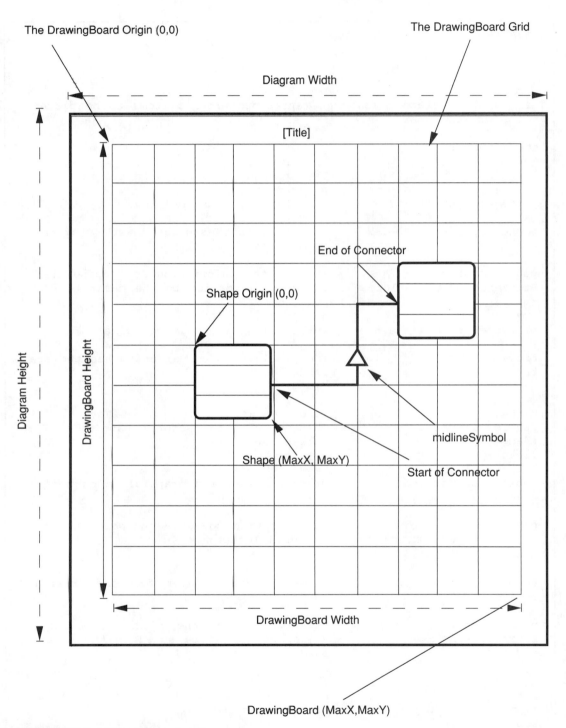

FIGURE 12-5 The parts of a diagram.

```
Class Name:        GraphicItem
Version:        1
Base Classes:

Description:
This is an abstract class that represents graphic items to be placed
on the drawing board.

Data Members:
  Member Name                     Description
  protected int startX            The starting location grid column.

  protected int startY            Starting location grid row.

  protected string theText        The basic test associated with a graphic
                                  item

  public static                   This is the information for maping the
  PrinterInfo printerInfo         logical information to the paper to be
                                  printed.

  protected double scale          Current logical units per pixel.

  protected double                The pixels per logical unit when the scale
  basicScale                      is 1.

Member Functions:
  Member Name                     Description
  public virtual void             Changes scale to factor * baseScale. Then
  changeScale(double              calls draw.
  factor)

  public virtual void             Draws the specific graphicItem on the
  draw(UI_DISPLAY * device)       screen.

  public virtual void             This function moves the graphic item to
  move(int newGridX,int           the grid location.
  newGridY)

  public virtual void             Takes the graphic item from the drawing
  remove()                        board.

  public const char *             Puts the data in the graphic item into a
  toString(string &               string so it can be saved to the data
                                  base.

  targetString)

  public virtual void             Reads the source string and converts it to
  fromString(string &             graphic item data.
  sourceString)
```

FORM 12-6   GraphicItem class.

public int maxX()	Returns the right most logical point on the item.
public int maxY()	Returns the maximum logical Y value within the item. Note maxX and maxY are relative to startX and startY.

FORM 12-6 *(continued).*

```
Class Name:         SimpleShape
Version:         1
Base Classes:
public GraphicItem


Description:
The base class for simple geometric shapes. Contains the common data
and values for each type of simple shape.

Data Members:
 Member Name                Description
 protected pointList        Contains a list of the physical points
 physicalPoints             define this shape. How the points are used
                            depend on the individual draw function.

 protected pointList        List of logical points that make up the
 logicalPoints              shape. The logical points are relative to
                            the grid at startX and startY.


Member Functions:
 Member Name                Description
 public virtual void        Draws the specific shape on the device.
 draw(UI_DISPLAY * device)

 public virtual void        Moves the graphic item to the new location.
 move(int newGridX,int
 newGridY)

 public const char *        Pure virtual function. Puts the shape data
 toString(string &          into targetString and returns the string
 targetString)              pointer.

 public virtual void        Reads shape data from string.
 fromString(string &
 sourceString)
```

FORM 12-7 SimpleShape class.

`public virtual void changeScale(double factor)`	Changes scale to factor * baseScale. Then calls draw.
`public int maxX()`	Returns the right most logical point on the shape.
`public int maxY()`	Returns the maximum logical Y value within the shape. Note maxX and maxY are relative to startX and startY.

FORM 12-7   *(continued).*

```
Class Name:        ComplexShape
Version:        1
Base Classes:
public GraphicItem


Description:
A complex shape is a list of simple shapes. All shapes are placed
relative to startX, start Y.

Data Members:
 Member Name              Description
 protected shapeList      Contains a list of the simple shapes that
 simpleShapes             define this shape.

The member functions listed for SimpleShapes are defined in
ComplexShapes.

The member functions call the corresponding function for each member
of shapeList.
```

FORM 12-8   ComplexShape class.

> **Find**—Searches for classes or functions that meet specific criteria, connects to current symbol. This will use the librarian search window.

Symbol

> **Alternate**—Allows user to change symbol to an alternate symbol. (See the middle picture in Figure 12-9.)
>
> **Description**—Allows user to edit the description of the symbol. The specific types of symbol descriptor classes are diagramed in Figure 12-10. The top picture of Figure 12-11 illustrates a sample description window, created by the ClassDescriptionWin class.
>
> **Change**—Allows the user to change the selected symbol to a different type of symbol. For example, a Coad and Yourdon Class may be changed to a Coad and Yourdon Class and Object.

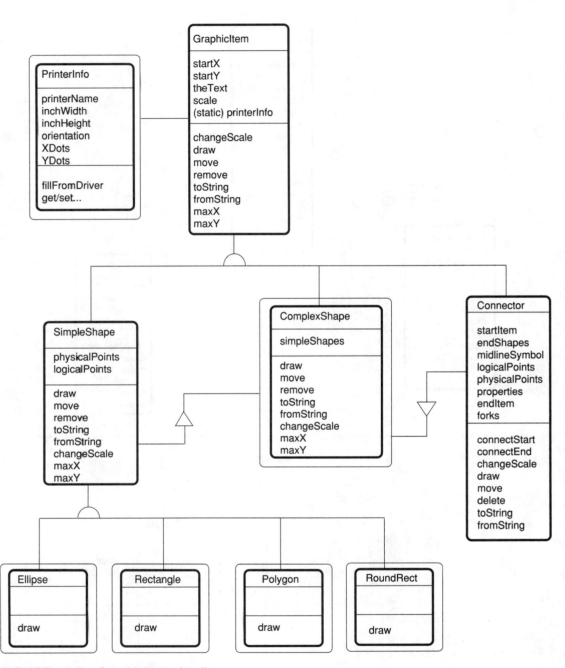

FIGURE 12-6 GraphicItem details.

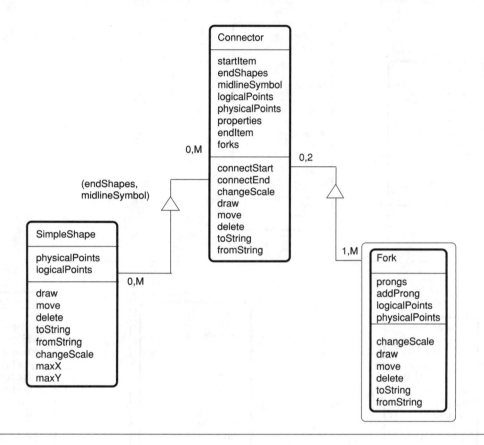

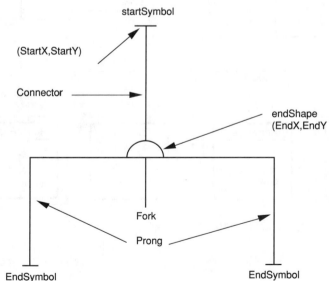

FIGURE 12-7   Connector details.

```
Class Name:         Connector
Version:         1
Base Classes:
public GraphicItem



Description:
A connector is a line or curve that connects two symbols or graphic
items.

Data Members:
  Member Name                     Description
  protected string                The location and identity of the starting
  startItem                       symbol or grahic item.

  protected ShapeList             Simple shapes at the end of the connector.
  endShapes

  protected SimpleShape           The shape occurs on the line.
  midlineSymbol

  protected PointList             List of logical points that make up the
  logicalPoints                   connector.

  protected PointList             List of physical points that make up the
  physicalPoints                  connector.

  protected string                Color, line width, line style, etc.
  properties

  protected string endItem        Location and identifier of the ending item.
  protected ForkList forks


Member Functions:
  Member Name                     Description
  public virtual void             Starts the connection by assigning the
  connectStart(string             first logical points to the appropriate
  startingItem,int                point relative to the starting item.
  logicalX,int logicalY)          Assigns startingItem to startItem.

  public virtual void             Sets the ending item. Calculates the
  connectEnd(string               logical points between startItem and
  endItem,int logicalX,int        endItem.
  logicalY)
```

FORM 12-9 Connector class.

`public virtual void`
`placeMidline(int`
`logicalX,int logicalY)`
	Places the appropriate midline symbol on the drawing board and adjusts the logical points accordingly.

`public virtual void`
`setAnchor(int`
`logicalX,int logicalY)`
	Places a constant point on the drawing board. This point will not move unless the user moves it. The line or curve willalways go from the previous point to this point.

`public virtual void`
 	
`display)`
	Draws the line or curve from the starting item to the ending item by way of any midline symbols or anchored points.

`public virtual void`
`move(point`
`startingLogicalPoint,point`
`endingLogicalPoint)`
	Move has no real meaning for complete connectors. Individual points can be moved, however. This function does so, then calls draw.

`public virtual void` `remove()`	Removes this connector from the drawing board.

`public const char *`
`toString(string &`
`targetString)`
	Converts connector data to string form and puts it in targetString. Returns string.ptr().

`public virtual void`
`fromString(string &`
`sourceString)`
	Fills the data in the connector from the sourceString.

FORM 12-9 *(continued).*

```
Class Name:        Fork
Version:        1
Base Classes:

Description:
The fork is a list of connectors originating from a common point. The
common point is an end point of a connector.

Data Members:
  Member Name                   Description
  protected ConnectorList       Each prong is a connector in its own
  prongs right.

  protected Point               All prongs start at the logicalStart. The
  logicalStart                  logicalStart is relative to the end of
                                the connector.
```

FORM 12-10 Fork class.

protected Point physicalStart	Physical start of all prongs.

```
Member Functions:
  Member Name                    Description
```

public virtual void changeScale(double factor)	Changes the scale of the physical points and all the prongs associated with a fork.
public virtual void draw(UI_DISPLAY * display)	Draws all the prongs on the display device.
public virtual void remove()	Removes fork (and all prongs) from the drawing board.
public const char * toString(string & targetString)	Writes fork and prong data to targetString. Returns a pointer to the targetString data.
public virtual void fromString(string & sourceString)	Fills fork data from source string.

FORM 12-10   *(continued).*

Select—Lists all the symbols in the diagram and lets the user select one ore more and make them current.

Shapes—Allows the user to alter the shapes within a symbol. Figure 12-12 shows a symbol editor. This is described further in another section.

View

Zoom In—Shows more detail, but less of the drawing board. The symbols and the grid will be larger.

Zoom Out—Shows less detail, but more of the drawing board. The symbols and the grid will be larger.

Grid—Turns the grid on and off. Figure 12-9 shows the grid turned on.

Symbol

Description—Views the description associated with symbol.

Diagram—Brings up diagram associated with symbol. It is possible that a particular symbol may represent another diagram entirely. For example, a collapsed Coad and Yourdon subject may explode to a different diagram containing a fully expanded version of the same subject.

Alternate Symbol—Lists alternate symbols associated with selected symbol.

List—Displays a list of symbols in the diagram.

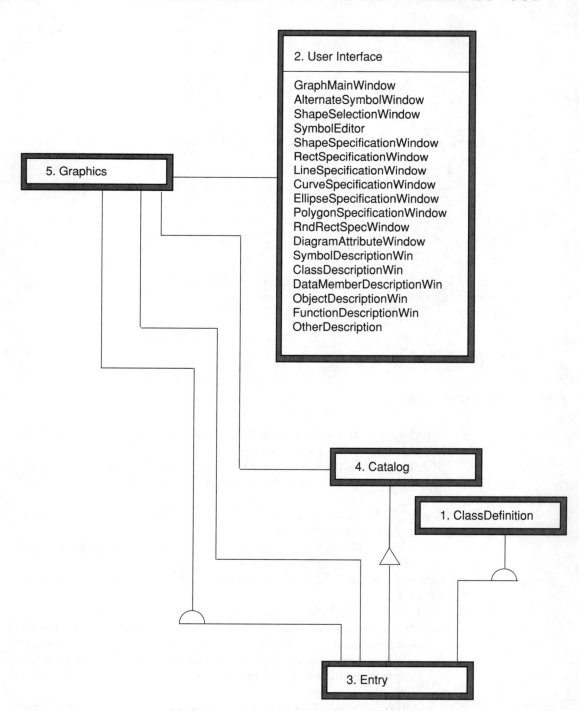

FIGURE 12-8   SOOT CASE graphic tool user interface in relation to other subjects.

Main Window: : GraphMainWindow

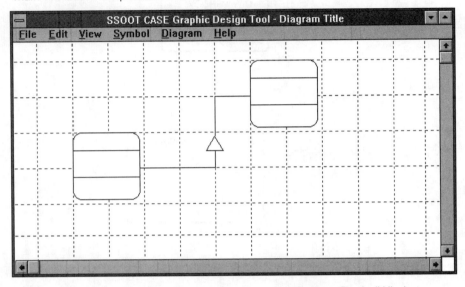

Selector Window to Allow a Symbol Change : AlternateSymbolWindow

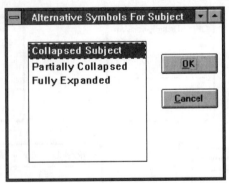

Window to Allow Selection of Shape: ShapeSelectionWindow

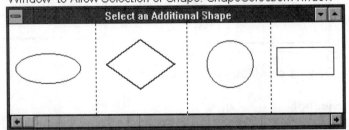

FIGURE 12-9 User interface windows.

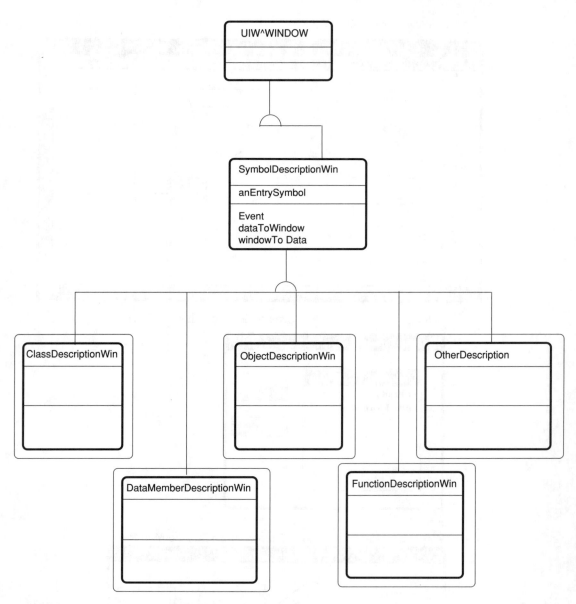

FIGURE 12-10 Descriptor windows describe symbols.

Symbol
> **Add**
>> **Class**—Adds a class symbol to the drawing board.
>> **Object**—Adds an object symbol to the drawing board.
>> **Function**—Adds a stand-alone function symbol to the drawing board.
>> **Member Function**—Adds a member function symbol to a drawing board.

ClassDescriptionWin

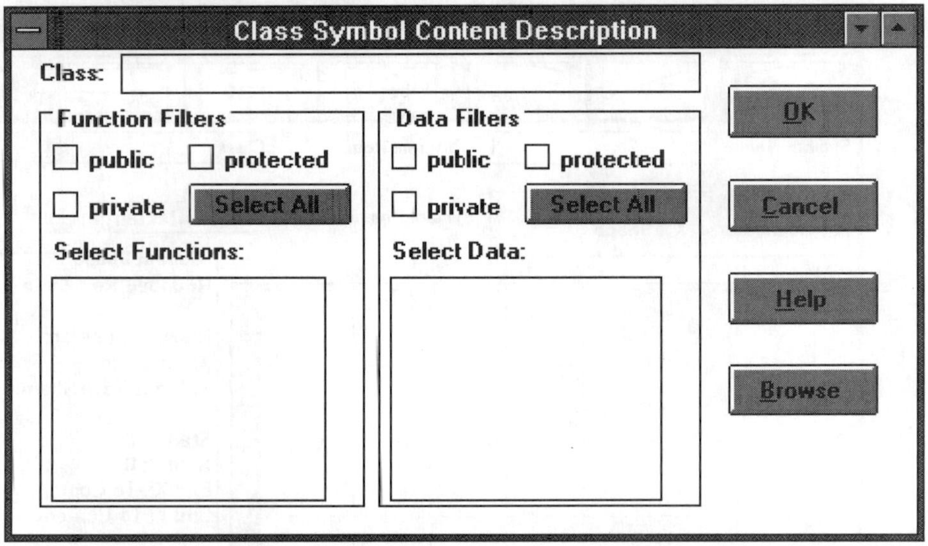

Class Symbol Content Description

Class: [_____]

Function Filters
- ☐ public   ☐ protected
- ☐ private   [Select All]

Select Functions:

Data Filters
- ☐ public   ☐ protected
- ☐ private   [Select All]

Select Data:

[OK]

[Cancel]

[Help]

[Browse]

DiagramAttributeWindow

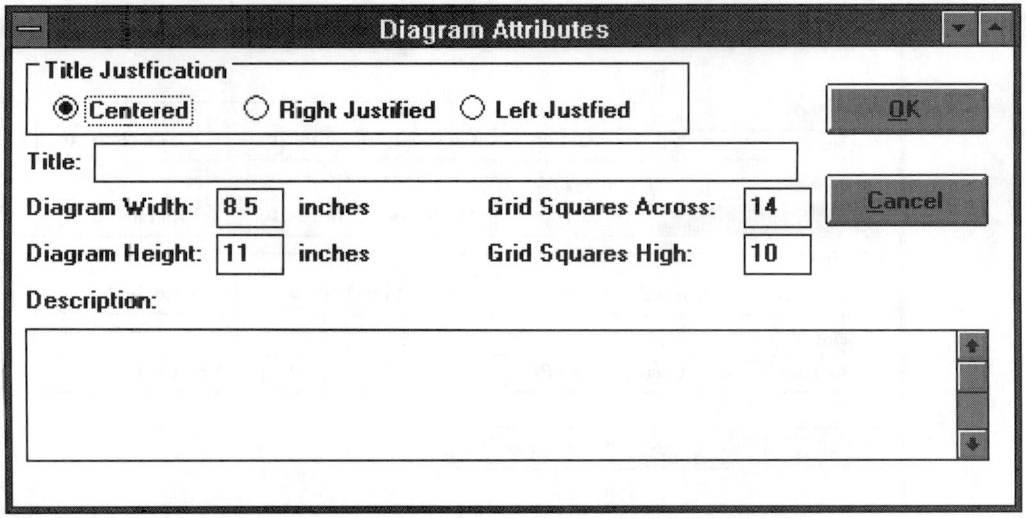

Diagram Attributes

Title Justfication
- ⦿ Centered   ○ Right Justified   ○ Left Justfied

Title: [_____]

Diagram Width: [8.5] inches   Grid Squares Across: [14]

Diagram Height: [11] inches   Grid Squares High: [10]

Description:

[OK]

[Cancel]

FIGURE 12-11   Description windows.

SymbolEditor

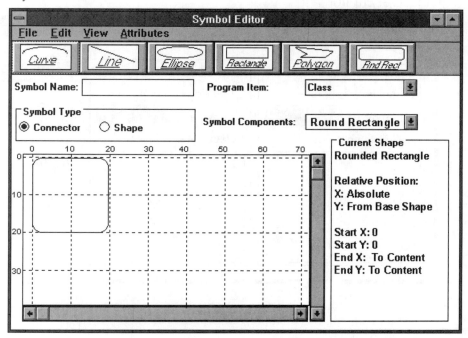

RectSpecificationWindow

FIGURE 12-12   Symbol editor windows.

Data—Adds a data member symbol to a drawing board.

Inheritance—Adds an inheritance symbol to the drawing board.

Communication—Adds a communication symbol to the drawing board.

Other Shape—Allows selection of user-defined shape to add to the drawing board. The last picture in Figure 12-9 shows a ShapeSelectionWindow.

Other Connector—Allows selection of user-defined connector to add to the drawing board.

Create—Allows the user to create a new symbol. Figure 12-12 shows the main window of the Symbol Editor. Section 12.5.2 describes this in more detail.

Connect

Alternate—Allows user to connect selected symbol to an alternate symbol. This will be used by the **Edit | Symbol | Alternate** menu selection.

Class Description—Allows user to connect a class description to a symbol. The picture of the window at the bottom of Figure 12-11 shows a ClassDescriptionWin. By using the Browse button, the user can browse through the class catalog using the browser from the previous chapter.

Function Description—Allows user to connect a function description to a symbol. The user can search for a function in the catalog.

Other Description—Allows user to connect a textual description to a symbol.

Diagram—Allows user to associate a new or existing diagram with a symbol. The user can search the catalog for an existing diagram or create another one.

Diagram—Invokes the diagram attribute window. Figure 12-11 shows the DiagramAttributeWindow.

Help—Invokes the help system.

12.5.2 Symbol Builder

The symbol builder is the portion of the SSOOT CASE Graphic Tool that makes it notation-independent. I've preloaded the Coad and Yourdon symbols, but you can use this section to enter the symbols for your own notation of choice. You can also use the symbol builder to create symbols for structure charts, data flow diagrams, etc.

A symbol is a ComplexShape or a Connector. The Symbol Editor lets the user describe a strategy for drawing the shapes that make up the symbol. The top of Figure 12-12 shows the main window of the Symbol Editor. The buttons along the top of the Symbol Editor let the user add simple shapes or lines to the symbol. The SymbolEditor main window has a menu with the following items:

File

   New Symbol—Lets the user create a new type of symbol.

   Load Symbol—Lets the user load an existing symbol from the catalog.

   Save Symbol—Saves a type of symbol into the catalog.

   Save As—Saves the symbol with a new name in the catalog.

Edit

   Cut—Removes a shape from the editor for later placement into the drawing.

   Copy—Copies a shape from the editor, without removing it, for later placement into the drawing.

   Paste—Places a shape that has been copied or cut into the drawing.

   Delete—Removes a shape from the editor.

View

   Zoom In—Shows more detail, but less of the drawing area. The symbols and the grid will be larger.

   Zoom Out—Shows less detail, but more of the drawing area. The symbols and the grid will be larger.

Attributes

   Grid

      Visible—Makes the grid visible.

      Invisible—Makes the grid visible.

      Color—Changes the color of the grid.

   Points—Invokes the shape specific specification window. I'll discuss the details of shape specification windows later in this section.

   Text—Defines the location of the symbol specific text within a shape. For example, if the symbol is to be a class or object, the user can specify where to put the class name, member functions or data members.

   Line Thickness—Gives five line thickness options for drawing shapes and connectors: Very Thin, Thin, Medium, Thick, and Very Thick.

   Line Ends —Allows user to select arrows, squares, circles, or other common simple shapes.

   Midline Symbol—Allows user to select from a variety of simple shapes to put in the center of a connector.

   Line Color—In DOS, this depends on the selected printer. If the user has selected a color version of one of the supported printers, colors will be available. While no formal methodology uses color for any sort of meaning, you should be able to take advantage of the color capabilities of your equipment for your own extensions. In Windows, the color and dithering will be taken care of by the device drivers in Windows.

   Line Style

      Solid —When this is selected, the lines in the shapes and connectors are solid, as normal.

      Dashed—When this is selected the lines in the shapes and connectors are dashed.

      Long Dashed—When this is selected the lines in the shapes and connectors are dashed. The lines between the spaces are longer than the normal dashed lines.

Users can add shapes to the symbol with the buttons under the menu. They don't draw shapes with a mouse as in a standard drawing program. Instead, each shape is drawn based on instructions in a specification window. Each type of shape has its own specification window. The bottom window in Figure 12-12 shows a rectangle specification window.

Shapes can be positioned in either absolute or relative coordinates. Absolute coordinates start with the origin in the upper left corner of the grid. Shapes can also be positioned relative to other shapes in the symbol. The first shape placed on a symbol is the base shape. If the first shape in a symbol is specified as being relative to the base shape, it will be drawn relative to the previous symbol.

If a shape is specified as having an EndX sized to content, the shape will be as wide as the longest line of text within the shape. If EndY is marked as size to content, the height of the shape will be defined by the number of lines of text contained within the shape.

Figure 12-13 shows the user interface classes for the Symbol Editor. The details are deferred to the programmer.

12.5.3   Interface to Browser

In Figure 12-11 the ClassDescriptionWin has a Browse button. Figure 12-14 shows what happens when the Browser button is selected. The Browser from the previous chapter, minus the file editing capabilities, can be used to find the class the user wants. The user can find the appropriate class, ancestor, or descendant to associate with the symbol.

12.5.4   Database Interface

There are two types of things that need to be stored in the database: diagrams and the list of possible symbols. Figure 12-15 shows how we can store the diagram in the catalog. If a diagram is made into an entry, it can be converted to record, and a record can be stored in the catalog. Here's the catch: Although we have several types of things in a diagram, we only have one record for each diagram, so we need to hold the symbols, connectors, and other contained items in variable length fields. Form 12-11 defines the record layouts used in the toRecord and fromRecord methods. Form 12-12 defines the string syntax for the symbols embedded in the drawing board.

The Symbols are created with the Symbol Editor and stored in the catalog as a SymbolEntry. Figure 12-16 shows the SymbolEntry family tree. Form 12-13 defines the record layout used in toRecord and fromRecord methods.

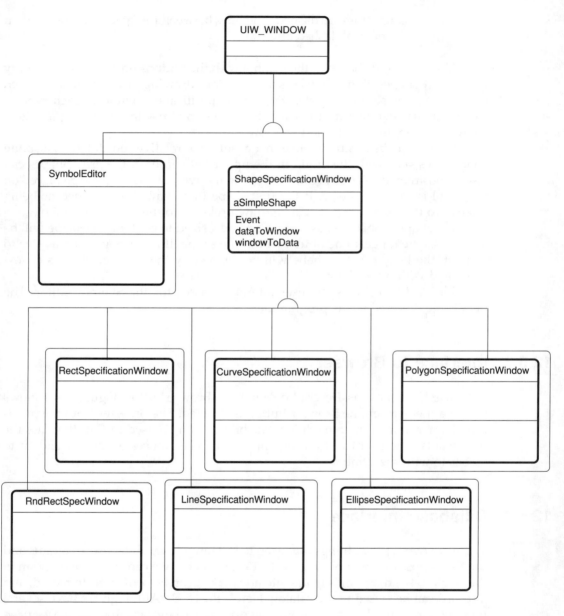

FIGURE 12-13   Symbol builder classes.

12.6   GUIDE TO SOURCE CODE

The subdirectory, CHAP12, contains the source code and executables for this chapter. The file README.12 lists the files, their purposes, and any differences from the design listed in this chapter and its implementation in code.

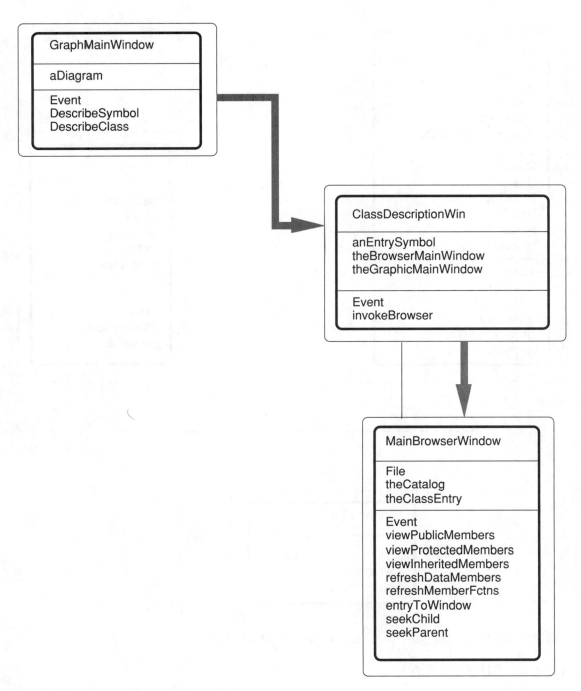

FIGURE 12-14   Invoking the browser.

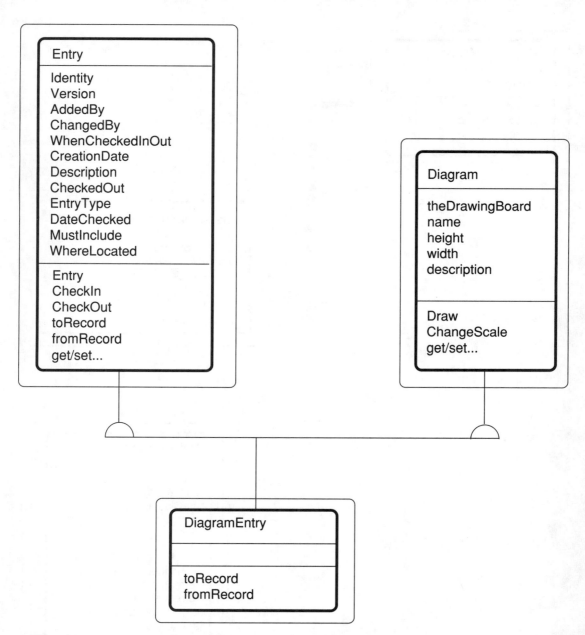

FIGURE 12-15   A DiagramEntry lets us keep track of diagrams.

12.7   SUMMARY

This chapter defines the classes and objects required to build a graphic design tool that interfaces with the entries in the SSOOT CASE Catalog. There are two basic

```
Record: DiagramEntry

Field Name        Data Type        Purpose

Identity          String           This and the version uniquely identify the
                                   diagram.

Version           Long             Version of diagram being stored.

Name              String           Name (title) of diagram.

Height            Long             Height of diagram in inches.

Width             Long             Width of diagram in inches.

description       String           Description of diagram.

Record: DrawingBoard

Identity          String           This and the version uniquely identify the
                                   drawing board.

Version           Long             Version of diagram being stored.

squaresHigh       Long             Number of grid squares high.

squaresWide       Long             Number of grid squares wide.

gridSize          Real             Size of grid in inches.

entrySymbols      String           String of entry symbols. (See syntax below)

graphicItems      String           String of graphic items. (See syntax below)

textBlocks        String           String of text blocks. (See syntax below)

scale             Real             Pixels per logical unit.
```

FORM 12-11   Record layout for diagram.

types of classes defined here, shapes and connectors. These shapes and connectors are placed on a diagram within the drawing board.

The user interface design is reviewed by examining the screen dumps and menu selections. The chapter then examines the details of how the information in the graphic items would be stored in the database.

```
For GraphicItem:

{GraphicItem,(startX,startY), "theText," {SimpleShape | ComplexShape|
Connector}}

For SimpleShape:

{ Ellipse|Rectangle|Polygon|RoundRect, {properties}, {logicalPoints}}

For logicalPoints:

{(x,y),(x,y). . .}

For ComplexShape:

{ComplexShape,{GraphicItem,GraphicItem,. . .}}

For Connector:

{Connector,{"startItem",{SimpleShape,...},{SimpleShapes},{logicalPoints},{properties},"endItem",{forks}}

For Properties:

{color,lineStyle,lineThickness}

For Forks:

{Fork,{(x,y)},{Connector,. . .}}

For EntrySymbols:

{EntrySymbol,{"Class"|"Function",Identifier,Version},{"member filter
string","member filter string"},

{"Symbol Name"},{TextBlock, . . .}}

For TextBlock:

{TextBlock, (x,y),"the text,"{properties}}

For Symbol:

{Symbol, "Symbol Identifier,""Program Item,""Symbol Type," {GraphicItem,
. . . }}
```

FORM 12-12　String syntax for items

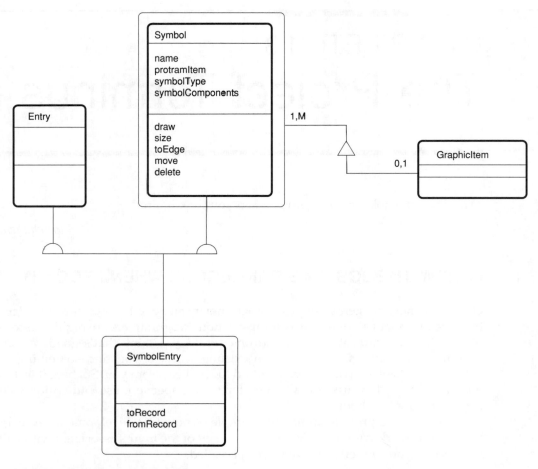

FIGURE 12-16 The SymbolEntry class.

Record: SymbolEntry		
Field Name	**Data Type**	**Purpose**
Identifier	String	This and version uniquely identify the symbol entry.
Version	Long	The version of the SymbolEntry being stored.
Name	String	The name of the symbol.
SymbolType	String	Program component this symbol represents.
symbol/Components	String	The graphic items that make up the symbol.

FORM 12-13 Layout of SymbolEntry record.

CHAPTER 13
The Project Terminus

"You knew the job was dangerous when you took it, Fred."

Superchicken.

13.1 I KNEW THE JOB WAS DANGEROUS WHEN I TOOK IT

One of the most dangerous things a programmer can do to his own ego is to place his code in front of all of his peers for inspection. Programmers are highly susceptible to the "I can do it better" syndrome. Frankly, I think that's good. We all benefit from attempts to improve on existing work. If you find something in SSOOT CASE you can do better, great! I'd like to hear from you. So, here it is, the book and the disk, warts and all, open for your inspection, use and critique. Be gentle, it's my first book.

I've tried to provide an honest example of how OO development can help you in your work without trying to sell you any of the myths associated with OO hype. Only you can tell how well I've succeeded.

13.2 POSSIBLE SSOOT CASE ENHANCEMENTS

13.2.1 Perfectly Satisfied Users

The users have now been using SSOOT CASE in their OO development. As you can see in Figure 13-1, they love it and are perfectly satisfied with it. Well, almost. Here's the user's wish list for things they'd like to see improved, changed or reworked.

1. More Entry types. The users would like to be able to have other types of entries in the library. For example, a change request Entry to allow the developers to match version variants with requests made by users and programmers.
2. Support for template classes and functions.

FIGURE 13-1 The users are perfectly satisfied with SSOOT CASE.

3. Support for embedded classes. Classes and structures can have classes, enums, and other structures embedded in them. SSOOT CASE should recognize and handle that.
4. Support for projects. There is no way to tell which projects are using or have used the classes and functions in the library. This would be helpful.
5. The ability to import and export entries. Since we have the ability to use different catalogs, it would be helpful if we could transfer data between the catalogs.
6. The ability to create custom reports.
7. Defect tracking. Classes and functions have defects. Defect tracking capabilities with the Class entries and Function entries would help with quality assurance.

8. Interface to SCM. The librarian would be more helpful with an interface to automated source code management system.
9. The graphic tool should draw hierarchies automatically.
10. We need an "Undo" on the edit menus.

13.2.2 The Developers Respond to the Users Requests

You can tell from Figure 13-2 that the development team is anxious to get to work on the enhancements. Most of us consider program maintenance the least fun part of programming. But that's where many of us spend the most time.

One of the goals of Object Engineering is to decrease maintenance efforts. I don't think enough data has been collected on the subject to prove that it does; however, my intuition tells me it will.

It is the project team's responsibility to prioritize and analyze the enhancement list in the previous section and keep data on what it takes to make the requested changes. I'd like to invite you to become part of the development team. Feel free to take on some of those enhancements listed above. If you're using this book as part of a class, some of those enhancements would make great projects.

13.3   WHERE YOU CAN GO FROM HERE

I've presented you with a fairly large collection of classes that model OOP components. If you're a programmer's tool developer, or if you like developing your own tools, you can use them to create additional tools. Here are some suggestions that come to mind:

- A cross reference utility
- A code formatter
- A defect tacking system
- A change request tracking system

I hope this list will inspire more ideas. Even though I felt that Zinc and Pinnacle were the best tools for the job when I built SOOT CASE, I'd like to see how independent the problem domain is from the library code. If you decide to port this code to another set of libraries, I'd love to hear from you.

13.4   CLOSING REMARKS

CASE has suffered from being over sold when it was introduced. Lately, I've been seeing articles in professional journals with titles like "The Failure of CASE" and "The CASE of the Broken Promise." When it was new, CASE was the magic wand that would solve all of our programming problems.

FIGURE 13-2   The developers are anxious to enhance SSOOT CASE.

CASE hasn't failed. I remember drawing structure charts by hand and agonizing over changes I now take for granted. CASE is not the final solution. It's one more tool that can make our lives a little easier. That's what I've tried to do with SSOOT CASE. I didn't try to give you everything to magically create perfect programs; I did try to give you a set of software tools that would make your life easier.

OOP has gotten more than its share of hype. I hope it doesn't suffer from a sudden reality crash when people realize that it's not a panacea either. Its one more thing that can make programming better.

When I came up with the idea for this book, I wanted to combine OOP and CASE to create a synergistic set of tools in which the combination of OOP and CASE would make a programmer's life better than either could separately. Here it is, I hope you like it.

APPENDIX A
OO and C++ Sources

CLASS LIBRARY SOURCES

Here is a list of the sources for the C++ classes I used but did not build. I'll include a small review of each one.

Pinnacle Relational Engine

The Pinnacle Relational Engine functions are examples of good, modular, manageable code. Pinnacle has data structures and functions that operate on those structures. The people at Vermont Database Corporation have wrapped those functions and structures into C++ classes.

The core Pinnacle functions are written in portable C, so it's available for a wide variety of platforms. Some of these include, but are not limited to, Windows, UNIX, VMS, and DOS. Pinnacle is available for both multi-user and single-user platforms. If you want to use it in multi-user mode, or if you work on a platform besides Windows or DOS and you want to use SSOOT CASE, contact Vermont Database Corporation for the Pinnacle version you need.

Pinnacle is a commercial (as opposed to Shareware) product, but a free trial disk is available from Vermont Database Corporation for the asking. The trial diskette will suffice if you want to modify some of these programs yourself. If you want to do any real work with SSOOT CASE, however, you'll need the fully functional version.

> Pinnacle Relational Engine
> Vermont Database Corporation
> 400 Upper Hollow Hill Road
> Stowe, VT 05672
> 1-800-822-4437

Zinc Application Framework

The Zinc Application Framework is a C++ user interface library from Zinc Software Inc. It supports several popular platforms. Zinc's primary feature is a C++

class library. It consists of class definitions, object code, and source code for those classes. The class library is designed so that your application only needs to have one set of source code for writing applications for several platforms. Zinc comes with a core library and "keys" for each platform you want to support. Each key consists of libraries and source files for a specific platform.

In SSOOT CASE, I used Zinc Version 3.5 with the DOS and Windows keys. You can change platforms with minimal source code changes by simply buying another key. Contact Zinc for the list of currently available platforms.

The other major feature that comes with Zinc is the Zinc Designer. The Zinc Designer is a program that allows the programmer to draw windows, dialogues, menus, bitmaps etc. Using the designer is faster than writing the equivalent source code. It allows the programmer to make better "Look and Feel" decisions. You can look through chapters 9, 11 and 12 and see how I used the designer.

The Zinc documentation consists of three books: The Programmer's Guide, The Programmer's Tutorial, and The Programmer's Reference. It also includes a Quick Reference Guide containing a class hierarchy and a list of the most common constructors, flags, and event information.

The Programmer's Guide provides a good overview of the concepts in the Zinc Application Framework. It is a short book that hits the most important points of the library. It also contains a user's guide to the Zinc Designer.

The Programmer's Tutorial is a clear and simple book to help the programmer get started. It is short enough to stay interesting. That is a major accomplishment when you consider that it not only contains lessons on using the Zinc Library, but a C++ and Object-Oriented design tutorial as well. The examples are excellent. They are clear, and many are useful building blocks for your own applications.

The Programmer's Reference is a well-organized book that covers most of the classes that come with Zinc.

Zinc Application Framework
Zinc Software Incorporated
405 South 100 East, 2nd Floor
Pleasant Grove, Utah 84062
1-800-638-8665

Online Services

When I need a type of class in a hurry, and when I am curious about what other C++ programmers are up to, I look online. I use two services primarily, CompuServe and BIX.

CompuServe

CompuServe has several areas in which to look for C++ classes. These are the forums I most often use to do just that:

Computer Language Forum - GO CLFORUM
Dr. Dobb's Forum - GO DDJFORM
Borland C++ for Windows Forum - GO BCPPWIN
Borland C++/DOS Forum - GO BCPPDOS
IBM Programming Forum - GO IBMPRO

These are just the ones I use a lot. To get a comprehensive list, type "FIND OOP" or "FIND C++" at the command line.

CompuServe
1-800-848-8199

BIX

I didn't use anything specifically from BIX in SSOOT CASE. I did, however, read the conferences and download candidate classes for use in SSOOT CASE. BIX has comments and thoughts from some of the "Big Names" in OOP and C++: Stroustrup, Booch, Lippman.

I look in the following conferences and file listing areas for C++ and OO topics:

ood
c.plus.plus
microsoft
borland

You can learn more about BIX by contacting them.

BIX, General Videotex Corporation
103 Massachusetts Ave.
Cambridge, MA 02138
1-800-695-4775

C++/OO Training

I'm listing companies that provide OO training here as a service to you so you don't have to spend a great deal of time looking for addresses and phone numbers. I'm not being paid to list them and neither is the publisher. I've had contact with some of them, and others I've only heard of. You'll need to decide for yourself if you can use their services.

Object International
8140 N. MoPac Expwy., 4-200
Austin, TX 78759
512-795-0202

Peter Coad, co-inventor of the Coad and Yourdon OO notation is the chairman of Object International. If you want training in Coad and Yourdon OOA or OOD, you might want to check them out.

Technology Exchange Company
Route 128
One Jacob Way
Reading, MA 01867
1-800-662-4282

I only know TEC from their brochures, however, they have an impressive list of instructors, advisors, and technical editors.

Rational
3320 Scott Boulevard
Santa Clara, CA 95054
1-800-767-3237

Rational of Santa Clara, CA supports the Booch methodology. This isn't really surprising since Grady Booch is on the staff at Rational. If you want to know more about OOD Booch style, you might want to call them.

APPENDIX B

Commercial OO CASE Tools

Please note that the inclusion of a product in this appendix does not necessarily imply an endorsement. I'm simply passing on leads for you to explore. You must determine the suitability of each tool for your specific needs.

Object International of Austin Texas has a couple of tools that support the Coad and Yourdon notation, OOATool, and (by the time this book is in print) OODTool. These tools are available for several platforms including MS-Windows, Unix, and Mac.

Object International
8140 N. MoPac Expwy., 4-200
Austin, TX 78759
512-795-0202

Interactive Development Environments of San Francisco, CA supports the OOSD notation in their CASE tool. Their primary platform at the time of this writing is UNIX with X-Windows.

Interactive Development Environments
595 Market Street, 10th Floor
San Francisco, CA 94105
1-800-888-4331

Rational of Santa Clara, CA supports the Booch notation in their Rose CASE tools. The Rose system is X-Windows based and MS-Windows based. I saw a demonstration of Rose in Chicago. The tool was impressive enough, but what I was really impressed with was the practical knowledge of the Rational developers.

Rational
3320 Scott Boulevard
Santa Clara, CA 95054
1-800-767-3237

System Architect from Popkin Software and Systems Inc. supports more than just OO techniques. It supports traditional diagrams, Booch diagrams, and Coad and Yourdon diagrams. At the time of this writing, it is available for MS-Windows and OS/2.

Popkin Software & Systems Inc.
11 Park Place
New York, NY 10007
1-212-571-3434

APPENDIX C
Recommended Reading

"Evolve or die; Those who can take seminars. Those who *must*, read books."

From the beginning of PC Techniques *Bookstream,*
a regular feature of *PC Techniques* magazine.

Obviously one book won't teach you everything you need to know about OO development. In this appendix, I'll recommend some additional reading on the topics of C++ , OO Development and CASE tools. I'll include a short comment about each recommendation.

C++ PROGRAMMING

Introductory Books

Teach Yourself . . . C++ **by Al Stevens, MIS Press, 1990.**

Al is the C columnist for *Dr. Dobb's Journal.* This was the first C++ book I could relate to. I'd had one C++ class, and I was completely lost. I bought this book because I liked Al's column. I found it to be clear and to the point. His examples, while short, were useful and logical. If you have a C programming background, I would strongly recommend this book for learning C++.

C++ Primer, 2nd Edition **by Stan B. Lippman, Addison-Wesley, 1991.**

This book has a more comprehensive coverage of C++ than Al's book. Stan doesn't assume you already know C. This was where I first learned about C++ templates. It is a good cross between a reference book and a tutorial.

Advanced C++ and Reference Books

C++ Programming Guidelines by Thomas Plum and Dan Saks, Plum Hall, 1991.

Having a standard coding convention can help turn C++ source code into valuable system documentation. This book provides a good set of guidelines for such conventions. The guidelines are logical, and local variations are possible. I like the fact that they provide a "justification" section for each guideline. It's easier to accept a standard if you know why it's being suggested. The C++ experience these two men share in this book could take years for an individual or small company to accumulate.

Borland C++ 3.0 Programmer's Guide, Borland International, 1991.

You probably won't be able to find this if you don't use the Borland C++ compiler. It has a great C++ language description, though. Chapters 1 through 5 aren't very Borland specific. I found them to be an excellent reference for even non-compiler specific language questions.

Developing C++ Software by Russel Winder, John Wiley & Sons, 1991.

This book is written as a text book. The author uses it to teach a first year computer science course and as part of a master's program. It may be a fine introductory book if you have an instructor's guidance, but it has too much information crammed into it to be a beginning tutorial. It has good coverage of the C++ language, good code examples, and a good index. I used it as a language reference.

Periodicals

C++ Report, published by SIGS Publications Group, Inc., New York, NY.

This journal has some big names in the C++ and OO world flying on its mast head. It's full of C++ news, tips, and caveats. It has columns on object-oriented topics like design and databases. All in all, I've found the columns, articles and editorials to be informative and well written.

The C++ Journal, published by The C++ Journal Inc., Port Washington, NY.

This journal also covers C++ news, tips and caveats. It's published quarterly. Although they cover the same types of topics as *The C++ Report* the content and style are different. While *The C++ Report* is about C++ in general, *The C++ Journal* seems to be about programming in C++. The difference is subtle, but the two magazines complement each other.

The C Users Journal, **published by R&D Publications, Lawrence, KS.**

One could argue (and many have) that C++ is essentially a just a new version of C. The *C Users Journal* covers C and C++, topics. If you program in C and plan to move to C++, or plan to program in both C and C++ you should find some very useful columns and articles.

OBJECT-ORIENTED TOPICS

General

A Book of Object-Oriented Knowledge **by Brian Henderson-Sellers, Prentice Hall, 1992.**

I found *A Book of Object-Oriented Knowledge* about three quarters of my way through writing this book. It has a good general overview of OOA, OOD, and a very short overview of OOP. I didn't use any information from it for this book, so I didn't include it in the bibliography.

Object Orientation: Concepts, Languages, Databases, User Interfaces **by Setrag Khoshafian and Razmik Abnous, John Wiley & Sons, 1990.**

This book explores the ramifications of object orientation in its various facets. It is a book about OO philosophy with a tie to the "real world." It explains the "whys" of object orientation as much as the "whats" and "hows."

OO Analysis and OO Design

Object Oriented Analysis, 2nd Edition **and** *Object Oriented Design* **by Peter Coad and Ed Yourdon, Prentice-Hall, 1991.**

In Chapter 3 I covered a very little bit about what the Coad and Yourdon OO methodology was about. These two books cover the Coad/Yourdon methodology in complete detail. I looked into the notation, but these books look into the details how to use the notation effectively.

Object-Oriented Design with Applications **by Grady Booch, Benjamin/ Cummings, 1991.**

This book is considered a standard in OOD. It is the definitive work on the Booch method of OOD. I personally feel that it is a little long on theory and a little short on application, but I have no doubt you will find it to be useful and informative.

Periodicals

Dr. Dobb's Journal, **published by Miller Freeman, Inc., San Mateo, CA.**

Dr. Dobb's Journal is a magazine for software professionals. It addresses more topics than just OOP, and it doesn't have OO topics in every issue. However, there is more to the software profession than just OOP. The articles and columns cover a wide range of practical tips and advice, including OO topics when they're appropriate.

PC Techniques, **published by The Coriolis Group, Inc., Scottsdale, AZ.**

PC Techniques is not as formal as some other programming magazines. It has a very personal style with articles and columns that address real needs of individual programmers. This magazine does not focus specifically on OO topics, but its articles and columns address them regularly.

APPENDIX D
The Code

```
//////////////////////////////////////////////////////////////////////
// Listing  : 6-1
// Filename : CLSDFN.H
// Purpose  : Class definition classes
//////////////////////////////////////////////////////////////////////
#ifndef CLSDFN_H
#define CLSDEFN_H
#include <iostream.h>
#include <arrays.h>
#include <fstream.h>
const int maxIdLen = 33; //Really, it's 32, but we need the nil terminator
typedef char IdString[maxIdLen]; // These hold identifiers, and modifiers
enum memberTypes { unknown, isFunction, isData };


//////////////////////////////////////////////////////////////////////
// Author         : David Brumbaugh
// Class Name     : ClassMemberDefinition
// Creation Date  : 7/10/92
// Catagories     : Model, Abstract
// Purpose        : Classes contain two kinds of members, functions and
//                  data. This class has the common features of both.
//
// Major Public Methods:
//    ClassMemberDefinition: Constructor
//    <: For sorting (Required by BIDS library)
//    ==: For comparing values (Required by BIDS library)
//    makeTemplate: (pure) Generate an "empty" source code version of member
//    toSource: (pure) Generates a definition of the member within the class
//    fromSource: (pure) Reads the source code and fills this class's data
//    shouldMakeTemplate: (pure) Should this member be have a template made?
//    getName - What is this thing called?
//    getAccessSpecifier - (public,protected or private)
//    getTypeSpecifiers - (const,int, virtual etc.)
//    getOwningClass - Name of the class that contains this member
//    getType - What is this, a function or data member?
//
// Major Data Items:
//
//    isA:  a function or data member?
//    name: What is this thing called?
//    typeSpecifiers: (const,int, virtual etc.)
//    accessSpecifer : public, private, protected
//    owningClass    : name of class that owns member
//
//////////////////////////////////////////////////////////////////////

class ClassMemberDefinition
{
    protected:
        IdString name,
            accessSpecifier,
            typeSpecifiers,
            owningClass;
```

```
        memberTypes type;
        static IdString lastTypeSpec;
        char ptrSpec[7]; // Six levels of indirection should be plenty
        virtual void movePtrSpec();
        // Move the pointer spec from the name to the type
        static int numInstances; // Debugging variable to validate memory
                                 // management
    public:
        ClassMemberDefinition(char *className);
        virtual operator < (ClassMemberDefinition &c);
        virtual operator == (ClassMemberDefinition &c) const;
        memberTypes isA() { return type; }
        virtual void makeTemplate(ostream &out) = 0;
        virtual void toSource(ostream &out,int withAccess = 0,
        int newType = 0) = 0;
        virtual int shouldMakeTemplate() = 0;
        virtual void fromSource(istream &in, char *accessSpec) = 0;
        const char *getName() { return name; }
        const char *getTypeSpec() { return typeSpecifiers; }
        const char *getAccessSpec() { return accessSpecifier; }
        const char *getOwner() { return owningClass; }
        static void showCount() { cout << numInstances << '\n'; }
        // showCount is a debugging function only

        virtual ~ClassMemberDefinition() { --numInstances; }
};


////////////////////////////////////////////////////////////////////
// Author        : David Brumbaugh
// Class Name    : MemberFunctionDefinition
// Creation Date : 7/10/92
// Catagories    : Model
// Purpose       : Defines a class's member function
//
// Major Public Methods:
//     MemberFunctionDefinition: Constructor
//     ==: Overloaded from parent class
//   makeTemplate: Overloaded
//    toSource: Overloaded
//   fromSource: Overloaded
//   shouldMakeTemplate: Overloaded
//
// Major Data Items:
//    parameters: List of parameters
//   num_params: Number of parameters in function
//    suffix: End of function definition like: "= 0", "const", or "{..}"
//     expandInline: Should we include inline functions in the template?
//                Some people put the inline code in the header.
////////////////////////////////////////////////////////////////////

struct paramDefinition
{
    IdString typeSpecifiers; // int, char *, etc.
    IdString name; // Parameter name
    IdString defaultValue;
```

```
};

const int maxNumParameters = 25; //For now, maybe later we'll use a BIDS list

class MemberFunctionDefinition: public ClassMemberDefinition
{
    protected:
        int expandInline;
        int num_params;
        IdString suffix;
        paramDefinition parameters[maxNumParameters];
        virtual void makeTypeAndName(istream &in);//Get typeSpec, name from in
        virtual void makeParamList(istream &in);// Make parameter list from in
        virtual void makeSuffix(istream &in); // Things like = 0, const, {..}
    public:
        MemberFunctionDefinition(char *className, istream *in = NULL,
        char *accessSpec = NULL, int expInline = 0);
        virtual shouldMakeTemplate();
        virtual operator == (ClassMemberDefinition &c) const;
        virtual void makeTemplate(ostream &out);
        virtual void toSource(ostream &out, int withAccess = 0,
        int newType = 0);
        virtual void fromSource(istream &in, char *accessSpec = NULL);

};

//////////////////////////////////////////////////////////////////////
// Author       : David Brumbaugh
// Class Name   : DataMemberDefinition
// Creation Date : 7/10/92
// Catagories   : Model
// Purpose      : Model of the data member declaration
//
// Major Public Methods:
//     DataMemberDefinition: Constructor
//   makeTemplate: Overloaded
//    toSource: Overloaded
//   fromSource: Overloaded
//   shouldMakeTemplate: Overloaded
// Major Data Items:
//   None specific to this class
//////////////////////////////////////////////////////////////////////

class DataMemberDefinition : public ClassMemberDefinition
{
    public:
        virtual shouldMakeTemplate();
        DataMemberDefinition(char *className, istream *in = NULL,
        char *accessSpec = NULL);
        virtual void makeTemplate(ostream &out);
        virtual void toSource(ostream &out, int withAccess = 0,
        int newType = 0);
        virtual void fromSource(istream &in, char *accessSpec = NULL);

};
```

```
///////////////////////////////////////////////////////////////////
// Author        : David Brumbaugh
// Class Name    : ClassDefinition
// Creation Date : 7/10/92
// Catagories    : Model
// Purpose       : Defines a C++ Class, this model will be used for a
// series of OO Case Tools.
//
// Major Public Methods:
//        ClassDefinition: Constructor
//      fromSource: Reads source file and builds class definition
//      toSource : Builds class defintion as in a header file
//      makeTemplate : Builds empty function descriptions and static data
//                     declarations for this class.
//
// Major Data Items:
//      name: Class name
//      ancestors: List of ancestors' names and their access specs
//      members: List of class members
//      commentSource: stream from which to draw comment templates
//      optionFlags: User preferences on how to use class
///////////////////////////////////////////////////////////////////

const int maxAncestors = 5; // Quintuple inheritance is enough for now
struct AncestorSpec
{
    char baseSpecifier[20]; // public, private, virtual ...
    IdString name; // Class name of ancestor
};

typedef BI_ArrayAsVector<ClassMemberDefinition *> MemberList;
const unsigned ExpandInline = 0x0001, UseComments = 0x002;

class ClassDefinition
{
    private: // The "private" keyword is redundant, but included for clarity
        int forwardDeclaration; // TRUE if this is not really a class but a
                                // forward declartion
        static int noInstances; // We're keeping track of the number of
                                // Instances of this class for debugging
                                // purposes.
    protected:
        virtual int getClassName(istream &in);
        virtual void getAncestors(istream &in);
        virtual void getMembers(istream &in);
        virtual void putComment(ostream &out,const char *what,
        const char *id);
        IdString name;
        AncestorSpec ancestors[maxAncestors];
        int numAncestors;
        MemberList members;
        istream *commentSource;
        // OptionFlags
        unsigned expandInline : 1, // Exapand inline functions in source?
```

```
            useComments: 1;

    public:
        ClassDefinition(istream *in = NULL, unsigned options = 0,
        char *commentFile = NULL);
        virtual void fromSource(istream &in);
        virtual void toSource(ostream &out);
        virtual void makeTemplate(ostream &out);
        virtual    ~ClassDefinition();
};


#endif


/////////////////////////////////////////////////////////////////////
// Listing   : 6-2
// Filename  : ClsDfn.CPP
// Purpose   : Class definition classes
/////////////////////////////////////////////////////////////////////

#include "DEFNFILE.H"
#include <STDLIB.H>
#include <utility.h> // C functions that I still like to use
#include <string.h>
#include <strstrea.h>
#include <stdio.h>

/* = = = = = = = = = ClassMemberDefinition Data   = = = = = = = = = = = = */

IdString ClassMemberDefinition::lastTypeSpec;
int ClassMemberDefinition::numInstances = 0;

/* = = = = = = = = = ClassMemberDefinition methods  = = = = = = = = = = = */
/////////////////////////////////////////////////////////////////////
// Author: David Brumbaugh
// Method Name: ClassMemberDefinition
// Creation Date: 7/13/92
// Purpose: Constructor, initialize data members;
//
// Return Value: None
// Parameters:
//   Type                 Name
     Purpose/Description                 Default Value
//   char *               className    Name of the class to        None
//                                      which the member belongs
/////////////////////////////////////////////////////////////////////


ClassMemberDefinition::ClassMemberDefinition(char *className)
{
  type = unknown;
    memset(ptrSpec,0,sizeof(ptrSpec));
    memset(name,0,sizeof(name));
```

```
    memset(accessSpecifier,0,sizeof(accessSpecifier));
    memset(typeSpecifiers,0,sizeof(typeSpecifiers));
    strcpy(owningClass,className);
    // ====> For debugging only <==== \\
            ++numInstances;
    // ============================== \\
}


//////////////////////////////////////////////////////////////////////
// Author: David Brumbaugh
// Method Name: operator <
// Creation Date:  7/12/92
// Purpose: For sorting ClassMemberDefinitions.
//            BIDS requires a < operator for any sorted contained classes.
//            The sort order for members is:
//                accessSpecifier,typeSpecifiers
//         That allows similar members to be grouped together.
//
// Return Value: 1 or 0 depending on the condition
// Parameters:
//  Type                      Name      Purpose/Description      Default Value
//  ClassMemberDefinition & c           Value being compared     None
//////////////////////////////////////////////////////////////////////

ClassMemberDefinition::operator < (ClassMemberDefinition &c)
{
    int cmp = strcmp(accessSpecifier,c.accessSpecifier);
    // This is so we can group private, protected and public members
    // together.
    if (cmp < 0)
        return 1;
    else if (cmp == 0)
    {
        cmp = strcmp(typeSpecifiers,c.typeSpecifiers);
        return (cmp < 0);
    }
    else
        return 0;
}

//////////////////////////////////////////////////////////////////////
// Author: David Brumbaugh
// Method Name: operator ==
// Creation Date:  7/12/92
// Purpose: For comparing ClassMemberDefinitions. BIDS requires a ==
// operator for most contained classes.
//    If a class member has the same name it matches. This will be overloaded
//  in the MemberFunctionDefn class.
//
// Return Value: 0 or Non-0
// Parameters:
//  Type                      Name      Purpose/Description      Default Value
//  ClassMemberDefinition &    c        Value being compared     None
```

```
//////////////////////////////////////////////////////////////////////

ClassMemberDefinition::operator == (ClassMemberDefinition &c) const
{
    if (this == &c) // This really isn't necessary, but it shows how
        return 1;   // to use "this". Obviously if the address of "c" and
                    // "this" match we have the same object. Therefore,
                    // they must be equal. So, we return non-zero.
    if (type == c.type)
        return(strcmp(name,c.name) == 0);
    else
        return(0);
}
//////////////////////////////////////////////////////////////////////
// Author: David Brumbaugh
// Method Name: movePtrSpec
// Creation Date: 8/14/92
// Purpose: Move the pointer specifers from the name to type specifers
//
// Return Value: void
// Parameters: None
//////////////////////////////////////////////////////////////////////


void ClassMemberDefinition::movePtrSpec()
{
    //The pointer and reference characters are part of the type.
    int len = strlen(ptrSpec);
    while (name[0] == '*' || name[0] == '&')
    {
        ptrSpec[len++] = name[0];
        rmvstr(name,1);
    }

    // But we're keeping the pointer specs seperately
    char *check;
    while ((check = strchr(typeSpecifiers,'*')) != NULL ||
     (check = strchr(typeSpecifiers,'&')) != NULL)
    {
        ptrSpec[len++] = *check;
        rmvstr(check,1);
    }


}

/* = = = = = = = = = =  MemberFunctionDefn methods  = = = = = = = = = = = */
//////////////////////////////////////////////////////////////////////
// Author: David Brumbaugh
// Method Name: MemberFunctionDefinition
// Creation Date: 7/13/92
// Purpose: Constructor
//
// Return Value:
// Parameters:
```

```
//   Type              Name            Purpose/Description        Default Value
//   char *            className       Name of owning class       None
//
//   istream *         in              Source code stream from    NULL
//                                     which to build definition.
//
//   int               expInline       If non-0, expand inline    0
//                                     w code in source file
////////////////////////////////////////////////////////////////////////

MemberFunctionDefinition::MemberFunctionDefinition(char *className,
istream *in, char *accessSpec,int expInline):ClassMemberDefinition(className)
{
    type = isFunction;
    expandInline = expInline;
    num_params = 0;
    memset(parameters,0,sizeof(parameters));
    memset(suffix,0,sizeof(suffix));
    if (in)
        fromSource(*in,accessSpec);
}


////////////////////////////////////////////////////////////////////////
// Author: David Brumbaugh
// Method Name: operator ==
// Creation Date:  7/12/92
// Purpose: For comparing ClassMemberDefinitions. BIDS requires a ==
// operator for most contained classes.
//    If a class member has the same name it matches. This will be overloaded
//  in the MemberFunctionDefn class.
//
// Return Value: 0 or Non-0
// Parameters:
//  Type                          Name     Purpose/Description        Default Value
//  ClassMemberDefinition &        c        Value being compared
None
////////////////////////////////////////////////////////////////////////

MemberFunctionDefinition::operator == (ClassMemberDefinition &c) const
{
    if (type == c.isA()) //Both must be member functions
    {
        // Now we'll compare apples and apples
        MemberFunctionDefinition *mfd = (MemberFunctionDefinition *) &c;
        if (strcmp(name,mfd->name) == 0)
        {
            if (strcmp(typeSpecifiers,mfd->typeSpecifiers) == 0)
            {
                if (num_params == mfd->num_params)
                {
                    if (memcmp(parameters,mfd->parameters,sizeof(parameters)))
                        return 1;
                }
            }
        }
```

```
        }
    }
    return 0;
}

//////////////////////////////////////////////////////////////////////////
// Author: David Brumbaugh
// Method Name: makeTemplate
// Creation Date: 7/13/92
// Purpose: Creates a set of empty functions for the class.
// When it is called it will create the following template on the output
// stream:
//          typeSpecifications owningClass::name(parameters)
//          {
//          }
//
// Return Value: none
// Parameters:
//   Type             Name            Purpose/Description    Default Value
//   ostream &        out             Where the template is  None
//                                    going.
//////////////////////////////////////////////////////////////////////////

void MemberFunctionDefinition::makeTemplate(ostream &out)
{
    // Do we make templates out of this functions definition?
    if ( ! shouldMakeTemplate())
    {
        return;
    }

    // The keyword "virtual" does not go into the templates
    IdString typeSpec;
    strcpy(typeSpec,typeSpecifiers);
    char *c;
    if ((c = strstr(typeSpec,"virtual")) != NULL)
        rmvstr(c,7); // Remove the "virtual" from the type

    // Neither does the keyword "static"
    if ((c = strstr(typeSpec,"static")) != NULL)
        rmvstr(c,6); // Remove the "static" from the type

    // Put the template on the stream;
    out << skpblk(trim(typeSpec)) << ' ' << ptrSpec << owningClass;
    out << "::" << name << '(';
    for(int i = 0; i < num_params; ++i)
    {
        out << trim(parameters[i].typeSpecifiers) << ' ';
        out << parameters[i].name;
        if (i != num_params -1)
            out << ',';
    }
    out << ')' << "\n{\n}\n\n";

}
```

```
//////////////////////////////////////////////////////////////////////
// Author: David Brumbaugh
// Method Name: toSource
// Creation Date: 7/14/92
// Purpose: Creates a declaration within the class definition.
// When it is called it will create the following template on the output
// stream:
//        [accessSpecifier:]
//         typeSpecifications name(parameters);
//
// Return Value: none
// Parameters:
//  Type            Name            Purpose/Description    Default Value
//  ostream &       out             Where the prototype is None
//                                  going.
//
//  int             withAccess      Will include the access 0 (false)
//                                  specifiation
//  int             newType         If non-0, this data    0
//                                  type is different that
//                                  the previous one.
//////////////////////////////////////////////////////////////////////


void MemberFunctionDefinition::toSource(ostream &out, int withAccess,
int newType)
{
    if (withAccess)
        out << accessSpecifier << ":\n";

    if (newType)
        out << '\t' << skpblk(trim(typeSpecifiers));

    out << ' ';
    if (strlen(ptrSpec))
        out << ptrSpec;
    out << name << '(';
    for(int i = 0; i < num_params; ++i)
    {
        out << trim(parameters[i].typeSpecifiers) << ptrSpec;
        if (strlen(ptrSpec))
            out << ' ';
        out << parameters[i].name;
        if (strlen(parameters[i].defaultValue))
            out << " = " << parameters[i].defaultValue;
        if (i != num_params -1)
            out << ',';
    }
    out << ")" << suffix << '\n';
}


//////////////////////////////////////////////////////////////////////
// Author: David Brumbaugh
// Method Name: shouldMakeTemplate
```

```
// Creation Date: 7/14/92
// Purpose: Returns non-0 if we should generate a template for this function.
//
// Return Value: 0 or Non-0
// Parameters: None
//////////////////////////////////////////////////////////////////////////

MemberFunctionDefinition::shouldMakeTemplate()
{
    // Check inline sometimes people like to put those in headers
    if (! expandInline)
        if (strstr(typeSpecifiers,"inline"))
            return 0;

    // Check the suffix:
        // We don't want to make templates for pure virtual functions
    if (strchr(suffix,'0'))
        return 0;
        // We don't want functions already expanded in the header either
    if (strchr(suffix, '{'))
        return 0;
    return 1;
}


//////////////////////////////////////////////////////////////////////////
// Author: David Brumbaugh
// Method Name: fromSource
// Creation Date: 7/14/92
// Purpose: Fills data members from "in", where "in" is a stream
// of source code such as that found in a class definintion. Assumes the
// following:
//          1. The stream starts at the begining of function definition
//          2. The source code is syntactically correct
//          3. All comments have been removed
//          4. The stream contains only the function defintion
//
//
// Return Value: None
// Parameters:
// Type           Name        Purpose/Description       Default Value
// istream &      in          Stream which contains     None
//                            the defintion
// char *         accessSpec  access specifier          NULL (ie,"private")
//////////////////////////////////////////////////////////////////////////

void MemberFunctionDefinition::fromSource(istream &in, char *accessSpec)
{
    in.unsetf(ios::skipws);
    if (! accessSpec)
        strcpy(accessSpecifier,"private");
    else
        strcpy(accessSpecifier,accessSpec);
    makeTypeAndName(in);
    makeParamList(in);
```

```
    makeSuffix(in);
}


//////////////////////////////////////////////////////////////////////
// Author: David Brumbaugh
// Method Name: makeTypeAndName
// Creation Date: 7/16/92
// Purpose: Fills the type and name data members from the input stream
// Supports "fromSource"
//
// Return Value: None
// Parameters:
//   Type         Name        Purpose/Description       Default Value
//   istream &    in          Stream which contains     None
//                            the defintion
//////////////////////////////////////////////////////////////////////

void MemberFunctionDefinition::makeTypeAndName(istream &in)
{
    int done = 0;
    IdString work, prev;
    char typeNameBuff[100];
    //Enough for a full type and several modifiers
    memset(typeNameBuff,0,sizeof(typeNameBuff));
    char *check;
    prev[0] = '\0';
    name[0] = '\0';
    in.getline(typeNameBuff,sizeof(typeNameBuff) ,'('); // Read up to paren
    istrstream  typeNameIn(typeNameBuff); //Streams are easier to work with
    do
    {
        typeNameIn >> work >> ws; // Trim the trailing white space
        if (typeNameIn.eof())
            done = 1;
        if (strlen(prev)) // Have we got any type info yet?
        {
            if ( strcmp(prev,"operator") != 0 )
            {
                strcat(typeSpecifiers,prev);
                strcat(typeSpecifiers," ");
            }
            else
                strcpy(name,prev);
        }
        strcpy(prev,work); // Save work, it may be a type spec or name
        if (done)
        {
            if (strlen(typeSpecifiers))
                strcpy(lastTypeSpec,typeSpecifiers);
            else
                strcpy(typeSpecifiers,lastTypeSpec);
            strcat(name,prev); // The last string is usually the name
        }
    } while (! done);
```

```
    movePtrSpec(); // Fix the pointer specifiers if they exist

}

//////////////////////////////////////////////////////////////////////
// Author: David Brumbaugh
// Method Name: makeParamList
// Creation Date: 7/16/92
// Purpose: Fills parameter list from "in"
//
// Return Value: None
// Parameters:
// Type          Name        Purpose/Description        Default Value
// istream &     in          Stream which contains      None
//                           the definition
//
//////////////////////////////////////////////////////////////////////

void MemberFunctionDefinition::makeParamList(istream &in)
{
    int done = 0, level = 0, i = 0;
    char work[100], prev[100];
    char paramBuffer[512], // Surely this will be enough
        *check; // Check for value in string with this one
    prev[0] = '\0';
    if (in.peek() == '(')
        in.ignore(); // Skip the initial open paren
    ++level;
    memset(paramBuffer,'\0',sizeof(paramBuffer));
    in >> ws;
    do
    {
        in >> paramBuffer[i];
        if (paramBuffer[i] == '(')
            ++level;
        else if (paramBuffer[i] == ')')
            —level;
        if (level == 0)
            paramBuffer[i] = '\0';
        ++i;
    } while(level > 0);

    trim(paramBuffer);
    istrstream  params(paramBuffer);
    do
    {
        if (! params.getline(work,sizeof(work),','))
        {
            done = 1;
            break;
        }
        if ((check = strchr(work,'=')) != NULL) //Do we have a default value?
        {
            *check = '\0';
```

```
            ++check;
            strcpy(parameters[num_params].defaultValue,skpblk(trim(check)));
        }
        check = strtok(work," "); // get the first token
        if (check)
            strcpy(prev,check);

        // The last word we get is probably the name
        // All the others probably type specs.
        while ((check = strtok(NULL," ")) != NULL)
        {
            strcat(parameters[num_params].typeSpecifiers,prev);
            strcat(parameters[num_params].typeSpecifiers," ");
            strcpy(prev,check);
        }
        // However, if there is only one word in the parameter list,
        // it's a type spec. Since we're not keeping track of all types,
        // (This is only a pseudo-parser, not a full compiler.) we'll
        // assume that the last word is the name.
        // We also need to move the pointer indicators over to the "type"
        int ptrI = 0;
        int len = strlen(parameters[num_params].typeSpecifiers);
        while (prev[ptrI] == '*' || prev[ptrI] == '&')
        {
            parameters[num_params].typeSpecifiers[len++] = prev[ptrI++];
            parameters[num_params].typeSpecifiers[len] = '\0';
        }
        strcpy(parameters[num_params++].name,&prev[ptrI]);

    } while (! done);
}
///////////////////////////////////////////////////////////////////////
// Author: David Brumbaugh
// Method Name: makeSuffix
// Creation Date: 7/20/92
// Purpose: Fills suffix from "in"
//    (Things like "= 0", "const", "{.." etc.
//
// Return Value: None
// Parameters:
//  Type            Name        Purpose/Description      Default Value
//  istream &       in          Stream which contains    None
//                              the definition
//
///////////////////////////////////////////////////////////////////////

void MemberFunctionDefinition::makeSuffix(istream &in)
{
    int done = 0;
    char work[512];
    work[0] = 0;
    in >> ws;
    do
    {
```

```
        in >> work >> ws;
        if (in.eof())
            done = 1;
        if (work[0] == ';' || work[0] == '{' )
        {
            done = 1;
            if (work[0] == '{')
            {
                strcpy(suffix, "{ }");
                // We're not going to keep all the inline code
            }
            // If we've come to a semi colon or '{' we're done with this type
            lastTypeSpec[0] = 0;
        }
        else
        {
            strcat(suffix,trim(work));
            strcat(suffix," ");
        }
        if (done && ! strchr(suffix,'{') && ! strchr(suffix,';'))
            strcat(suffix,";");
    } while( ! done);
}


/* = = = = = = = = = = = DataMemberDefinition Methods = = = = = = = = = */

//////////////////////////////////////////////////////////////////////
// Author: David Brumbaugh
// Method Name: DataMemberDefinition
// Creation Date: 7/20/92
// Purpose: Constructor
//
// Return Value:
// Parameters:
// Type            Name          Purpose/Description      Default Value
// char *          className      Class to which this     None
//                                member belongs
// istream *       in             Source of data          NULL
//////////////////////////////////////////////////////////////////////

DataMemberDefinition::DataMemberDefinition(char *className, istream *in,
char *accessSpec):ClassMemberDefinition(className)
{
    type = isData;
    if (in)
        fromSource(*in,accessSpec);
}

//////////////////////////////////////////////////////////////////////
// Author: David Brumbaugh
// Method Name: shouldMakeTemplate
// Creation Date: 7/20/92
// Purpose: Return true if this data member should go into the class's
```

```
// source code template. In this case, only "static" members should
// go into the function.
//
// Return Value: 1 or 0
// Parameters: None
//
/////////////////////////////////////////////////////////////////////
DataMemberDefinition::shouldMakeTemplate()
{
    if (strstr(typeSpecifiers,"static"))
        return 1;
    else
        return 0;
}


/////////////////////////////////////////////////////////////////////
// Author: David Brumbaugh
// Method Name: makeTemplate
// Creation Date: 7/20/92
// Purpose: Create data member defintion templates
//
// Return Value: none
// Parameters:
// Type         Name          Purpose/Description       Default Value
// ostream &    out           Where to send template
/////////////////////////////////////////////////////////////////////

void DataMemberDefinition::makeTemplate(ostream &out)
{
   if (shouldMakeTemplate())
   {
       IdString typeSpec;
       strcpy(typeSpec,typeSpecifiers);
       rmvstr(strstr(typeSpec,"static"),6);
       out << skpblk(typeSpec) << ptrSpec << ' ' << owningClass;
       out << "::" << name << "\n";
   }
}


/////////////////////////////////////////////////////////////////////
// Author: David Brumbaugh
// Method Name: fromSource
// Creation Date: 7/20/92
// Purpose: Fills data members from "in", where "in" is a stream
// of source code such as that found in a class definintion. Assumes the
// following:
//         1. The stream starts at the begining of a data definition
//         2. The source code is syntactically correct
//         3. All comments have been removed
//         4. The stream contains only the data definition
//
// Return Value: None
// Parameters:
// Type          Name          Purpose/Description        Default Value
// istream &     in            Source stream              None
```

```
//    char *          accessSpec     access specifier          NULL (ie,"private")
///////////////////////////////////////////////////////////////////

void DataMemberDefinition::fromSource(istream &in, char *accessSpec)
{
    int done = 0;
    char c, *check;
    int i = 0;
    IdString work, prev;
    prev[0] = '\0';
    if (accessSpec)
        strcpy(accessSpecifier,accessSpec);
    else
        strcpy(accessSpecifier,"private");

    in.unsetf(ios::skipws);
    in >> ws;
    do
    {
        in >> c;
        if (c == ';' || c == ',' || in.eof())
        {
            work[i] = '\0';
            i = 0;
            done = 1;
            in >> ws; //Skip the white space
        }
        else if (! isspace(c))
            work[i++] = c;
        else // We have a space
        {
            work[i] = '\0';
            i = 0;
            in >> ws; // Get rid of the rest of the white space;
            if (strlen(prev) && !done) // Have we got any type info yet?
            {
                strcat(typeSpecifiers,prev);
                strcat(typeSpecifiers," ");
            }
            strcpy(prev,work); // Save work, it may be a type spec or name
        }
        if (done)
        {
            if (strlen(typeSpecifiers))
                strcpy(lastTypeSpec,typeSpecifiers);
            else
                strcpy(typeSpecifiers,lastTypeSpec);
            strcpy(name,prev); // The last string is the name
        }
    } while (! done);

    movePtrSpec(); // Fix up the pointer specifier if it exists

}
```

```
///////////////////////////////////////////////////////////////////////
// Author: David Brumbaugh
// Method Name: toSource
// Creation Date: 7/20/92
// Purpose: Creates data member definitions within class definition
//
// Return Value: None
// Parameters:
//  Type           Name        Purpose/Description              Default Value
//  ostream &      out         Where to write the data          None
//  int                        withAccess If non-0 include access  0
//                             specifier in source
//  int            newType     If non-0, this data              0
//                             type is different that
//                             the previous one.
///////////////////////////////////////////////////////////////////////

void DataMemberDefinition::toSource(ostream &out, int withAccess, int newType)
{
    if (withAccess)
        out << accessSpecifier << ":\n";
    if (newType)
        out << '\t' << skpblk(typeSpecifiers) << ' ';
    out << ptrSpec << name;
}
/* = = = = = = = = = = = ClassDefinition Methods = = = = = = = = = = = = */
///////////////////////////////////////////////////////////////////////
// Author: David Brumbaugh
// Method Name: ClassDefinition
// Creation Date: 7/22/92
// Purpose: Constructor
//
// Return Value: None
// Parameters:
//  Type         Name         Purpose/Description              Default Value
//  istream *    in           Class source code ie:            NULL
//                            class   <name>:
//                            In stream starts here^
//  unsigned     options      Flags for how to build class     0
//                            Valid values:
//                            ExpandInline
//                            UseComment
//  char *    CommentFile  File name of comment template NULL
///////////////////////////////////////////////////////////////////////

ClassDefinition::ClassDefinition(istream *in, unsigned options,
char *commentFile):members(5,0,5),numAncestors(0)
{
    expandInline = options & ExpandInline ? 1 : 0;
    useComments = options & UseComments ? 1 : 0;
    forwardDeclaration = 0;
    memset(ancestors,'\0',sizeof(ancestors));

    IdString look;
```

```
    if (commentFile)
        commentSource = new ifstream(commentFile);
    else
        commentSource = NULL;

    if (in)
    {

        fromSource(*in);
    }
}

//////////////////////////////////////////////////////////////////
// Author: David Brumbaugh
// Method Name: fromSource
// Creation Date: 7/20/92
// Purpose: Fills class definition from "in", where "in" is a stream
// of source code such as that found in a class definintion. Assumes the
// following:
//          1. The stream starts at the begining of a data definition
//          2. The source code is syntactically correct
//          3. All comments have been removed
//
// Return Value: None
// Parameters:
//   Type          Name           Purpose/Description       Default Value
//   istream &     in             Source stream             None
//////////////////////////////////////////////////////////////////

void ClassDefinition::fromSource(istream &in)
{
    in.unsetf(ios::skipws); // Don't automatically skip the whitespace
    if (getClassName(in))
        getAncestors(in);
    if (forwardDeclaration)
        return;
    getMembers(in);
}

//////////////////////////////////////////////////////////////////
// Author: David Brumbaugh
// Method Name: getClassName
// Creation Date: 7/22/92
// Purpose: Reads class name from stream. Leaves the stream in postion to
// read ancestors.
//
// Return Value: Non 0 if it has ancestors
// Parameters:
//   Type          Name           Purpose/Description       Default Value
//   istream &     in             Class source              None
//////////////////////////////////////////////////////////////////

int ClassDefinition::getClassName(istream &in)
{
```

```
char *tmpName = tmpnam(NULL); // Open a temporary work file
fstream temp(tmpName, ios::in | ios::trunc | ios::out);

in >> ws; // Skip passed all the initial white space
char c;

while (in >> c)
{   // The class name is the first token before the ':' or '{'
    if (c != ':' && c != '{' && c != ';')
        temp << c;
    else
        break;
}
if (c == ';')
{
    forwardDeclaration = 1;
}
IdString work;
temp.seekg(0L,ios::beg);
do
{   // Skip through to the last token
    temp >> work >> ws;
} while ( ! temp.eof());

strcpy(name, work);
temp.rdbuf()->close();
remove(tmpName);
return (c == ':');  // If our last character was a colon, we need to read
                    // ancestsors

}

//////////////////////////////////////////////////////////////////////////
// Author: David Brumbaugh
// Method Name: getAncestors
// Creation Date: 7-23-92
// Purpose: Read the ancestor list from the input stream
//
// Return Value: none
// Parameters:
// Type          Name       Purpose/Description              Default Value
// istream &     in         Stream containing class definition   None
//////////////////////////////////////////////////////////////////////////

void ClassDefinition::getAncestors(istream &in)
{
    char *validBaseSpecs[] = { "virtual","public","private","protected",0 };


    in >> ws; // Skip the initial white space
    IdString work;
    int i = 0, done = 0;
    do
    {
```

```
        in >> work[i];
        if ( isspace(work[i]))
        {
            work[i] = '\0';
            i = 0;
            if (in_list(work,validBaseSpecs) > -1)
            {
                strcat(ancestors[numAncestors].baseSpecifier,work);
                strcat(ancestors[numAncestors].baseSpecifier," ");
            }
            else // If it's not a base specifer it must be a base class
            {
                strcpy(ancestors[numAncestors++].name,work);
            }
            in >> ws; // Skip the rest of the white space
        }
        else if (work[i] == ',' || work[i] == '{' )
        {
            done = (work[i] == '{');
            work[i] = '\0';
            i = 0;
            if (strlen(work))
                strcpy(ancestors[numAncestors++].name,work);
        }
        else
            ++i;
    } while (! done && ! in.eof());

}

//////////////////////////////////////////////////////////////////
// Author: David Brumbaugh
// Method Name: getMembers
// Creation Date: 7/26/92
// Purpose: Create member list
//
// Return Value: None
// Parameters:
// Type            Name           Purpose/Description      Default Value
// istream &       in             Member source            None
//////////////////////////////////////////////////////////////////

void ClassDefinition::getMembers(istream &in)
{
    char *tmpName = tmpnam(NULL); // Open a temporary work file
    fstream temp(tmpName, ios::in | ios::trunc | ios::out);
    char c;
    memberTypes curMember;
    IdString accessSpecifier;
    char work[512];
    int i = 0;
    char *validAccessSpecs[] = {"private","public","protected",'\0'};

    strcpy(accessSpecifier,"private"); // Default specifier
```

```
in >> ws; // Skip passed all the initial white space
do
{
    curMember = isData; // Assume it's a data member
    while (in >> c)
    {
        if (c == '}') // All done?
            break;
        if ( c == ':')
        {   // We've been reading an access specifier
            work[i] = '\0'; i = 0;
            in >> ws;
            if (in_list(skpblk(trim(work)),validAccessSpecs) != -1)
                strcpy(accessSpecifier,work);
        }
        else if (c != ';' && c != '{' && c != ',')
        { // The declararion ends with a ; or {  or ,
            if (c == '(')
            {
                curMember = isFunction;
                // Pick up all the parameters
                int level = 1;
                do
                {
                    work[i++] = c;
                    in >> c;
                    if (c == ')')
                        —level;
                    else if (c == '(')
                        ++level;
                } while( level > 0);
            }
            // temp << c;
            work[i++] = c; // Build a word in the working buffer
        }
        else
        { // We've got a whole "word" to remember
            work[i] = '\0';
            temp << work << ' ';
            work[0] = '\0'; i = 0;
            in >> ws; // Skip the white space
            temp << c; // Put the declaration terminator into temp
            if ( c == '{')
            {   // Let's get to the end of the inline function
                int level = 1;
                while ( level > 0)
                {
                    in >> c >> ws;
                    if (c == '{')
                        ++level;
                    else if (c == '}')
                        —level;
                }
                if (c == '}') // We don't want to terminate the loop
```

```
                          c = 0;
                }
            break; // We're ready to build the member
        }
    }
    if (c != '}')
    {
        temp.seekg(OL,ios::beg); // Rewind the file for member declarations
        if (curMember == isFunction)
            members.add(new MemberFunctionDefinition(name,&temp,
            accessSpecifier,expandInline));
        else
        {
            members.add(new DataMemberDefinition(name,&temp,
            accessSpecifier));
        }
        in >> ws; // Skip the white space to the next token
        temp.close(); // Clean up the temp file and start over
        temp.open(tmpName,ios::in | ios::out | ios::trunc);
    }
    } while(c != '}');
    temp.close();
    remove(tmpName);
}

////////////////////////////////////////////////////////////////////
// Author: David Brumbaugh
// Method Name: toSource
// Creation Date: 7/26/92
// Purpose: Creates a source description of class
//
// Return Value: None
// Parameters:
//   Type          Name          Purpose/Description      Default Value
//   ostream &      out           Where to put the source  None
////////////////////////////////////////////////////////////////////

void ClassDefinition::toSource(ostream &out)
{
    char c;
    char currAccessSpec[12], currTypeSpec[40];

    putComment(out,"Class:",name);
    out << "class" << ' ' << name << ' ';
    if (numAncestors)
    {
        out  << ':' << ' ';
        for (int i = 0; i < numAncestors; ++i)
        {
            out << ancestors[i].baseSpecifier << ' ' <<
            ancestors[i].name << ' ';
            if (i == (numAncestors - 1))
                out << "\n{\n";
            else
```

```
                            out << ", ";
              }
      }
      currAccessSpec[0] = '\0';
      currTypeSpec[0] = '\0';
      memberTypes lastMember = unknown;

      int newAccessSpec = 0, newTypeSpec = 0;
      for ( int i = 0; i < members.getItemsInContainer(); ++i)
      {
          if (strcmp(currAccessSpec,members[i]->getAccessSpec()))
          {
              strcpy(currAccessSpec,members[i]->getAccessSpec());
              newAccessSpec = 1;
          }
          if (strcmp(currTypeSpec,members[i]->getTypeSpec()))
          {
              strcpy(currTypeSpec,members[i]->getTypeSpec());
              newTypeSpec = 1;
          }

          if (lastMember == isData && newTypeSpec)
              out << ";\n";
          else if (lastMember == isData)
              out << ',';
          members[i]->toSource(out, newAccessSpec, newTypeSpec);
          newAccessSpec = 0;
          newTypeSpec = 0;
          lastMember = members[i]->isA();
      }
      out << "\n};\n";

}

////////////////////////////////////////////////////////////////////////
// Author: David Brumbaugh
// Method Name: putComment
// Creation Date: 7/27/92
// Purpose: Puts the comment template before the class or method
//
// Return Value: void
// Parameters:
//   Type           Name       Purpose/Description      Default Value
//   ostream &      out        Target for comment
////////////////////////////////////////////////////////////////////////

void ClassDefinition::putComment(ostream &out, const char *what,
const char *id)
{
    char c;
    if (! useComments)
      return;
    out << "//";
    for (int i = 0; i < 76; ++i)
```

```
            out << '/';
        out << '\n';
        out << "// " << what << ' ' << id << '\n';
        if (commentSource)
        {
            do
            {
                *commentSource >> c;
                out << c;
            } while(! commentSource->eof() );
            commentSource->clear();
            commentSource->seekg(0L,ios::beg);
        }
        out << "//";
        for (i = 0; i < 76; ++i)
            out << '/';
        out << '\n';
    }


    ////////////////////////////////////////////////////////////////////////
    // Author: David Brumbaugh
    // Method Name: makeTemplate
    // Creation Date: 7/27/92
    // Purpose: Create a source file with empty functions and static data
    // declaration for this class
    //
    // Return Value: None
    // Parameters:
    // Type           Name        Purpose/Description        Default Value
    // ostream &      out         Target for source code     None
    ////////////////////////////////////////////////////////////////////////

    void ClassDefinition::makeTemplate(ostream &out)
    {
        if (forwardDeclaration)
            return;
        putComment(out,"Source For Class:",name);
        for ( int i = 0; i < members.getItemsInContainer(); ++i)
        {
            if (members[i]->isA() == isFunction &&
                members[i]->shouldMakeTemplate())
                putComment(out,"Method: ", members[i]->getName());
            members[i]->makeTemplate(out);
        }
    }


    ////////////////////////////////////////////////////////////////////////
    // Author: David Brumbaugh
    // Method Name: ~ClassDefinition
    // Creation Date: 7/27/92
    // Purpose: Destructor
    //
    // Return Value:  None
    // Parameters: None
```

```
//
///////////////////////////////////////////////////////////////////////

ClassDefinition::~ClassDefinition()
{
    if (commentSource)
        delete commentSource;
    for (int i = 0; i < members.getItemsInContainer(); ++i)
        delete members[i];
        // Because members is a list of POINTERS and not a list of members,
        // we need to clean it up ourselves.
}


///////////////////////////////////////////////////////////////////////
// Listing  : 6-3
// Filename    : DEFNFILE.H
// Purpose   : Class definition file declaration
///////////////////////////////////////////////////////////////////////

///////////////////////////////////////////////////////////////////////
// Author        : David Brumbaugh
// Class Name   : ClassDefnFile
// Creation Date: 7/31/92
// Catagories    : Model
// Purpose       : Models the header file that contains classes
//                 Can build class templates for any or all classes
//                 defined in the header file.
//
// Major Public Methods:
//    ClassDefnFile       : Constructor
//    getIoStream          : Returns i/o stream
//  startOfClass        : Positions stream input stream at the start of a
//                        class
//  addClassToMake      : put class name into classes to have templates
//                        created
//  makeClassDefinitions : Create class selected definition templates.
//
// Major Data Items:
// classesToMake        : List of classes the user wants to have templates
//                        made of.
// anIoStream           : Stream with header information
//
// aClassDefinition     : A working variable for class definition
// classesInStream      : List of classes & offsets in the stream
// options              : Flags for specific class options for classes in
//                        the header.
///////////////////////////////////////////////////////////////////////
#ifndef DEFNFILE_H
#define DEFNFILE_H
#include "clsdfn.h"
#include <stdio.h>
#include <strng.h>
#include <string.h>
```

```
struct classOffset
{
    public:
        String className;
        long offset;

    operator ==(const classOffset &i) // Necessary for membership in BI_Array
    { return (className == i.className); }

};

typedef BI_ArrayAsVector<classOffset> ClassOSList;
typedef BI_ArrayAsVector<String> IdList;


class ClassDefnFile
{
    protected:
        unsigned options;
        iostream *anIoStream;
        IdList classesToMake;
        ClassDefinition *aClassDefinition;
        ClassOSList classesInStream;
        void init(istream &in, unsigned options);
        //Initialize the class: called by the constructors
        void removeComments(istream &in); // Remove comments from header
        void findClasses(); // Locate the start of each class in the iostream
        char *getClassName(); // Get the name of the class from the iostream
        char tempName[L_tmpnam];
        // We need to remember this, so we can delete the temporary file
    public:
        iostream *getIoStream() { return anIoStream; }
        void addClassToMake(const char *className);
        ClassDefnFile(const char *fileName, unsigned options = 0);
        ClassDefnFile(istream &inputStream, unsigned options = 0);
        int startOfClass(const char *className);
        void makeClassTemplates(char *outFileName, int makeAll = 0);
        void makeClassTemplates(ostream &out, int makeAll = 0);
        ~ClassDefnFile();
};

#endif


////////////////////////////////////////////////////////////////////////
// Listing  : 6-4
// Filename  : DEFNFILE.CPP
// Purpose   : Source code for ClassDefnClass
////////////////////////////////////////////////////////////////////////

#include "DEFNFILE.H"
#include <string.h>
#include <strstrea.h>
////////////////////////////////////////////////////////////////////////
```

```
// Author: David Brumbaugh
// Method Name: ClassDefnFile
// Creation Date: 8/5/92
// Purpose: Constructor
//
// Parameters:
//   Type        Name          Purpose/Description         Default Value
//   char *      fileName       Name of header file         None
//////////////////////////////////////////////////////////////////////////

ClassDefnFile::ClassDefnFile(const char *fileName, unsigned options):
classesToMake(10,0,10),classesInStream(10,0,10)
{
    ifstream in(fileName);
    init(in,options);
}
//////////////////////////////////////////////////////////////////////////
// Author: David Brumbaugh
// Method Name: ClassDefnFile
// Creation Date: 8/5/92
// Purpose: Constructor
//
// Parameters:
//   Type        Name       Purpose/Description         Default Value
//   istream &   in         Stream with class info      None
//////////////////////////////////////////////////////////////////////////

ClassDefnFile::ClassDefnFile(istream &inputStream,unsigned options):
classesToMake(10,0,10),classesInStream(10,0,10)
{
    init(inputStream,options);
}
//////////////////////////////////////////////////////////////////////////
// Author: David Brumbaugh
// Method Name:
// Creation Date:
// Purpose:
//
// Return Value:
// Parameters:
//   Type        Name          Purpose/Description         Default Value
//   char *      className      Name of classes to make     None
//////////////////////////////////////////////////////////////////////////

void ClassDefnFile::addClassToMake(const char *className)
{
    classesToMake.add(className);
}
//////////////////////////////////////////////////////////////////////////
// Author: David Brumbaugh
// Method Name: startOfClass
// Creation Date: 8/6/92
// Purpose: Locate a particular class within the working iostream
//
```

```
// Return Value: 1 if found, 0 if not
// Parameters:
//   Type        Name              Purpose/Description        Default Value
//   char *      className         Name of class to find      None
//                                 find the start of.
/////////////////////////////////////////////////////////////////////

int ClassDefnFile::startOfClass(const char *className)
{
    classOffset co;
    co.className = className;
    if (classesInStream.hasMember(co))
    {
        for (int i = 0; i < classesInStream.getItemsInContainer(); ++i)
            if (classesInStream[i].className == className)
            {
                // Set both the get and put pointers in the stream
                anIoStream->seekg(classesInStream[i].offset);
                anIoStream->seekp(classesInStream[i].offset);
                return 1;
            }
    }
    return 0;
}


/////////////////////////////////////////////////////////////////////
// Author: David Brumbaugh
// Method Name: removeComments
// Creation Date: 8/6/92
// Purpose: Removes comments from original input as it moves the rest
// of the file into anIoStream
//
// Return Value: None
// Parameters:
//   Type          Name         Purpose/Description        Default Value
//   istream &     in           Original input file        None
/////////////////////////////////////////////////////////////////////

void ClassDefnFile::removeComments(istream &in)
{
    char c, endChar;
    int inComment = 0;

    in.unsetf(ios::skipws);

    do
    {
        in >> c;
        if (c == '/')
        {
            if (in.peek() == '/')
            {
                endChar = '\n';
                inComment = 1;
```

```
                    }
                    else if (in.peek() == '*')
                    {
                        endChar = '*';
                        inComment = 1;
                    }
                    else
                        inComment = 0;

                    while(inComment)
                    {
                        in >> c;
                        if (c == endChar)
                        {
                            if (c == '\n')
                            {
                                inComment = 0;
                                c = ' ';
                            }
                            else if (in.peek() == '/')
                            {
                                in.ignore();
                                inComment = 0;
                                c = ' ';
                            }
                        }
                    }
                }
            *anIoStream << c;
        } while (! in.eof());
}


//////////////////////////////////////////////////////////////////////////
// Author: David Brumbaugh
// Method Name: makeClassTemplates
// Creation Date: 8/7/92
// Purpose: Create templates for selected classes in a header file
//
// Return Value: None
// Parameters:
//   Type       Name              Purpose/Description        Default Value
//   char *     outFileName       Name of destination        None
//   int        makeAll           If TRUE, make templates     0 (FALSE)
//                                for all the classes in
//                                in the file, otherwise
//                                make only those in the
//                                classesToMake list.
//////////////////////////////////////////////////////////////////////////

void ClassDefnFile::makeClassTemplates(char *outFileName, int makeAll)
{
    fstream outFile(outFileName, ios::in | ios::trunc | ios::out);
    makeClassTemplates(outFile,makeAll);
}
```

```
/////////////////////////////////////////////////////////////////////
// Author: David Brumbaugh
// Method Name: makeClassTemplates
// Creation Date: 8/8/92
// Purpose: See above
//
// Return Value: None
// Parameters:
//   Type            Name        Purpose/Description      Default Value
//   ostream &       out         Destinaiton of template  None
//   int             makeAll     If TRUE, make templates  0 (FALSE)
//                               for all the classes in
//                               in the file, otherwise
//                               make only those in the
//                               classesToMake list.
/////////////////////////////////////////////////////////////////////

void ClassDefnFile::makeClassTemplates(ostream &out, int makeAll)
{
    if (! makeAll)
    {
        for(int i = 0; i < classesToMake.getItemsInContainer(); ++i)
        {
            if (startOfClass(classesToMake[i]))
            {
                aClassDefinition = new ClassDefinition(anIoStream,options);
                aClassDefinition->makeTemplate(out);
                delete aClassDefinition;
            }
        }
    }
    else
    {
        for(int i = 0; i < classesInStream.getItemsInContainer(); ++i)
        {
            anIoStream->clear(); // Clear out the eof and other flags
            anIoStream->seekg(classesInStream[i].offset, ios::beg);
            anIoStream->seekp(classesInStream[i].offset, ios::beg);
            aClassDefinition = new ClassDefinition(anIoStream,options);
            aClassDefinition->makeTemplate(out);
            delete aClassDefinition;
        }

    }
}


/////////////////////////////////////////////////////////////////////
// Author: David Brumbaugh
// Method Name: init
// Creation Date: 8/5/92
// Purpose: Initialize the header file
//
// Return Value:  None
// Parameters:
```

```
//  Type         Name         Purpose/Description        Default Value
//  istream &    in           Input stream               None
//////////////////////////////////////////////////////////////////////

void ClassDefnFile::init(istream &in, unsigned opt)
{
    tmpnam(tempName);
    options = opt;
    anIoStream = new fstream(tempName, ios::in | ios::trunc | ios::out);
    removeComments(in);
    findClasses();
}


//////////////////////////////////////////////////////////////////////
// Author: David Brumbaugh
// Method Name: ~ClassDefnFile()
// Creation Date: 8/5/92
// Purpose: Destructor
//
//////////////////////////////////////////////////////////////////////

ClassDefnFile::~ClassDefnFile()
{
    delete anIoStream;
    remove(tempName);
}


//////////////////////////////////////////////////////////////////////
// Author: David Brumbaugh
// Method Name: findClasses
// Creation Date: 8/5/92
// Purpose: Identify classes and loctations within cleaned stream
//
// Return Value:  None
// Parameters: None
//////////////////////////////////////////////////////////////////////
void ClassDefnFile::findClasses()
{
    char work[256];
    classOffset co;
    long offset;

    anIoStream->seekg(0L);
    while (! anIoStream->eof())
    {
        *anIoStream >> ws >> work >> ws;
        if (strcmp(work,"class") == 0)
        {

            co.offset = anIoStream->tellg();
            co.className = getClassName();
            classesInStream.add(co);
        }
    }
}
```

```
//////////////////////////////////////////////////////////////////
// Author: David Brumbaugh
// Method Name: getClassName
// Creation Date: 8/8/92
// Purpose: Get the class name out of the io stream
//
// Return Value: Name of the class
// Parameters: None
//
//////////////////////////////////////////////////////////////////

char *ClassDefnFile::getClassName()
{
    char tmpBuff[512];
    static IdString name;

    strstream temp(tmpBuff, sizeof(tmpBuff), ios::in | ios::out);

    *anIoStream >> ws; // Skip passed all the initial white space
    char c;

    while (*anIoStream >> c)
    {   // The class name is the first token before the ':' or '{' or ';'
        if (c != ':' && c != '{' && c != ';')
            temp << c;
        else
            break;
    }

    IdString work;
    temp.seekg(0L,ios::beg);
    do
    {   // Skip through to the last token
        temp >> work >> ws;
    } while ( ! temp.eof());

    strcpy(name, work);

    return name;
}


//////////////////////////////////////////////////////////////////
// Listing  : 6-5
// Filename   : MAIN.CPP
// Purpose    : Main function for Class Function Template Application
//////////////////////////////////////////////////////////////////

#include <stdio.h>
#include <CTYPE.H>
#include "defnfile.h"
#include <stacks.h>
#include <strng.h>

static void showHelp()
```

```
{
    cout << "C<className | ALL> :\n";
    cout << "Specifiy Which Class to Make Template of or ALL classes\n\n";
    cout << "I : Expand Inline functions in the template\n\n";
    cout << "M[<commentFile>] : Put comments in the template\n\n";
    cout << "H<headerFile> : Specify which file to use as input\n\n";
    cout << "O<outputFile> : Specify destination for template\n";
}

void main(int argc, char **argv)
{
    if (argc < 2)
    {
        cout << "Usage:" << argv[0] << "{C<className | ALL>}\n";
        cout << "[I] [M<commentFile>] [H<headerFile>] [O<outputFile>]\n";
        cout << "Where:\n\n";
        showHelp();
        exit(0);
    }
    char inFile[80], outFile[80], work[80], commentFile[80],
    *cmmFile;
    unsigned useComments = 0, expandInline = 0, useAll = 0;
    BI_StackAsList<String> classStack;

    cmmFile = NULL;
    // OK, so the main driver is procedural, not object-oriented
    inFile[0] = '\0';
    for (int i=1; i < argc; ++i)
    {
        switch(toupper(argv[i][0]))
        {
            case 'O':
                strcpy(outFile,++argv[i]);
            break;
            case 'H':
                strcpy(inFile,++argv[i]);
            break;
            case 'I':
                expandInline = 1;
            break;
            case 'C':
                if (strcmpi(++argv[i],"ALL") == 0)
                    useAll = 1;
                else
                    classStack.push(argv[i]);
            break;
            case 'M':
                useComments = 1;
                ++argv[i];
                if (*argv[i])
                {
                    strcpy(commentFile,argv[i]);
                    cmmFile = commentFile;
                }
```

```
            break;
        case '?':
            showHelp();
        break;
        default:
            cout << "Usage:" << argv[0] << "{C<className | \"ALL\">}\n";
            cout << "[I] [H<headerFile>] [O<outputFile>]\n";
        }
    }

    unsigned optionFlags =
    (expandInline ? ExpandInline:0) | (useComments ? UseComments:0);

    ClassDefnFile *cd;
    if (strlen(inFile))
        cd = new ClassDefnFile(inFile, optionFlags);
    else
        cd = new ClassDefnFile(cin, optionFlags);

    if ( ! useAll)
        while (! classStack.isEmpty())
            cd->addClassToMake(classStack.pop());

    if (strlen(outFile))
        cd->makeClassTemplates(outFile,useAll,cmmFile);
    else
        cd->makeClassTemplates(cout,useAll,cmmFile);

    delete cd;
}


//////////////////////////////////////////////////////////////////////
// Listing  : 6-6
// Filename    : CH6-6
// Purpose     : Demonstrate overloading caveats in inheritance
//////////////////////////////////////////////////////////////////////
#include <iostreams.h>

/* =========================================
    This file will not compile properly.
    =========================================*/
class C1
{
    protected:
        int x;
    public:
        void setX(int x1) { x = x1; }
        virtual int foo(int y) { return y; }
};

class C2 : public C1
{
    public:
```

```cpp
        virtual int foo() { return x; }
};

void main()
{
    C2 c2;
    c2.setX(5);
    cout << c2.foo(10) << '\n';
}


//////////////////////////////////////////////////////////////////////
// Listing  : 6-7
// Filename    : CH6-7.CPP
// Purpose     : Demonstrate constructors and destructors in
//               single inheritance.
//////////////////////////////////////////////////////////////////////
#include <iostream.h>

class C1
{
    public:
        C1() { cout << "C1\n"; }
        ~C1() { cout << "~C1\n"; }
};

class C2: public C1
{
    public:
        C2() { cout << "C2\n"; }
        virtual ~C2() { cout << "~C2\n"; }
};

class C3: public C2
{
    public:
        C3() { cout << "C3\n"; }
        ~C3() { cout << "~C3\n"; }
};

void main()
{
    cout << "Start of Program\n";
    C3 c3;
    cout << "Creating C3 on C1*\n";
    C1 *c1 = new C3;
    cout << "Killing it\n";
    delete c1;
    cout << "Creating C3 on C2*\n";
    C2 *c2 = new C3;
    cout << "Killing it\n";
    delete c2;
    cout << "End of Program\n";
```

```
}
/* =========================================================================
                        Output From Above Program


Start of Program
C1
C2
C3
Creating C3 on C1*
C1
C2
C3
Killing it
~C1
Creating C3 on C2*
C1
C2
C3
Killing it
~C3
~C2
~C1
End of Program
~C3
~C2
~C1


============================================================================*/



//////////////////////////////////////////////////////////////////////
// Listing  : 6-8
// Filename   : CH6-8.CPP
// Purpose    : Demonstrate non-default of constructors in
//            single inheritance.
//////////////////////////////////////////////////////////////////////
#include <iostream.h>

class C1
{
    protected:
        int x;
    public:
        C1(int y) { x = y; cout << "\nC1\n"; }
};

class C2: C1
{
    public:
        C2():C1(2) { cout << "\nC2\n" << "x =" << x; }
};
```

```
void main()
{
    C2 c2;
}
/* ========================================================================
                    Output From Above Program

C1

C2
x =2



=========================================================================*/


///////////////////////////////////////////////////////////////////////
// Listing  : 6-9
// Filename  : CH6-9.CPP
// Purpose   : Demonstrate scope resolution operator in
//              single inheritance.
///////////////////////////////////////////////////////////////////////
#include <iostream.h>

class C1
{
    protected:
        int x;
    public:
        void showX() { cout << x << '\n'; }
        C1(int y) { x = y; cout << "C1\n"; }
};

class C2: public C1
{
    public:
        void showX() { cout << "overloaded" << '\n'; }
        C2():C1(2) { cout << "C2\n"; }
};


void main()
{
    C2 c2;
    c2.showX();
    c2.C1::showX();
}
/* ========================================================================
                    Output From Above Program

C1
C2
overloaded
2
```

```
===========================================================================*/


////////////////////////////////////////////////////////////////////
// Listing   : 6-10
// Filename  : CH6-10.CPP
// Purpose   : Show ambiguity problems in multipe inheritance with a
//             a common ancestor.
////////////////////////////////////////////////////////////////////
#include <iostream.h>
#include <string.h>

class C1
{
    protected:
        char childClass[10];
    public:
        virtual void showChildClass() { cout << childClass << '\n'; }
        C1(const char* y = "NONE")
        { strcpy(childClass,y);
        cout << "C1\n" << "Child Class = " << y << '\n'; }
};

class C2: public C1
{

    public:
        virtual void showChildClass() { cout << "overloaded in C2" << '\n'; }
        C2():C1("C2") { cout << "C2\n"; }
};

class C3: public C1
{
    public:
        virtual void showChildClass() { cout << "overloaded in C3" << '\n'; }
        C3():C1("C3") { cout << "C3\n"; }
};

class C4: public C2, public C3
{
    public:
        C4() { cout << "C4\n"; }
};

void main()
{
    C4 c4;

    c4.showChildClass();
//Error: Member is ambiguous: 'C2::showChildClass' and 'C3::showChildClass'

    c4.C1::showChildClass();
//Error: 'C1' is not a public base class of 'C4'
```

```
}
/* ==========================================================================
                            Output From Above Program


===========================================================================*/


//////////////////////////////////////////////////////////////////////
// Listing  : 6-11
// Filename   : CH6-11.CPP
// Purpose    : Show ambiguity resolution in multipe inheritance with a
//              a common ancestor.
//////////////////////////////////////////////////////////////////////
#include <iostream.h>
#include <string.h>

class C1
{
    protected:
        char childClass[10];
    public:
        virtual void showChildClass() { cout << childClass << '\n'; }
        C1(const char* y = "NONE")
        { strcpy(childClass,y);
        cout << "C1 Child Class = " << y << '\n'; }
};

class C2: public C1
{

    public:
        virtual void showChildClass() { cout << "overloaded in C2" << '\n'; }
        C2():C1("C2") { cout << "C2\n"; }
};

class C3: public C1
{
    public:
        virtual void showChildClass() { cout << "overloaded in C3" << '\n'; }
        C3():C1("C3") { cout << "C3\n"; }
};

class C4: public C2, public C3
{
    public:
        C4() { cout << "C4\n"; }
        virtual void showChildClass()
        { C2::showChildClass(); C3::showChildClass(); }
};

void main()
{
    C4 c4;
```

```
    c4.showChildClass();
/*
    This still doesn't work:
    c4.C1::showChildClass();
*/
}
/* ==========================================================================
                         Output From Above Program
C1 Child Class = C2
C2
C1 Child Class = C3
C3
C4
overloaded in C2
overloaded in C3



===========================================================================*/



////////////////////////////////////////////////////////////////////////////
// Listing  : 6-12
// Filename  : CH6-12.CPP
// Purpose   : Show virtual base class use in multiple inheritance with a
//             a common ancestor.
////////////////////////////////////////////////////////////////////////////
#include <iostream.h>
#include <string.h>

class C1
{
    protected:
        char childClass[10];
    public:
        virtual void showChildClass() { cout << childClass << '\n'; }
        C1(const char* y = "NONE")
        { strcpy(childClass,y);
        cout << "C1 Child Class = " << y << '\n'; }
};

class C2: public virtual C1
{

    public:
        virtual void showChildClass() { cout << "overloaded in C2" << '\n'; }
        C2():C1("C2") { cout << "C2\n"; }
};

class C3: public virtual C1
{
    public:
        virtual void showChildClass() { cout << "overloaded in C3" << '\n'; }
        C3():C1("C3") { cout << "C3\n"; }
};
```

```
//
// Major Public Methods:
//      push - Puts something on the stack.
//      pop  - Takes something off the stack and returns it.
//      isEmpty -returns TRUE on an empty stack.
//
// Major Data Items:
//   stack - Array of <T> to hold the data
//   top - Array index indicating top of stack
/////////////////////////////////////////////////////////////////////

#include <iostream.h>

const int maxStack = 100;

template <class T> class Stack
{
    protected:
        int top;
        T stack[maxStack];
    public:
        Stack():top(-1) {}
        virtual void push(const T &t) { stack[++top] = t; }
        virtual T &pop() { return stack[top—]; }
        virtual int isEmpty() { return top < 0; }
};

void main()
{
    Stack<int> anIntStack;
    Stack<float> aFloatStack;

    for (int i = 0; i < 5; ++i)
        anIntStack.push(i);
    for (float f = 1.1; f < 2.2; f += 0.1)
        aFloatStack.push(f);

    while(! anIntStack.isEmpty())
        cout << anIntStack.pop() << '\n';

    while(! aFloatStack.isEmpty())
        cout << aFloatStack.pop() << '\n';

}

/* =============================================================================
                        Output For Program Listed Above

4
3
2
1
0
2.1
```

```
2
1.9
1.8
1.7
1.6
1.5
1.4
1.3
1.2
1.1
  ========================================================================= */


////////////////////////////////////////////////////////////////////////
// Listing  : 6-15
// Filename    : CH6-15.CPP
// Purpose    : Demonstrate class templates and inheritance
////////////////////////////////////////////////////////////////////////

////////////////////////////////////////////////////////////////////////
// Author      : David Brumbaugh
// Class Name  : Stack<T>
// Creation Date: August '92
// Catagories  : Container
// Purpose      : Provide LIFO stack for any type. Note that T must have
//                a valid assignment operator.
//
// Major Public Methods:
//        push - Puts something on the stack.
//      pop  - Takes something off the stack and returns it.
//      isEmpty -returns TRUE on an empty stack.
//
// Major Data Items:
//     stack - Array of <T> to hold the data
//   top - Array index indicating top of stack
////////////////////////////////////////////////////////////////////////

#include <iostream.h>

const int maxStack = 10;

template <class T> class Stack
{
    protected:
        int top;
        T stack[maxStack];
    public:
        Stack():top(-1) {}
        virtual void push(const T &t) { stack[++top] = t; }
        virtual T &pop() { return stack[top-]; }
        virtual int isEmpty() { return top < 0; }
};

////////////////////////////////////////////////////////////////////////
```

```
// Author      : David Brumbaugh
// Class Name  : FloatStack
// Creation Date: August '92
// Catagories  : Container
// Purpose     : Stack of floats
//
// Major Public Methods:
//   average - Returns the average of the all the values in the stack
//
// Major Data Items: None, they're all inherited from the base class
///////////////////////////////////////////////////////////////////

class FloatStack: public virtual Stack<float>
{
    public:
        virtual float average();
};

float FloatStack::average()
{
    float total = 0.0;

    if (isEmpty())
        return 0.0;

    for (int i = 0; i <= top; ++i)
        total += stack[i];

    return(total/(top+1));
}

// A SafeStack is just like a stack but it has saftey features to prevent
// Over and underflow. See the comments for Stack<T> for details.

template <class T> class SafeStack: public virtual Stack<T>
{
    protected:
        int isSafeToPush() { return (top < maxStack-1); }
        int isSafeToPop() { return (top >= 0); }
    public:
        virtual void push(const T &t)
        { if (isSafeToPush()) Stack<T>::push(t);}
        virtual T &pop()
        {
            if (isSafeToPop())
                return Stack<T>::pop();
            // This generates a warning. Someday soon, compilers will
            // implement good exeption handling with try,throw and catch
            // for this stuff.
        }
}

void main()
{
```

```
    SafeStack<int> anIntStack;
    FloatStack aFloatStack;

    for (int i = 0; i < 15; ++i)
        anIntStack.push(i);
    for (float f = 1.5; f < 2.0; f += 0.1)
        aFloatStack.push(f);

    while(! anIntStack.isEmpty())
        cout << anIntStack.pop() << '\n';

    cout << "The average of aFloatStack is " << aFloatStack.average();
}

/* ========================================================================
                        Output For Program Listed Above
9
8
7
6
5
4
3
2
1
0
The average of aFloatStack is 1.7


  ====================================================================== */


//////////////////////////////////////////////////////////////////////
// Listing  : 6-16
// Filename   : CH6-16.CPP
// Purpose    : Demonstrate class templates and inheritance. A class
//              template can inherit from a non-template.
//////////////////////////////////////////////////////////////////////

//////////////////////////////////////////////////////////////////////
// Author        : David Brumbaugh
// Class Name    : Stack<T>
// Creation Date: August '92
// Catagories    : Container
// Purpose         : Provide LIFO stack for any type. Note that T must have
//                   a valid assignment operator. In this case we inherit
//                   from a useless base class to explain how it works.
//
// Major Public Methods:
//      push - Puts something on the stack.
//      pop  - Takes something off the stack and returns it.
//      isEmpty -returns TRUE on an empty stack.
//
// Major Data Items:
//     stack - Array of <T> to hold the data
```

```cpp
//  top - Array index indicating top of stack
////////////////////////////////////////////////////////////////////////

#include <iostream.h>

class Base
{
    public:
        Base() { cout << "Base class initialized\n"; }

};

const int maxStack = 10;

template <class T> class Stack : Base
{
    protected:
        int top;
        T stack[maxStack];
    public:
        Stack():top(-1) {}
        virtual void push(const T &t) { stack[++top] = t; }
        virtual T &pop() { return stack[top-]; }
        virtual int isEmpty() { return top < 0; }
};


// A SafeStack is just like a stack but it has saftey features to prevent
// Over and underflow. See the comments for Stack<T> for details.

template <class T> class SafeStack: public virtual Stack<T>
{
    protected:
        int isSafeToPush() { return (top < maxStack-1); }
        int isSafeToPop() { return (top >= 0); }
    public:
        virtual void push(const T &t)
        { if (isSafeToPush()) Stack<T>::push(t);}
        virtual T &pop()
        {
            if (isSafeToPop())
                return Stack<T>::pop();
            // This generates a warning. Someday soon, compilers will
            // implement good exeption handling with try,throw and catch
            // for this stuff.
        }
}

void main()
{
    SafeStack<int> anIntStack;

    for (int i = 0; i < 15; ++i)
        anIntStack.push(i);
```

```
    while(! anIntStack.isEmpty())
        cout << anIntStack.pop() << '\n';


}

/* ==========================================================================
                        Output For Program Listed Above
Base class initialized
9
8
7
6
5
4
3
2
1
0

========================================================================= */


Listing 9-1

create ssootlib.db
addtab * Entry "Entry in the SSOOT CASE Library Catalog"
addcol * * Identity "Specific Indentifier" "%s" NULL "String NoNulls Indexed"
addcol * * Version "Version of Identifier" "%s" NULL "Integer NoNulls Indexed"
addkey * * IDVersion +Identity+Version Unique
addcol * * Name "Entry Name" "%s" NULL "String Indexed NoNulls"
addcol * * Description "Entry Description" "%s" NULL "String"
addcol * * CheckedOut "Checked In or Out" NULL NULL "Integer"
addcol * * DateAdded "Date Entry Entered" NULL NULL "Integer"
addcol * * ChangedBy "Person who changed" "%s" NULL "String NoNulls Indexed"
addcol * * AddedBy "Person who added this entry" "%s" NULL "String"
addcol * * EntryType "Is it a Class or Function Entry?" "%s" NULL "String"
addcol * * DateChecked "Date Last Checked In/Out" NULL NULL "Integer"
addcol * * WhereLocated "File path to source" "%s"  NULL "String"
addcol * * MustInclude "File path to header" "%s" NULL "String"

addtab * FunctionEntry "Addional Function Data"
addcol * * Identity "Specific Indentifier" "%s" NULL "String NoNulls Indexed"
addcol * * Version "Version of Identifier" "%s" NULL "Integer NoNulls Indexed"
addkey * * IDVersion +Identity+Version Unique
addcol * * Parameters "List of parameters" "%s" NULL "String"
addcol * * ReturnType "Return type" "%s" NULL "String"
addcol * * ReturnVal "The meaning of the return value" "%s" NULL "String"
addcol * * SourcePath "File Path to Source Code" "%s" NULL "String"
addcol * * Specification "Specification if it's a function" "%s" NULL "String"
addcol * * ParamDescriptions "Parameter descriptions" "%s" NULL "String"

addtab * ClassEntry "Additional Class Data"
addcol * * Identity "Specific Indentifier" "%s" NULL "String NoNulls Indexed"
addcol * * Version "Version of Identifier" "%s" NULL "Integer NoNulls Indexed"
```

```
addkey * * IDVersion +Identity+Version Unique
addcol * * BaseClasses "List of base classes" "%s" NULL "String"
addcol * * ClassSpec "class,struct or union" "%s" NULL "String"

addtab * ClassMember "Member Data (Function & Data)"
addcol * * Identity "Specific Indentifier" "%s" NULL "String NoNulls"
addcol * * Version "Version of Identifier" "%s" NULL "Integer NoNulls"
addkey * * IDVersion +Identity+Version
addcol * * Name      "Name of class member" "%s" NULL "NoNulls String"
addcol * * OwningClass "Name of class that owns this one" "%s" NULL "String NoNulls"
addcol * * AccessSpecifier "public, private, etc." "%s" NULL "String NoNulls
                           Indexed"
addcol * * TypeSpecifiers "const, int, virtual, etc." "%s" NULL "String"
addcol * * MemberType "Function or Data" "%s" NULL "String Indexed"
addcol * * PtrSpec "Pointer Specifications" "%s" NULL "String"
addcol * * Suffix "Function Member Only" "%s" NULL "String"
addcol * * Specification "Specification if it's a function" "%s" NULL "String"
addcol * * Parameters "List of parameters (Fn Member Only)" "%s" NULL "String"
addcol * * ReturnVal "The meaning of the typespecifier (Fn Mem)" "%s" NULL "String"
addcol * * Description "Description of Member" "%s" NULL "String"
addcol * * SourcePath "File Path to Source Code" "%s" NULL "String"


exit


///////////////////////////////////////////////////////////////////
// Listing  : 10-1
// Filename  : D_List.H
// Purpose   : Defines an implementation independent protocol for list
//            access.
///////////////////////////////////////////////////////////////////

///////////////////////////////////////////////////////////////////
//
// Class Name: template <class R> class D_List
//
// Creation Date: 6/2/92
// Purpose: List Class Template
//         R is a record of any type
//         Note that this class is both generic and abstract
//
//
// Major Public Methods:
//  at_top         Return TRUE if current member is top member.
//   at_end        Return TRUE if current member is last member.
//   is_empty      Return TRUE if LIST is empty, FALSE otherwise.
//   find          Search the list for a member meeting "condition"
//                 If not found, return FALSE and don't change currency.
//   prev          Make the member previous to this one current. If
//                 current member is top, do nothing.
//   next          Make the member after this one current. If
//                 current member is last, do nothing.
//   seek          Search to a position in the list. Use like fseek.
```

```
//     top               Make the top member current.
//     end               Make the last member current.
//     add               Add a new member to the list.  Return TRUE on success.
//     replace           Replace data in current member. Return TRUEE on success.
//     current           Return the current member.
//     total             Return the total number of members int the list.
//     tell              Return the position, from the start of the list
//                       of the current member. The top member is 0.
//
// Major Data Items:
//     <class R> buffer       Holds a working Record
//
//////////////////////////////////////////////////////////////////////////////

#ifndef D_LIST_H
#define D_LIST_H
#include <stddef.h>
enum Boolean {false, true};
enum SeekStart { from_top, from_here, from_end };

template <class R>
class D_List {
    protected:
        R buffer;
    public:
    virtual  Boolean at_top()
        { return ((Boolean) (tell() == 0L));}
    virtual    Boolean at_end() = 0;
    virtual  Boolean is_empty()
        { return ((Boolean) (total() == 0L)); }
    virtual     Boolean find(char *condition) = 0;
    virtual void prev() = 0,
            next() = 0,
            seek(long where, SeekStart start = from_top) = 0,
            top() = 0,
            end() = 0;
    virtual Boolean add(R &member) = 0,
                  replace(R &member) = 0;
    virtual void remove() = 0;
    virtual R current() = 0;
    virtual    long total() const = 0,
            tell() const = 0;
    virtual R &operator[] (long where)
    { seek(where,from_top); buffer = current(); return buffer; }
    virtual R &operator[] (char *key)
    {
        if (find(key))
            buffer = current();
        return buffer;
    }
};

#endif
```

```
///////////////////////////////////////////////////////////////////////
// Listing   : 10-2
// Filename  : LISTIMP.H
// Purpose   : Implementation of D_List using Borland's ArrayAsVector
///////////////////////////////////////////////////////////////////////

///////////////////////////////////////////////////////////////////////
// Author         : David Brumbaugh
// Class Name     : ListImp
// Creation Date: 10/4/92
// Catagories    : Container, Adapter, Abstract
// Purpose        : Template container class. I'm using the D_List interface
//                 to unify list activity to isolate the application from
//                 compiler specific libraries.
//
// Major Public Methods:
// Inherited and overloaded from D_List.
//
// Major Data Items:
//     anIterator : Iterator to navigate Borland's list
///////////////////////////////////////////////////////////////////////
#ifndef LISTIMP_H
#define LISTIMP_H
#include "D_List.H"
#include <ARRAYS.H>

template <class R>
class ListImp: public D_List<R>
{
    protected:
        int curr; // Current postion in the list
        BI_ArrayAsVector<R> anArray;
    public:
        ListImp():anArray(1,0,1) { curr = 0; }
        virtual    Boolean at_end()
        { return (Boolean) (curr == anArray.getItemsInContainer());}
        virtual  Boolean is_empty()
            { return (Boolean) anArray.isEmpty(); }
        virtual    Boolean find(char *) {return false;} // Unused for now
        virtual void prev() { if (--curr < 0)  curr = 0; }
        virtual void next() { if (++curr >=  total()) curr = total() - 1; }
        virtual void seek(long where, SeekStart start = from_top);
        virtual void top() {curr = 0;}
        virtual void end() {curr = total() - 1; }
        virtual Boolean add(R &member)
                { anArray.add(member); return true; }
        virtual Boolean  replace(R &member)
                        { anArray[curr] = member; return true; }
        virtual void remove() { anArray.destroy(curr); }
        virtual R current() { return anArray[curr]; }
        virtual    long total() const { return anArray.getItemsInContainer();}
        virtual long tell() const { return curr; }
        virtual R &operator[] (long where) { return anArray[where]; }
};
```

```
template <class R>
void ListImp<R>::seek(long where, SeekStart start)
{
    if (start == from_top)
        curr = where;
    else if (start == from_end)
        curr = (total() - 1) - where;
    else
        curr += where;
}

#endif


//////////////////////////////////////////////////////////////////////////
// Listing  : 10-3
// Filename   : CLSDFN.H
// Purpose    : Update of ClassDefinition classes using D_List decendents
//              and the string class.
//////////////////////////////////////////////////////////////////////////
#ifndef CLSDFN_H
#define CLSDFN_H
#include <iostream.h>
#include <arrays.h>
#include <fstream.h>
#include "str.h"
#include "ListImp.h"
#include "DRECRD.H"

const int maxIdLen = 33; //Really, it's 32, but we need the nil terminator
typedef char IdString[maxIdLen]; // These hold identifiers, and modifiers
enum memberTypes { unknown, isFunction, isData };


//////////////////////////////////////////////////////////////////////////
// Author       : David Brumbaugh
// Class Name    : ClassMemberDefinition
// Creation Date: 7/10/92
// Catagories    : Model, Abstract
// Purpose        : Classes contain two kinds of members, functions and
//                  data. This class has the common features of both.
//
// Major Public Methods:
//    ClassMemberDefinition: Constructor
//    <: For sorting (Required by BIDS library
//    ==: For comparing values (Required by BIDS library)
//    makeTemplate: (pure) Generate an "empty" source code version of member
//    toSource: (pure) Generates a definition of the member within the class
//    fromSource: (pure) Reads the source code and fills this class's data
//    shouldMakeTemplate: (pure) Should this member be have a template made?
//    getName - What is this thing called?
//    getAccessSpecifier - (public,protected or private)
//    getTypeSpecifiers - (const,int, virtual etc.)
//    getOwningClass - Name of the class that contains this member
```

```
//     getTypeSpec - What is this, a function or data member?
//     isA:  a function or data member?
//     get/setDescription - Assigns and retrieves description.
//
// Major Data Items:
//
//     type:  a function or data member?
//     name: What is this thing called?
//     typeSpecifiers: (const,int, virtual etc.)
//     accessSpecifier: public, private, protected
//     owningClass : name of class that owns member
//     description: A textual description of the member.
//     ptrSpec: The pointer specification, we need to keep track of these
//              separately because when we parse the class, we need to
//              remember the base type specification when it is
//              implied by listing.
//
////////////////////////////////////////////////////////////////////////

class ClassMemberDefinition
{
    protected:
        IdString name;
        IdString owningClass;
        string    accessSpecifier,
            typeSpecifiers;
        memberTypes type;
        string description;
        static string lastTypeSpec;
        char ptrSpec[7]; // Six levels of indirection should be plenty
    public:
        ClassMemberDefinition(const char *className = NULL);
        virtual operator < (ClassMemberDefinition &c);
        virtual operator == (ClassMemberDefinition &c) const;
        memberTypes isA() { return type; }
        virtual void makeTemplate(ostream &out) = 0;
        virtual void toSource(ostream &out,int withAccess = 0,
        int newType = 0) = 0;
        virtual int shouldMakeTemplate() = 0;
        virtual void fromSource(istream &in, char *accessSpec) = 0;
        const char *getName() { return &name[0]; }
        const char *getTypeSpec() { return typeSpecifiers.ptr(); }
        const char *getAccessSpec() { return accessSpecifier.ptr(); }
        const char *getOwner() { return &owningClass[0]; }
        const char *getPtrSpec() { return ptrSpec; }
        void setName(const char *nm) { strcpy(name,nm); }
        void setTypeSpec(const char *ts) { typeSpecifiers = ts; }
        void setAccessSpec(const char *as) { accessSpecifier= as; }
        void setOwner(const char *o) { strcpy(owningClass,o); }
        virtual void movePtrSpec(); // Move the pointer spec
                                    // from the name or the type
        virtual void fromRecord(D_Record &record);
        virtual D_Record toRecord(const char *id, long version);
        virtual const char *getDescription() {return description.ptr();}
```

```
        virtual void setDescription(const char *s)
        { description = s; }

};


/////////////////////////////////////////////////////////////////////
// Author         : David Brumbaugh
// Class Name     : ParamDefinition
// Purpose        : Defines function and method parameters
//
// Major Public Methods:
//     operator == : Returns non-0 if the types match.
//
// Major Data Items:
//     typeSpecifiers: Data type of parameter
//     name : Name of parameter
//     defaultValue : Default value of the parameter
//     description  : Textual descriptio of puropose of parameter
/////////////////////////////////////////////////////////////////////


struct ParamDefinition
{
    string typeSpecifiers; // int, char *, etc.
    string name; // Parameter name
    string defaultValue;
    string description;
    operator == (ParamDefinition &c) const
    { return (typeSpecifiers == c.typeSpecifiers); }
    // If the type specs match in a parameter, it's "the same"

};

/////////////////////////////////////////////////////////////////////
// Author       : David Brumbaugh
// Class Name   : ParamList
// Purpose      : List of parameters.
//
// Major Public Methods:
//       toSource - Generates a parameter list in source code format
//       fromSource - Fills the ParamList from source code
//       toString - Generates a string with the parameters in it.
//       fromString - Generates a list of parameters from a string.
//       getDescField - Generates a list of descriptions, delimieted by
//                      a verticle tab character.
//       fillDescField - fills the list of descriptiosn from a v tab
//                       delimited field.
/////////////////////////////////////////////////////////////////////


class ParamList: public ListImp<ParamDefinition>
{
    public:
```

```
        virtual void toSource(ostream &out, Boolean withNames = true,
        Boolean withDefaults = false);
        virtual void fromSource(istream &in);
        virtual const char *toString(Boolean withNames = true,
        Boolean withDefaults = false);
        virtual void fromString(const char *);
        operator ==(const ParamList &p) const;
        const char *getDescField();
        void fillDescriptions(const char *str);

};
///////////////////////////////////////////////////////////////////
// Author        : David Brumbaugh
// Class Name    : MemberFunctionDefinition
// Creation Date: 7/10/92
// Catagories    : Model
// Purpose        : Defines a class's member function
//
// Major Public Methods:
//     MemberFunctionDefinition: Constructor
//    ==: Overloaded from parent class
//   makeTemplate: Overloaded
//    toSource: Overloaded
//   fromSource: Overloaded
//   shouldMakeTemplate: Overloaded
//
// Major Data Items:
//   parameters: List of parameters
//   suffix: End of function definition like: "= 0", "const", or "{..}"
//   expandInline: Should we include inline functions in the template?
//                 Some people put the inline code in the header.
//   returnValue:  String describing meaning of return value
//   sourceFile :  String specifing file in which the body of this member
//                 exists.
///////////////////////////////////////////////////////////////////

class MemberFunctionDefinition: public ClassMemberDefinition
{
    protected:
        int expandInline;
        string suffix;
        ParamList parameters;
        string specification;
        virtual void makeTypeAndName(istream &in);//Get typeSpec, name from in
        virtual void makeParamList(istream &in);// Make parameter list from in
        virtual void makeSuffix(istream &in); // Things like = 0, const, {..}
        string returnValue;
        string sourceFile;
    public:
        MemberFunctionDefinition(const char *className = NULL,
        istream *in = NULL,char *accessSpec = NULL, int expInline = 0);
        virtual shouldMakeTemplate();
        virtual operator == (ClassMemberDefinition &c) const;
        virtual void makeTemplate(ostream &out);
```

```
        virtual void toSource(ostream &out, int withAccess = 0,
        int newType = 0);
        virtual void fromSource(istream &in, char *accessSpec = NULL);
        virtual void fromRecord(D_Record &record);
        virtual D_Record toRecord(const char *id, long version);
        virtual ParamList &getParams() { return parameters; }
        virtual void setSpecification(const char *spec)
        { specification = spec; }
        virtual const char *getSpecification()
        { return specification.ptr(); }
        virtual void setReturnValue(const char *rv)
        { returnValue = rv; }
        const char *getReturnValue() { return returnValue.ptr(); }
        virtual void setSourceFile(const char *sf)
        { sourceFile = sf; }
        const char *getSourceFile() { return sourceFile.ptr(); }
        const char *getSuffix() { return suffix.ptr(); }
        void setSuffix(const char *sfx) { suffix = sfx; }


};


//////////////////////////////////////////////////////////////////
// Author        : David Brumbaugh
// Class Name    : DataMemberDefinition
// Creation Date: 7/10/92
// Catagories    : Model
// Purpose       : Model of the data member declaration
//
// Major Public Methods:
// DataMemberDefinition: Constructor
// makeTemplate: Overloaded
// toSource: Overloaded
// fromSource: Overloaded
// shouldMakeTemplate: Overloaded
// Major Data Items:
// None specific to this class
//////////////////////////////////////////////////////////////////

class DataMemberDefinition : public ClassMemberDefinition
{
    public:
        virtual shouldMakeTemplate();
        DataMemberDefinition(const char *className = NULL,
        istream *in = NULL, char *accessSpec = NULL);
        virtual void makeTemplate(ostream &out);
        virtual void toSource(ostream &out, int withAccess = 0,
        int newType = 0);
        virtual void fromSource(istream &in, char *accessSpec = NULL);

};
```

```
//////////////////////////////////////////////////////////////////////
// Author        : David Brumbaugh
// Class Name     : ClassDefinition
// Creation Date: 7/10/92
// Catagories     : Model
// Purpose        : Defines a C++ Class, this model will be used for a
// series of OO Case Tools.
//
// Major Public Methods:
//      ClassDefinition: Constructor
//      fromSource: Reads source file and builds class definition
//      toSource : Builds class defintion as in a header file
//      makeTemplate : Builds empty function descriptions and static data
//                      declarations for this class.
//
// Major Data Items:
//      name: Class name
//      ancestors: List of ancestors' names and their access specs
//      members: List of class members
//      commentSource: stream from which to draw comment templates
//      optionFlags: User preferences on how to use class
//      classSpec : "class", "struct" or "union"
//////////////////////////////////////////////////////////////////////

struct BaseClassSpec
{
    string baseSpecifier; // public, private, virtual ...
    IdString name; // Class name of ancestor
    operator == (BaseClassSpec &c) const
    { return (baseSpecifier == c.baseSpecifier && strcmp(name,c.name) == 0); }
};

typedef ListImp<BaseClassSpec> BaseClassList;
class MemberList : public  ListImp<ClassMemberDefinition *>
{
/*    public:
        virtual ~MemberList();
        virtual MemberList &operator = (const MemberList &memList);
*/
};
const unsigned ExpandInline = 0x0001, UseComments = 0x002;

class ClassDefinition
{
    protected:
        int forwardDeclaration; // TRUE if this is not really a class but a
                                // forward declartion
        virtual int getClassName(istream &in);
        virtual void getMembers(istream &in);
        virtual void putComment(ostream &out,const char *what,
        const char *id);
        IdString name;
        BaseClassList baseClasses;
        MemberList members;
```

```
            istream *commentSource;
            string classSpec; // class, union, or struct
            // OptionFlags
            unsigned expandInline : 1, // Exapand inline functions in source?
                useComments : 1;

        public:
            ClassDefinition(const char *cSpec = "class", istream *in = NULL,
            unsigned options = 0, char *commentFile = NULL);
            virtual    ~ClassDefinition();
            // Interface to "real world"
            virtual void fromSource(istream &in);
            virtual void toSource(ostream &out);
            virtual void makeTemplate(ostream &out);
            void setCommentSource(istream *i)
            { if (commentSource) delete commentSource; commentSource = i; }
            virtual void getParents(istream &in);
            // Member and Base Class List access
            virtual Boolean add(ClassMemberDefinition *cmd)
            {
                return members.add(cmd);
            }
            virtual MemberList &getMembers() { return members; }
            virtual BaseClassList &getBaseClasses() { return baseClasses; }
            // Class Specification & Name Access
            virtual void setClassSpec(const char *cSpec) {classSpec = cSpec;}
            const char *getClassSpec() { return classSpec.ptr(); }
            void setName(const char *nm) { strcpy(name,nm); }
            const char *getName() { return &name[0]; }
            // Interface to Options
            virtual void setOption(unsigned option,Boolean value)
            { if (option == UseComments) useComments = value;
            if (option == ExpandInline) expandInline = value;
            }
            Boolean getUseComments() { return (Boolean) useComments; }
            Boolean getExpandInline() { return (Boolean) expandInline; }
            int isAForwardDeclaration() { return forwardDeclaration; }

    };


    #endif

    //////////////////////////////////////////////////////////////////////
    // Listing  : 10-4
    // Filename   : ClsDfn.CPP
    // Purpose    : Class definition classes, Modified to use ListImp and string
    //////////////////////////////////////////////////////////////////////

    #include "DEFNFILE.H"
    #include <STDLIB.H>
    #include <utility.h>

    #include <stdio.h>
```

```
#include <strstrea.h>
/* = = = = = = = = = ClassMemberDefinition Data   = = = = = = = = = = = */

string ClassMemberDefinition::lastTypeSpec;

/* = = = = = = = = = ClassMemberDefinition methods  = = = = = = = = = = */
//////////////////////////////////////////////////////////////////////
// Author: David Brumbaugh
// Method Name: ClassMemberDefinition
// Creation Date: 7/13/92
// Purpose: Constructor, initialize data members;
//
// Return Value: None
// Parameters:
//  Type          Name           Purpose/Description        Default Value
//  char *        className       Name of the class to       None
//                                which the member belongs
//////////////////////////////////////////////////////////////////////

ClassMemberDefinition::ClassMemberDefinition(const char *className)
{
    type = unknown;
    memset(ptrSpec,0,sizeof(ptrSpec));
    memset(name,0,sizeof(name));
    strcpy(owningClass,className);
}



//////////////////////////////////////////////////////////////////////
// Author: David Brumbaugh
// Method Name: operator <
// Creation Date:  7/12/92
// Purpose: For sorting ClassMemberDefinitions.
//          BIDS requires a < operator for any sorted contained classes.
//          The sort order for members is:
//              accessSpecifier,typeSpecifiers
//          That allows similar members to be grouped together.
//
// Return Value: 1 or 0 depending on the condition
// Parameters:
//  Type                     Name     Purpose/Description       Default Value
//  ClassMemberDefinition & c         Value being compared      None
//////////////////////////////////////////////////////////////////////

ClassMemberDefinition::operator < (ClassMemberDefinition &c)
{
    if (accessSpecifier < c.accessSpecifier)
        return 1;
    else if (accessSpecifier == c.accessSpecifier)
    {
        return (typeSpecifiers == c.typeSpecifiers);
    }
    else
```

```
        return 0;
}

///////////////////////////////////////////////////////////////////
// Author: David Brumbaugh
// Method Name: operator ==
// Creation Date:  7/12/92
// Purpose: For comparing ClassMemberDefinitions. BIDS requires a ==
// operator for most contained classes.
//     If a class member has the same name it matches. This will be overloaded
//  in the MemberFunctionDefn class.
//
// Return Value: 0 or Non-0
// Parameters:
//  Type                        Name      Purpose/Description        Default Value
//  ClassMemberDefinition & c             Value being compared       None
///////////////////////////////////////////////////////////////////

ClassMemberDefinition::operator == (ClassMemberDefinition &c) const
{
    if (this == &c) // This really isn't necessary, but it shows how
        return 1;    // to use "this". Obviously if the address of "c" and
                     // "this" match we have the same object. Therefore,
                     // they must be equal. So, we return non-zero.
    if (type == c.type)
        return(strcmp(name,c.name) == 0);
    else
        return(0);
}
///////////////////////////////////////////////////////////////////
// Author: David Brumbaugh
// Method Name: movePtrSpec
// Creation Date: 8/14/92
// Purpose: Move the pointer specifers from the name or type specifers
//
// Return Value: void
// Parameters: None
///////////////////////////////////////////////////////////////////


void ClassMemberDefinition::movePtrSpec()
{
    //The pointer and reference characters are part of the type.
    int len = strlen(ptrSpec);
    while (name[0] == '*' || name[0] == '&')
    {
        ptrSpec[len++] = name[0];
        rmvstr(name,1);
    }

    // But we're keeping the pointer specs seperately
    char *check;
    while ((check = strchr(typeSpecifiers.ptr(),'*')) != NULL ||
    (check = strchr(typeSpecifiers.ptr(),'&')) != NULL)
```

```
        {
            ptrSpec[len++] = *check;
            rmvstr(check,1);
        }

}

////////////////////////////////////////////////////////////////
// Author: David Brumbaugh
// Method Name: fromRecord
// Creation Date: 11/92
// Purpose: Fills the class member from a D_Record. Basicly, this is
// just a data transfer function.
//
// Return Value: void
// Parameters:
//   D_Record record : The record being filled from
////////////////////////////////////////////////////////////////
void ClassMemberDefinition::fromRecord(D_Record &record)
{
    strcpy(name,record["Name"]);
    strcpy(owningClass,record["OwningClass"]);
    accessSpecifier = (const char *) record["AccessSpecifier"];
    typeSpecifiers = (const char *) record["TypeSpecifiers"];
    if ( stricmp((const char *) record["MemberType"], "data") == 0)
        type = isData;
    else
        type = isFunction;
    strcpy(ptrSpec,record["PtrSpec"]);
    description = (const char *) record["Description"];
}

////////////////////////////////////////////////////////////////
// Author: David Brumbaugh
// Method Name: toRecord
// Creation Date: 11/92
// Purpose: Fills the D_Record from the ClassMemberDefinion.
// Basicly, this is just a data transfer function.
//
// Return Value: D_Record record : The record being filled from
// Parameters: None
////////////////////////////////////////////////////////////////

D_Record ClassMemberDefinition::toRecord(const char *id, long version)
{
    D_Record record;
    record.add(D_Field("Identity",id));
    record.add(D_Field("Version", version));
    record.add(D_Field("Name",name));
    record.add(D_Field("OwningClass",owningClass));
    record.add(D_Field("AccessSpecifier",accessSpecifier.ptr()));
    record.add(D_Field("TypeSpecifiers", typeSpecifiers.ptr()));
    if (type == isData)
        record.add(D_Field("MemberType","data"));
```

```
    else
        record.add(D_Field("MemberType", "function"));
    record.add(D_Field("PtrSpec",ptrSpec));
    record.add(D_Field("Description",description.ptr()));
    return record;
}


/* = = = = = = = = = =  MemberFunctionDefn methods  = = = = = = = = = = = */
//////////////////////////////////////////////////////////////////////
// Author: David Brumbaugh
// Method Name: MemberFunctionDefinition
// Creation Date: 7/13/92
// Purpose: Constructor
//
// Return Value:
// Parameters:
//   Type            Name            Purpose/Description        Default Value
//   char *          className       Name of owning class       None
//
//   istream *       in              Source code stream from    NULL
//                                   which to build definition.
//
//   int             expInline       If non-0, expand inline    0
//                                   code in source file
//////////////////////////////////////////////////////////////////////

MemberFunctionDefinition::MemberFunctionDefinition(const char *className,
istream *in, char *accessSpec,int expInline):ClassMemberDefinition(className)
{
    type = isFunction;
    expandInline = expInline;
    if (in)
        fromSource(*in,accessSpec);
}



//////////////////////////////////////////////////////////////////////
// Author: David Brumbaugh
// Method Name: operator ==
// Creation Date:  7/12/92
// Purpose: For comparing ClassMemberDefinitions. BIDS requires a ==
// operator for most contained classes.
//    If a class member has the same name it matches. This will be overloaded
//   in the MemberFunctionDefn class.
//
// Return Value: 0 or Non-0
// Parameters:
//   Type                    Name      Purpose/Description        Default Value
//   ClassMemberDefinition & c         Value being compared       None
//////////////////////////////////////////////////////////////////////

MemberFunctionDefinition::operator == (ClassMemberDefinition &c) const
{
    if (type == c.isA()) //Both must be member functions
```

```
        {
            // Now we'll compare apples and apples
            MemberFunctionDefinition *mfd = (MemberFunctionDefinition *) &c;
            if (strcmp(name,mfd->name) == 0)
            {
                if ( ! (parameters == mfd->parameters))
                    return 0;
            }
            return 1;
        }
        return 0;
}


/////////////////////////////////////////////////////////////////////////
// Author: David Brumbaugh
// Method Name: makeTemplate
// Creation Date: 7/13/92
// Purpose: Creates a set of empty functions for the class.
// When it is called it will create the following template on the output
// stream:
//        typeSpecifications owningClass::name(parameters)
//            {
//            }
//
// Return Value: none
// Parameters:
//   Type           Name              Purpose/Description    Default Value
//   ostream &      out               Where the template is  None
//                                    going.
/////////////////////////////////////////////////////////////////////////

void MemberFunctionDefinition::makeTemplate(ostream &out)
{
    // Do we make templates out of this functions definition?
    if ( ! shouldMakeTemplate())
    {
        return;
    }

    // The keyword "virtual" does not go into the templates
    string tempTypeSpecifiers = typeSpecifiers;
    int c = tempTypeSpecifiers.Index("virtual");
    if (c >= 0)
        tempTypeSpecifiers.Delete(c,7);

    // Neither does the keyword "static"
    c = tempTypeSpecifiers.Index("static");
    if (c >= 0)
        tempTypeSpecifiers.Delete(c,6);

    // Put the template on the stream;
    out << tempTypeSpecifiers.Trim() << ' ' << ptrSpec << owningClass;
    out << "::" << name;
    out << parameters.toString(true,false);
```

```
    suffix.Trim();
    if (suffix == "const")
        out << ' ' << suffix;

    out << "\n{\n}\n\n";


}


//////////////////////////////////////////////////////////////////////
// Author: David Brumbaugh
// Method Name: toSource
// Creation Date: 7/14/92
// Purpose: Creates a declaration within the class definition.
// When it is called it will create the following template on the output
// stream:
//    [accessSpecifier:]
//        typeSpecifications name(parameters);
//
// Return Value: none
// Parameters:
//  Type            Name            Purpose/Description     Default Value
//  ostream &       out             Where the prototype is  None
//                                  going.
//
//  int             withAccess      Will include the access 0 (false)
//                                  specifiation
//  int             newType         If non-0, this data     0
//                                  type is different that
//                                  the previous one.
//////////////////////////////////////////////////////////////////////


void MemberFunctionDefinition::toSource(ostream &out, int withAccess,
int newType)
{
    if (withAccess)
        out << accessSpecifier << ":\n";

    if (newType)
    {

        out << '\t' << typeSpecifiers.Trim();
    }
    out << ' ';
    if (strlen(ptrSpec))
        out << ptrSpec;
    out << name;
    out << parameters.toString(true,true);
    out << suffix << '\n';
}


//////////////////////////////////////////////////////////////////////
// Author: David Brumbaugh
```

```
// Method Name: shouldMakeTemplate
// Creation Date: 7/14/92
// Purpose: Returns non-0 if we should generate a template for this function.
//
// Return Value: 0 or Non-0
// Parameters: None
/////////////////////////////////////////////////////////////////////

MemberFunctionDefinition::shouldMakeTemplate()
{
    // Check inline sometimes people like to put those in headers
    if (! expandInline)
        if (typeSpecifiers.Index("inline") > 0)
            return 0;

    // Check the suffix:
        // We don't want to make templates for pure virtual functions
    if (strchr(suffix.ptr(),'0'))
        return 0;
        // We don't want functions already expanded in the header either
    if (strchr(suffix.ptr(), '{'))
        return 0;
    return 1;
}


/////////////////////////////////////////////////////////////////////
// Author: David Brumbaugh
// Method Name: fromSource
// Creation Date: 7/14/92
// Purpose: Fills data members from "in", where "in" is a stream
// of source code such as that found in a class definintion. Assumes the
// following:
//          1. The stream starts at the begining of function definition
//          2. The source code is syntactically correct
//          3. All comments have been removed
//          4. The stream contains only the function defintion
//
//
// Return Value: None
// Parameters:
//    Type            Name           Purpose/Description         Default Value
//    istream &       in             Stream which contains       None
//                                   the defintion
//    char *          accessSpec     access specifier            NULL (ie,"private")
/////////////////////////////////////////////////////////////////////

void MemberFunctionDefinition::fromSource(istream &in, char *accessSpec)
{
    in.unsetf(ios::skipws);
    if (! accessSpec)
        accessSpecifier = "private";
    else
        accessSpecifier = accessSpec;
    makeTypeAndName(in);
```

```
    makeParamList(in);
    makeSuffix(in);
}


//////////////////////////////////////////////////////////////////////
// Author: David Brumbaugh
// Method Name: makeTypeAndName
// Creation Date: 7/16/92
// Purpose: Fills the type and name data members from the input stream
// Supports "fromSource"
//
// Return Value: None
// Parameters:
//   Type        Name            Purpose/Description        Default Value
//   istream &   in              Stream which contains      None
//                               the defintion
//////////////////////////////////////////////////////////////////////

void MemberFunctionDefinition::makeTypeAndName(istream &in)
{
    int done = 0;
    IdString work, prev;
    char typeNameBuff[100];
    //Enough for a full type and several modifiers
    memset(typeNameBuff,0,sizeof(typeNameBuff));
    char *check;
    prev[0] = '\0';
    name[0] = '\0';
    in.getline(typeNameBuff,sizeof(typeNameBuff) ,'('); // Read up to paren
    istrstream  typeNameIn(typeNameBuff); //Streams are easier to work with
    do
    {
        typeNameIn >> work >> ws; // Trim the trailing white space
        if (typeNameIn.eof())
            done = 1;
        if (strlen(prev)) // Have we got any type info yet?
        {
            if ( strcmp(prev,"operator") != 0 )
            {
                typeSpecifiers += prev;
                typeSpecifiers += " ";
            }
            else
                strcpy(name,prev);
        }
        strcpy(prev,work); // Save work, it may be a type spec or name
        if (done)
        {
            if (typeSpecifiers.Len())
                lastTypeSpec = typeSpecifiers;
            else
                typeSpecifiers = lastTypeSpec;
            strcat(name,prev); // The last string is usually the name
        }
```

```
    } while (! done);

    movePtrSpec(); // Fix the pointer specifiers if they exist

}

////////////////////////////////////////////////////////////////////
// Author: David Brumbaugh
// Method Name: makeParamList
// Creation Date: 7/16/92
// Purpose: Fills parameter list from "in"
//
// Return Value: None
// Parameters:
//  Type           Name        Purpose/Description        Default Value
//  istream &      in          Stream which contains      None
//                             the defintion
//
////////////////////////////////////////////////////////////////////

void MemberFunctionDefinition::makeParamList(istream &in)
{
    parameters.fromSource(in);
}
////////////////////////////////////////////////////////////////////
// Author: David Brumbaugh
// Method Name: makeSuffix
// Creation Date: 7/20/92
// Purpose: Fills suffix from "in"
//    (Things like "= 0", "const", "{.." etc.
//
// Return Value: None
// Parameters:
//  Type           Name        Purpose/Description        Default Value
//  istream &      in          Stream which contains      None
//                             the defintion
//
////////////////////////////////////////////////////////////////////

void MemberFunctionDefinition::makeSuffix(istream &in)
{
    int done = 0;
    char work[512];
    work[0] = 0;
    in >> ws;
    do
    {
        in >> work >> ws;
        if (in.eof())
            done = 1;
        if (work[0] == ';' || work[0] == '{' )
        {
            done = 1;
```

```
            if (work[0] == '{')
            {
                suffix = "{ }";
                // We're not going to keep all the inline code
            }
            // If we've come to a semi colon or '{' we're done with this type
            lastTypeSpec[0] = 0;
        }
        else
        {
            suffix += trim(work);
            suffix += " ";
        }
        if (done && ! strchr(suffix.ptr(),'{') && ! strchr(suffix.ptr(),';'))
            suffix += ";";
    } while( ! done);
}


////////////////////////////////////////////////////////////////////////
// Author: David Brumbaugh
// Method Name: fromRecord
// Creation Date: 11/92
// Purpose: Fills the member function data from a D_Record
//
// Return Value: void
// Parameters: D_Record from which member is being filled.
////////////////////////////////////////////////////////////////////////

void MemberFunctionDefinition::fromRecord(D_Record &record)
{
    ClassMemberDefinition::fromRecord(record);
    specification = (const char *) record["Specification"];
    suffix = (const char *) record["Suffix"];
    parameters.fromString(record["Parameters"]);
    returnValue = (const char *) record["ReturnVal"];

}


////////////////////////////////////////////////////////////////////////
// Author: David Brumbaugh
// Method Name: toRecord
// Creation Date: 11/92
// Purpose: Fills a D_Record from the member function data
//
// Return Value: D_Record created by this function
// Parameters: None
////////////////////////////////////////////////////////////////////////

D_Record MemberFunctionDefinition::toRecord(const char *id, long version)
{
    D_Record record = ClassMemberDefinition::toRecord(id,version);
    record.add(D_Field("Specification",specification.ptr()));
    record.add(D_Field("Suffix",suffix.ptr()));
    record.add(D_Field("Parameters", parameters.toString(true,true)));
```

```
    record.add(D_Field("ReturnVal",returnValue.ptr()));
    record.add(D_Field("SourcePath",sourceFile.ptr()));
    return record;
}


/* = = = = = = = = = = = DataMemberDefinition Methods = = = = = = = = = */

/////////////////////////////////////////////////////////////////////
// Author: David Brumbaugh
// Method Name: DataMemberDefinition
// Creation Date: 7/20/92
// Purpose: Constructor
//
// Return Value:
// Parameters:
//  Type        Name        Purpose/Description     Default Value
//  char *      className    Class to which this    None
//                           member belongs
//  istream *   in           Source of data         NULL
/////////////////////////////////////////////////////////////////////

DataMemberDefinition::DataMemberDefinition(const char *className, istream *in,
char *accessSpec):ClassMemberDefinition(className)
{
    type = isData;
    if (in)
        fromSource(*in,accessSpec);
}


/////////////////////////////////////////////////////////////////////
// Author: David Brumbaugh
// Method Name: shouldMakeTemplate
// Creation Date: 7/20/92
// Purpose: Return true if this data member should go into the class's
// source code template. In this case, only "static" members should
// go into the function.
//
// Return Value: 1 or 0
// Parameters: None
//
/////////////////////////////////////////////////////////////////////
DataMemberDefinition::shouldMakeTemplate()
{
    if (typeSpecifiers.Index("static") >= 0)
        return 1;
    else
        return 0;
}


/////////////////////////////////////////////////////////////////////
// Author: David Brumbaugh
// Method Name: makeTemplate
```

```
// Creation Date: 7/20/92
// Purpose: Create data member defintion templates
//
// Return Value: none
// Parameters:
//   Type          Name        Purpose/Description       Default Value
//   ostream &     out         Where to send template
//////////////////////////////////////////////////////////////////////

void DataMemberDefinition::makeTemplate(ostream &out)
{
    if (shouldMakeTemplate())
    {
        string tempTypeSpecifiers = typeSpecifiers;
        int i = tempTypeSpecifiers.Index("static");
        if ( i >= 0)
            tempTypeSpecifiers.Delete(i,6);
        out << tempTypeSpecifiers.Trim() << ' ' << ptrSpec << ' ';
        out << owningClass << "::" << name << "\n";
    }
}


//////////////////////////////////////////////////////////////////////
// Author: David Brumbaugh
// Method Name: fromSource
// Creation Date: 7/20/92
// Purpose: Fills data members from "in", where "in" is a stream
// of source code such as that found in a class definintion. Assumes the
// following:
//        1. The stream starts at the begining of a data definition
//        2. The source code is syntactically correct
//        3. All comments have been removed
//        4. The stream contains only the data definition
//
// Return Value: None
// Parameters:
//   Type          Name        Purpose/Description       Default Value
//   istream &     in          Source stream             None
//   char *        accessSpec  access specifier          NULL (ie,"private")
//////////////////////////////////////////////////////////////////////

void DataMemberDefinition::fromSource(istream &in, char *accessSpec)
{
    int done = 0;
    char c, *check;
    int i = 0;
    char work[50], prev[50];
    prev[0] = '\0';
    if (accessSpec)
        accessSpecifier = accessSpec;
    else
        accessSpecifier = "private";

    in.unsetf(ios::skipws);
```

```
    in >> ws;
    do
    {
        in >> c;
        if (c == ';' || c == ',' || in.eof())
        {
            work[i] = '\0';
            i = 0;
            done = 1;
            in >> ws; //Skip the white space
        }
        else if (! isspace(c))
            work[i++] = c;
        else // We have a space
        {
            work[i] = '\0';
            i = 0;
            in >> ws; // Get rid of the rest of the white space;
            if (strlen(prev) && !done) // Have we got any type info yet?
            {
                typeSpecifiers += prev;
                typeSpecifiers + " ";
            }
            strcpy(prev,work); // Save work, it may be a type spec or name
        }
        if (done)
        {
            if (typeSpecifiers.Len())
                lastTypeSpec = typeSpecifiers;
            else
                typeSpecifiers = lastTypeSpec;
            strcpy(name,prev); // The last string is the name
        }
    } while (! done);

    movePtrSpec(); // Fix up the pointer specifier if it exists

}

///////////////////////////////////////////////////////////////////
// Author: David Brumbaugh
// Method Name: toSource
// Creation Date: 7/20/92
// Purpose: Creates data member definitions within class definition
//
// Return Value: None
// Parameters:
// Type            Name           Purpose/Description         Default Value
// ostream &       out            Where to write the data     None
// int             withAccess     If non-0 include access     0
//                                specifier in source
// int             newType        If non-0, this data         0
//                                type is different that
//                                the previous one.
```

```
///////////////////////////////////////////////////////////////////

void DataMemberDefinition::toSource(ostream &out, int withAccess, int newType)
{
    if (withAccess)
        out << accessSpecifier << ":\n";
    if (newType)
        out << '\t' << typeSpecifiers << ' ';
    out << ptrSpec << name;
}

/* = = = = = = = = = = = ClassDefinition Methods = = = = = = = = = = = = */
///////////////////////////////////////////////////////////////////
// Author: David Brumbaugh
// Method Name: ClassDefinition
// Creation Date: 7/22/92
// Purpose: Constructor
//
// Return Value: None
// Parameters:
// Type        Name          Purpose/Description           Default Value
// istream *   in            Class source code ie:         NULL
//                           class  <name>:
//                           In stream starts here^
// unsigned    options       Flags for how to build class  0
//                           Valid values:
//                           ExpandInline
//                           UseComment
// char *      CommentFile   File name of comment template NULL
///////////////////////////////////////////////////////////////////

ClassDefinition::ClassDefinition(const char *cSpec, istream *in,
unsigned options, char *commentFile)
{
    name[0] = '\0';
    classSpec = cSpec;
    expandInline = options & ExpandInline ? 1 : 0;
    useComments = options & UseComments ? 1 : 0;
    forwardDeclaration = 0;

    //IdString look;
    if (commentFile)
        commentSource = new ifstream(commentFile);
    else
        commentSource = NULL;

    if (in)
    {

        fromSource(*in);
    }
}


///////////////////////////////////////////////////////////////////
```

```
// Author: David Brumbaugh
// Method Name: fromSource
// Creation Date: 7/20/92
// Purpose: Fills class definition from "in", where "in" is a stream
// of source code such as that found in a class definintion. Assumes the
// following:
//          1. The stream starts at the begining of a data definition
//          2. The source code is syntactically correct
//          3. All comments have been removed
//
// Return Value: None
// Parameters:
//  Type            Name            Purpose/Description     Default Value
//  istream &       in              Source stream           None
/////////////////////////////////////////////////////////////////////

void ClassDefinition::fromSource(istream &in)
{
    in.unsetf(ios::skipws); // Don't automatically skip the whitespace
    if (getClassName(in))
        getParents(in);
    if (forwardDeclaration)
        return;
    getMembers(in);
}


/////////////////////////////////////////////////////////////////////
// Author: David Brumbaugh
// Method Name: getClassName
// Creation Date: 7/22/92
// Purpose: Reads class name from stream. Leaves the stream in postion to
// read baseClasses.
//
// Return Value: Non 0 if it has baseClasses
// Parameters:
//  Type            Name            Purpose/Description     Default Value
//  istream &       in              Class source            None
/////////////////////////////////////////////////////////////////////

int ClassDefinition::getClassName(istream &in)
{
    char *tmpName = tmpnam(NULL); // Open a temporary work file
    fstream temp(tmpName, ios::in | ios::trunc | ios::out);

    in >> ws; // Skip passed all the initial white space
    char c;

    while (in >> c)
    {   // The class name is the first token before the ':' or '{'
        if (c != ':' && c != '{' && c != ';')
            temp << c;
        else
            break;
    }
```

```
        if (c == ';')
        {
            forwardDeclaration = 1;
        }
        else
        {
            forwardDeclaration = 0;
        }
        IdString work;
        temp.seekg(0L,ios::beg);
        do
        {   // Skip through to the last token
            temp >> work >> ws;
        } while ( ! temp.eof());

        strcpy(name, work);
        temp.rdbuf()->close();
        remove(tmpName);
        return (c == ':');  // If our last character was a colon, we need to read
                            // ancestsors


}

///////////////////////////////////////////////////////////////////////////////
// Author: David Brumbaugh
// Method Name: getParents
// Creation Date: 7-23-92
// Purpose: Read the base class list from the input stream
//
// Return Value: none
// Parameters:
// Type         Name      Purpose/Description                Default Value
// istream &    in        Stream containing class definition None
///////////////////////////////////////////////////////////////////////////////

void ClassDefinition::getParents(istream &in)
{

// Clear out the base class list to start
    while(baseClasses.total())
    {
        baseClasses.top();
        baseClasses.remove();
    }

    char *validBaseSpecs[] = { "virtual","public","private","protected",0 };

    in >> ws; // Skip the initial white space
    IdString work;
    int i = 0, done = 0;
    BaseClassSpec  *aBaseClassSpec = new BaseClassSpec;
    // A working structure
    do
    {
```

```
        in >> work[i];
        if ( isspace(work[i]) || in.eof())
        {
            work[i] = '\0';
            i = 0;
            if (in_list(work,validBaseSpecs) > -1)
            {
                aBaseClassSpec->baseSpecifier += work;
                aBaseClassSpec->baseSpecifier += " ";
            }
            else if (strlen(work))
            {  // If it's not a base specifer it must be a base class
                strcpy(aBaseClassSpec->name,skpblk(trim(work)));
                aBaseClassSpec->baseSpecifier.Trim();
                baseClasses.add(*aBaseClassSpec);
                delete aBaseClassSpec;
                aBaseClassSpec = new BaseClassSpec;
            }
            in >> ws; // Skip the rest of the white space
        }
        else if (work[i] == ',' || work[i] == '{' )
        {
            done = (work[i] == '{');
            work[i] = '\0';
            i = 0;
            if (strlen(work))
            {
                strcpy(aBaseClassSpec->name,skpblk(trim(work)));
                aBaseClassSpec->baseSpecifier.Trim();
                baseClasses.add(*aBaseClassSpec);
                delete aBaseClassSpec;
                aBaseClassSpec = new BaseClassSpec;
            }
            in >> ws; // skip white space after the comma
        }
        else
            ++i;
    } while (! done && ! in.eof());

    /*
    chg - 3/14
    if (aBaseClassSpec)
        delete aBaseClassSpec;
    */

}

/////////////////////////////////////////////////////////////////
// Author: David Brumbaugh
// Method Name: getMembers
// Creation Date: 7/26/92
// Purpose: Create member list
//
// Return Value: None
```

```
// Parameters:
// Type           Name         Purpose/Description        Default Value
// istream &      in           Member source             None
////////////////////////////////////////////////////////////////////

void ClassDefinition::getMembers(istream &in)
{
    char *tmpName = tmpnam(NULL); // Open a temporary work file
    fstream temp(tmpName, ios::in | ios::trunc | ios::out);
    char c;
    memberTypes curMember;
    IdString accessSpecifier;
    char work[512];
    int i = 0;
    char *validAccessSpecs[] = {"private","public","protected",'\0'};

    strcpy(accessSpecifier,"private"); // Default specifier

    in >> ws; // Skip passed all the initial white space
    do
    {
        curMember = isData; // Assume it's a data member
        while (in >> c)
        {
            if (c == '}') // All done?
                break;
            if ( c == ':')
            {   // We've been reading an access specifier
                work[i] = '\0'; i = 0;
                in >> ws;
                if (in_list(skpblk(trim(work)),validAccessSpecs) != -1)
                    strcpy(accessSpecifier,work);
            }
            else if (c != ';' && c != '{' && c != ',')
            { // The declararion ends with a ; or {  or ,
                if (c == '(')
                {
                    curMember = isFunction;
                    // Pick up all the parameters
                    int level = 1;
                    do
                    {
                        work[i++] = c;
                        in >> c;
                        if (c == ')')
                            --level;
                        else if (c == '(')
                            ++level;
                    } while( level > 0);
                }
                // temp << c;
                work[i++] = c; // Build a word in the working buffer
            }
            else
```

```
            { // We've got a whole "word" to remember
                work[i] = '\0';
                temp << work << ' ';
                work[0] = '\0'; i = 0;
                in >> ws; // Skip the white space
                temp << c; // Put the declaration terminator into temp
                if ( c == '{')
                {    // Let's get to the end of the inline function
                    int level = 1;
                    while ( level > 0)
                    {
                        in >> c >> ws;
                        if (c == '{')
                            ++level;
                        else if (c == '}')
                            —level;
                    }
                    if (c == '}') // We don't want to terminate the loop
                        c = 0;
                }
                break; // We're ready to build the member
            }
        }
        if (c != '}')
        {
            temp.seekg(0L,ios::beg); // Rewind the file for member declarations
            if (curMember == isFunction)
            {
                ClassMemberDefinition *t =
                new MemberFunctionDefinition(name,&temp, accessSpecifier,
                expandInline);
                // I'll save a warning and assign the temp myself
                members.add(t);
            }
            else
            {
                ClassMemberDefinition *t =
                new DataMemberDefinition(name,&temp,accessSpecifier);
                members.add(t);
            }
            in >> ws; // Skip the white space to the next token
            temp.close(); // Clean up the temp file and start over
            temp.open(tmpName,ios::in | ios::out | ios::trunc);
        }
    } while(c != '}');
    temp.close();
    remove(tmpName);
}

//////////////////////////////////////////////////////////////////////
// Author: David Brumbaugh
// Method Name: toSource
// Creation Date: 7/26/92
// Purpose: Creates a source description of class
```

```
//
// Return Value: None
// Parameters:
//   Type              Name            Purpose/Description          Default Value
//   ostream &         out             Where to put the source      None
//////////////////////////////////////////////////////////////////////

void ClassDefinition::toSource(ostream &out)
{
    char c;
    char currAccessSpec[12], currTypeSpec[40];

    string spec = classSpec+':';
    spec.toUpper();
    putComment(out,spec.ptr(),name);
    out << classSpec << ' ' << name << ' ';
    if (baseClasses.total())
    {
        out  << ':' << ' ';
        for (int i = 0; i < baseClasses.total(); ++i)
        {
            out << baseClasses[i].baseSpecifier << ' ' <<
            baseClasses[i].name << ' ';
            if (i == (baseClasses.total() - 1))
                out << "\n{\n";
            else
                out << ", ";
        }
    }
    else
        out << "\n{\n";
    currAccessSpec[0] = '\0';
    currTypeSpec[0] = '\0';
    memberTypes lastMember = unknown;

    int newAccessSpec = 0, newTypeSpec = 0;
    for ( int i = 0; i < members.total(); ++i)
    {
        if (strcmp(currAccessSpec,members[i]->getAccessSpec()))
        {
            strcpy(currAccessSpec,members[i]->getAccessSpec());
            newAccessSpec = 1;
        }
        if (strcmp(currTypeSpec,members[i]->getTypeSpec()))
        {
            strcpy(currTypeSpec,members[i]->getTypeSpec());
            newTypeSpec = 1;
        }

        if (lastMember == isData && newTypeSpec)
            out << ";\n";
        else if (lastMember == isData)
            out << ',';
        else if (lastMember != isData && i != 0)
```

```
        {
            newTypeSpec = 1;
        }
        members[i]->toSource(out, newAccessSpec, newTypeSpec);
        newAccessSpec = 0;
        newTypeSpec = 0;
        lastMember = members[i]->isA();
    }
    out << "\n};\n";

}

//////////////////////////////////////////////////////////////////////
// Author: David Brumbaugh
// Method Name: putComment
// Creation Date: 7/27/92
// Purpose: Puts the comment template before the class or method
//
// Return Value: void
// Parameters:
//   Type          Name      Purpose/Description        Default Value
//   ostream &     out       Target for comment
//////////////////////////////////////////////////////////////////////

void ClassDefinition::putComment(ostream &out, const char *what,
const char *id)
{
    char c;
    if (! useComments)
    return;
    out << "//";
    for (int i = 0; i < 76; ++i)
        out << '/';
    out << '\n';
    out << "// " << what << ' ' << id << '\n';
    if (commentSource)
    {
        do
        {
            *commentSource >> c;
            out << c;
        } while(! commentSource->eof() );
        commentSource->clear();
        commentSource->seekg(0L,ios::beg);
    }
    out << "//";
    for (i = 0; i < 76; ++i)
        out << '/';
    out << '\n';
}

//////////////////////////////////////////////////////////////////////
// Author: David Brumbaugh
// Method Name: makeTemplate
```

```
// Creation Date: 7/27/92
// Purpose: Create a source file with empty functions and static data
// declaration for this class
//
// Return Value: None
// Parameters:
//   Type            Name          Purpose/Description          Default Value
//   ostream &       out           Target for source code       None
/////////////////////////////////////////////////////////////////////////

void ClassDefinition::makeTemplate(ostream &out)
{
    if (forwardDeclaration)
        return;
    putComment(out,"Source For Class:",name);
    for ( int i = 0; i < members.total(); ++i)
    {
        if (members[i]->isA() == isFunction &&
            members[i]->shouldMakeTemplate())
            putComment(out,"Method: ", members[i]->getName());
        members[i]->makeTemplate(out);
    }
}


/////////////////////////////////////////////////////////////////////////
// Author: David Brumbaugh
// Method Name: ~ClassDefinition
// Creation Date: 7/27/92
// Purpose: Destructor
//
// Return Value:  None
// Parameters: None
//
/////////////////////////////////////////////////////////////////////////

ClassDefinition::~ClassDefinition()
{
    if (commentSource)
        delete commentSource;
    for (int i = 0; i < members.total(); ++i)
        delete members[i];
        // Because members is a list of POINTERS and not a list of members,
        // we need to clean it up ourselves.
}

//—————————— Param List ——————————

void ParamList::toSource(ostream & out,Boolean withNames,Boolean withDefaults)
{
    out <<  '(';

    for(int i = 0; i < total(); ++i)
    {
        out << anArray[i].typeSpecifiers.Trim() << ' ';
```

```
            if (withNames)
                out << anArray[i].name;
            if (anArray[i].defaultValue.Len() && withDefaults)
                out << " = " << anArray[i].defaultValue;
            if (i != (total() -1))
                out << ',';
        }
    out << ')';
}

void ParamList::fromSource(istream & in)
{
    int done = 0, level = 0, i = 0;
    char work[100], prev[100];
    char paramBuffer[512], // Surely this will be enough
        *check; // Check for value in string with this one

    anArray.flush(); // We chould be starting over
    top(); // So we start over
    prev[0] = '\0';
    if (in.peek() == '(')
        in.ignore(); // Skip the initial open paren
    ++level;
    memset(paramBuffer,'\0',sizeof(paramBuffer));
    in >> ws;
    do
    {
        in >> paramBuffer[i];
        if (paramBuffer[i] == '(')
            ++level;
        else if (paramBuffer[i] == ')')
            —level;
        if (level == 0)
            paramBuffer[i] = '\0';
        ++i;
    } while(level > 0 && ! in.eof());
    if (in.eof())
        return;
    trim(paramBuffer);
    istrstream  params(paramBuffer);
    ParamDefinition *paramDef;
    do
    {
        paramDef = new ParamDefinition;
        if (! params.getline(work,sizeof(work),','))
        {
            done = 1;
            delete paramDef;
            break;
        }
        if ((check = strchr(work,'=')) != NULL) //Do we have a default value?
        {
            *check = '\0';
            ++check;
```

```
            paramDef->defaultValue = skpblk(trim(check));
        }
        check = strtok(work," "); // get the first token
        if (check)
            strcpy(prev,check);

        // The last word we get is probably the name
        // All the others probably type specs.
        while ((check = strtok(NULL," ")) != NULL)
        {
            paramDef->typeSpecifiers += prev;
            paramDef->typeSpecifiers += " ";
            strcpy(prev,check);
        }
        // However, if there is only one word in the parameter list,
        // it's a type spec. Since we're not keeping track of all types,
        // (This is only a pseudo-parser, not a full compiler.) we'll
        // assume that the last word is the name.
        // We also need to move the pointer indicators over to the "type"
        int ptrI = 0;
        while (prev[ptrI] == '*' || prev[ptrI] == '&')
        {
            paramDef->typeSpecifiers += prev[ptrI++];
        }
        paramDef->typeSpecifiers.Trim();

        paramDef->name = trim(skpblk(&prev[ptrI]));
        add(*paramDef);

        delete paramDef;
    } while (! done);

}

const char *ParamList::toString(Boolean withNames,Boolean withDefaults)
{
    string r;
    r += '(';
    for( int i = 0; i < total(); ++i)
    {
        r += anArray[i].typeSpecifiers.Trim();
        if (withNames)
        {
            r +=  " ";
            r += anArray[i].name;
        }
        if (withDefaults && anArray[i].defaultValue.Len() > 0)
        {
            r +=  " = ";
            r += anArray[i].defaultValue;
        }
        if (i != total() - 1)
            r += ',';
    }
```

```
    r += ')';
    static string r1;
    r1 = r;
    return r1.ptr();
}

void ParamList::fromString(const char *s)
{
    string ss(s);
    istrstream in(ss.ptr());
    in.unsetf(ios::skipws);
    in >> ws; // We'll skip the first white space
    fromSource(in);
}

ParamList::operator == (const ParamList &p) const
{
    if (total() != p.total())
        return 0;
    for(int x = 0; x < total(); ++x)
    {
        if (anArray[x].typeSpecifiers != p[x].typeSpecifiers)
            return 0;
    }
    return 1;
}

const char *ParamList::getDescField()
{
    string descField;
    for (int i = 0; i < total(); ++i)
    {
        descField += anArray[i].description;
        descField += (char) 11;
        // 11 is a Vertical TAB in ASCII, a logical seperator
    }
    static string s;
    s = descField;
    return s.ptr();
}

void ParamList::fillDescriptions(const char *str)
{
    char *buffer = new char[strlen(str) + 1];
    char *strBuff = new char[strlen(str) + 1];
    strcpy(strBuff,str);
    istrstream descripField(strBuff);
    for (int i = 0; i < total(); ++i)
    {
        descripField.getline(buffer,strlen(strBuff)+1,(char) 11);
        anArray[i].description = buffer;
    }
    delete buffer;
    delete strBuff;
```

```
}

/*
MemberList::~MemberList()
{ for (int i = 0; i < total(); ++i) delete anArray[i];
} // Clear out the member list


MemberList &MemberList::operator = (const MemberList &memList)
{
    int tot = total();
    ClassMemberDefinition *cmd;

    // Clear out the existing stuff
    for (int i = 0; i < tot; ++i)
    {
        cmd = anArray[i];
        delete cmd;
    }
    anArray.flush();
    // Add new stuff
    MemberFunctionDefinition *mfd1, *mfd2;
    DataMemberDefinition *dmd1, *dmd2;
    for (i = 0; i < memList.total(); ++i)
    {
        cmd = memList.anArray[i];
        if (cmd->isA() == isData)
        {
            dmd1 = new DataMemberDefinition;
            dmd2 = (DataMemberDefinition *) cmd;
            *dmd1 = *dmd2;
            add((ClassMemberDefinition *) dmd1);
        }
        else
        {
            mfd1 = new MemberFunctionDefinition;
            mfd2 = (MemberFunctionDefinition *) cmd;
            *mfd1 = *mfd2;
            add((ClassMemberDefinition *)mfd1);
        }
    }
    return *this;
}

*/


//////////////////////////////////////////////////////////////////
// Listing  : 10-5
// Filename    : DEFNFILE.H
// Purpose  : Class definition file declaration
//////////////////////////////////////////////////////////////////

#ifndef DEFNFILE_H
```

```
#define DEFNFILE_H
#include "clsdfn.h"
#include "listimp.h"
#include <stdio.h>
#include <str.h>
#include <string.h>
#include "FUNCDEF.H"

// Offset of class within the file.
struct classOffset
{
    public:
        string classSpec; // class, union, struct ...
        string className; // Name of class
        long offset;       // Where in the file

    operator ==(const classOffset &i) // Necessary for membership in BI_Array
    { return (className == i.className); }

};

// Offset of function prototype within the file.
struct FunctOffset
{
        string name;   // Name of function
        ParamList parameters; // List of function parameters
        long offset;            // Offset within the file.
        operator ==(const FunctOffset &fo) const;
        void makeName(istream *in); // Make name from source
        void makeParamList(istream *in);  // Make parameter list from source
        // Maybe this should have been a class?
};

typedef ListImp<classOffset> ClassOSList;
typedef ListImp<FunctOffset> FunctOSList;
typedef ListImp<string> IdList;

//////////////////////////////////////////////////////////////////////
// Author        : David Brumbaugh
// Class Name    : HeaderFileDefn
// Creation Date: 7/31/92
// Catagories    : Model
// Purpose       : Models the header file that contains classes
//                 Can build class templates for any or all classes
//                 defined in the header file.
//
// Major Public Methods:
//   HeaderFileDefn      : Constructor
//   getIoStream         : Returns i/o stream
//   startOfClass        : Positions stream input stream at the start of a
//                         class
//   addClassToMake      : put class name into classes to have templates
//                         created
//   makeClassDefinitions : Create class selected definition templates.
```

```
//
// Major Data Items:
// classesToMake          : List of classes the user wants to have templates
//                           made of.
// anIoStream             : Stream with header information
//
// aClassDefinition       : A working variable for class definition
// classesInStream        : List of classes & offsets in the stream
// options                 : Flags for specific class options for classes in
//                           the header.
//////////////////////////////////////////////////////////////////////////////

class HeaderFileDefn
{
    protected:
        unsigned options;
        iostream *anIoStream;
        IdList classesToMake;
        ClassDefinition *aClassDefinition;
        FunctionDefinition *aFunctionDefinition;
        ClassOSList classesInStream;
        FunctOSList functionsInStream;
        void init(istream &in, unsigned options);
        //Initialize the class: called by the constructors
        void removeComments(istream &in); // Remove comments from header
        void findClasses(); // Locate the start of each class in the iostream
        void findFunctions(); // Locate the start of each function
        char *getClassName(); // Get the name of the class from the iostream
        char tempName[L_tmpnam];
        // We need to remember this, so we can delete the temporary file
        void skipBlock(); //Skip a class or template in the header file
        void skipPreprocessorCommand(); // You know ...
        FunctOffset *buildFunctOffset(long os); // Builds a FunctOffset struct
    public:
        iostream *getIoStream() { return anIoStream; }
        void addClassToMake(const char *className);
        HeaderFileDefn(const char *fileName, unsigned options = 0);
        HeaderFileDefn(istream &inputStream, unsigned options = 0);
        int startOfClass(const char *className);
        void makeClassTemplates(char *outFileName, int makeAll = 0,
        char *commentFile = NULL);
        void makeClassTemplates(ostream &out, int makeAll = 0,
        char *commentFile = NULL);
        FunctOSList *getFunctionList() { return &functionsInStream; }
        ClassOSList *getClassList() { return &classesInStream; }
        ~HeaderFileDefn();
};

#endif


//////////////////////////////////////////////////////////////////////////////
// Listing  : 10-6
// Filename : DEFNFILE.CPP
```

```
// Purpose    : Source code for ClassDefnClass
//////////////////////////////////////////////////////////////////////

#include "DEFNFILE.H"
#include <string.h>
#include <strstrea.h>
#include <utility.h>
//////////////////////////////////////////////////////////////////////
// Author: David Brumbaugh
// Method Name: HeaderFileDefn
// Creation Date: 8/5/92
// Purpose: Constructor
//
// Parameters:
//  Type        Name            Purpose/Description        Default Value
//  char *      fileName        Name of header file        None
//////////////////////////////////////////////////////////////////////

HeaderFileDefn::HeaderFileDefn(const char *fileName, unsigned options)
{
    ifstream in(fileName);
    init(in,options);
}
//////////////////////////////////////////////////////////////////////
// Author: David Brumbaugh
// Method Name: HeaderFileDefn
// Creation Date: 8/5/92
// Purpose: Constructor
//
// Parameters:
//  Type         Name     Purpose/Description        Default Value
//  istream &    in       Stream with class info     None
//////////////////////////////////////////////////////////////////////

HeaderFileDefn::HeaderFileDefn(istream &inputStream,unsigned options)
{
    init(inputStream,options);
}
//////////////////////////////////////////////////////////////////////
// Author: David Brumbaugh
// Method Name:  addClassToMake
// Creation Date:  8/92
// Purpose: Put a class name into a list to be built
//
// Return Value: None
// Parameters:
//  Type        Name            Purpose/Description        Default Value
//  char *      className        Name of classes to make    None
//////////////////////////////////////////////////////////////////////

void HeaderFileDefn::addClassToMake(const char *className)
{
    string temp(className); // Make my own teporary and save the warning
    classesToMake.add(temp);
```

```
}
////////////////////////////////////////////////////////////////////
// Author: David Brumbaugh
// Method Name: startOfClass
// Creation Date: 8/6/92
// Purpose: Locate a particular class within the working iostream
//
// Return Value: index if found, -1 if not
// Parameters:
// Type         Name            Purpose/Description          Default Value
// char *       className        Name of class to find        None
//                               find the start of.
////////////////////////////////////////////////////////////////////

int HeaderFileDefn::startOfClass(const char *className)
{
    classOffset co;
    co.className = className;
    for (int i = 0; i < classesInStream.total(); ++i)
        if (classesInStream[i].className == className)
        {
            // Set both the get and put pointers in the stream
            anIoStream->seekg(classesInStream[i].offset);
            anIoStream->seekp(classesInStream[i].offset);
            return i;
        }
    return -1;
}


////////////////////////////////////////////////////////////////////
// Author: David Brumbaugh
// Method Name: removeComments
// Creation Date: 8/6/92
// Purpose: Removes comments from original input as it moves the rest
// of the file into anIoStream
//
// Return Value: None
// Parameters:
// Type         Name            Purpose/Description          Default Value
// istream &    in               Original input file          None
////////////////////////////////////////////////////////////////////

void HeaderFileDefn::removeComments(istream &in)
{
    char c, endChar;
    int inComment = 0;

    in.unsetf(ios::skipws);

    do
    {
        in >> c;
        if (c == '/')
        {
```

```
        if (in.peek() == '/')
        {
            endChar = '\n';
            inComment = 1;
        }
        else if (in.peek() == '*')
        {
            endChar = '*';
            inComment = 1;
        }
        else
            inComment = 0;

        while(inComment)
        {
            in >> c;
            if (c == endChar)
            {
                if (c == '\n')
                {
                    inComment = 0;
                    c = '\n'; // Let's maintain line integrity.
                }
                else if (in.peek() == '/')
                {
                    in.ignore();
                    inComment = 0;
                    c = ' ';
                }
            }
        }
    }
    *anIoStream << c;
  } while (! in.eof());
}

////////////////////////////////////////////////////////////////////////
// Author: David Brumbaugh
// Method Name: makeClassTemplates
// Creation Date: 8/7/92
// Purpose: Create templates for selected classes in a header file
//
// Return Value: None
// Parameters:
//   Type         Name          Purpose/Description         Default Value
//   char *       outFileName   Name of destination         None
//   int          makeAll       If TRUE, make templates      0 (FALSE)
//                              for all the classes in
//                              in the file, otherwise
//                              make only those in the
//                              classesToMake list.
////////////////////////////////////////////////////////////////////////

void HeaderFileDefn::makeClassTemplates(char *outFileName, int makeAll,
```

```
char *commentFile)
{
    fstream outFile(outFileName, ios::in | ios::trunc | ios::out);
    makeClassTemplates(outFile,makeAll,commentFile);
}

////////////////////////////////////////////////////////////////////
// Author: David Brumbaugh
// Method Name: makeClassTemplates
// Creation Date: 8/8/92
// Purpose: See above
//
// Return Value: None
// Parameters:
//   Type           Name           Purpose/Description        Default Value
//   ostream &      out            Destinaiton of template    None
//   int            makeAll        If TRUE, make templates     0 (FALSE)
//                                 for all the classes in
//                                 in the file, otherwise
//                                 make only those in the
//                                 classesToMake list.
////////////////////////////////////////////////////////////////////

void HeaderFileDefn::makeClassTemplates(ostream &out, int makeAll,
char *commentFile)
{
    if (! makeAll)
    {
        for(int i = 0; i < classesToMake.total(); ++i)
        {
            int s;
            if ( (s = startOfClass(classesToMake[i].ptr())) >= 0)
            {
                aClassDefinition =
                new ClassDefinition(classesInStream[s].classSpec.ptr(),
                anIoStream, options, commentFile);
                aClassDefinition->makeTemplate(out);
                delete aClassDefinition;
            }
        }
    }
    else
    {
        for(int i = 0; i < classesInStream.total(); ++i)
        {
            anIoStream->clear(); // Clear out the eof and other flags
            anIoStream->unsetf(ios::skipws); // Put this one back
            anIoStream->seekg(classesInStream[i].offset, ios::beg);
            anIoStream->seekp(classesInStream[i].offset, ios::beg);
            aClassDefinition =
            new ClassDefinition(classesInStream[i].classSpec.ptr(),
            anIoStream, options,commentFile);
            aClassDefinition->makeTemplate(out);
            delete aClassDefinition;
```

```
        }

    }
    // Assume we always want to make the standalone functions
    for (int i = 0; i < functionsInStream.total(); ++i)
    {
        anIoStream->clear();
        anIoStream->unsetf(ios::skipws);
        anIoStream->seekg(functionsInStream[i].offset, ios::beg);
        anIoStream->seekp(functionsInStream[i].offset, ios::beg);
        aFunctionDefinition =
        new FunctionDefinition(anIoStream);
        aFunctionDefinition->makeTemplate(out);
        delete aFunctionDefinition;
    }
}

//////////////////////////////////////////////////////////////////
// Author: David Brumbaugh
// Method Name: init
// Creation Date: 8/5/92
// Purpose: Initialize the header file
//
// Return Value:  None
// Parameters:
//  Type         Name          Purpose/Description      Default Value
//  istream &    in            Input stream             None
//////////////////////////////////////////////////////////////////

void HeaderFileDefn::init(istream &in, unsigned opt)
{
    tmpnam(tempName);
    options = opt;
    anIoStream = new fstream(tempName, ios::in | ios::trunc | ios::out);
    anIoStream->unsetf(ios::skipws);
    removeComments(in);
    findClasses();
    findFunctions();
}

//////////////////////////////////////////////////////////////////
// Author: David Brumbaugh
// Method Name: ~HeaderFileDefn()
// Creation Date: 8/5/92
// Purpose: Destructor
//
//////////////////////////////////////////////////////////////////

HeaderFileDefn::~HeaderFileDefn()
{
    delete anIoStream;
    remove(tempName);
}
```

```
//////////////////////////////////////////////////////////////////
// Author: David Brumbaugh
// Method Name: findClasses
// Creation Date: 8/5/92
// Purpose: Identify classes and loctations within cleaned stream
//
// Return Value:  None
// Parameters: None
//////////////////////////////////////////////////////////////////
void HeaderFileDefn::findClasses()
{
    char work[256];
    classOffset co;
    long offset;

    anIoStream->seekg(0L);
    while (! anIoStream->eof())
    {
        *anIoStream >> ws >> work >> ws;
        if ((strcmp(work,"class") == 0) || (strcmp(work,"struct") == 0)
        || strcmp(work,"union")  == 0)
        {
            co.classSpec = work;
            co.offset = anIoStream->tellg();
            co.className = getClassName();
            classesInStream.add(co);
        }
    }
}


//////////////////////////////////////////////////////////////////
// Author: David Brumbaugh
// Method Name: getClassName
// Creation Date: 8/8/92
// Purpose: Get the class name out of the io stream
//
// Return Value: Name of the class
// Parameters: None
//
//////////////////////////////////////////////////////////////////

char *HeaderFileDefn::getClassName()
{
    char tmpBuff[512];
    static IdString name;

    strstream temp(tmpBuff, sizeof(tmpBuff), ios::in | ios::out);

    *anIoStream >> ws; // Skip passed all the initial white space
    char c;

    while (*anIoStream >> c)
    {   // The class name is the first token before the ':' or '{' or ';'
        if (c != ':' && c != '{' && c != ';')
```

```
                temp << c;
            else
                break;
        }

        IdString work;
        temp.seekg(0L, ios::beg);
        do
        {   // Skip through to the last token
            temp >> work >> ws;
        } while ( ! temp.eof());

        strcpy(name, work);

        return name;
    }

//////////////////////////////////////////////////////////////////////
// Author: David Brumbaugh
// Method Name: findFunctions
// Creation Date: 10/17/92
// Purpose: Locate the start of each function
//
// Return Value: None
// Parameters: None
//
//////////////////////////////////////////////////////////////////////
void HeaderFileDefn::findFunctions()
{
    char work[256];
    long offset;
    static char *blocks[] = { "class", "struct", "union", "template", NULL };
    anIoStream->seekg(0L);
    anIoStream->clear();
    anIoStream->unsetf(ios::skipws);
    while (! anIoStream->eof())
    {
        offset = anIoStream->tellg();
        *anIoStream >> ws >> work >> ws;
        if (work[0] == '#')
            skipPreprocessorCommand();
        else if (in_list(work, blocks) >= 0)
            skipBlock();
        else // If it's not one of the above, it must be a function prototype
        {
            FunctOffset *fo = buildFunctOffset(offset);
            if (fo)
            {
                functionsInStream.add(*fo);
                delete fo;
            }
        }
    }
}
```

```
///////////////////////////////////////////////////////////////////
// Author: David Brumbaugh
// Method Name: skipPreprocessorCommand
// Creation Date: 10/17/92
// Purpose: Locate the end of a preprocessor
//
// Return Value: None
// Parameters:
// Type            Name     Puropose
// const char *    work     Contains what's been read so far
//
///////////////////////////////////////////////////////////////////

void HeaderFileDefn::skipPreprocessorCommand()
{
    // Normally, the preprocessor command only takes one line
    // However it could have a '\\' at the end and take up the
    // next line. Also, the #else, #endif directive doesn't have anything
    // after it, so it is complete.
    // So...
    // Let's be sure we didn't skip over an important '\n'
    anIoStream->seekg(-1L, ios::cur);

    int done = 0;
    char c,prevC = 0;
    while (! done)
    {
        *anIoStream >> c;
        if (c == '\n' && prevC != '\\' || anIoStream->eof())
            done = 1;
        else
            prevC = c;
    }

}

///////////////////////////////////////////////////////////////////
// Author: David Brumbaugh
// Method Name: skipClass
// Creation Date: 10/17/92
// Purpose: Skip passed a class definition in a header file
//
// Return Value: None
// Parameters: None
//
///////////////////////////////////////////////////////////////////

void HeaderFileDefn::skipBlock()
{
    // We have the "class" or "template" keyword
    // So let's find the { } enclosing the body

    int done = 0;
    char c;
```

```
    int level = 0;
    while (! done)
    {
        *anIoStream >> c;
        if ( c == '{')
            ++level;
        else if ( c == '}')
        {
            —level;
            done = level == 0;
        }
        else if ( level == 0 && c == ';')
            done = 1; // It could be a declaration or assignment of some sort.
        else if (anIoStream->eof())
            done = 1;
    }


}

///////////////////////////////////////////////////////////////////
// Author: David Brumbaugh
// Method Name: buildFunctOffset
// Creation Date: 10/17/92
// Purpose: Builds the FuncOffset structure
//
// Return Value: FunctOffset * that was built or NULL if there is no
// function there.
//
// Parameters:
// Type     Name        Purpose
// long     offset      Start of potential function definition.
///////////////////////////////////////////////////////////////////

FunctOffset *HeaderFileDefn::buildFunctOffset(long offset)
{
    FunctOffset *aFunctOffset;
    anIoStream->seekg(offset); // Start over at the begining.
    char *stopTokens = ";{,="; // Each of these could indicate that we don't
                               // Really have a function.
    int done = 0;
    char c;
    do
    {
        *anIoStream >> c;
        if (strchr(stopTokens,c) || anIoStream->eof())
            return NULL;
        else if (c == '(') // We really do have a function
        {
            aFunctOffset = new FunctOffset;
            aFunctOffset->offset = offset;
            aFunctOffset->makeName(anIoStream);
            aFunctOffset->makeParamList(anIoStream);
```

```
            done = 1;
        }

    } while (! done);
    return aFunctOffset;
}

/*——————— FunctOffset Methods ——————*/
////////////////////////////////////////////////////////////////////////
// Author: David Brumbaugh
// Method Name: makeName
// Creation Date: 10/18/92
// Purpose: Get the name of the function out of the stream.
//
// Return Value: None
// Parameters:
//  Type           Name        Purpose/Description         Default Value
//  istream *      in          Source of function name     None
////////////////////////////////////////////////////////////////////////

void FunctOffset::makeName(istream *in)
{
    char nBuff[100], work[100];
    int done = 0;

    in->seekg(offset); //Start over again
    in->getline(nBuff,100,'('); // We've got the type and name
    istrstream  nameIn(nBuff); //Streams are easier to work with
    do
    {
        nameIn >> work >> ws; // Trim the trailing white space
        if (nameIn.eof())
            done = 1;
        if ( strcmp(work,"operator") == 0 )
            name = work;
        if (done)
        {
            if (name.Len() != 0)
                name += ' ';
            name += work; // The last string is usually the name
        }
    } while (! done);

    // Fix the pointer specifiers if they exist
    while(name[0] == '*' || name[0] == '&')
        name.Delete(0,1);
}

////////////////////////////////////////////////////////////////////////
// Author: David Brumbaugh
// Method Name: makeParamList
// Creation Date: 10/19/92
// Purpose: Get the list of parameters from the input file.
//
```

```
// Return Value:
// Parameters:
//    Type          Name              Purpose/Description        Default Value
//
////////////////////////////////////////////////////////////////////////

void FunctOffset::makeParamList(istream *in)
{
    parameters.fromSource(*in);
}


////////////////////////////////////////////////////////////////////////
// Author: David Brumbaugh
// Method Name: ==
// Creation Date: 10/19/92
// Purpose:  Compares structures for equality
//
// Return Value: True if the names and parameter types match
// Parameters:
//  Type              Name    Purpose/Description          Default Value
//  FunctOffset &     fo      Structure to compare
////////////////////////////////////////////////////////////////////////

FunctOffset::operator ==(const FunctOffset &fo) const
{
    return (name == fo.name && parameters == fo.parameters);
}



////////////////////////////////////////////////////////////////////////
// Listing  :10-7
// Filename   :FuncDef.H
// Purpose    : Class Declaration of function definition in .h files.
////////////////////////////////////////////////////////////////////////

#ifndef FUNCDEF_H
#define FUNCDEF_H
#include "clsdfn.h"
////////////////////////////////////////////////////////////////////////
// Author        : David Brumbaugh
// Class Name    : FunctionDefinition
// Creation Date: 10/10/92
// Catagories    : Model
// Purpose       : Models the fucntion declarations within a header file.
//
// Major Public Methods:
//     toSource : Generates a definition of the
//  fromSource: Reads the source code and fills this class's data
//  makeTemplate: Generate an "empty" source code version of function
//  ==: For comparing values
//
// Major Data Items:
//
//   type:  a function or template function?
```

```
//    name: What is this thing called?
//    typeSpecifiers: (const,int, etc.)
//    parameters: List of parameters
//    suffix: End of function definition like: "const"
//
//////////////////////////////////////////////////////////////////////

enum functionTypes {isUnknow, isStandaloneFunction };

class FunctionDefinition
{
    protected:
        IdString name;
        string typeSpecifiers;
        string returnValue; // What does the return type mean?
        functionTypes type;
        char ptrSpec[7]; // Six levels of indirection should be plenty
        virtual void movePtrSpec();
        // Move the pointer spec from the name to the type
        string suffix;
        ParamList parameters;
        virtual void makeTypeAndName(istream &in);//Get typeSpec, name from in
        virtual void makeParamList(istream &in);// Make parameter list from in
        virtual void makeSuffix(istream &in); // Things like = 0, const, {..}
        string specification; // Textual description of Function.

    public:
        functionTypes isA() { return type; }
        FunctionDefinition(istream *in = NULL);
        const char *getName() { return name; }
        virtual void setName(const char *n) { strcpy(name,n); }
        const char *getTypeSpec() { return typeSpecifiers.ptr(); }
        void setTypeSpec(const char *type) { typeSpecifiers = type; }
        const char *getSpecification() { return specification.ptr(); }
        void setSpecification(const char *spec) { specification = spec; }
        virtual operator == (FunctionDefinition &c) const;
        virtual void makeTemplate(ostream &out, Boolean withComments = false,
        const char *description = NULL);
        virtual void toSource(ostream &out);
        virtual void fromSource(istream &in);
        virtual void addParameter(ParamDefinition &paramDefn)
        {
            parameters.add(paramDefn);
        }
        virtual ParamList &getParamList() { return parameters; }
        const char *getSuffix() { return suffix.ptr(); }
        void setSuffix(const char *sfx) {suffix = sfx; }

};


#endif
```

```
//////////////////////////////////////////////////////////////////
// Listing  : 10-8
// Filename   : FUNCDEF.CPP
// Purpose   : Souce code for FunctionDefinition classes
//////////////////////////////////////////////////////////////////

#include "funcdef.h"
#include <strstream.h>
#include <utility.h>
//////////////////////////////////////////////////////////////////
// Author: David Brumbaugh
// Method Name: FunctionDefinition
// Creation Date: 10/92
// Purpose: Constructor
//
// Return Value:
// Parameters:
//  Type            Name               Purpose/Description       Default Value
//  istream *       in                 Source code stream from   NULL
//                                     which to build definition.
//
//  int             expInline          If non-0, expand inline   0
//                                     code in source file
//////////////////////////////////////////////////////////////////

FunctionDefinition::FunctionDefinition(istream *in)
{
    name[0] = '\0';
    type = isStandaloneFunction;
    ptrSpec[0] = '\0';
    if (in)
        fromSource(*in);
}


//////////////////////////////////////////////////////////////////
// Author: David Brumbaugh
// Method Name: operator ==
// Creation Date:  10/92
// Purpose: For comparing ClassMemberDefinitions. BIDS requires a ==
// operator for most contained classes.
//    If a class member has the same name it matches. This will be overloaded
//  in the MemberFunctionDefn class.
//
// Return Value: 0 or Non-0
// Parameters:
//  Type                      Name    Purpose/Description        Default Value
//  ClassMemberDefinition &   c       Value being compared       None
//////////////////////////////////////////////////////////////////

FunctionDefinition::operator == (FunctionDefinition &c) const
{
    if (type == c.isA()) //Both must be functions
    {
```

```
        // Now we'll compare apples and apples
        FunctionDefinition *mfd = (FunctionDefinition *) &c;
        if (strcmp(name,mfd->name) == 0)
        {
            if ( ! (parameters == mfd->parameters) )
                return 0;
        }
        return 1;
    }
    return 0;
}


/////////////////////////////////////////////////////////////////////////
// Author: David Brumbaugh
// Method Name: makeTemplate
// Creation Date: 10/92
// Purpose: Creates a set of empty functions for the class.
// When it is called it will create the following template on the output
// stream:
//        typeSpecifications owningClass::name(parameters)
//          {
//          }
//
// Return Value: none
// Parameters:
//  Type          Name      Purpose/Description      Default Value
//  ostream &     out        Where the template is    None
//                           going.
/////////////////////////////////////////////////////////////////////////

void FunctionDefinition::makeTemplate(ostream &out,
Boolean withComments, const char *description)
{
    string tempTypeSpecifiers = typeSpecifiers;

    int e = tempTypeSpecifiers.Index("extern");
    if (e >= 0) // extern doesn't go into the .cpp file
        tempTypeSpecifiers.Delete(e,6);

    if (withComments)
    {
        int p; // Position within a string
        // Comment Block:
        out << "/*\n";
        out << "Function Name: " << name << '\n';
        if (description)
        {
            string descr(description);
            do
            {
                p = descr.Index('\r');
                if (p != -1)
                    descr.Delete(p,1);
            }while (p != -1);
```

```
            out << "Description: " << descr << "\n\n";
        }
    out << "Return Type: " <<  tempTypeSpecifiers << ": ";
    out << returnValue << '\n';
    out << "Parameters: ";
    if (parameters.total() == 0)
        out << "none\n";
    else
        out << '\n';
    for (int i = 0; i < parameters.total(); ++i)
    {
        out << '\t' << parameters[i].typeSpecifiers;
        out << ' ' << parameters[i].name;
        if (parameters[i].defaultValue.Len())
            out << " = " << parameters[i].defaultValue;
        if (parameters[i].description.Len())
        {
            do
            {
                p = parameters[i].description.Index('\r');
                if (p != -1)
                    parameters[i].description.Delete(p,1);
            }while (p != -1);
            out << ": " << parameters[i].description;
        }
        out << '\n';
    }
    out << "*/\n\n";
}

// Put the template on the stream;
out << tempTypeSpecifiers.Trim() << ' ' << ptrSpec;
out << name;
out << parameters.toString(true, false);
out << "\n{\n}\n\n";

}


//////////////////////////////////////////////////////////////////////
// Author: David Brumbaugh
// Method Name: toSource
// Creation Date: 10/92
// Purpose: Creates a declaration within the class definition.
// When it is called it will create the following template on the output
// stream:
//    [accessSpecifier:]
//        typeSpecifications name(parameters);
//
// Return Value: none
// Parameters:
//  Type           Name                Purpose/Description      Default Value
//  ostream &      out                 Where the prototype is   None
//                                     going.
```

```
//
//   int          withAccess       Will include the access 0 (false)
//                                 specifiation
//   int          newType          If non-0, this data      0
//                                 type is different that
//                                 the previous one.
////////////////////////////////////////////////////////////////////

void FunctionDefinition::toSource(ostream &out)
{
    out << typeSpecifiers;
    out << ' ';
    if (strlen(ptrSpec))
        out << ptrSpec;
    out << name;
    out << parameters.toString(true, true);
    out  << suffix << '\n';
}


////////////////////////////////////////////////////////////////////
// Author: David Brumbaugh
// Method Name: fromSource
// Creation Date: 10/92
// Purpose: Fills data members from "in", where "in" is a stream
// of source code such as that found in a class definintion. Assumes the
// following:
//        1. The stream starts at the begining of function definition
//        2. The source code is syntactically correct
//        3. All comments have been removed
//        4. The stream contains only the function defintion
//
//
// Return Value: None
// Parameters:
//   Type          Name          Purpose/Description        Default Value
//   istream &     in            Stream which contains      None
//                               the defintion
//   char *        accessSpec    access specifier           NULL (ie,"private")
////////////////////////////////////////////////////////////////////

void FunctionDefinition::fromSource(istream &in)
{
    in.unsetf(ios::skipws);
    makeTypeAndName(in);
    makeParamList(in);
    makeSuffix(in);
}


////////////////////////////////////////////////////////////////////
// Author: David Brumbaugh
// Method Name: makeTypeAndName
// Creation Date: 10/92
```

```
// Purpose: Fills the type and name data members from the input stream
// Supports "fromSource"
//
// Return Value: None
// Parameters:
//  Type          Name      Purpose/Description        Default Value
//  istream &     in        Stream which contains      None
//                          the defintion
/////////////////////////////////////////////////////////////////

void FunctionDefinition::makeTypeAndName(istream &in)
{
    int done = 0;
    IdString work, prev;
    char typeNameBuff[100];
    //Enough for a full type and several modifiers
    memset(typeNameBuff,0,sizeof(typeNameBuff));
    char *check;
    prev[0] = '\0';
    name[0] = '\0';
    in.getline(typeNameBuff,sizeof(typeNameBuff) ,'('); // Read up to paren
    istrstream  typeNameIn(typeNameBuff); //Streams are easier to work with
    do
    {
        typeNameIn >> work >> ws; // Trim the trailing white space
        if (typeNameIn.eof())
            done = 1;
        if (strlen(prev)) // Have we got any type info yet?
        {
            if ( strcmp(prev,"operator") != 0 )
            {
                typeSpecifiers += prev;
                typeSpecifiers += " ";
            }
            else
                strcpy(name,prev);
        }
        strcpy(prev,work); // Save work, it may be a type spec or name
        if (done)
        {
            strcat(name,prev); // The last string is usually the name
        }
    } while (! done);

    movePtrSpec(); // Fix the pointer specifiers if they exist

}

/////////////////////////////////////////////////////////////////
// Author: David Brumbaugh
// Method Name: makeParamList
// Creation Date: 10/92
// Purpose: Fills parameter list from "in"
//
```

```
// Return Value: None
// Parameters:
//   Type            Name            Purpose/Description      Default Value
//   istream &       in              Stream which contains    None
//                                   the defintion
//
//////////////////////////////////////////////////////////////////////

void FunctionDefinition::makeParamList(istream &in)
{
    parameters.fromSource(in);
}
//////////////////////////////////////////////////////////////////////
// Author: David Brumbaugh
// Method Name: makeSuffix
// Creation Date: 10/92
// Purpose: Fills suffix from "in"
//    (Things like "= 0", "const", "{.." etc.
//
// Return Value: None
// Parameters:
//   Type            Name            Purpose/Description      Default Value
//   istream &       in              Stream which contains    None
//                                   the defintion
//
//////////////////////////////////////////////////////////////////////

void FunctionDefinition::makeSuffix(istream &in)
{
    int done = 0;
    char work[512];
    work[0] = 0;
    in >> ws;
    do
    {
        in >> work >> ws;
        if (in.eof())
            done = 1;
        if (work[0] == ';' || work[0] == '{' )
        {
            done = 1;
            if (work[0] == '{')
            {
                suffix = "{ }";
                // We're not going to keep all the inline code
            }
        }
        else
        {
            suffix += trim(work);
            suffix += " ";
        }
        if (done && ! strchr(suffix.ptr(),'{') && ! strchr(suffix.ptr(),';'))
            suffix += ";";
```

```
    } while( ! done);
}

////////////////////////////////////////////////////////////////////
// Author: David Brumbaugh
// Method Name: movePtrSpec
// Creation Date: 10/92
// Purpose: Move the pointer specifers from the name to type specifers
//
// Return Value: void
// Parameters: None
////////////////////////////////////////////////////////////////////


void FunctionDefinition::movePtrSpec()
{
    //The pointer and reference characters are part of the type.
    int len = strlen(ptrSpec);
    while (name[0] == `*' || name[0] == `&')
    {
        ptrSpec[len++] = name[0];
        rmvstr(name,1);
    }

    // But we're keeping the pointer specs seperately
    char *check;
    while ((check = strchr(typeSpecifiers.ptr(),'*')) != NULL ||
    (check = strchr(typeSpecifiers.ptr(),'&')) != NULL)
    {
        ptrSpec[len++] = *check;
        rmvstr(check,1);
    }

}



////////////////////////////////////////////////////////////////////
// Listing  : 10-9
// Filename    : Entry.H
// Purpose     : Class description of Entry
////////////////////////////////////////////////////////////////////
#ifndef ENTRY_H
#define ENTRY_H

////////////////////////////////////////////////////////////////////
// Author      : David Brumbaugh
// Class Name   : Entry
// Creation Date: 10/20/92
// Catagories   : Model
// Purpose       : An Entry into the class catalog
//
// Major Public Methods:
//
// Major Data Items:
```

```
//          string identity - An identifier for this Entry. Also the name.
//          string description - Text desribing this Entry
//          string version - Which verstion of the Entry is this
//          Boolean checkedOut - True if this Entry is checked out
//          Date creationDate - Date this Entry was created
//          string addedBy - Name of user who added this Entry
//          string changedBy - Name of user who last changed this Entry
//          Date whenCheckedInOut - When this was last checked in or Out
//          string mustInclude - Drive, directory, file names of any files that
//                          must be included for this Entry
//          string whereLocated - Drive, directory file names of Entries code
//          string entryType - Class or Function
//////////////////////////////////////////////////////////////////////


#include "DATECLS4.H"
#include "str.h"
#include "clsdfn.h"
#include "funcdef.h"
class Catalog;

class Entry
{
    protected:
        string identity;
        string description;
        long version;
        Boolean checkedOut;
        Date creationDate;
        string addedBy;
        string changedBy;
        Date whenCheckedInOut;
        string whereLocated;
        string mustInclude;
        string entryType;
    public:
        const char *getIdentity() { return identity.ptr(); }
        void setIdentity(const char *id) { identity = id; }
        Date getCreationDate() { return creationDate; }
        void getCheckOutStatus(char *whoChngd, Date &when,
        Boolean &stat)
        { strcpy(whoChngd, changedBy.ptr()); when = whenCheckedInOut;
        stat = checkedOut; }
        virtual Boolean  checkOut(Catalog &cat, char *who);
        virtual Boolean  checkIn(Catalog &cat,Boolean makeNewVersion,
        char *who);
        const char *getLocation() { return whereLocated.ptr(); }
        void setLocation(const char *loc) { whereLocated = loc; }
        long getVersion() { return version; }
        const char *getInclude() { return mustInclude.ptr(); }
        void setInclude(const char *incl) { mustInclude = incl; }

        const char *getId() { string s = identity + ' ' + version;
```

```
                            return s.ptr(); }
        virtual void setDescription(const char *desc) { description = desc; }
        virtual void getDescription(string &desc) { desc = description; }
        virtual void setAddedBy(const char *who) { addedBy = who; }
        virtual void getAddedBy(string &who) { who = addedBy; }
        virtual void setChangedBy(const char *who) { changedBy = who; }
        virtual void getChangedBy(string &who) { who = changedBy; }
        virtual D_Record toRecord();
        virtual void fromRecord(D_Record &record);
        virtual void setVersion(long vers) { version = vers; }
        virtual long getVerstion() { return version; }
        Entry():version(0), checkedOut(::true)
        { // Default to today unless retrieved.
        whenCheckedInOut.Set(); creationDate.Set();
        }
};

//////////////////////////////////////////////////////////////////////
// Author        : David Brumbaugh
// Class Name    : ClassEntry
// Creation Date : 11/92
// Catagories    : Model
// Purpose       : An Entry in the catalog that records the data
//                 associated with a C++ class
//
// Major Public Methods:
//    toRecord - Converts Entry to a D_Record
//    fromRecord - Reads an builds a ClassEntry from a D_Record
//
// Major Data Items:
//    (All inherited)
//////////////////////////////////////////////////////////////////////


class ClassEntry : public Entry, public ClassDefinition
{
    public:
        ClassEntry(){entryType = "class";}
        virtual D_Record toRecord();
        virtual D_Record toRecord(D_Record &classPart);
        virtual void fromRecord(D_Record &record);
};

//////////////////////////////////////////////////////////////////////
// Author        : David Brumbaugh
// Class Name    : FunctionEntry
// Creation Date: 11/92
// Catagories    : Model
// Purpose       : An Entry in the catalog that records the data
//                 associated with a C++ stand alone function.
//
// Major Public Methods:
//    toRecord - Converts Entry to a D_Record
//    fromRecord - Reads an builds a ClassEntry from a D_Record
```

```
//
// Major Data Items:
//    returnValue - Description of what the function returns
///////////////////////////////////////////////////////////////////

class FunctionEntry : public Entry, public FunctionDefinition
{
    protected:
        string sourcePath; // Location of source code file
    public:
        FunctionEntry(){entryType = "function";}
        virtual D_Record toRecord();
        virtual D_Record toRecord(D_Record &fnRecord);
        virtual void fromRecord(D_Record &record);
        void setReturnValue(char *rv) {  returnValue = rv; }
        void getReturnValue(string &rv) { rv = returnValue; }
        void setSourcePath(const char *thePath) { sourcePath = thePath; }
        void getSourcePath(string &thePath) { thePath = sourcePath; }
};


#endif


///////////////////////////////////////////////////////////////////
// Listing   : 10-10
// Filename   : Entry.CPP
// Purpose    : Source code for Entry class
///////////////////////////////////////////////////////////////////

#include "Entry.H"
#include "strstream.h"
#include "catalog.h"
#include <alloc.h>
#include <ui_win.hpp>

/*============================ Entry ==================================*/

///////////////////////////////////////////////////////////////////
// Author: David Brumbaugh
// Method Name: checkOut
// Creation Date: 10/24/92
// Purpose: Check the entry out of the catalog so the user can modify
// it.
//
// Return Value: True on success false on failure
// Parameters:
//   Type          Name       Purpose/Description            Default Value
//   Catalog &     cat        Catalog being checked out of   None
//   char *        who        User checking it out           None
///////////////////////////////////////////////////////////////////

Boolean Entry::checkOut(Catalog &cat,char *who)
{
```

```
    if (checkedOut)
        return false; // Already checked out

    string search = "Entry == '";
    search += identity + "'";
    search += "&& Version == ";
    search += string(version);

    if (cat.find(search.ptr()))
    {
        checkedOut = true;
        whenCheckedInOut.Set(); // Today's date
        changedBy = who;
        D_Record entryRecord = toRecord();
        return((cat.replace(entryRecord)));
    }
    return false;
}

//////////////////////////////////////////////////////////////////////
// Author: David Brumbaugh
// Method Name: checkIn
// Creation Date: 10/24/92
// Purpose: Check the entry into the catalog after the user updates
// it.
//
// Return Value:
// Parameters:
//  Type            Name              Purpose/Description        Default Value
//  Catalog &       cat               Catalog being checked into    None
//  Boolean         makeNewVersion    True if a copy is to be made   None
//  char *          who               Name of user checking it in    None
//////////////////////////////////////////////////////////////////////

Boolean Entry::checkIn(Catalog & cat, Boolean makeNewVersion,char * who)
{
    if (makeNewVersion)
    {
        string selection = "Identity == '" + identity;
        selection += "' && ";
        cat.select(selection.ptr());
        cat.set_order("Version");
        cat.end();
        checkedOut = false;
        whenCheckedInOut.Set(); // Today's date
        creationDate.Set();
        D_Record entry = cat.current();
        version = ((long) entry["Version"]) + 1;
        changedBy = who;
        addedBy = who;
        return(cat.add(toRecord()));
    }
    else if (checkedOut)
    {
```

```
            string search = "Identity == '";
            search += identity + "' ";
            search += "&& Version == ";
            search += string(version);
            if (cat.find(search.ptr()))
            {
                checkedOut = false;
                whenCheckedInOut.Set(); // Today's date
                changedBy = who;
                D_Record entryRecord = toRecord();
                return((cat.replace(entryRecord)));
            }
        }
        return false;
}
///////////////////////////////////////////////////////////////////////
// Author: David Brumbaugh
// Method Name: toRecord
// Creation Date: 10/24/92
// Purpose: Puts Entry data into a D_Record
//
// Return Value: D_Record - Record converted to
// Parameters: none
///////////////////////////////////////////////////////////////////////

D_Record Entry::toRecord()
{
    D_Record dr;

    dr.add(D_Field("Version",version));
    dr.add(D_Field("Name", identity.ptr()));
    dr.add(D_Field("Identity",identity.ptr()));
    dr.add(D_Field("Description",description.ptr()));
    dr.add(D_Field("CheckedOut", (long) checkedOut));
    dr.add(D_Field("DateAdded",  creationDate.julDate()));
    dr.add(D_Field("ChangedBy", changedBy.ptr()));
    dr.add(D_Field("AddedBy",addedBy.ptr()));
    dr.add(D_Field("EntryType",entryType.ptr()));
    dr.add(D_Field("WhereLocated", whereLocated.ptr()));
    dr.add(D_Field("MustInclude", mustInclude.ptr()));
    dr.add(D_Field("DateChecked", whenCheckedInOut.julDate()));

    return dr;
}

///////////////////////////////////////////////////////////////////////
// Author: David Brumbaugh
// Method Name: fromRecord
// Creation Date: 10/24/92
// Purpose: Fills Entry data from a D_Record
//
// Return Value: None
// Parameters:
//  Type           Name            Purpose/Description          Default Value
```

```
// D_Record &    record        Record converted from        None
////////////////////////////////////////////////////////////////////

void Entry::fromRecord(D_Record  &record)
{
    identity = (const char *) record["Identity"];
    description = (const char *) record["Description"];
    version = (long) record["Version"];
    checkedOut = (Boolean) ((long) record["CheckedOut"]);
    whenCheckedInOut.Set((long) record["DateChecked"]);
    creationDate.Set((long) record["DateAdded"]);
    addedBy = (const char *) record["AddedBy"];
    changedBy = (const char *) record["ChangedBy"];
    whereLocated = (const char *) record["WhereLocated"];
    mustInclude = (const char *) record["MustInclude"];
    entryType = (const char *) record["EntryType"];

}


/*=========================== ClassEntry ===========================*/

////////////////////////////////////////////////////////////////////
// Author: David Brumbaugh
// Method Name: toRecord
// Creation Date: 11/3/92
// Purpose: Converts a ClassEntry to a D_Record
//
// Return Value: The D_Record converted to
// Parameters: None
//
////////////////////////////////////////////////////////////////////

D_Record ClassEntry::toRecord()
{
    if (identity.Len() == 0)
        identity = name; // The identity is the original name, if the name
                         // changes, the identity stays the same
    entryType = classSpec;
    D_Record dr = Entry::toRecord();
    dr["Name"] = name;
    string baseClassBuffer;
    for (int i = 0; i < baseClasses.total(); ++i)
    {
        baseClassBuffer += baseClasses[i].baseSpecifier;
        baseClassBuffer += ' ';
        baseClassBuffer += baseClasses[i].name;
        if (i != (baseClasses.total() - 1))
            baseClassBuffer += ',';
    }
    dr.add(D_Field("BaseClasses",baseClassBuffer.ptr()));
    dr.add(D_Field("ClassSpec",classSpec.ptr()));
    return (dr);
}
```

```
/////////////////////////////////////////////////////////////////////
// Author: David Brumbaugh
// Method Name: toRecord
// Creation Date: 11/3/92
// Purpose: Converts a ClassEntry to a pair of D_Records, one for Entry
// and one for for the ClssEntry
//
// Return Value: The D_Record converted to the Entry
// Parameters: D_Record &clRec. The record converted to a ClassEntry rec.
//
/////////////////////////////////////////////////////////////////////

D_Record ClassEntry::toRecord(D_Record &clEntry)
{
    if (identity.Len() == 0)
        identity = name; // The identity is the original name, if the name
                         // changes, the identity stays the same

    entryType = classSpec;
    D_Record dr = Entry::toRecord();
    dr["Name"] = name;

    clEntry.add(D_Field("Identity",identity.ptr()));
    clEntry.add(D_Field("Version", version));
    string baseClassBuffer;
    for (int i = 0; i < baseClasses.total(); ++i)
    {
        baseClassBuffer += baseClasses[i].baseSpecifier;
        baseClassBuffer += ' ';
        baseClassBuffer += baseClasses[i].name;
        if (i != (baseClasses.total() - 1))
            baseClassBuffer += ',';
    }
    clEntry.add(D_Field("BaseClasses",baseClassBuffer.ptr()));
    clEntry.add(D_Field("ClassSpec",classSpec.ptr()));
    return (dr);
}

/////////////////////////////////////////////////////////////////////
// Author: David Brumbaugh
// Method Name: fromRecord
// Creation Date: 11/3/92
// Purpose: Fills the class Entry data from a specific record.
//
// Return Value: None
// Parameters:
//  Type           Name      Purpose/Description            Default Value
//  D_Record &     record    The record being converted from   NULL
/////////////////////////////////////////////////////////////////////

void ClassEntry::fromRecord(D_Record & record)
{
    Entry::fromRecord(record);
    strcpy(name, (const char *) record["Name"]);
```

```
    string bcB = (const char *)record["BaseClasses"];
    istrstream baseClassBuff(bcB.ptr());
    baseClassBuff.unsetf(ios::skipws);
    getParents(baseClassBuff);
    classSpec = (const char *) record["ClassSpec"];


}

/*========================= FunctionEntry ===============================*/

//////////////////////////////////////////////////////////////////////
// Author: David Brumbaugh
// Method Name: toRecord
// Creation Date: 11/92
// Purpose: Converts a FunctionEntry into a D_Record.
//
// Return Value: the D_Record
// Parameters: None
//
//////////////////////////////////////////////////////////////////////

D_Record FunctionEntry::toRecord()
{
    if (identity.Len() == 0)
        identity = name; // The identity is the original name, if the name
                         // changes, the idetnity stays the same

    D_Record dr = Entry::toRecord();
    dr.add(D_Field("Parameters", parameters.toString(true,true)));
    dr.add(D_Field("ReturnType", typeSpecifiers.ptr()));
    dr.add(D_Field("ReturnValue", returnValue.ptr()));
    dr.add(D_Field("SourcePath", sourcePath.ptr()));
    dr.add(D_Field("Specification",specification.ptr()));
    dr.add(D_Field("ParamDescriptions",parameters.getDescField()));
    return dr;
}
//////////////////////////////////////////////////////////////////////
// Author: David Brumbaugh
// Method Name: toRecord
// Creation Date: 11/92
// Purpose: Converts a FunctionEntry into two D_Records,
//          the Entry D_Record and the FunctionEntry D_Record
//          That way we can save the records sperartely.
//
// Return Value: The Entry D_Record
// Parameters: D_Record &fnRecord - The FuncitonEntry D_Record
//
//////////////////////////////////////////////////////////////////////

D_Record FunctionEntry::toRecord(D_Record &fnRecord)
{
    if (identity.Len() == 0)
        identity = name; // The identity is the original name, if the name
                         // changes, the idetnity stays the same
```

```
    D_Record er = Entry::toRecord();

    fnRecord.add(D_Field("Identity",identity.ptr()));
    fnRecord.add(D_Field("Version",version));
    fnRecord.add(D_Field("Parameters", parameters.toString(true,true)));
    fnRecord.add(D_Field("ReturnType", typeSpecifiers.ptr()));
    fnRecord.add(D_Field("ReturnVal", returnValue.ptr()));
    fnRecord.add(D_Field("SourcePath", sourcePath.ptr()));
    fnRecord.add(D_Field("Specification",specification.ptr()));
    fnRecord.add(D_Field("ParamDescriptions",parameters.getDescField()));

    return er;
}

/////////////////////////////////////////////////////////////////////
// Author: David Brumbaugh
// Method Name: fromRecord
// Creation Date: 11/92
// Purpose: Transfers data from D_Record into FunctinEntry
//
// Return Value: None
// Parameters:
//   Type            Name        Purpose/Description            Default Value
//   D_Record &      record      The record being transfere from   None
/////////////////////////////////////////////////////////////////////

void FunctionEntry::fromRecord(D_Record & record)
{
    Entry::fromRecord(record);
    strcpy(name, (const char *) record["Name"]);
    parameters.fromString(record["Parameters"]);
    typeSpecifiers = (const char*) record["ReturnType"];
    returnValue = (const char *)record["ReturnValue"];
    sourcePath = (const char *)record["SourcePath"];
    specification = (const char *)record["Specification"];
    parameters.fillDescriptions(record["ParamDescriptions"]);
}


/////////////////////////////////////////////////////////////////////
// Listing   : 10-11
// Filename  : DRecrd.H
// Purpose   : D_Record class description
/////////////////////////////////////////////////////////////////////

#ifndef DRECRD_H
#define DRECRD_H

#include <string.h>
#include <stddef.h>
#include "listimp.h"

/////////////////////////////////////////////////////////////////////
// Author        : David Brumbaugh
```

```
// Class Name    : D_Field
// Creation Date: 10/20/92
// Catagories    : Adapter
// Purpose       : Supports D_Record
//
// Major Public Methods:
//  = Assignment
//  == Comparison
//  Cast functions to long, double, string and Binary objects
//  Constructor
//  get/setName assigns, gets field name
//  getType, gets field type
//
// Major Data Items:
//   type : What is it? long, double, string or binary
//   union:
//       unassignedFld - No value at all
//       lngVal - Value if it's a long or int
//       dblVal - Value if it's a float or double
//       strVal - Value if it's a string
//       binFld - Value if it's binary
/////////////////////////////////////////////////////////////////

enum FieldType { unassignedFld, lngFld, dblFld, strFld, binFld };

struct BinObj
{
    size_t bytes;
    void *data;
};

class D_Field
{
    protected:
        char *name;
        FieldType type;
        union
        {
            long lngVal;
            double dblVal;
            char *strVal;
            BinObj binVal;
        }; // Values
        void reset() { if (type == strFld && strVal)
                        delete strVal;
                       type = unassignedFld;
                       strVal = NULL;
                     }
    public:
        void setName(const char *s)
        { if (name)
            delete name;
        name = new char[strlen(s) + 1]; strcpy(name,s); }
        D_Field() { type = unassignedFld; name = NULL; strVal = NULL;
```

```
++count; }

D_Field(char *nm, long l):name(NULL), type(unassignedFld)
    { setName(nm); *this = l; ++count; }
D_Field(char *nm, double d):name(NULL), type(unassignedFld)
    { setName(nm); *this = d; ++count; }
D_Field(char *nm, const char *s):name(NULL), type(unassignedFld)
    { setName(nm); *this = s; ++count; }
D_Field(char *nm, BinObj &bin):name(NULL), type(unassignedFld)
    { setName(nm); *this = bin; ++count; }
D_Field(D_Field &df);
static int count;

~D_Field()
{
    —count;
    if (name)
        delete name;
    if (type == strFld && strVal)
        delete strVal;
}
// Not responsible for binary objects

operator == (D_Field &d) const
{ return (strcmp(name,d.name) == 0); }

long operator = (const long &l)
{ reset(); lngVal = l; type = lngFld; return l; }
double operator = (const double &d)
{ reset(); dblVal = d; type = dblFld; return d; }
const char * operator = (const char *s)
{
    if (type == strFld && strVal == s)
        return strVal;

    char *tmp;
    if (type == strFld && strVal)
        tmp = strVal;
    else
        tmp = NULL;

    strVal = new char[strlen(s) + 1]; strcpy(strVal,s); type = strFld;
    if (tmp)
        delete tmp;

    return strVal;
}
BinObj operator = (BinObj &binO)
{ reset(); binVal = binO; type = binFld; return binO; }
D_Field operator = (D_Field &df);
operator long() {return lngVal; }
operator double() { return dblVal; }
operator const char *() { return strVal; }
operator BinObj() { return binVal; }
```

```
        const char *getName() { return name; }
        FieldType getType() { return type; }
};


/////////////////////////////////////////////////////////////////////
// Author      : David Brumbaugh
// Class Name  : D_Record
// Creation Date : 10/20/92
// Catagories  : Adapter
// Purpose     : The record class acts as a "universal" protocol to
// any number of database libraries.
//
// Major Public Methods:
//        operator [] : Gets a specific field
//        find : Gets a named field.
// Major Data Items:
/////////////////////////////////////////////////////////////////////

class D_Record : public ListImp<D_Field>
{
    public:
        virtual D_Field &operator[] (char *fld)
        { find(fld); return anArray[curr]; }
        virtual D_Field &operator[] (long where) { return anArray[where]; }
        virtual    Boolean find(char *fldName);
};
#endif


/////////////////////////////////////////////////////////////////////
// Listing  : 10-12
// Filename : DRECRD.CPP
// Purpose  : D_Field and D_Record member functions.
/////////////////////////////////////////////////////////////////////
#include "DRECRD.H"

int D_Field::count = 0;

// D_Field assignment operator.
D_Field    D_Field::operator = (D_Field &df)
{
    if (df.name)
        setName(df.name);
    // type = df.type;
    switch(df.type)
    {
        case lngFld:
            *this = (long) df;
        break;
        case dblFld:
            *this = (double) df;
        break;
        case strFld:
```

```
            *this = (const char*) df;
        break;
        case binFld:
            *this = (BinObj) df;
        break;
    }
    return *this;
}

//D_Field copy constructor
D_Field::D_Field(D_Field &df):name(NULL),type(unassignedFld)
{
    ++count;

    if (df.name)
        setName(df.name);
    // type = df.type;
    switch(df.type)
    {
        case lngFld:
            *this = (long) df;
        break;
        case dblFld:
            *this = (double) df;
        break;
        case strFld:
            *this = (const char*) df;
        break;
        case binFld:
            *this = (BinObj) df;
        break;
    }
}

/////////////////////////////////////////////////////////////////////
// Author: David Brumbaugh
// Method Name: find
// Creation Date: 10/23/92
// Purpose: Finds a field
//
// Return Value: True on success
// Parameters:
//   Type           Name        Purpose/Description        Default Value
//   char *         fldName     Name of field to find      None
/////////////////////////////////////////////////////////////////////

Boolean D_Record::find(char *fldName)
{
    int oldCur;
    oldCur = curr;
    for (curr = 0; curr < total(); ++curr)
    {
        if (strcmp(anArray[curr].getName(), fldName) == 0)
            return true;
```

```
    }
    curr = oldCur;
    return false;
}


//////////////////////////////////////////////////////////////////
// Listing   : 10-13
// Filename  : Catalog.H
// Purpose   : Catalog class
//////////////////////////////////////////////////////////////////

#ifndef CATALOG_H
#define CATALOG_H
#include "RECLIST.H"
#include "DRECRD.H"
#include "ENTRY.H"


//////////////////////////////////////////////////////////////////
// Author        : David Brumbaugh
// Class Name    : Catalog
// Creation Date: 10/24/92
// Catagories    : Model, Container
// Purpose       : Contains Entries in the SSOOT CASE Librarian
//  A catalog is list of datbase entries. The current implementaion
//  of RecList is a kind of Pinnacle Data Manager List.
//  Through a particular Entry, all other types of Entries are
//  accessable.
//
// Major Public Methods:
//  Catalog - Constructor
//
// Major Data Items:
// RecList ClassEntry - The ClassEntry table
// RecList FunctionEntry - The FunctionEntry table
// RecList ClassMember - The ClassMember table
//////////////////////////////////////////////////////////////////

// Forward declaration.
class ClassEntry;
class FunctionEntry;

class Catalog : public RecList
{
    protected:
        RecList *theClassEntryTbl; // The ClassEntry table
        RecList *theFunctionEntryTbl; // The FunctionEntry table
        RecList *theClassMemberTbl; // The ClassMember table
    public:
        Catalog(database &db):RecList(db,"Entry"){}
        Boolean deleteEntry(string ident, long version);
        virtual Boolean getEntry(ClassEntry &clEntry);
        virtual Boolean getEntry(FunctionEntry &fnEntry);
        virtual Boolean setEntry(ClassEntry &clEntry);
```

```
            virtual Boolean setEntry(FunctionEntry &fnEntry);
            virtual const char *getSummary();
};

#endif


//////////////////////////////////////////////////////////////////////
// Listing  : 10-14
// Filename    : CATALOG.CPP
// Purpose    : Source code for catalog class.
//////////////////////////////////////////////////////////////////////

#include "catalog.h"
#include <ui_win.hpp>
#include <alloc.h>
//////////////////////////////////////////////////////////////////////
// Author: David Brumbaugh
// Method Name: getEntry
// Creation Date: 11/92
// Purpose: Get the current from the catalog
//
// Return Value: True on success
// Parameters:
//  Type                Name        Purpose/Description         Default Value
//  ClassEntry &        clEntry     Destination ClassEntry      None
//////////////////////////////////////////////////////////////////////

Boolean Catalog::getEntry(ClassEntry &clEntry)
{
    theClassEntryTbl = new RecList(*db,"ClassEntry");
    D_Record dr = current();
    string etype = (const char *)dr["EntryType"];
    if (etype != "class" && etype != "struct" && etype != "union")
    {
        delete theClassEntryTbl;
        return false;
    }
    string selString = "Identity == '" + string((const char *)dr["Identity"]);
    selString += "' &&";
    selString += ("Version == " + string((long) dr["Version"]));
    if (theClassEntryTbl->find(selString.ptr()))
    {
        D_Record clEntryRec = theClassEntryTbl->current();
        // We'll combine the two records
        dr.add(clEntryRec["BaseClasses"]);
        dr.add(clEntryRec["ClassSpec"]);

        // Fill the Entry data from the combined records
        clEntry.fromRecord(dr);

        // Fill the members up
        theClassMemberTbl = new RecList(*db,"ClassMember");
        ClassMemberDefinition *cmd;
```

```
        theClassMemberTbl->select(selString.ptr());
        theClassMemberTbl->set_order("IDVersion");
        int totalMem = theClassMemberTbl->total();

        int i;
        for (i = 0, theClassMemberTbl->top(); i < totalMem;
        ++i, theClassMemberTbl->next())
        {
            D_Record memRecord = theClassMemberTbl->current();
            if (strcmp(memRecord["MemberType"],"data") == 0)
            {
                cmd = new DataMemberDefinition((const char *)dr["Name"]);
                cmd->fromRecord(memRecord);
                clEntry.add(cmd);
            }
            else
            {
                cmd = new MemberFunctionDefinition((const char *)dr["Name"]);
                cmd->fromRecord(memRecord);
                clEntry.add(cmd);
            }

        }
        theClassMemberTbl->clear_select();
        delete theClassMemberTbl;
    }
    delete theClassEntryTbl;
    return true;
}


/////////////////////////////////////////////////////////////////////////
// Author: David Brumbaugh
// Method Name: getEntry
// Creation Date: 11/92
// Purpose: Get a function entry from the catalog
//
// Return Value: None
// Parameters:
//  Type             Name      Purpose/Description           Default Value
//  FunctionEntry &  fnEntry   The functionEntry to fill      None
/////////////////////////////////////////////////////////////////////////

Boolean Catalog::getEntry(FunctionEntry &fnEntry)
{
    D_Record dr = current();
    string etype = (const char *)dr["EntryType"];
    if (etype != "function")
        return false;
    theFunctionEntryTbl = new RecList(*db,"FunctionEntry");
    string selString = "Identity == '" + string((const char *)dr["Identity"]);
    selString += "' && ";
    selString += ("Version == " + string((long) dr["Version"]));
    if (theFunctionEntryTbl->find(selString.ptr()))
    {
```

```
        D_Record fnEntryRec = theFunctionEntryTbl->current();
        // We'll combine the two records
        dr.add(fnEntryRec["Parameters"]);
        dr.add(fnEntryRec["ReturnType"]);
        dr.add(fnEntryRec["ReturnVal"]);
        dr.add(fnEntryRec["SourcePath"]);
        dr.add(fnEntryRec["Specification"]);
        dr.add(fnEntryRec["ParamDescriptions"]);
        // Fill the Entry data from the combined records
        fnEntry.fromRecord(dr);
    }
    delete theFunctionEntryTbl;
    return true;
}


/////////////////////////////////////////////////////////////////////
// Author: David Brumbaugh
// Method Name: deleteEntry
// Creation Date: 11/92
// Purpose: Removes an entry from the catalog.
//
// Return Value: True if it is successful
// Parameters:
//   Type          Name         Purpose/Description          Default Value
//   string        ident        Identity of entry to be deleted  None
//   long          version      Version of the specific entry    None
/////////////////////////////////////////////////////////////////////

Boolean Catalog::deleteEntry(string ident, long version)
{
    string selString = "Identity == '" + ident;
    selString += ("' && Version == " + string(version));
    if (! find(selString.ptr()))
    {
        return false;
    }
    D_Record dr = current();
    string etype = (const char *)dr["EntryType"];
    if (etype == "function")
    {
        theFunctionEntryTbl = new RecList(*db,"FunctionEntry");
        if (theFunctionEntryTbl->find(selString.ptr()))
            theFunctionEntryTbl->remove();
        remove();
        delete theFunctionEntryTbl;
        return true;
    }
    else
    {
        // We've got a class. The class members need to be removed first
        theClassMemberTbl = new RecList(*db,"ClassMember");
        theClassMemberTbl->select(selString.ptr());
        theClassMemberTbl->set_order("IDVersion");
        int totalMem = theClassMemberTbl->total();
```

```
        int i;
        for(i = 0, theClassMemberTbl->top(); i < totalMem;
        ++i)
        {
            theClassMemberTbl->remove();
        }
        theClassMemberTbl->clear_order();
        theClassMemberTbl->clear_select();
        delete theClassMemberTbl;

        theClassEntryTbl = new RecList(*db,"ClassEntry");

        if (theClassEntryTbl->find(selString.ptr()))
        {
            theClassEntryTbl->remove();
            remove();
            delete theClassEntryTbl;
            return true;
        }
        delete theClassEntryTbl;
    }
    return false;
}


//////////////////////////////////////////////////////////////////////
// Author: David Brumbaugh
// Method Name: setEntry
// Creation Date: 11/92
// Purpose: Puts an Entry back into the catalog.
//
// Return Value: True if it is successful
// Parameters:
// Type              Name          Purpose/Description      Default Value
// ClassEntry &      clEntry       The class entry being    None
//                                 put into the catalog.
//////////////////////////////////////////////////////////////////////

Boolean Catalog::setEntry(ClassEntry  &clEntry)
{
    // We may have one of these already so we'll delete this entry
    deleteEntry(clEntry.getIdentity(), clEntry.getVersion());

    // We'll put the basic entry and the class entry records in first
    D_Record clRec;
    D_Record baseEntry = clEntry.toRecord(clRec);
    if (! add(baseEntry) )
        return false; // problem

    theClassEntryTbl = new RecList(*db,"ClassEntry");
    if (! theClassEntryTbl->add(clRec))
    {
        delete theClassEntryTbl;
        return false; // problem
    }
```

```
    delete theClassEntryTbl;

    // Now we need to store the members
    ClassMemberDefinition *aClassMem; // We need to have a place to start
    DataMemberDefinition  *aDataMem; // It could be a data member
    MemberFunctionDefinition *aMemFctn; // Or a member function
    MemberList &memList = clEntry.getMembers();
    theClassMemberTbl =  new RecList(*db,"ClassMember");
    for (int i = 0; i < memList.total(); ++i)
    {
        aClassMem = memList[i];
        if (aClassMem->isA() == isFunction)
        {
            aMemFctn = (MemberFunctionDefinition *)aClassMem;
            D_Record memRec = aMemFctn->toRecord(clEntry.getIdentity(),
            clEntry.getVersion());
            if (! theClassMemberTbl->add(memRec) )
            {
                delete theClassMemberTbl;
                return false;
            }
        }
        else
        {
            aDataMem =(DataMemberDefinition *) aClassMem;
            D_Record memRec = aDataMem->toRecord(
            clEntry.getIdentity(), clEntry.getVersion());
            if (! theClassMemberTbl->add(memRec) )
            {
                delete theClassMemberTbl;
                return false;
            }
        }
    }
    delete theClassMemberTbl;
    return true;

}
//////////////////////////////////////////////////////////////////
// Author: David Brumbaugh
// Method Name: setEntry
// Creation Date: 11/92
// Purpose: Puts a function entry into the catalog.
//
// Return Value: True on success
// Parameters:
//  Type                Name        Purpose/Description     Default Value
//  FunctionEntry       fnEntry     Function entry to go    None
//                                  into the catalog.
//////////////////////////////////////////////////////////////////

Boolean Catalog::setEntry(FunctionEntry &fnEntry)
{
    // We may have one of these already so we'll delete this entry
```

```
    deleteEntry(fnEntry.getIdentity(), fnEntry.getVersion());


    // We'll put the basic entry and the class entry records in first
    D_Record fnRec;
    D_Record baseEntry = fnEntry.toRecord(fnRec);

    if (! add(baseEntry) )
        return false; // problem

    theFunctionEntryTbl = new RecList(*db,"FunctionEntry");

    if (! theFunctionEntryTbl->add(fnRec))
    {
        delete theFunctionEntryTbl;
        return false; // problem
    }

    delete theFunctionEntryTbl;
    return true;
}

///////////////////////////////////////////////////////////////////////
// Author: David Brumbaugh
// Method Name: getSummary
// Creation Date: 11/92
// Purpose: Returns a summary of the current record consising of:
//          EntryType Name (Paramters) Version In/Out DateChecked ChangedBy
//
// Return Value: A summary string as listed above.
// Parameters: None
//
///////////////////////////////////////////////////////////////////////

const char *Catalog::getSummary()
{
    // Get the current record.

    D_Record curr = current();


    // Concatinate the record fields into a summary string
    string theSummary = (const char *) curr["EntryType"];

    theSummary += ' ';
    theSummary += (const char *) curr["Name"];


    // If it is a function, we need to get the parameters

    theFunctionEntryTbl = new RecList(*db,"FunctionEntry");
    if (stricmp(curr["EntryType"], "function") == 0)
    {
        string selString = "Identity == '" +
```

```
                              string((const char *) curr["Identity"]);
        selString += "' && Version == ";
        selString += string((long) curr["Version"]);

        if (! theFunctionEntryTbl->find(selString.ptr()))
        {
            delete theFunctionEntryTbl;
            return " ";
        }
        D_Record fnEntryRec = theFunctionEntryTbl->current();
        theSummary +=
                string((const char *)fnEntryRec["Parameters"]);
    }
    delete theFunctionEntryTbl;

    // Continue the concatination
    theSummary += (";"+string((long) curr["Version"]));
    if ((long) curr["CheckedOut"])
        theSummary += " Out ";
    else
        theSummary += " In  ";
    Date d = (long) curr["DateChecked"];
    theSummary += d.formatDate(MDY);

    // The static string keeps us from loosing it on the return
    static string rval;
    rval = theSummary;

    return rval.ptr();
}


/////////////////////////////////////////////////////////////////////
// Listing  : 10-15
// Filename : RecList.H
// Purpose  : Pfm_List of records
/////////////////////////////////////////////////////////////////////

/////////////////////////////////////////////////////////////////////
// Author        : David Brumbaugh
// Class Name    : RecList
// Creation Date : 10/23/92
// Catagories    : Adapter, Device Interface
// Purpose       : List of "Generic" Records
//
// Major Public Methods:
// current - Loads a record from the database
// replace - Puts a record into the databse
//
// Major Data Items:
// None
/////////////////////////////////////////////////////////////////////

#ifndef RECLIST_H
```

```
#define RECLIST_H
#ifdef _Windows
#define BORLANDC 1
#define PFM_DLL 1
#endif
#include "PFM_LIST.H"
#include "DRECRD.H"
extern void TheErrorFunction();
extern void TheBadErrorFunction(char *msg);



class RecList : public Pfm_List<D_Record>
{
    public:
        RecList(database &open_db, char *table_name):
        Pfm_List<D_Record>(open_db,table_name){ initError(); }
        RecList(DBTAB db_table):Pfm_List<D_Record>(db_table)
        { initError(); }

        virtual Boolean replace(D_Record &rec);
        virtual D_Record current();
        static void initError();
        static Boolean initErrorDone;


};

#endif


//////////////////////////////////////////////////////////////////
// Listing  : 10-16
// Filename : RECLIST.CPP
// Purpose  : Source code for the RecList class
//////////////////////////////////////////////////////////////////

#define PFM_CLASSLIB
#include "RECLIST.H"
#include <str.h>
#include <ui_win.hpp>

// Assign the error function
Boolean RecList::initErrorDone = false;

//////////////////////////////////////////////////////////////////
// Author: David Brumbaugh
// Method Name: initError
// Purpose: Assigns the errror functions to the data base.
//
// Return Value: None
// Parameters:   None
//
//////////////////////////////////////////////////////////////////
```

```
void RecList::initError()
{
    if (! initErrorDone)
    {
        DB_SetErrorFunc(TheErrorFunction);
        DB_SetUserExit(TheBadErrorFunction);
        initErrorDone = ::true;
    }
}

//////////////////////////////////////////////////////////////////
// Author: David Brumbaugh
// Method Name: current
// Creation Date: 11/92
// Purpose: Return the current record int the database
//
// Return Value: The current D_Record.
// Parameters: NONE
//
//////////////////////////////////////////////////////////////////

D_Record RecList::current()
{
    D_Field currFld;
    firstcolumn();
    buffer.top();
    while( ! buffer.is_empty())
        buffer.remove();

    while(nextcolumn())
    {
        column col = currentcolumn();
        currFld.setName(col.name());
        unsigned long colType = DB_GetType(col.c) & TypeMask;
        switch(colType)
        {
            case Integer:
                currFld = (long) col;
            break;
            case Real:
                currFld = (double) col;
            break;
            case String:
                currFld = (_charp) col;
            break;
            case User:
            case Blob:
                blob b = col;
                BinObj bobj;
                bobj.bytes = b.len;
                bobj.data = malloc(b.len);
                memmove(bobj.data,b.p,b.len);
                currFld = bobj;
            break;
```

```
            case Null:
            // Sometimes columns don't have a type and then we don't want
            // to keep it.
            case Key:
            // A key isn't really a column, but one or more other columns
                continue;
        }

        if (get_error() == DB_OK)
            buffer.add(currFld);
    }
    return buffer;
}

//////////////////////////////////////////////////////////////////////
// Author: David Brumbaugh
// Method Name: replace
// Creation Date: 11/92
// Purpose: Replace tha current record with D_Record
//
// Return Value: True if successful. False otherwise.
// Parameters:
//   Type            Name      Purpose/Description        Default Value
//   D_Record &      rec       The record being replaced  None
//////////////////////////////////////////////////////////////////////


Boolean RecList::replace(D_Record & rec)
{
    for(int i = 0; i < rec.total(); ++i)
    {
        // The column constructor doesn't accept const char *, needs char *
        column c((table)*this,(char *)rec[i].getName());

        switch(rec[i].getType())
        {
            case lngFld:
                c = (long) rec[i];
            break;
            case dblFld:
                c = (double) rec[i];
            break;
            case strFld:
                string s((const char *) rec[i]);
                c = s.ptr();
            break;
            case binFld:
                BinObj bobj = (BinObj) rec[i];
                blob b;
                b.len = bobj.bytes;
                b.p = bobj.data;
                c = b;
            break;
        }
```

```
        if (get_error() != DB_OK)
            return false;
    }

    return ((Boolean) (get_error() == DB_OK));
}


////////////////////////////////////////////////////////////////////////
// Listing : 10-17
// Filename: Pfm_List.H
// Purpose : Definition of List to be implemented as a Pfm Table
// Note: By putting the body and the defintino into one file I'm using
// the default compiler settings for templates. If the same template
// instance is encounted more than one, they'll be merged.
////////////////////////////////////////////////////////////////////////


////////////////////////////////////////////////////////////////////////
// Author         : David Brumbaugh
//
// Class Name     : template <class R> Pfm_List
// Creation Date: 6/2/92
// Purpose        : Implements the D_List protocol using Pinnacle File
//                  Manager
//
// Major Public Methods:
//    thThose requiring overload from D_List
//    The constructors and destructors reflect the need for PFM info
//
//    select: Limits the list to the members with the selected criteria
//            affects first, next, total;
//    clear_select: Clears the selection critera from the table.
//    set_order: Assigns the column by which the list will be ordered.
//    clear_order: Assures that the list is in the original order
//    commit: Commits changes to the database.
//    rollback: rolls back changes from the database.
//
//      Database Specific Methods:
//         const database &DBHandle()       Returns class's database
//         column getColumn(const char *name) Returns named column
//
// Major Data Items:
//   database db , database that owns the table especially
//
////////////////////////////////////////////////////////////////////////

#ifndef PINCLASS_H
#define PINCLASS_H

// Pinnacle has a string class but I'm using another one with the same name
// elsewhere. So, I'll just change the name of Pinnacle's string.
#define string PFM_String
#define PFM_LARGE //Let pinnacle know we're using the large model.
#define UCHAR PFM_UCHAR // The pinnacle defines a UHAR differently
```

```cpp
// #define BORLANDC 1
// #define PFM_DLL 1
#include <pinnacle.h>
#undef string
#undef UCHAR

#include "D_list.H"



template <class R>
class Pfm_List: public D_List<R>, protected table  {
protected:
    database *db;
    Boolean is_at_top, // Flags
            is_at_bottom;

public:
// Constructors and Destructors
        Pfm_List(database &open_db, char *table_name);
        Pfm_List(DBTAB db_table);

// Database Specific Methods
//    const database &DBHandle() {return db;}
    column getColumn(const char *columnName);
    void commit() { db->commit(); } // OK, so table commits the whole database
    void rollback() { db->rollback(); } // And we rollback the database too

//  List Status overloaded
    virtual Boolean at_top()
        { return( is_at_top); }
    virtual Boolean at_end()
        { return( is_at_bottom); }
    virtual long tell() const;
    virtual long total() const;

//  List Navigation
    virtual Boolean find(char *condition)
    { return (Boolean) DB_Find(t,condition); }
    virtual void prev(), next(),
                top(),  end(),
                seek(long where, SeekStart start = from_top);
    virtual void select(char *criteria) { DB_Filter(t,criteria); }
    virtual void clear_select() { clearfilters(); }
    virtual void set_order(char *col) { orderby(col);    DB_FirstRow(t); }
    virtual void clear_order() { unordered(); }

//  Interface to and from List
    virtual Boolean add(R &record);
    virtual Boolean replace(R &record) = 0;
    virtual void remove();
    virtual R current() = 0;

};
```

```
/* ===================== PFM_List Body ================================ */

//////////////////////////////////////////////////////////////////////////
// Author: David Brumbaugh
//
// Method Name: Pfm_List<R>::Pfm_list
// Creation Date: 6/2/92
// Purpose: Constructor that uses an open database during instansiation
//
// Return Value: None
//
// Parameters:
//   Type           Name            Purpose/Description        Default Value
//   ----           ----            ------------------         -------------
//   database &     open_db         Handle of already opened   None
//                                  Database
//   char           *table_name     Name of Table to be used   None
//////////////////////////////////////////////////////////////////////////

template <class R>
Pfm_List<R>::Pfm_List(database &open_db, char *table_name):table(open_db,
table_name)
{
    db = &open_db;

    // Position the list at "the top"
    DB_FirstRow(t);
    DB_NextRow(t,DBNEXT);
    is_at_top = true;
    is_at_bottom = false;


}

//////////////////////////////////////////////////////////////////////////
// Author: David Brumbaugh
//
// Method Name: Pfm_List<R>::Pfm_list
// Creation Date: 6/2/92
// Purpose: Constructor that uses an open database and
//          existing table during instansiation
//
// Return Value: None
//
// Parameters:
//   Type    Name            Purpose/Description        Default Value
//   ----    ----            ------------------         -------------
//   DB &    open_db         Handle of already opened
//                           Database
//   DBTAB &db_table         Table to be used
//////////////////////////////////////////////////////////////////////////

template <class R>
Pfm_List<R>::Pfm_List(DBTAB db_table):
```

```
    if (nextrow()) // If nextrow() is non-0 we aren't at the bottom yet
    {
        is_at_bottom = false;
    }
    else // We've gone off the bottom
    {
        is_at_bottom = true;
        if (total() > 1L) // We have some left
        {
            is_at_top = false; // Therefore we're not at the top
        }
    }

}


///////////////////////////////////////////////////////////////////////
// Author: David Brumbaugh
// Method Name: Pfm_List<R>::top()
// Creation Date: 6/3/92
// Purpose: Set currency to top row of table
//
// Return Value: none
// Parameters: none
//
///////////////////////////////////////////////////////////////////////

template <class R>
void Pfm_List<R>::top()
{
    firstrow();
    nextrow();
    is_at_top = true;
    if (total() > 1L)
        is_at_bottom = false;

}

///////////////////////////////////////////////////////////////////////
// Author: David Brumbaugh
// Method Name: Pfm_List<R>::end()
// Creation Date: 6/3/92
// Purpose: Set currency to last row of table
//
// Return Value: none
// Parameters: none
//
///////////////////////////////////////////////////////////////////////

template <class R>
void Pfm_List<R>::end()
{
    forallrows(t);
```

```
    prevrow();
    is_at_bottom = true;
    if (total() > 1L)
        is_at_top = false;

}


/////////////////////////////////////////////////////////////////////
// Author: David Brumbaugh
//
// Method Name: Pfm_List<R>::add
// Creation Date: 6/3/92
// Purpose: Add a record to the list
//
// Return Value: TRUE if successful, FALSE otherwise
// Parameters:
//  Type        Name            Purpose/Description        Default Value
//  —           ————            ————————————               ————————
//  Any         record          Any type of record to be   none
//     (See class header)       added
/////////////////////////////////////////////////////////////////////


template <class R>
Boolean Pfm_List<R>::add(R &record)
{
    if (DB_AddRow(t) != DB_OK)
    {
        return(false);
    }
    return(replace(record));
}


/////////////////////////////////////////////////////////////////////
// Author: David Brumbaugh
// Method Name: Pfm_List<R>::remove()
// Creation Date: 6/3/92
// Purpose: Delete current row from table
//
// Return Value: none
// Parameters: none
//
/////////////////////////////////////////////////////////////////////

template <class R>
void Pfm_List<R>::remove()
{
    delrow();
    nextrow();
}


/////////////////////////////////////////////////////////////////////
// Author: David Brumbaugh
```

```
// Method Name: seek
// Creation Date: 6/3/92
// Purpose: Search to a specific offset into the list
//
// Return Value: none
// Parameters:
//   Type              Name              Purpose/Description          Default Value
//   ——                ————————          ———————————                  ————
//   long              where             Tells Postion to Seek To     from_top
//   SeekStart         start             Tells where to begin seek:
//                                       from_top, from_here, from_end
/////////////////////////////////////////////////////////////////////

template <class R>
void Pfm_List<R>::seek(long where, SeekStart start)
{
    long i;
    switch(start)
    {
        case from_top:
            top();
        case from_here:
        for (i = 0; i < where; ++i)
            nextrow();
        break;
        case from_end:
            end();
        for (i = 0; i < where; ++i)
            nextrow(-1);
        break;
    }

}


#endif


/////////////////////////////////////////////////////////////////////
// Listing  : 10-18
// Filename    : LibMWin.HPP
// Purpose     : Class definition of the main window.
/////////////////////////////////////////////////////////////////////

#ifndef LIBMWIN_HPP
#define LIBMWIN_HPP

#include <ui_win.hpp>
#define USE_SSOOT_LIB1
#include "ssootlib.hpp"
#undef USE_SSOOT_LIB1
#include "catlist.hpp"
#include "FNDEFWIN.HPP"
#include "CLSDFWIN.HPP"
```

```
// Librarian Main Window Event Constants - These constants match the
// Menu item values in the SSOOTLIB.DAT SSOOT_LIB_1 resource.

const int OpenCatalogEvent = 11001;
const int NewCatalogEvent = 10002;
const int ImportFromHeaderEvent = 10003;
const int PrintEvent = 10004;
const int PrintSetupEvent = 10005;
const int ExitEvent = 10006;

const int SelectEvent = 20001;
const int FindEvent = 20002;
const int OrderByEvent = 20003;
const int AddClassEvent = 20004;
const int AddFunctionEvent = 20005;
const int EditEntryEvent = 20006;
const int DeleteEntryEvent = 20007;

const int AddUserEvent = 31001;
const int EditUserEvent = 31002;
const int DeleteUserEvent= 31003;


////////////////////////////////////////////////////////////////////
// Author        : David Brumbaugh
// Class Name    : LibMainWindow
// Creation Date: 11/92
// Catagories    : User Interface
// Purpose       : Main window for SSOOT CASE Libraian
//
// Major Public Methods:
//      Event - Handles menu items etc.
//      LibMainWindow - Constructor
//      getCatalog - Gets the current catalog
//      setCatalog - Assigns a catalog to the window
//      refreshCatList - Rebuilds the catalog display list
//      scrollCatList - Scrolls the catalog list.
//      currentCatListPos - Returns the index of the current list value.
//
// Major Data Items:
//      db - The database
//      theCatalog - The catalog being viewed
//      theCatalogList - The window containing the catalog list
//      anEntryWindow - Edit window for class and function entries
//      fnEntry - FunctionEntry being edited or added.
//      clsEntry - ClassEntry being edited or added.
////////////////////////////////////////////////////////////////////


class LibMainWindow : public UIW_WINDOW
{
    protected:
        database db;
```

```
    Catalog *theCatalog;
    CATALOG_LIST *theCatalogList;
    UIW_WINDOW *anEntryWindow;
    FunctionEntry *fnEntry;
    ClassEntry *clsEntry;
    // Actions on the File Menu
    virtual void openCatalog();
    virtual void newCatalog() {}
    virtual void importFromHeader() {}
    virtual void print() {}
    virtual void printSetup() {}
    // Actions on the Catalog Menu
    virtual void addFunction()
    {    anEntryWindow = new FunctionDefnWindow(this);
        *windowManager + anEntryWindow;
    }
    virtual void addClass()
    {      anEntryWindow = new ClassDefnWindow(this);
        *windowManager + anEntryWindow;
    }
    virtual void select();
    virtual void orderBy() {}
    virtual void find();
    virtual void editEntry();
    virtual void deleteEntry();
    // Actions on the Utilities Menu

    virtual void addUser() {}
    virtual void editUser() {}
    virtual void deleteUser(){}
public:
    LibMainWindow(char *catalogName = NULL);
    ~LibMainWindow() {if (theCatalog) delete theCatalog;
    if (fnEntry) delete fnEntry; if (clsEntry) delete clsEntry;}
    virtual EVENT_TYPE Event(const UI_EVENT &event);
    Catalog *getCatalog() { return theCatalog; }
    void setCatalog(Catalog *aCatalog)
    { if (theCatalog) delete theCatalog;
    theCatalog = aCatalog; }
    void refreshCatList()
    {
    theCatalogList->Destroy();
    theCatalogList->newTotal();
    theCatalogList->Event(Recreate);
    }
    void scrollCatList(int numRecords)
    {
        UI_EVENT sEvent(S_VSCROLL);
        sEvent.scroll.delta = numRecords;
        theCatalogList->Event(sEvent);
    }
    int currentCatListPos()
    {
        return(theCatalogList->Index(theCatalogList->Current()));
```

```
        }

};


#endif


///////////////////////////////////////////////////////////////////
// Listing : 10-19
// Filename : LibMwin.CPP
// Purpose  : Source Code for the LibMainWindow class
///////////////////////////////////////////////////////////////////


///////////////////////////////////////////////////////////////////
// Author: David Brumbaugh
// Method Name: LibMainWindow
// Creation Date: 11/92
// Purpose: Constructor
//
// Parameters:
// Type       Name             Purpose/Description        Default Value
// char *     catalogName      Name of catalog associated NULL
//                             with library.
///////////////////////////////////////////////////////////////////


#include "LibMwin.HPP"
#include "dialog.hpp"
#include "searchwi.h"
#include "direct.hpp"

LibMainWindow::LibMainWindow(char *catalogName):
UIW_WINDOW("SSOOTLIB~SSOOT_LIB_1"), db(catalogName,"rw"), theCatalog(NULL),
fnEntry(NULL),clsEntry(NULL)
{
    if (catalogName)
    {
        theCatalog = new Catalog(db);
        theCatalog->set_order("IDVersion");
        theCatalogList = new CATALOG_LIST(theCatalog);
        *this + theCatalogList;
    }
}


///////////////////////////////////////////////////////////////////
// Author: David Brumbaugh
// Method Name: Event
// Creation Date: 11/92
// Purpose: Maps the menu selection to the
//          appropriate member functions.
//
// Return Value: Event type, as per Zinc Standard
// Parameters: Event to be processed.
```

```
//
//////////////////////////////////////////////////////////////////

EVENT_TYPE LibMainWindow::Event(const UI_EVENT &event)
{
    switch(event.type)
    {
    // File Menu Events
        case OpenCatalogEvent:
            openCatalog();
        break;
        case NewCatalogEvent:
            newCatalog();
        break;
        case ImportFromHeaderEvent:
            importFromHeader();
        break;
        case PrintEvent:
            print();
        break;
        case PrintSetupEvent:
            printSetup();
        break;
        case ExitEvent:
            eventManager->Put(L_EXIT);
        break;
    //Catalog Menu Events
        case SelectEvent:
            select();
        break;
        case FindEvent:
            find();
        break;
        case OrderByEvent:
            orderBy();
        break;
        case AddClassEvent:
            addClass();
        break;
        case AddFunctionEvent:
            addFunction();
        break;
        case EditEntryEvent:
            editEntry();
        break;
        case DeleteEntryEvent:
            deleteEntry();
        break;
    // Utility Menu Events
        case AddUserEvent:
            addUser();
        break;
        case EditUserEvent:
            editUser();
```

```
        break;
        case DeleteUserEvent:
            deleteUser();
        break;
    // Other Events
        case FILE_FOPEN:
        {
            char *catalogName = (char *) event.data;
            DB theDB = DB_Open (catalogName,"rw",20);
            if (theDB)
            {
                db.close();
                db.x = theDB;
                *this - theCatalogList;
                delete theCatalogList;
                setCatalog(new Catalog(db));
                theCatalogList = new CATALOG_LIST(theCatalog);
                *this + theCatalogList;

                // refreshCatList();
            }

        }
        break;
        default:
            return UIW_WINDOW::Event(event);
    }
    return event.type;
}


//////////////////////////////////////////////////////////////////////
// Author: David Brumbaugh
// Method Name: find
// Creation Date: 11/92
// Purpose: Starts the EntrySearchWindow to find a particular entry.
//
// Return Value: None
// Parameters: None
//
//////////////////////////////////////////////////////////////////////

void LibMainWindow::find()
{
    *windowManager +
        new EntrySearchWindow(this,::true);
}

//////////////////////////////////////////////////////////////////////
// Author: David Brumbaugh
// Method Name: select
// Creation Date: 11/92
// Purpose: Starts the EntrySearchWindow to find a list of entries
//
// Return Value: None
```

```
// Parameters: None
//
//////////////////////////////////////////////////////////////////////

void LibMainWindow::select()
{
    *windowManager +
        new EntrySearchWindow(this,::false);
}



//////////////////////////////////////////////////////////////////////
// Author: David Brumbaugh
// Method Name: editEntry
// Creation Date: 11/92
// Purpose:  Edits the current entry.
//
// Return Value: None
// Parameters: None
//
//////////////////////////////////////////////////////////////////////

void LibMainWindow::editEntry()
{
    eventManager->DeviceState(E_MOUSE,DM_WAIT);
    ENTRY_ELEMENT *elem = theCatalogList->Current();
    if (elem)
    {
        theCatalog->seek(elem->recordNumber);
        D_Record theEntry = theCatalog->current();
        string etype = (const char *)theEntry["EntryType"];

        if (etype == "function")
        {
            if (fnEntry)
                delete fnEntry;
            fnEntry = new FunctionEntry;
            if (theCatalog->getEntry(*fnEntry))
            {
                anEntryWindow = new FunctionDefnWindow(this, fnEntry);
                *windowManager + anEntryWindow;
            }
            eventManager->DeviceState(E_MOUSE,DM_VIEW);
            return;
        }
        else
        {
            if (clsEntry)
                delete clsEntry;
            clsEntry = new ClassEntry;
            if (theCatalog->getEntry(*clsEntry))
            {
                anEntryWindow = new ClassDefnWindow(this,clsEntry);
```

```
                        *windowManager + anEntryWindow;
                }
                eventManager->DeviceState(E_MOUSE,DM_VIEW);
                return;
        }
    }
}

//////////////////////////////////////////////////////////////////////
// Author: David Brumbaugh
// Method Name: deleteEntry
// Creation Date: 12/92
// Purpose: Deletes the current entry
//
// Return Value: None
// Parameters: None
//
//////////////////////////////////////////////////////////////////////

void LibMainWindow::deleteEntry()
{
    ENTRY_ELEMENT *elem = theCatalogList->Current();
    if (elem)
    {
        theCatalog->seek(elem->recordNumber);
        D_Record theEntry = theCatalog->current();

        DIALOG_WINDOW dialog("Confirm", "QUESTION",
        DIF_YES|DIF_NO,    "Do you want to delete entry:\r\n\r\n%s %ld?",
        (const char *)theEntry["Identity"], (long) theEntry["Version"] );
        if (dialog.Response() == DIALOG_NO)
            return;
        eventManager->DeviceState(E_MOUSE,DM_WAIT);
        theCatalog->deleteEntry((const char *)theEntry["Identity"],
        (long) theEntry["Version"]);
        refreshCatList();
        eventManager->DeviceState(E_MOUSE,DM_VIEW);
    }

}
//////////////////////////////////////////////////////////////////////
// Author: David Brumbaugh
// Method Name: openCatalog
// Creation Date: 3/93
// Purpose: Opens a new catalog
//
// Return Value: None
// Parameters: None
//
//////////////////////////////////////////////////////////////////////


void LibMainWindow::openCatalog()
{
```

```
// Event map table.
 #ifdef _WINDOWS
 static UI_EVENT_MAP vlistEventMapTable[] =
 {
     { ID_WINDOW_OBJECT,    L_UP,       WM_KEYDOWN,      GRAY_UP_ARROW },,
     { ID_WINDOW_OBJECT,    L_UP,       WM_KEYDOWN,      WHITE_UP_ARROW },,
     { ID_WINDOW_OBJECT,    L_DOWN,     WM_KEYDOWN,      GRAY_DOWN_ARROW },,
     { ID_WINDOW_OBJECT,    L_DOWN,     M_KEYDOWN,       WHITE_DOWN_ARROW },,
     { ID_WINDOW_OBJECT,    L_PGUP,     WM_KEYDOWN,      GRAY_PGUP },,
     { ID_WINDOW_OBJECT,    L_PGUP,     WM_KEYDOWN,      WHITE_PGUP },,
     { ID_WINDOW_OBJECT,    L_PGDN,     WM_KEYDOWN,      GRAY_PGDN },,
     { ID_WINDOW_OBJECT,    L_PGDN,     WM_KEYDOWN,      WHITE_PGDN },,
     { ID_WINDOW_OBJECT,    L_LEFT,     WM_KEYDOWN,      GRAY_LEFT_ARROW },,
     { ID_WINDOW_OBJECT,    L_LEFT,     WM_KEYDOWN,      WHITE_LEFT_ARROW },,
     { ID_WINDOW_OBJECT,    L_RIGHT,    WM_KEYDOWN,      GRAY_RIGHT_ARROW },,
     { ID_WINDOW_OBJECT,    L_RIGHT,    WM_KEYDOWN,      WHITE_RIGHT_ARROW },,
     { ID_WINDOW_OBJECT,    L_TOP,      MM_KEYDOWN,      GRAY_HOME },,
     { ID_WINDOW_OBJECT,    L_TOP,      WM_KEYDOWN,      WHITE_HOME },,
     { ID_WINDOW_OBJECT,    L_BOTTOM,   WM_KEYDOWN,      GRAY_END },,
     { ID_WINDOW_OBJECT,    L_BOTTOM,   WM_KEYDOWN,      WHITE_END },,
     { ID_WINDOW_OBJECT,    L_PREVIOUS, WM_CHAR,         BACKTAB },,
     { ID_WINDOW_OBJECT,    L_NEXT,     WM_CHAR,         TAB },,
     { ID_WINDOW_OBJECT,    L_SELECT,   WM_CHAR,         4   ENTER },,

     // End of array.
     { ID_END, 0, 0, 0 }
 };
 #endif


/////////////////////////////////////////////////////////////////////
// Author: David Brumbaugh
// Method Name:   ENTRY_ELEMENT
// Purpose: constructor
//
// Return Value: None
// Parameters:
//   Type   Name                      Purpose/Description
//   int    left, top, width, _height   Dimensions of element
/////////////////////////////////////////////////////////////////////

ENTRY_ELEMENT::ENTRY_ELEMENT(int left, int top, int width, int _height,
int length) :
        UIW_STRING(left, top, width, "", length, STF_NO_FLAGS, WOF_NO_FLAGS),
    height(_height)
{
    // Set up event map table for Windows.
#ifdef _WINDOWS
    eventMapTable = vlistEventMapTable;
#endif

}
```

```
//////////////////////////////////////////////////////////////////////
// Author: David Brumbaugh
// Method Name: Event
// Purpose: Handles events sent to the ENTRY_ELEMENT
//
// Return Value: The event type processed
// Parameters:
//  Type            Name       Purpose/Description          Default Value
//  UI_EVENT &      event      The event to process         None
//////////////////////////////////////////////////////////////////////

EVENT_TYPE ENTRY_ELEMENT::Event(const UI_EVENT &event)
{
    EVENT_TYPE ccode = LogicalEvent(event, ID_WINDOW_OBJECT);

    switch (ccode)
    {
        case S_INITIALIZE:
        UIW_STRING::Event(event);
        if (display && !display->isText)
            relative.bottom = relative.top + height;
        break;

#ifdef _WINDOWS
    // Let the parent window handle these keyboard events.
    case L_UP:
    case L_DOWN:
    case L_NEXT:
    case L_PREVIOUS:
    case L_PGUP:
    case L_PGDN:
    case L_TOP:
    case L_BOTTOM:
        return parent->Event(event);

#endif

    default:
        ccode = UIW_STRING::Event(event);
        break;
    }

    // Return the control code.
    return (ccode);
}
//////////////////////////////////////////////////////////////////////
// Author: David Brumbaugh
// Method Name: CATALOG_LIST
// Purpose: constructor
//
// Return Value: None
// Parameters:
```

```
// Type            Name          Purpose/Description              Default Value
// Catalog *       aCatalog      Catalog associated with this     NULL
//                               list window
/////////////////////////////////////////////////////////////////////

CATALOG_LIST::CATALOG_LIST(Catalog *aCatalog) :
        UIW_WINDOW(2,1, 55, 6, WOF_BORDER), numberShowing(0),
        currentPosition(0), numberOfRecords(0), lastRecord(-1)
{
    // Set up event map table for Windows.
#ifdef _WINDOWS
    eventMapTable = vlistEventMapTable;
#endif

    *this + new UIW_SCROLL_BAR(0,0,0,0);
    // Associate the database, get the total number of records.
    if (aCatalog)
    {
        theCatalog = aCatalog;
        numberOfRecords = aCatalog->total();
    }


}


/////////////////////////////////////////////////////////////////////
// Author: David Brumbaugh
// Method Name: Event
// Purpose: Processes the catalog list event
/////////////////////////////////////////////////////////////////////


EVENT_TYPE CATALOG_LIST::Event(const UI_EVENT &event)
{
    EVENT_TYPE ccode = LogicalEvent(event, ID_WINDOW);
    switch (ccode)
    {
        case Recreate:
        case S_CREATE:
        {
            UI_REGION region;
            if (ccode != Recreate)
                UIW_WINDOW::Event(event);

        // Get the available drawing region of the window.
#ifdef _WINDOWS
        RECT rect;
        GetClientRect(screenID, &rect);
        region.Assign(rect);

#else
        region = clipList.First()->region;
#endif
        // Calculate the number of elements that will fit in the list.
        int lineHeight = display->TextHeight("Mxq", screenID, font)
```

```
                        + display->preSpace + display->postSpace;

        int newNumberShowing = (region.bottom - region.top + display->preSpace +
        display->postSpace);
        newNumberShowing /= lineHeight;
        if (display->isText)
                newNumberShowing++;

        // Set the current item and currentPosition.
        numberShowing = newNumberShowing;

        currentPosition = First() ? First()->recordNumber : 0;
        int index = Current() ? Index(Current()) : 0;

        // Check for sizing the window that clips the current item.
        if (index > numberShowing - 1)
        {
                currentPosition += (numberShowing - 1);
                index = numberShowing - 1;
        }
        else currentPosition += index;
        Destroy();
        int right = region.right - region.left + 1;

        for (int line = 0; line < numberShowing; line++)
        {
                ENTRY_ELEMENT *element = new ENTRY_ELEMENT(0,
                    line * lineHeight, right, lineHeight, 100);
                 element->woStatus |= (WOS_GRAPHICS | (line == index ? WOS_CURRENT
                                    : 0));
                LoadRecord(element, currentPosition - index + line);
                Add(element);
        }
        // Set scroll bar range.
#ifdef _WINDOWS
         SetScrollRange(screenID, SB_VERT, 0, numberOfRecords - 1, FALSE);
         SetScrollPos(screenID, SB_VERT, First()->recordNumber, TRUE);
                 ccode = Event(UI_EVENT(S_REDISPLAY));


#else
        if (vScroll)
        {
            UI_EVENT sEvent(S_VSCROLL_SET);
            sEvent.scroll.minimum = 0;
            sEvent.scroll.maximum = numberOfRecords - 1;
            sEvent.scroll.current = currentPosition;
            sEvent.scroll.delta = 1;
            sEvent.scroll.showing = numberShowing - 1;
            vScroll->Event(sEvent);
        }
#endif


        }
```

```
            break;

      case S_VSCROLL:
          {
          UI_EVENT sEvent(S_VSCROLL);

          // Figure the delta we actually need to scroll.
          sEvent.scroll.delta = event.scroll.delta;
          if ((!currentPosition && sEvent.scroll.delta < 0) ||
             (currentPosition == numberOfRecords - 1 && sEvent.scroll.delta > 0))
               return ccode;

          currentPosition += sEvent.scroll.delta;
          if (currentPosition < 0)
          {
              sEvent.scroll.delta -= currentPosition;
              currentPosition = 0;
          }
          else if (currentPosition > numberOfRecords - 1)
          {
              sEvent.scroll.delta -= (currentPosition - (numberOfRecords - 1));
              currentPosition = numberOfRecords - 1;
          }
          // Update the scroll bar thumb and scroll the list.
          MoveScrollBar(sEvent.scroll.delta);
          ScrollList(sEvent.scroll.delta);
          if (currentPosition == 0 && Current() != First())
              Add(First());

#ifdef _WINDOWS
                  Event(UI_EVENT(S_REDISPLAY));
#endif

          }
          break;

      case L_PREVIOUS:
      case L_UP:
          if (Current() != First())
          {
              currentPosition—;
              MoveScrollBar(-1);
              Add(Current()->Previous());
          }
          else if (currentPosition)
          {
              UI_EVENT sEvent(S_VSCROLL);
              sEvent.scroll.delta = -1;
              Event(sEvent);
          }
          break;

      case L_NEXT:
      case L_DOWN:
```

```
        if (Current() != Last() && Current()->recordNumber != numberOfRecords - 1)
        {
                currentPosition++;
                MoveScrollBar(1);
                Add(Current()->Next());
        }
        else if (currentPosition < numberOfRecords - 1)
        {
                UI_EVENT sEvent(S_VSCROLL);
                sEvent.scroll.delta = 1;
                Event(sEvent);
            }
        break;

        case L_PGUP:
        case L_PGDN:
            {
          UI_EVENT sEvent(S_VSCROLL);
          sEvent.scroll.delta = ccode == L_PGUP ? -(numberShowing - 1)
                  : numberShowing - 1;
         Event(sEvent);
        }
        break;

        case L_TOP:
        case L_BOTTOM:
            {
            UI_EVENT sEvent(S_VSCROLL);
            sEvent.scroll.delta = ccode == L_TOP ? -(numberOfRecords - 1)
                : numberOfRecords - 1;
            Event(sEvent);
            }
            break;

        case L_BEGIN_SELECT:
            {
            // Update position and scroll bar if new item selected with mouse.
            if (!clipList.First()->region.Overlap(event.position))
                return UIW_WINDOW::Event(event);

            UI_WINDOW_OBJECT *oldElement = Current();
            UIW_WINDOW::Event(event);
            UI_WINDOW_OBJECT *newElement = Current();
            if (newElement != oldElement && newElement->Inherited(ID_STRING))
            {
                int delta = (Index(newElement) - Index(oldElement));
                if (delta > 0)
                    currentPosition += Max(0, delta);
                else if (delta < 0)
                    currentPosition += Min(0, delta);
                MoveScrollBar(delta);
            }
            }
            break;
```

```
        default:

#ifdef _WINDOWS
    // Convert WINDOWS Scroll messages to S_VSCROLL events.
    if(event.type == E_MSWINDOWS && event.message.message == WM_VSCROLL)
    {
        UI_EVENT sEvent(S_VSCROLL);

        switch(event.message.wParam)
        {
        case SB_LINEUP:
            sEvent.scroll.delta = -1;
            break;
        case SB_LINEDOWN:
            sEvent.scroll.delta = 1;
            break;
        case SB_PAGEUP:
            sEvent.scroll.delta = -(numberShowing - 1);
            break;
        case SB_PAGEDOWN:
            sEvent.scroll.delta = numberShowing - 1;
            break;
        case SB_THUMBPOSITION:
          sEvent.scroll.delta = LOWORD(event.message.lParam) - currentPosition;
            break;
        default:
            sEvent.scroll.delta = 0;
        break;
        }
        if (sEvent.scroll.delta)
            return Event(sEvent);
    }
#endif
        ccode = UIW_WINDOW::Event(event);
    }

    // Return the control code.
    return (ccode);
}

void CATALOG_LIST::LoadRecord(ENTRY_ELEMENT *element, int recordNumber)
{

    // Load the record from the file.
    if (recordNumber > numberOfRecords - 1)
        element->DataSet(-1, "");
    else if (theCatalog && recordNumber > -1)
    {
        // Mildly optimized seek.
        if ((recordNumber == (lastRecord + 1)) && recordNumber != 0 )
            theCatalog->next();
        else if (recordNumber == (lastRecord - 1))
            theCatalog->prev();
```

```
            else if (recordNumber == theCatalog->total())
                theCatalog->end();
            else if (recordNumber == 0)
            {
                theCatalog->top();
            }
            else
                theCatalog->seek(recordNumber);


            char *text = new char[200];
            strcpy(text,theCatalog->getSummary());
            element->DataSet(recordNumber, text);
            delete text;
        }
        lastRecord = recordNumber;


}

#pragma argsused
void CATALOG_LIST::MoveScrollBar(int delta)
{

#ifdef _WINDOWS
        SetScrollPos(screenID, SB_VERT, currentPosition, TRUE);
#else
        UI_EVENT sEvent(S_VSCROLL);
        sEvent.scroll.delta = delta;
        if (vScroll)
            vScroll->Event(sEvent);
#endif

}


void CATALOG_LIST::ScrollList(int delta)
{
        if (delta == 1)
        {
            // Scroll down 1 record in the list.
          for (ENTRY_ELEMENT *object = First(); object && object->Next(); object =
            object->Next())
                    object->DataSet(object->Next());
                if (Last()->recordNumber != -1)
                    LoadRecord(Last(), Last()->recordNumber + 1);
        }
        else if (delta == -1)
        {
            // Scroll or move highlight bar up 1 record in the list.
            if (First()->recordNumber == 0 && Current() != First())
            {
                Add(Current()->Previous());
                return;
```

```
        }
        if (First()->recordNumber)
      for (ENTRY_ELEMENT *object = Last(); object && object->Previous(); object
                              = object->Previous())
          if (object->Previous()->recordNumber != -1)
              object->DataSet(object->Previous());
        LoadRecord(First(), First()->recordNumber -1);
    }
    else if (delta < 0 && First()->recordNumber == 0 && First() != Current())
    {
        // Page up to First record in list.
        Add(First());
        MoveScrollBar(-Index(Current()));
        currentPosition = 0;
    }
    else
    {
        // Page up or Page down .
        int recordNumber =  Max(0, currentPosition - Index(Current()));
      for (ENTRY_ELEMENT *object = First(); object;   object = object->Next())
              LoadRecord(object, recordNumber++);
    }


}


//////////////////////////////////////////////////////////////////////
// Listing  : 10-22
// Filename : ClsDfWin.HPP
// Purpose  : Function Definiton Window
//////////////////////////////////////////////////////////////////////
#include <alloc.h>
#ifndef CLSDFWIN_HPP
#define CLSDFWIN_HPP
#include "defnfile.h"
//////////////////////////////////////////////////////////////////////
// Author       : David Brumbaugh
// Class Name   : FunctionDefnWindow
// Creation Date : 12/92
// Catagories   : User Interface
// Purpose      : Allows creation and editing of data in the
//                FunctionDefinition
//
// Major Public Methods:
//  Event - Handles event processing in this window
//  FunctionDefnWindow - Constructor
//
//
// Major Data Items:
//  aFunctionEntry - The function entry being edited.
//////////////////////////////////////////////////////////////////////


#include <ui_win.hpp>
```

```
#define USE_CLASS_DEF_WIN
#include "ssootlib.hpp"
#undef USE_CLASS_DEF_WIN
#include "Entry.H"
#include "dediag.h"
#include "rptstup.h"

class LibMainWindow;


// Librarian Function Definiton Window Event Constants -
// These constants match the Menu item values in the
// SSOOTLIB.DAT CLASS_DEF_WIN resource.

// File Menu Events
// These values repeated here for convience
/*
const int ToSourceEvent = 10001;
const int MakeTemplateEvent = 10002;
const int MakeFromSourceEvent = 10003;
const int ReserveEvent = 10004;
const int PrintEntryEvent = 10005;

// Options Menu Events
const int UseCommentsEvent = 20011;
*/
const int NewUseCommentsEvent = 20015;
const int ExpandInlineEvent = 20014;
const int SetupReportEvent = 20013;

// Buttons
/*
const int OKBtn = 3001;
const int CancelBtn = 3000;
*/
const int AddMemDataBtn = 10101;
const int EditMemDataBtn = 10102;
const int DelMemDataBtn = 10103;
const int AddMemFctnBtn = 10104;
const int EditMemFctnBtn = 10105;
const int DelMemFctnBtn = 10106;

class ClassDefnWindow : public UIW_WINDOW
{
    protected:
    // Connections to Other Objects
        ClassEntry *aClassEntry;
        HeaderFileDefn *aHeaderFileDefn;
        MemberFunctionDefinition *fctnMem;
        ReportSetup theReportSetup;

    // For communication to Other Windows
        LibMainWindow *mainWindow;
        DataEntryDialog *dataEntryWindow;
```

```
    // State variables
        Boolean changedDataList,
                changedFctnList,
                needToDelete;
        Boolean wantsComments,
                wantsInlineExpansion;
    // Working variables
        string originalParameters; // For cancelEdit and cancelAdd
        string originalParamDescrip;

        unsigned char dataIndexes[125], // Working variables
                    fctnIndexes[125]; // to keep track of where
                                      // the members are in the windows.

        Boolean stuffChanged; // Has anything in the window been changed?
        // Data Transfer
        virtual void entryToWindow();
        virtual void windowToEntry();

        // File Menu
        virtual void toSource();
        virtual void makeFromSource();
        virtual void makeTemplate();
        virtual void reserve() {}
        virtual void print();

        // Options Menu
        virtual void useComments();
        virtual void expandInline();
        virtual void reportSetup();

        // Buttons
        virtual void handleCancel();
        virtual void handleOK();
        virtual void editMemData();
        virtual void addMemData();
        virtual void delMemData();
        virtual void editMemFctn();
        virtual void addMemFctn();
        virtual void delMemFctn();

        // Support
        virtual void completeEditData();
        virtual void completeAddData();
        virtual void updateDataList();
        virtual void updateFctnList();
        virtual void completeMakeFromSource();
        virtual void updateMemberIndexes();
        virtual void completeSetupReport();
        virtual Boolean dataChanged();
        virtual void printFctnSpecs(ofstream *out);

    public:
    // Communicate between windows
```

```cpp
        virtual EVENT_TYPE Event(const UI_EVENT &event);
        virtual void cancelAddFctn();
        virtual void cancelEditFctn();
        virtual void completeAddFctn();
        virtual void completeEditFctn();

        ClassDefnWindow (LibMainWindow *lmw,
        ClassEntry *ce = NULL) :
        UIW_WINDOW("SSOOTLIB~CLASS_DEF_WIN"),mainWindow(lmw)
        {
            changedDataList = ::true; // There is a data member of this
            changedFctnList = ::true; // window's ancestor also called 'true'
                                      // so, we're using the scope resolution
                                      // operator.
            wantsComments = false;
            wantsInlineExpansion = false;
            aHeaderFileDefn = NULL;
            stuffChanged = false;
            if (!ce)
            {
                needToDelete = ::true;
                aClassEntry = new ClassEntry;
            }
            else
            {
                needToDelete = false;
                aClassEntry = ce;
            }
        }
        virtual ~ClassDefnWindow() {
        if (needToDelete) delete aClassEntry;
        if (aHeaderFileDefn) delete aHeaderFileDefn;
    }
};

#endif


/////////////////////////////////////////////////////////////////////
// Listing  : 10-23
// Filename : ClsDfWin.CPP
// Purpose  : Source code for  Class Definition Window
/////////////////////////////////////////////////////////////////////

#include "CLSDFWIN.HPP"
#include "LIBMWIN.HPP"
#include "DEDIAG.H"
#include "dialog.hpp"
#include <fstream.h>
#include <strstream.h>
#include "memfnwin.hpp"
#include "txtrpt.h"
extern void TheBadErrorFunction(char *msg);
```

```
//////////////////////////////////////////////////////////////////
// Author: David Brumbaugh
// Method Name: Event
// Creation Date: 12/92
// Purpose: Handles Event processing for the FunctionDefnWindow
//
// Return Value: Event type to process
// Parameters: Event to be processed
//
//////////////////////////////////////////////////////////////////

EVENT_TYPE ClassDefnWindow::Event(const UI_EVENT &event)
{

    switch(event.type)
    {
        // File Menu Events
        case ToSourceEvent:
            toSource();
        break;
        case MakeTemplateEvent:
            makeTemplate();
        break;
        case MakeFromSourceEvent:
            makeFromSource();
        break;
        case ReserveEvent:
            reserve();
        break;
        case PrintEntryEvent:
            print();
        break;
        // Option Menu Events
        case ExpandInlineEvent:
            expandInline();
        break;
        case NewUseCommentsEvent:
            useComments();
        break;

        case SetupReportEvent:
            reportSetup();
        break;
        // Buttons
        case OKBtn:
            handleOK();
        break;
        case CancelBtn:
            handleCancel();
        break;
        case AddMemDataBtn:
            addMemData();
        break;
        case EditMemDataBtn:
```

```
                editMemData();
            break;
            case DelMemDataBtn:
                delMemData();
            break;
            case AddMemFctnBtn:
                addMemFctn();
            break;
            case EditMemFctnBtn:
                editMemFctn();
            break;
            case DelMemFctnBtn:
                delMemFctn();
            break;

            case S_INITIALIZE:
                if (aClassEntry)
                    entryToWindow();
            case S_REDISPLAY:
            case S_CURRENT:
                if (changedDataList || changedFctnList)
                    updateMemberIndexes();
                if (changedDataList)
                    updateDataList();
                if (changedFctnList)
                    updateFctnList();

            default:
                return UIW_WINDOW::Event(event);
        }
        return event.type;
}

//////////////////////////////////////////////////////////////////////
// Author: David Brumbaugh
// Method Name: windowToEntry
// Creation Date: 11/92
// Purpose: Transfer data from the window to the aFunctionEntry data
//              member.
//
// Return Value: None
// Parameters: None
//
//////////////////////////////////////////////////////////////////////

void ClassDefnWindow::windowToEntry()
{
    UIW_STRING *theString = (UIW_STRING *) Get("CLASS_NM");
    aClassEntry->setName(theString->DataGet());

    UIW_TEXT *theText = (UIW_TEXT *) Get("BASE_CLASS_LIST");
    istrstream anIStream(theText->DataGet());
    anIStream.unsetf(ios::skipws);
    aClassEntry->getParents(anIStream);
```

```
        UIW_COMBO_BOX *aCBox = (UIW_COMBO_BOX *) Get("CLASS_TYPE");
        theString = (UIW_STRING *) aCBox->Current();
        aClassEntry->setClassSpec(theString->DataGet());

        theString = (UIW_STRING *) Get("HDR_FILE_SPC");
        aClassEntry->setInclude(theString->DataGet());

        theString = (UIW_STRING *) Get("SRC_SPC_STR");
        aClassEntry->setLocation(theString->DataGet());

        theText = (UIW_TEXT *) Get("CLASS_DESC");
        aClassEntry->setDescription(theText->DataGet());

        UIW_INTEGER *theInt = (UIW_INTEGER *) Get("VRSN_FLD");
        aClassEntry->setVersion(theInt->DataGet());

}
/////////////////////////////////////////////////////////////////
// Author: David Brumbaugh
// Method Name: updateDataList
// Creation Date: 12/92
// Purpose: Updates the data member list on the screen
//
// Return Value: None
// Parameters: None
//
/////////////////////////////////////////////////////////////////

void ClassDefnWindow::updateDataList()
{
    DataMemberDefinition *dataMemDefn;
    UIW_VT_LIST *theList = (UIW_VT_LIST *) Get("MEM_DATA_LIST");
    theList->Destroy();
    MemberList &members = aClassEntry->getMembers();
    string dataSpec;
    for (int i = 0; i < members.total(); ++i)
    {
        dataMemDefn = (DataMemberDefinition *) members[i];
        if ( dataMemDefn->isA() != isData)
            continue;
        dataSpec = dataMemDefn->getAccessSpec() + string(' ');
        dataSpec += dataMemDefn->getTypeSpec();
        dataSpec +=    dataMemDefn->getPtrSpec()
        + string(' ');
        dataSpec += dataMemDefn->getName();
        theList->Add(new UIW_STRING(0,0,50,dataSpec.ptr()));

    }
    changedDataList = ::false;
    theList->Event(UI_EVENT(S_REDISPLAY));

}

/////////////////////////////////////////////////////////////////
```

```
// Author: David Brumbaugh
// Method Name: updateMemberIndexes
// Creation Date: 12/92
// Purpose: Updates the member index lists
//
// Return Value: None
// Parameters: None
//
///////////////////////////////////////////////////////////////////


void ClassDefnWindow::updateMemberIndexes()
{
    int d = 0, f = 0;
    MemberList &members = aClassEntry->getMembers();
    for (int i = 0; i < members.total(); ++i)
    {
        DataMemberDefinition *dataMemDefn =
        (DataMemberDefinition *) members[i];
        if ( dataMemDefn->isA() == isData)
            dataIndexes[d++] = i;
        else
            fctnIndexes[f++] = i;
    }


}

///////////////////////////////////////////////////////////////////
// Author: David Brumbaugh
// Method Name: updateFctnList
// Creation Date: 12/92
// Purpose: Updates the parameter list on the screen
//
// Return Value: None
// Parameters: None
//
///////////////////////////////////////////////////////////////////

void ClassDefnWindow::updateFctnList()
{
    MemberFunctionDefinition *memFctnDefn;
    UIW_VT_LIST *theList = (UIW_VT_LIST *) Get("MEM_FCTN_LIST");
    theList->Destroy();
    MemberList &members = aClassEntry->getMembers();
    string fctnSpec;
    for (int i = 0; i < members.total(); ++i)
    {
        memFctnDefn = (MemberFunctionDefinition *) members[i];
        if ( memFctnDefn->isA() == isData)
            continue;
        ParamList &parameters = memFctnDefn->getParams();
        fctnSpec = memFctnDefn->getAccessSpec() + string(' ');
        fctnSpec += memFctnDefn->getTypeSpec();
```

```
            fctnSpec += memFctnDefn->getPtrSpec() + string(' ');
            fctnSpec += memFctnDefn->getName();
            fctnSpec += parameters.toString();
            theList->Add(new UIW_STRING(0,0,50,fctnSpec.ptr()));

    }
    changedFctnList = ::false;
    theList->Event(UI_EVENT(S_REDISPLAY));
}


////////////////////////////////////////////////////////////////////////
// Author: David Brumbaugh
// Method Name: toSource
// Creation Date: 12/92
// Purpose: Converts class to header file code.
//
// Return Value: None
// Parameters: None
////////////////////////////////////////////////////////////////////////

void ClassDefnWindow::toSource()
{
    windowToEntry();
    string sourcePath =     aClassEntry->getInclude();
    sourcePath.Trim();
    if (sourcePath.Len() == 0)
    {
        DIALOG_WINDOW dialog("Incomplete Data", "ASTERISK",
        DIF_OK,    "You need a valid file name in the Header File field.");
        dialog.Response();
        return;
    }
    string descrip;
    aClassEntry->getDescription(descrip);
    string desc;
    aClassEntry->getDescription(desc);
    string commentString = "// ";
    string leftOver;
    while (wrapString(desc,leftOver,75))
    {
        commentString += desc;
        commentString += "\n// ";
        if (leftOver.Len())
            desc = leftOver;
    }
    commentString += desc;
    commentString += '\n';
    istrstream *istrm = new istrstream(commentString.ptr());
    istrm->unsetf(ios::skipws);
    aClassEntry->setCommentSource(istrm);

    ofstream out(sourcePath.ptr(),ios::app|ios::out);
    aClassEntry->toSource(out);
```

```
    aClassEntry->setCommentSource(NULL);   // Deletes the istrm stream
}

/////////////////////////////////////////////////////////////////////
// Author: David Brumbaugh
// Method Name: makeTemplate
// Creation Date: 12/92
// Purpose: Converts class to template source code.
//
// Return Value: None
// Parameters:   None
/////////////////////////////////////////////////////////////////////

void ClassDefnWindow::makeTemplate()
{
    windowToEntry();
    string sourcePath = aClassEntry->getLocation();
    sourcePath.Trim();
    if (sourcePath.Len() == 0)
    {
        DIALOG_WINDOW dialog("Incomplete Data", "ASTERISK",
        DIF_OK,    "You need a valid file name in the Source File field.");
        dialog.Response();
        return;
    }
    // Destructor will delete comment source
    ofstream out(sourcePath.ptr(),ios::app|ios::out);
    aClassEntry->makeTemplate(out);
}

/////////////////////////////////////////////////////////////////////
// Author: David Brumbaugh
// Method Name: makeFromSource and completeMakeFromSource
// Creation Date: 12/92
// Purpose: Builds class entry from header file
//
// Return Value: None
// Parameters:   None
/////////////////////////////////////////////////////////////////////

void ClassDefnWindow::makeFromSource()
{
    dataEntryWindow = new DataEntryDialog("SSOOTLIB~CLASS_HDR_LST_WIN",
    (UIW_WINDOW *) this,
    (void(UIW_WINDOW::*)()) &ClassDefnWindow::completeMakeFromSource);

    UIW_VT_LIST *theList = (UIW_VT_LIST *) dataEntryWindow->Get("CLASS_LST");
    windowToEntry();
    string sourcePath = aClassEntry->getInclude();
    sourcePath.Trim();
    if (sourcePath.Len() == 0)
    {
        DIALOG_WINDOW dialog("Incomplete Data", "ASTERISK",
        DIF_OK,    "You need a valid file name in the Header File field.");
```

```
        dialog.Response();
        return;
    }
    if (aHeaderFileDefn)
        delete aHeaderFileDefn;
    aHeaderFileDefn = new HeaderFileDefn(sourcePath.ptr());
    ClassOSList *classList = aHeaderFileDefn->getClassList();
    string theClass;
    for (int i = 0; i < classList->total(); ++i)
    {
        theClass = (*classList)[i].classSpec + ' '
                    + (*classList)[i].className;

        theList->Add(new UIW_STRING(0,0,50,theClass.ptr()));
    }
    *windowManager + dataEntryWindow;
}

void ClassDefnWindow::completeMakeFromSource()
{
    ClassOSList *classList = aHeaderFileDefn->getClassList();

    UIW_VT_LIST *theList = (UIW_VT_LIST *) dataEntryWindow->Get("CLASS_LST");
    int i = theList->Index(theList->Current());
    long offset = (*classList)[i].offset;
    iostream *anIoStream =      aHeaderFileDefn->getIoStream();
    anIoStream->clear();
    anIoStream->unsetf(ios::skipws);
    anIoStream->seekg(offset, ios::beg);
    anIoStream->seekp(offset, ios::beg);
    aClassEntry->fromSource(*anIoStream);
    delete aHeaderFileDefn;
    aHeaderFileDefn = NULL;
    if (aClassEntry->isAForwardDeclaration())
    {
        DIALOG_WINDOW dialog("Not a Complete Class", "ASTERISK",
        DIF_OK,    "The selected class is not fully defined.");
        dialog.Response();
        windowToEntry();
        return;
    }
    entryToWindow();
    changedDataList = ::true;
    changedFctnList = ::true;
    stuffChanged = ::true;
    Event(S_REDISPLAY);
}


//
// Menu Item: print
//
void ClassDefnWindow::print()
{
    if (theReportSetup.reportDest == 1 && theReportSetup.filename.Len())
```

```
        theReportSetup.tempFile = theReportSetup.filename;
else if (theReportSetup.reportDest != 1)
        theReportSetup.tempFile = tmpnam(NULL);
else
{
        UI_WINDOW_OBJECT::errorSystem->ReportError(windowManager,
        WOS_NO_STATUS, "File Error: %s", "No file specified");
        return;
}

ofstream rpt(theReportSetup.tempFile.ptr());

TextReport txtRpt(&rpt,"Class Definition Report %D%","%P%");
if (theReportSetup.reportFmt != 1)// Only interested in member functions.
{
        txtRpt.put("Class Name: ",false);
        txtRpt.put((char *)aClassEntry->getName(),::true);
        txtRpt.put("Version: ",false);
        string vers(aClassEntry->getVersion());
        txtRpt.put(vers.ptr(),::true);
        txtRpt.put("Base Classes: ",::true);
        BaseClassList &bases = aClassEntry->getBaseClasses();
        BaseClassSpec bcs;
        string line;
        for (int i = 0; i < bases.total(); ++i)
        {
                bcs = bases[i];
                line =  (bcs.baseSpecifier + " ") + bcs.name;
                txtRpt.put(line.ptr(),::true);
        }
        txtRpt.put("\n",::true);
        txtRpt.put("Description:",::true);
        string desc;
        aClassEntry->getDescription(desc);
        txtRpt.put(desc.ptr());
        txtRpt.put(" ",::true);

        txtRpt.put("Data Members:",::true);
        txtRpt.defineColumns(25,LEFT,2,LEFT,43,LEFT,-1);
        txtRpt.put("Member Name"," ","Description",NULL);
        // TheBadErrorFunction("Past the initial put");
        MemberList &members = aClassEntry->getMembers();
        string dataSpec;
        string memDesc;
        DataMemberDefinition *dataMemDefn;
        for (i = 0; i < members.total(); ++i)
        {
                dataMemDefn = (DataMemberDefinition *) members[i];
                if ( dataMemDefn->isA() != isData)
                        continue;
                dataSpec = dataMemDefn->getAccessSpec() + string(' ');
                dataSpec += dataMemDefn->getTypeSpec();
                dataSpec +=    dataMemDefn->getPtrSpec()
                + string(' ');
```

```
                    dataSpec += dataMemDefn->getName();
                    memDesc = dataMemDefn->getDescription();
                    txtRpt.put(dataSpec.ptr()," ",memDesc.ptr(),NULL);
                    txtRpt.put(" ",::true);
                }
1
            txtRpt.put(" ",::true);
            txtRpt.put("Member Functions:",::true);
            string fctnSpec;
            string fctnDesc;
            txtRpt.put("Member Name"," ", "Description",NULL);
            MemberFunctionDefinition *memFctnDefn;
            for (i = 0; i < members.total(); ++i)
            {
                memFctnDefn = (MemberFunctionDefinition *) members[i];
                if ( memFctnDefn->isA() == isData)
                    continue;
                ParamList &parameters = memFctnDefn->getParams();
                fctnSpec = memFctnDefn->getAccessSpec() + string(' ');
                fctnSpec += memFctnDefn->getTypeSpec();
                fctnSpec += memFctnDefn->getPtrSpec() + string(' ');
                fctnSpec += memFctnDefn->getName();
                fctnSpec += parameters.toString();
                fctnDesc = memFctnDefn->getDescription();
                txtRpt.put(fctnSpec.ptr()," ",fctnDesc.ptr(),NULL);
                txtRpt.put(" ",::true);
            }
        }
    if (theReportSetup.reportFmt == 2 || theReportSetup.reportFmt == 1)
    {
        txtRpt.newPage();
        printFctnSpecs(&rpt);
    }
    rpt.close();
    if (theReportSetup.reportDest != 1)
        remove(theReportSetup.tempFile.ptr());

}


// Prints the function specification
void ClassDefnWindow::printFctnSpecs(ofstream *out)
{
    TextReport *txtRpt;
    string fctnSpec;
    string fctnDesc, fullSpec, paramString;
    string divider('=',69);
    MemberFunctionDefinition *memFctnDefn;
    ParamDefinition paramDef;
    txtRpt = new
        TextReport(out,"Member Function Definition %D%","%P%");
    MemberList &members = aClassEntry->getMembers();
    for (int i = 0; i < members.total(); ++i)
    {
```

```
        memFctnDefn = (MemberFunctionDefinition *) members[i];
        if ( memFctnDefn->isA() == isData)
            continue;
        ParamList &parameters = memFctnDefn->getParams();
        fctnSpec = "Member Function: ";
        fctnSpec += memFctnDefn->getAccessSpec() + string(' ');
        fctnSpec += memFctnDefn->getTypeSpec();
        fctnSpec += memFctnDefn->getPtrSpec() + string(' ');
        fctnSpec += aClassEntry->getName();
        fctnSpec += "::";
        fctnSpec += (char *) memFctnDefn->getName();
        fctnSpec += (char *) parameters.toString();
        txtRpt->put(fctnSpec.ptr(),::true);
        txtRpt->put(" ",::true);
        fctnDesc = memFctnDefn->getDescription();
        txtRpt->put("Description:",::true);
        txtRpt->put(fctnDesc.ptr(),::true);
        txtRpt->put(" ",::true);
        txtRpt->put("Parameter Definition:",::true);
        if (! parameters.total())
            txtRpt->put("(No parameters)",::true);
        else
        {
            txtRpt->defineColumns(32,LEFT,2,LEFT,36,LEFT,-1);
            txtRpt->put("Parameter"," ","Definition");
            txtRpt->put(" ",::true);
            for (int p = 0; p < parameters.total(); ++p)
            {
                paramDef = parameters[p];
                paramString = paramDef.typeSpecifiers + " " + paramDef.name;
                if (paramDef.defaultValue.Len())
                {
                    paramString += " = ";
                    paramString += paramDef.defaultValue;
                }
                txtRpt->put(paramString.ptr()," ",
                paramDef.description.ptr(),NULL);
            }
        }
        txtRpt->put(" ",::true);
        if (strlen(memFctnDefn->getSpecification()))
        {
            txtRpt->put("Function Specification:",::true);
            txtRpt->put((char *)memFctnDefn->getSpecification(),::true);
        }
        else
        {
            txtRpt->put("(No Specification)",::true);
        }
        txtRpt->put(" ",::true);
        txtRpt->put(divider.ptr());


}
```

```
        delete txtRpt;

}

//
// Sets up the report type and destination
//
void ClassDefnWindow::reportSetup()
{
    dataEntryWindow = new DataEntryDialog("SSOOTLIB~CLS_RPT_SETUP",
    (UIW_WINDOW *) this,
    (void(UIW_WINDOW::*)()) &ClassDefnWindow::completeSetupReport);
    UIW_STRING *theString =
    (UIW_STRING *) dataEntryWindow->Get("DEST_FILE");
    if (theReportSetup.filename.Len())
        theString->DataSet(theReportSetup.filename.ptr());

    UIW_GROUP *theGroup = (UIW_GROUP *) dataEntryWindow->Get("RPT_DST_GRP");
    UIW_BUTTON *theButton0 = (UIW_BUTTON *) theGroup->Get("PRN_SEL");
    UIW_BUTTON *theButton1 = (UIW_BUTTON *) theGroup->Get("FILE_SEL");
    UIW_BUTTON *theButton2 = (UIW_BUTTON *) theGroup->Get("WIN_DEST");
    switch(theReportSetup.reportDest)
    {
        case 0:
            theButton0->woStatus |= WOS_SELECTED;
            theButton1->woStatus &= ~WOS_SELECTED;
            theButton2->woStatus &= ~WOS_SELECTED;
        break;
        case 1:
            theButton0->woStatus &= ~WOS_SELECTED;
            theButton1->woStatus |= WOS_SELECTED;
            theButton2->woStatus &= ~WOS_SELECTED;
        break;
        case 2:
            theButton0->woStatus &= ~WOS_SELECTED;
            theButton1->woStatus &= ~WOS_SELECTED;
            theButton2->woStatus |= WOS_SELECTED;
        break;
        default:
            theButton0->woStatus &= ~WOS_SELECTED;
            theButton1->woStatus &= ~WOS_SELECTED;
            theButton2->woStatus &= ~WOS_SELECTED;
        break;
    }
    theGroup = (UIW_GROUP *) dataEntryWindow->Get("RPT_FMT_GRP");
    theButton0 = (UIW_BUTTON *) theGroup->Get("CLASS_ONLY_BTN");
    theButton1 = (UIW_BUTTON *) theGroup->Get("FCTN_ONLY_BTN");
    theButton2 = (UIW_BUTTON *) theGroup->Get("FULL_RPT_BTN");
    switch(theReportSetup.reportFmt)
    {
        case 0:
            theButton0->woStatus |= WOS_SELECTED;
            theButton1->woStatus &= ~WOS_SELECTED;
            theButton2->woStatus &= ~WOS_SELECTED;
```

```
                break;
            case 1:
                theButton0->woStatus &= ~WOS_SELECTED;
                theButton1->woStatus |= WOS_SELECTED;
                theButton2->woStatus &= ~WOS_SELECTED;
            break;
            case 2:
                theButton0->woStatus &= ~WOS_SELECTED;
                theButton1->woStatus &= ~WOS_SELECTED;
                theButton2->woStatus |= WOS_SELECTED;
            break;
            default:
                theButton0->woStatus &= ~WOS_SELECTED;
                theButton1->woStatus &= ~WOS_SELECTED;
                theButton2->woStatus &= ~WOS_SELECTED;
            break;
        }


        *windowManager + dataEntryWindow;

    }

void ClassDefnWindow::completeSetupReport()
{
    UIW_STRING *theString =
    (UIW_STRING *) dataEntryWindow->Get("DEST_FILE");
    if (strlen(theString->DataGet()))
        theReportSetup.filename = theString->DataGet();

    UIW_GROUP *theGroup = (UIW_GROUP *) dataEntryWindow->Get("RPT_DST_GRP");
    UIW_BUTTON *theButton0 = (UIW_BUTTON *) theGroup->Get("PRN_SEL");
    UIW_BUTTON *theButton1 = (UIW_BUTTON *) theGroup->Get("FILE_SEL");
    UIW_BUTTON *theButton2 = (UIW_BUTTON *) theGroup->Get("WIN_DEST");

    if (theButton0->woStatus & WOS_SELECTED)
        theReportSetup.reportDest = 0;
    else if (theButton1->woStatus & WOS_SELECTED)
        theReportSetup.reportDest = 1;
    else if (theButton2->woStatus & WOS_SELECTED)
        theReportSetup.reportDest = 2;
    else
        theReportSetup.reportDest = 4;

    theGroup = (UIW_GROUP *) dataEntryWindow->Get("RPT_FMT_GRP");
    theButton0 = (UIW_BUTTON *) theGroup->Get("CLASS_ONLY_BTN");
    theButton1 = (UIW_BUTTON *) theGroup->Get("FCTN_ONLY_BTN");
    theButton2 = (UIW_BUTTON *) theGroup->Get("FULL_RPT_BTN");


    if (theButton0->woStatus & WOS_SELECTED)
        theReportSetup.reportFmt = 0;
    else if (theButton1->woStatus & WOS_SELECTED)
        theReportSetup.reportFmt = 1;
```

```
        else if (theButton2->woStatus & WOS_SELECTED)
            theReportSetup.reportFmt = 2;
        else
            theReportSetup.reportFmt = 4;


}

//////////////////////////////////////////////////////////////////////
// Author: David Brumbaugh
// Method Name: various
// Creation Date: 12/92
// Purpose: Handle button messages
//
// Return Value: None
// Parameters: None
//
//////////////////////////////////////////////////////////////////////

// Button OK

void ClassDefnWindow::handleOK()
{
    windowToEntry();
    eventManager->DeviceState(E_MOUSE,DM_WAIT);
    Catalog *theCatalog = mainWindow->getCatalog();
    theCatalog->setEntry(*aClassEntry);
    mainWindow->refreshCatList();
    eventManager->DeviceState(E_MOUSE, DM_VIEW);
    eventManager->Put(S_CLOSE);
}

// Button Cancel
void ClassDefnWindow::handleCancel()
{
    if (! dataChanged())
    {
        eventManager->Put(S_CLOSE);
    }
    else
    {
        DIALOG_WINDOW dialog("Data Has Changed", "EXCLAMATION",
        DIF_YES|DIF_NO,
                "Do you want to cancel without saving ?");
        if (dialog.Response() == DIALOG_NO)
            return;
        else
            eventManager->Put(S_CLOSE);
    }
}

// Return true if the data in the window has changed.

Boolean ClassDefnWindow::dataChanged()
```

```
{
    if (stuffChanged)
        return ::true;
    for (UI_WINDOW_OBJECT *object = First(); object; object = object->Next())
    {
        if (FlagSet(object->woStatus,WOS_CHANGED))
            return ::true;
    }
    return false;
}


// Transfer data from the class entry to the window.

void ClassDefnWindow::entryToWindow()
{
    UIW_STRING *theString = (UIW_STRING *) Get("CLASS_NM");
    theString->DataSet((char *) aClassEntry->getName());

    UIW_COMBO_BOX *aCBox = (UIW_COMBO_BOX *) Get("CLASS_TYPE");
    aCBox->Event(L_TOP);
    string eType = aClassEntry->getClassSpec();
    eType.Trim();
    if (eType == "struct")
    {
        aCBox->Event(L_DOWN);
    }
    else if (eType == "union")
        aCBox->Event(L_LAST);


    UIW_TEXT *theText = (UIW_TEXT *) Get("BASE_CLASS_LIST");
    BaseClassList &baseClasses = aClassEntry->getBaseClasses();
    string parents;
    if (baseClasses.total())
    {

        for (int i = 0; i < baseClasses.total(); ++i)
        {
            parents += baseClasses[i].baseSpecifier + ' ';
            parents += baseClasses[i].name;
            if (i != (baseClasses.total() - 1))
                parents += ", ";
        }
    }
    if (parents.Len())
        theText->DataSet(parents.ptr());

    UIW_INTEGER *theInt = (UIW_INTEGER *) Get("VRSN_FLD");
    int i = aClassEntry->getVersion();
    theInt->DataSet(&i);

    theString = (UIW_STRING *) Get("HDR_FILE_SPC");
    theString->DataSet((char *)aClassEntry->getInclude());
```

```
    theString = (UIW_STRING *) Get("SRC_SPC_STR");
    theString->DataSet((char *)aClassEntry->getLocation());

    theText = (UIW_TEXT *) Get("CLASS_DESC");
    string descrip;
    aClassEntry->getDescription(descrip);
    theText->DataSet(descrip.ptr());

}


// Put up a dialog box to edit the class member data

void ClassDefnWindow::editMemData()
{
    windowToEntry();
    dataEntryWindow = new DataEntryDialog("SSOOTLIB~DATA_MEMBER_WINDOW",
    (UIW_WINDOW *) this,
    (void(UIW_WINDOW::*)()) &ClassDefnWindow::completeEditData);

    UIW_VT_LIST *theList = (UIW_VT_LIST *) Get("MEM_DATA_LIST");
    int d = theList->Index(theList->Current());
    int i = dataIndexes[d];
    MemberList &memList = aClassEntry->getMembers();
    DataMemberDefinition *dataMem = (DataMemberDefinition *) memList[i];

    UIW_STRING *theString =
    (UIW_STRING *) dataEntryWindow->Get("OWNING_CLASS");
    theString->DataSet((char *)dataMem->getOwner());
    UIW_COMBO_BOX *aCBox =
    (UIW_COMBO_BOX *) dataEntryWindow->Get("ACCESS_SPEC");
    string anAccessSpec = dataMem->getAccessSpec();
    anAccessSpec.Trim();
    aCBox->Event(L_TOP);
    if (anAccessSpec == "private")
        aCBox->Event(L_DOWN);
    else if (anAccessSpec  == "public")
        aCBox->Event(L_LAST);

    theString = (UIW_STRING *) dataEntryWindow->Get("DATA_TYPE");
    string fullTypeSpec = dataMem->getTypeSpec() +
                        string(dataMem->getPtrSpec());
    theString->DataSet(fullTypeSpec.ptr());
    theString = (UIW_STRING *) dataEntryWindow->Get("MEM_NAME");
    theString->DataSet((char *) dataMem->getName());
    UIW_TEXT *theText = (UIW_TEXT *) dataEntryWindow->Get("PURPOSE");
    theText->DataSet((char *) dataMem->getDescription());

    *windowManager + dataEntryWindow;


}


void ClassDefnWindow::completeEditData()
```

```
{
    UIW_VT_LIST *theList = (UIW_VT_LIST *) Get("MEM_DATA_LIST");
    int d = theList->Index(theList->Current());
    int i = dataIndexes[d];
    MemberList &memList = aClassEntry->getMembers();
    DataMemberDefinition *dataMem = (DataMemberDefinition *) memList[i];

    UIW_COMBO_BOX *aCBox =
    (UIW_COMBO_BOX *)dataEntryWindow->Get("ACCESS_SPEC");
    UIW_STRING *theString = (UIW_STRING *) aCBox->Current();
    dataMem->setAccessSpec(theString->DataGet());
    theString = (UIW_STRING *) dataEntryWindow->Get("DATA_TYPE");
    dataMem->setTypeSpec(theString->DataGet());
    theString = (UIW_STRING *) dataEntryWindow->Get("MEM_NAME");
    dataMem->setName(theString->DataGet());
    UIW_TEXT *theText = (UIW_TEXT *) dataEntryWindow->Get("PURPOSE");
    dataMem->setDescription(theText->DataGet());

    changedDataList = ::true;
    stuffChanged = ::true;
#ifdef _Windows
    Event(S_REDISPLAY);
#endif


}

// Add a data member to the class definition

void ClassDefnWindow::addMemData()
{
    windowToEntry();
    dataEntryWindow = new DataEntryDialog("SSOOTLIB~DATA_MEMBER_WINDOW",
    (UIW_WINDOW *) this,
    (void(UIW_WINDOW::*)()) &ClassDefnWindow::completeAddData);
    UIW_STRING *theString =
    (UIW_STRING *) dataEntryWindow->Get("OWNING_CLASS");
    theString->DataSet((char *)aClassEntry->getName());


    *windowManager + dataEntryWindow;

}

void ClassDefnWindow::completeAddData()
{
    MemberList &memList = aClassEntry->getMembers();
    DataMemberDefinition *dataMem =
    new DataMemberDefinition(aClassEntry->getName());

    UIW_COMBO_BOX *aCBox =
    (UIW_COMBO_BOX *)dataEntryWindow->Get("ACCESS_SPEC");
    UIW_STRING *theString = (UIW_STRING *) aCBox->Current();
```

```
    dataMem->setAccessSpec(theString->DataGet());
    theString = (UIW_STRING *) dataEntryWindow->Get("DATA_TYPE");
    dataMem->setTypeSpec(theString->DataGet());
    theString = (UIW_STRING *) dataEntryWindow->Get("MEM_NAME");
    dataMem->setName(theString->DataGet());
    UIW_TEXT *theText = (UIW_TEXT *) dataEntryWindow->Get("PURPOSE");
    dataMem->setDescription(theText->DataGet());

    memList.add((ClassMemberDefinition *) dataMem);

    changedDataList = ::true;
    stuffChanged = ::true;
#ifdef _Windows
    Event(S_REDISPLAY);
#endif

}

// Delete member data from the class definition

void ClassDefnWindow::delMemData()
{
    UIW_VT_LIST *theList = (UIW_VT_LIST *) Get("MEM_DATA_LIST");
    int d = theList->Index(theList->Current());
    int i = dataIndexes[d];
    MemberList &memList = aClassEntry->getMembers();
    DataMemberDefinition *dataMem = (DataMemberDefinition *) memList[i];
    if (i < memList.total() && i >= 0)
    {
        string dataSpec = (string(dataMem->getTypeSpec() +
        string(dataMem->getPtrSpec()) + ' ')+
        string(dataMem->getName())));
        DIALOG_WINDOW dialog("Confirm", "QUESTION",
        DIF_YES|DIF_NO,
                "Delete DataMember:\r\n\r\n%s ?", dataSpec.ptr());
        if (dialog.Response() == DIALOG_NO)
            return;

        memList.seek(i);
        memList.remove();
    }
    changedDataList = ::true;
    updateDataList();

}

// Edit a member function definition

void ClassDefnWindow::editMemFctn()
{
    windowToEntry();
    UIW_VT_LIST *theList = (UIW_VT_LIST *) Get("MEM_FCTN_LIST");
    int f = theList->Index(theList->Current());
    int i = fctnIndexes[f];
```

```
    MemberList &memList = aClassEntry->getMembers();
    MemberFunctionDefinition *fctnMem =
    (MemberFunctionDefinition *) memList[i];
    originalParameters = fctnMem->getParams().toString(::true,::true);
    originalParamDescrip = fctnMem->getParams().getDescField();
    MemFunctionDefnWindow *memFctnWindow = new
  MemFunctionDefnWindow((char *)aClassEntry->getName(), this, fctnMem, false);
    *windowManager + memFctnWindow;

}

void ClassDefnWindow::completeEditFctn()
{
    changedFctnList = ::true;
    stuffChanged = ::true;
    updateFctnList();
    originalParameters = "";
    originalParamDescrip = "";

}
// Cancel the function edit

void ClassDefnWindow::cancelEditFctn()
{
    UIW_VT_LIST *theList = (UIW_VT_LIST *) Get("MEM_FCTN_LIST");
    int f = theList->Index(theList->Current());
    int i = fctnIndexes[f];
    MemberList &memList = aClassEntry->getMembers();
    MemberFunctionDefinition *fctnMem =
    (MemberFunctionDefinition *) memList[i];

    ParamList &pl = fctnMem->getParams();
    int t = pl.total();
    for (i = 0; i < t; ++i)
    {
        pl.seek(i); pl.remove();
    }
    pl.fromString(originalParameters.ptr());
    pl.fillDescriptions(originalParamDescrip.ptr());

}


// Cancel the add function

void ClassDefnWindow::cancelAddFctn()
{
    delete fctnMem;
}


// Add a member function to the class definition

void ClassDefnWindow::addMemFctn()
{
```

```
    windowToEntry();
    fctnMem = new MemberFunctionDefinition(aClassEntry->getName());
    MemFunctionDefnWindow *memFctnWindow = new
    MemFunctionDefnWindow((char *)aClassEntry->getName(), this,
    fctnMem, ::true);

    *windowManager + memFctnWindow;


}


void ClassDefnWindow::completeAddFctn()
{
    MemberList &memList = aClassEntry->getMembers();
    memList.add((ClassMemberDefinition *) fctnMem);
    changedFctnList = ::true;
    stuffChanged = ::true;
#ifdef _Windows
    Event(S_REDISPLAY);
#endif


}

// Delete the member function

void ClassDefnWindow::delMemFctn()
{
    windowToEntry();
    UIW_VT_LIST *theList = (UIW_VT_LIST *) Get("MEM_FCTN_LIST");
    int f = theList->Index(theList->Current());
    int i = fctnIndexes[f];
    MemberList &memList = aClassEntry->getMembers();
    MemberFunctionDefinition *fctnMem =
    (MemberFunctionDefinition *) memList[i];
    ParamList &pl = fctnMem->getParams();
    if (i < memList.total() && i >= 0)
    {
        string dataSpec =      string(fctnMem->getName());
        dataSpec += pl.toString();
        DIALOG_WINDOW dialog("Confirm", "QUESTION",
        DIF_YES|DIF_NO,
                "Delete Member Function:\r\n\r\n%s ?", dataSpec.ptr());
        if (dialog.Response() == DIALOG_NO)
            return;

        memList.seek(i);
        memList.remove();
    }
    changedFctnList = ::true;
    updateFctnList();


}
```

```
// Allows the user to select whether or not to use comments in the
// Output of the header or source file

void ClassDefnWindow::useComments()
{

    UIW_PULL_DOWN_MENU *mnu = (UIW_PULL_DOWN_MENU *) Get("CLS_DEFN_MENU");
    UIW_PULL_DOWN_ITEM *item = (UIW_PULL_DOWN_ITEM *) mnu->Get("CLS_OPT_ITM");
    UIW_POP_UP_ITEM *popup = (UIW_POP_UP_ITEM *) item->Get("USE_CMNTS");

    if ( (popup->woStatus & WOS_SELECTED) )
    {
        aClassEntry->setOption(UseComments,::true);
    }
    else
    {
        aClassEntry->setOption(UseComments,false);
    }
}


// Allows the user to select whether or not to expand inline functions
// in the source templates.

void ClassDefnWindow::expandInline()
{

    UIW_PULL_DOWN_MENU *mnu = (UIW_PULL_DOWN_MENU *) Get("CLS_DEFN_MENU");
    UIW_PULL_DOWN_ITEM *item = (UIW_PULL_DOWN_ITEM *) mnu->Get("CLS_OPT_ITM");
    UIW_POP_UP_ITEM *popup = (UIW_POP_UP_ITEM *) item->Get("EXP_INLINE");

    if (  (popup->woStatus & WOS_SELECTED) )
    {
        aClassEntry->setOption(ExpandInline,::true);
    }
    else
    {
        aClassEntry->setOption(ExpandInline,false);
    }


}


////////////////////////////////////////////////////////////////////
// Listing  : 10-24
// Filename   : DEDiag.H
// Purpose    : Class defintion of DataEntry dialog
////////////////////////////////////////////////////////////////////

////////////////////////////////////////////////////////////////////
// Author       : David Brumbaugh
// Class Name   : DataEntryDialog
```

```
// Creation Date: 12/92
// Catagories    : UI
// Purpose        : A general purpose dialog box that reads an object
//                  from a Zinc Designer data file. Assumes the following:
//                  1. Object is a Window
//                  2. Object has and OK button with a value of 3001
//                  3. Object has a CANCEL button with a value of 3000
//                  4. Both these buttons have the notify flag set to true.
//                  5. Object is MODAL (May not be strictly necessary)
//
// Major Public Methods:
//    DataEntryDialog - Constructor
//    lastButton - Tells the value of the last button pushed.
//
// Major Data Items:
//    buttonPushed - Last button pushed in data entry dialog
//    callBackFunction - Function to call when "OK" button is bushed.
//////////////////////////////////////////////////////////////////////
#ifndef DEDIAG_H
#define DEDIAG_H
#include <ui_win.hpp>

const EVENT_TYPE DEDG_OK = 3001,
                 DEDG_CANCEL = 3000;


class DataEntryDialog: public UIW_WINDOW
{
    protected:
        static EVENT_TYPE buttonPushed;
        void (UIW_WINDOW::*callBack)(); // A pointer to a void function
                                        // member of a UIW_WINDOW with
                                        // no parameters.
        UIW_WINDOW *callingObject;      // Object that originally invokes
                                        // this object.
    public:
        virtual EVENT_TYPE Event(const UI_EVENT &event);
        DataEntryDialog(char *object,
        UIW_WINDOW *win, void (UIW_WINDOW::*_callBack)() ) :
        UIW_WINDOW(object) {callingObject = win; callBack = _callBack; };
        // Assign the calling object and the call back function.

        static EVENT_TYPE lastButton() { return buttonPushed; }
};


#endif


//////////////////////////////////////////////////////////////////////
// Listing  : 10-25
// Filename   : DEDIAG.CPP
// Purpose    : DataEntryDialog source code
//////////////////////////////////////////////////////////////////////
```

```
////////////////////////////////////////////////////////////////////
// Author: David Brumbaugh
// Method Name: Event
// Creation Date: 12/92
// Purpose: Handles OK and CANCEL events
//
// Return Value: UI_EVENT processed or to be processed
// Parameters:
//   Type              Name         Purpose/Description      Default Value
//   const UI_EVENT &  event        Event to be processed    None
////////////////////////////////////////////////////////////////////
#include "dediag.h"

EVENT_TYPE DataEntryDialog::buttonPushed = 0;

EVENT_TYPE DataEntryDialog::Event(const UI_EVENT &event)
{
    switch(event.type)
    {
        case DEDG_OK:
            (callingObject->*callBack)();
        case DEDG_CANCEL:
            buttonPushed = event.type;
            eventManager->Put(S_CLOSE, Q_BEGIN);
        break;
        default:
            return UIW_WINDOW::Event(event);
    }
    return event.type;
}


////////////////////////////////////////////////////////////////////
// Listing  : 10-26
// Filename : TxtRpt.h
// Purpose  : Class definition for TextReport
////////////////////////////////////////////////////////////////////

////////////////////////////////////////////////////////////////////
// Author        : David Brumbaugh
// Class Name     : TextReport
// Creation Date: 3/93
// Catagories    : Interface
// Purpose        : Builds a text report
//
////////////////////////////////////////////////////////////////////


#ifndef TXTRPT_H
#define TXTRPT_H
#include "STR.H"

#ifndef D_LIST_H
```

```cpp
enum Boolean { false, true };
#endif

#define MAXCOLS 30


class TextReport
{
protected:
    ostream * out;
    int leftMargin,width,topMargin,bottomMargin,height;
    string header,footer;
    int headerJust, footerJust;
    int currentLine,currentPage, numColumns;
    int tabSize;
public:
    TextReport(ostream * out,char * _header = NULL,char * _footer = NULL,
    int _leftMargin = 5,int _topMargin = 5,int _bottomMargin = 0,
    int _height = 60,int _width = 70);
    ~TextReport();
    void put(char * outString,Boolean newLine = true,int _leftMargin = 0,
    int _rightMargin = 0);
    void setMargins(int left,int top,int bottom);
    void incLine();
    void newPage();
    void doHeader();
    void doFooter();
    void setTabSize(int _tabSize) { tabSize = _tabSize; }
protected:
    int colWidths[MAXCOLS];
    int colJust[MAXCOLS];
public:
    void defineColumns(int firstWidth,int firstJust, ...);
    void put(char * col1,char * col2, ...);
    void setFooter(char * footerString = NULL, int just = CENTER);
    void setHeader(char * aHeader = NULL, int just = CENTER);
    void setHW(int _height = 60,int _width = 70);

};

extern Boolean wrapString(string &origString, string &leftOver,
int width);

#endif


//////////////////////////////////////////////////////////////////////
// Listing  : 10-27
// Filename : TxtRpt.cpp
// Purpose  : Text Report Class  function code
//////////////////////////////////////////////////////////////////////


#include "listimp.h"
```

```
#include "txtrpt.h"
#include "utility.h"
#include "datecls4.h"
#include <stdarg.h>


typedef ListImp<string> stringList;

extern void TheBadErrorFunction(char *msg);

////////////////////////////////////////////////////////////////////
// Author: David Brumbaugh
// Method Name: TextReport
// Purpose: Constructor
//
////////////////////////////////////////////////////////////////////

TextReport::TextReport(ostream *_out,char * _header,
char * _footer,int _leftMargin,int _topMargin,int _bottomMargin,
int _height,int _width):out(_out),header(_header),footer(_footer),
leftMargin(_leftMargin),topMargin(_topMargin),bottomMargin(_bottomMargin),
height(_height),width(_width)
{
  tabSize = 4;
  currentLine = 0; currentPage = 1;
  memset(colWidths,0,sizeof(colWidths));
  memset(colJust,0,sizeof(colJust));
  headerJust = CENTER;
  footerJust = CENTER;
}
////////////////////////////////////////////////////////////////////
// Author: David Brumbaugh
// Method Name: ~TextReport
// Purpose: Destructor
////////////////////////////////////////////////////////////////////

TextReport::~TextReport()
{
    if (currentLine > 0)
        doFooter();
}


////////////////////////////////////////////////////////////////////
// Author: David Brumbaugh
// Method Name: put
// Purpose: Puts a string to the report stream.
//
// Return Value: None
// Parameters:
//   Type       Name           Purpose/Description             Default Value
//   char *     outString      String to put to out stream
//   Boolean    newLine        If true start new line after    true
//                             string.
//   int        _leftMargin    # chars to indent past normal   0
```

```
//                              margin
//  int          -rightMargin   # chars right of width to        0
//                              wrap line
///////////////////////////////////////////////////////////////

void TextReport::put(char * outString,Boolean newLine,
int _leftMargin,int _rightMargin)
{
    int maxLength = width - (_leftMargin + _rightMargin);
    // That's how long it can really be
    string pad(' ',leftMargin+_leftMargin);
    string orig = outString;
    Boolean done = false;
    string work,leftOver;
    orig.Sub("\r"," ");
    work = orig;
    char *notabs; // Fix up the tabs
    notabs = new char[work.Len() * tabSize]; // Worse case
    detab(notabs,work.ptr(),tabSize,(work.Len() * tabSize));
    work = notabs;
    delete notabs;

    int i;
    while (! done)
    {
        if (currentLine == 0)
            doHeader();
        // Move the line into work. It will go from work to out

        if ( wrapString(work,leftOver,maxLength) )
        {
            done = false;
            int nn;
            if ((nn = work.Index('\n')) > -1)
            {
                string errorMessage("New line in work at index");
                errorMessage += string((long) nn);
                TheBadErrorFunction(errorMessage.ptr());
            }
            *out << pad << work << '\n';
            work = leftOver;
            leftOver.Delete(0);
            incLine();
        }
        else
            done = true;

        if (done)
        {
            int nn;
            if ((nn = work.Index('\n')) > -1)
            {
                string errorMessage("New line in work at index ");
                errorMessage += string((long) nn);
```

```
                        TheBadErrorFunction(errorMessage.ptr());
                    }

                    *out << pad << work;
                    if (newLine)
                    {
                        *out << '\n'; incLine();
                    }
            }

        }
}

///////////////////////////////////////////////////////////////////////
// Author: David Brumbaugh
// Method Name: setMagins
// Purpose: Assigns new values to margins
//
///////////////////////////////////////////////////////////////////////

void TextReport::setMargins(int left,int top,int bottom)
{
    leftMargin = left; topMargin = top;
    bottomMargin = bottom;
}


///////////////////////////////////////////////////////////////////////
// Author: David Brumbaugh
// Method Name: incLine
// Purpose: Increments line count. Generates new page if necessary.
//
///////////////////////////////////////////////////////////////////////

void TextReport::incLine()
{
    if (currentLine == 0)
        doHeader();
    if (currentLine >= (height - bottomMargin - 1))
    {
        newPage();
    }
    else
        ++currentLine;
}
///////////////////////////////////////////////////////////////////////
// Author: David Brumbaugh
// Method Name:
// Creation Date:
// Purpose:
//
// Return Value:
// Parameters:
//    Type  Name            Purpose/Description      Default Value
//
```

```
//////////////////////////////////////////////////////////////////

void TextReport::newPage()
{
    for (int i = currentLine; i < height; ++i)
    {
        *out << '\n';
        if (i == (height - 1))
            doFooter();
    }
    ++currentPage;
    currentLine = 0;
}
//////////////////////////////////////////////////////////////////
// Author: David Brumbaugh
// Method Name: doHeader
// Purpose: Creates report header
//////////////////////////////////////////////////////////////////

void TextReport::doHeader()
{
    if (header.Len())
    {
        string hcopy = header;
        hcopy.Sub("%P%",string((long) currentPage));
        Date d("Today");
        hcopy.Sub("%D%",d.formatDate(FULL));
        hcopy.Justify(headerJust,width);
        string pad(' ',leftMargin);
        *out << pad << hcopy << '\n';
        ++currentLine;
    }
    for ( ; currentLine < topMargin; ++currentLine)
            *out << '\n';

}
//////////////////////////////////////////////////////////////////
// Author: David Brumbaugh
// Method Name: doFooter
// Purpose: Generates report footer
//////////////////////////////////////////////////////////////////

void TextReport::doFooter()
{
    if (footer.Len())
    {
        string fcopy = footer;
        fcopy.Justify(footerJust, width);
        fcopy.Sub("%P%",string((long) currentPage));
        Date d("Today");
        fcopy.Sub("%D%",d.formatDate(FULL));
        string pad(' ',leftMargin);
        *out << pad << fcopy;
    }
```

```
    *out << "\f\n";

}
////////////////////////////////////////////////////////////////////
// Author: David Brumbaugh
// Method Name: defineColumns
// Creation Date: Defines column widths and justification
////////////////////////////////////////////////////////////////////

void TextReport::defineColumns(int firstWidth, int firstJust, ...)
{
    numColumns = 0;
    memset(colWidths,0,sizeof(colWidths));
    memset(colJust,0,sizeof(colJust));
    va_list ap;
    int arg;
    va_start(ap, firstJust);
    colWidths[0] = firstWidth;
    colJust[0] = firstJust;
    ++numColumns;
    while ((arg = va_arg(ap,int)) != -1)
    {
        colWidths[numColumns] = arg;
        arg = va_arg(ap,int);
        colJust[numColumns++] = arg;
    }
    va_end(ap);

}
////////////////////////////////////////////////////////////////////
// Author: David Brumbaugh
// Method Name: put
// Purpose: Writes columns to report
//
////////////////////////////////////////////////////////////////////

typedef  char *  charPtr;

void TextReport::put(char * col1,char * col2, ...)
{
    va_list ap;
    va_start(ap, col2);

    string pad(' ',leftMargin);
    stringList columns;

    columns.add(string(col1));
    columns.add(string(col2));
    char *notabs;
    for (int i = 0; i < 2; ++i)
    {
        columns[i].Sub("\r"," ");
        notabs = new char[columns[i].Len() * tabSize]; // Worse case
        detab(notabs,columns[i].ptr(),tabSize,(columns[i].Len() * tabSize));
```

```
        columns[i] = notabs;
        delete notabs;
    }
    i = 2;
    int x;
    char *arg;

    while ((arg = va_arg(ap,charPtr)) != NULL  && i < numColumns )
    {
        columns.add(string(arg));
        columns[i].Sub("\r"," ");
        notabs = new char[columns[i].Len() * tabSize]; // Worse case
        detab(notabs,columns[i].ptr(),tabSize,(columns[i].Len() * tabSize));
        columns[i] = notabs;
        delete notabs;
        ++i;

    }
    va_end(ap);
    Boolean done = false;
    string line;
    int totLen, n;

    while (! done)
    {
        if (currentLine == 0)
            doHeader();
        for (i = 0; i < numColumns; ++i)
        {
            if (columns[i].Len() > colWidths[i])
            {
                string left;
                wrapString(columns[i],left,colWidths[i]);
                columns[i].Justify(colJust[i],colWidths[i]);
                line += columns[i];
                columns[i] = left;

            }
            else if((n = columns[i].Index("\n")) > -1)
            {
                string col = columns[i].SubStr(0,n);
                col.Justify(colJust[i],colWidths[i]);
                line += col;
                columns[i].Delete(0,n+1);
            }
            else
            {
                columns[i].Justify(colJust[i],colWidths[i]);
                line += columns[i];
                columns[i].Delete(0);
            }
        }

        *out << pad << line << '\n';
```

```
        incLine();
        line.Delete(0);
        totLen = 0;

        for (i = 0; i < numColumns; ++i)
            totLen+= columns[i].Len();
        if (totLen == 0)
            done = true;


    }

}

///////////////////////////////////////////////////////////////////////
// Author: David Brumbaugh
// Method Name: setFooter
// Purpose: Assigns string to footer
///////////////////////////////////////////////////////////////////////

void TextReport::setFooter(char * footerString, int just)
{
    footer = footerString;
    footerJust = just;
}


///////////////////////////////////////////////////////////////////////
// Author: David Brumbaugh
// Method Name: setHeader
// Purpose: Assigns a string to the header
///////////////////////////////////////////////////////////////////////

void TextReport::setHeader(char * aHeader, int just)
{
    header = aHeader;
    headerJust = just;
}


///////////////////////////////////////////////////////////////////////
// Author: David Brumbaugh
// Method Name: setHW
// Purpose: Sets the new height and width of the report
///////////////////////////////////////////////////////////////////////

void TextReport::setHW(int _height,int _width)
{
    height = _height;
    width = _width;
}


///////////////////////////////////////////////////////////////////////
// Author: David Brumbaugh
// Function Name: wrapString
// Purpose: Breaks a string at a particular width. Returns the left over
//          string.  Will break on white space if possible.
```

```
//
///////////////////////////////////////////////////////////////////////

Boolean wrapString(string &origString, string &leftOver, int width)
{
    int n;
    n = origString.Index("\n");
    if ((n > -1) && (n < width))
    {
        leftOver = origString.SubStr(n+1);
        origString.Delete(n);
        return true;
    }

    if (origString.Len() <= width)
        return false;

    for (int i = width - 1; i > 0; —i)
    {
        if (origString[i] == ' ')
        {
            leftOver = origString.SubStr(i+1);
            origString.Delete(i);
            return true;
        }
    }
    if ( i == 0)
    {
        leftOver = origString.SubStr(width-1);
        origString.Delete(width);
        return true;
    }
    return false;
}


///////////////////////////////////////////////////////////////////////
// Listing  : 10-28
// Filename : memfnwin.hpp
// Purpose  : Source code for function Definition Window
///////////////////////////////////////////////////////////////////////


///////////////////////////////////////////////////////////////////////
// Author       : David Brumbaugh
// Class Name   : MemFunctionDefnWindow
// Creation Date: 1/93
// Catagories   : User Interface
// Purpose      : Allows entry of class member function data
//
///////////////////////////////////////////////////////////////////////

#ifndef MEMFNWIN_HPP
```

```cpp
#define MEMFNWIN_HPP
#include <ui_win.hpp>
#include "clsdfn.h"
#define USE_MEM_FUNC_DEF
#include "ssootlib.hpp"
#undef USE_MEM_FUNC_DEF


class ClassDefnWindow;

class MemFunctionDefnWindow:  public UIW_WINDOW
{
    protected:
        // Working Variables
        MemberFunctionDefinition *aFunctionEntry;
        Boolean needToDelete;

        // Other Windows
        ClassDefnWindow  *mainWindow;
        DataEntryDialog *dataEntryWindow;
        // Changed State
        Boolean changedParamList;
        Boolean addingFunction;
        // Data Transfer
        virtual void entryToWindow();
        virtual void windowToEntry();
        // Buttons
        virtual void handleCancel()
        {if (addingFunction)
            mainWindow->cancelAddFctn();
        else
            mainWindow->cancelEditFctn();
        eventManager->Put(S_CLOSE);
        }
        virtual void handleOK();
        virtual void editParameter();
        virtual void addParameter();
        virtual void delParameter();
        virtual void specifyFunction();
        // Support
        virtual void completeSpecify();
        virtual void completeParamEdit();
        virtual void completeParamAdd();
        virtual void updateParamList();

    public:
        virtual EVENT_TYPE Event(const UI_EVENT &event);
        MemFunctionDefnWindow (char *className, ClassDefnWindow *mw,
        MemberFunctionDefinition *fe, Boolean doingAdd) :
        UIW_WINDOW("SSOOTLIB~MEM_FUNC_DEF"),mainWindow(mw)
            {
                addingFunction = doingAdd;
                changedParamList = ::true;
                aFunctionEntry = fe;
```

```
            UIW_STRING *theString =(UIW_STRING *) Get("OWNING_CLASS");
            theString->DataSet(className);

        }
};

#endif


//////////////////////////////////////////////////////////////////////
// Listing  : 10-29
// Filename : memfnwin.CPP
// Purpose  : Source code for member function Definition Window
//////////////////////////////////////////////////////////////////////

#include "CLSDFWIN.HPP"
#include "DEDIAG.H"
#include "dialog.hpp"
#include "MEMFNWIN.HPP"
#include "LibMWin.HPP"
#include <fstream.h>


//////////////////////////////////////////////////////////////////////
// Author: David Brumbaugh
// Method Name: Event
// Creation Date: 11/92
// Purpose: Handles Event processing for the MemFunctionDefnWindow
//
// Return Value: Event type to process
// Parameters: Event to be processed
//
//////////////////////////////////////////////////////////////////////

EVENT_TYPE MemFunctionDefnWindow::Event(const UI_EVENT &event)
{
    switch(event.type)
    {
        case OKBtn:
            handleOK();
        break;
        case CancelBtn:
            handleCancel();
        break;
        case AddParamBtn:
            addParameter();
        break;
        case EditParamBtn:
            editParameter();
        break;
        case DelParamBtn:
            delParameter();
        break;
        case SpecFctnBtn:
            specifyFunction();
```

```
            break;
        case S_INITIALIZE:
            if (aFunctionEntry)
                entryToWindow();
        case S_CURRENT:
        case S_REDISPLAY:
            if (changedParamList)
            {
                updateParamList();
            }
        default:
            return UIW_WINDOW::Event(event);
    }
    return event.type;
}

//////////////////////////////////////////////////////////////////////
// Author: David Brumbaugh
// Method Name: windowToEntry
// Creation Date: 11/92
// Purpose: Transfer data from the window to the aFunctionEntry data
//          member.
//
// Return Value: None
// Parameters: None
//
//////////////////////////////////////////////////////////////////////

void MemFunctionDefnWindow::windowToEntry()
{
    UIW_STRING *theString = (UIW_STRING *) Get("MEM_FCTN_NAME");
    aFunctionEntry->setName(theString->DataGet());

    theString = (UIW_STRING *) Get("MEM_FCTN_RTN_TYP");
    aFunctionEntry->setTypeSpec(theString->DataGet());

    theString = (UIW_STRING *) Get("MEM_FCTN_RTN_VAL");
    aFunctionEntry->setReturnValue(theString->DataGet());

    theString = (UIW_STRING *) Get("MEM_FCTN_SRC_STR");
    aFunctionEntry->setSourceFile(theString->DataGet());

    UIW_TEXT *theText = (UIW_TEXT *) Get("MEM_FCTN_DESC");
    aFunctionEntry->setDescription(theText->DataGet());

    UIW_COMBO_BOX *aCBox =
    (UIW_COMBO_BOX *) Get("MEM_FCTN_ACCESS_SPEC");
    theString = (UIW_STRING *) aCBox->Current();
    aFunctionEntry->setAccessSpec(theString->DataGet());

    theString = (UIW_STRING *) Get("MEM_FN_SUFFIX");
    string suffix = theString->DataGet();
    if ( suffix.Index('{') == -1)
        suffix += ';';
```

```
        aFunctionEntry->setSuffix(suffix.ptr());


}
//////////////////////////////////////////////////////////////////////
// Author: David Brumbaugh
// Method Name: updateParamList
// Creation Date: 12/92
// Purpose: Updates the parameter list on the screen
//
// Return Value: None
// Parameters: None
//
//////////////////////////////////////////////////////////////////////

void MemFunctionDefnWindow::updateParamList()
{
    ParamList &paramList = aFunctionEntry->getParams();
    ParamDefinition param;
    string theParam;
    UIW_VT_LIST *theList = (UIW_VT_LIST *) Get("MEM_FCTN_PARM_LST");
    theList->Destroy();
    UI_EVENT event;
    for(int i = 0; i < paramList.total(); ++i)
    {
        param = paramList[i];
        theParam = param.typeSpecifiers;
        theParam += " ";
        theParam += param.name;
        if (param.defaultValue.Len())
        {
            theParam += " = ";
            theParam += param.defaultValue;
        }
        theList->Add(new UIW_STRING(0,0,51,theParam.ptr(),
        -1, STF_NO_FLAGS, WOF_VIEW_ONLY));
    }
    changedParamList = ::false;
    theList->Event(UI_EVENT(S_REDISPLAY));

}



//////////////////////////////////////////////////////////////////////
// Author: David Brumbaugh
// Method Name: various
// Creation Date: 11/92
// Purpose: Handle button messages
//
// Return Value: None
// Parameters: None
//
//////////////////////////////////////////////////////////////////////
```

```
void MemFunctionDefnWindow::handleOK()
{
    windowToEntry();
    if (addingFunction)
        mainWindow->completeAddFctn();
    else
        mainWindow->completeEditFctn();
    eventManager->Put(S_CLOSE);
}

void MemFunctionDefnWindow::specifyFunction()
{
    dataEntryWindow = new DataEntryDialog("SSOOTLIB~FCTN_SPC_WIN",
    (UIW_WINDOW *) this,
    (void(UIW_WINDOW::*)()) &MemFunctionDefnWindow::completeSpecify);
    UIW_TEXT *theText = (UIW_TEXT *) dataEntryWindow->Get("FCTN_SPC");
    theText->DataSet((char *)aFunctionEntry->getSpecification());
    *windowManager + dataEntryWindow;

    // This is completed in "completeSpecify"
}

void MemFunctionDefnWindow::completeSpecify()
{
    UIW_TEXT *theText = (UIW_TEXT *) dataEntryWindow->Get("FCTN_SPC");
    aFunctionEntry->setSpecification(theText->DataGet());
}

// Transfers entry data to the window fields
void MemFunctionDefnWindow::entryToWindow()
{
    UIW_STRING *theString = (UIW_STRING *) Get("MEM_FCTN_NAME");

    theString->DataSet((char *) aFunctionEntry->getName());

    string suffix = aFunctionEntry->getSuffix();
    int si = suffix.Index(";");
    if (si > -1)
        suffix.Delete(si,1);
    theString = (UIW_STRING *) Get("MEM_FN_SUFFIX");
    theString->DataSet(suffix.ptr());

    UIW_COMBO_BOX *aCBox =
    (UIW_COMBO_BOX *) Get("MEM_FCTN_ACCESS_SPEC");
    string anAccessSpec = aFunctionEntry->getAccessSpec();
    anAccessSpec.Trim();
    aCBox->Event(L_TOP);
    if (anAccessSpec == "private")
        aCBox->Event(L_DOWN);
    else if (anAccessSpec == "public")
        aCBox->Event(L_LAST);


    theString = (UIW_STRING *) Get("MEM_FCTN_RTN_TYP");
```

```
    theString->DataSet((char *) aFunctionEntry->getTypeSpec());

    theString = (UIW_STRING *) Get("MEM_FCTN_RTN_VAL");
    string theRval=    aFunctionEntry->getReturnValue();
    theString->DataSet(theRval.ptr());

    theString = (UIW_STRING *) Get("MEM_FCTN_SRC_STR");
    string theSourcePath =
    aFunctionEntry->getSourceFile();
    theString->DataSet(theSourcePath.ptr());

    UIW_TEXT *theText = (UIW_TEXT *) Get("MEM_FCTN_DESC");
    string descrip =
    aFunctionEntry->getDescription();
    theText->DataSet(descrip.ptr());

}


// Edit a function parameter
void MemFunctionDefnWindow::editParameter()
{
    dataEntryWindow = new DataEntryDialog("SSOOTLIB~FCTN_PARAM",
    (UIW_WINDOW *) this,
    (void(UIW_WINDOW::*)()) &MemFunctionDefnWindow::completeParamEdit);

    UIW_VT_LIST *theList = (UIW_VT_LIST *) Get("MEM_FCTN_PARM_LST");
    int i = theList->Index(theList->Current());
    ParamList &paramList = aFunctionEntry->getParams();
    ParamDefinition param = paramList[i];

    UIW_STRING *theString = (UIW_STRING *) dataEntryWindow->Get("PARAM_TYPE");
    theString->DataSet(param.typeSpecifiers.ptr());
    theString = (UIW_STRING *) dataEntryWindow->Get("PARAM_NAME");
    theString->DataSet(param.name.ptr());
    theString = (UIW_STRING *) dataEntryWindow->Get("PARAM_DEF_VALUE");
    theString->DataSet(param.defaultValue.ptr());
    UIW_TEXT *theText = (UIW_TEXT *) dataEntryWindow->Get("PARAM_DEFN");
    theText->DataSet(param.description.ptr());

    *windowManager + dataEntryWindow;

}


void MemFunctionDefnWindow::completeParamEdit()
{
    ParamDefinition param;

    UIW_STRING *theString = (UIW_STRING *) dataEntryWindow->Get("PARAM_TYPE");
    param.typeSpecifiers = theString->DataGet();
    theString = (UIW_STRING *) dataEntryWindow->Get("PARAM_NAME");
    param.name = theString->DataGet();
    theString = (UIW_STRING *) dataEntryWindow->Get("PARAM_DEF_VALUE");
    param.defaultValue = theString->DataGet();
    param.defaultValue.Trim();
```

```
    UIW_TEXT *theText = (UIW_TEXT *) dataEntryWindow->Get("PARAM_DEFN");
    param.description = theText->DataGet();

    UIW_VT_LIST *theList = (UIW_VT_LIST *) Get("MEM_FCTN_PARM_LST");
    int i = theList->Index(theList->Current());
    ParamList &paramList = aFunctionEntry->getParams();
    paramList[i] = param;
    changedParamList = ::true;
#ifdef _Windows
    Event(S_REDISPLAY);
#endif
}


// Add a parameter to the function
void MemFunctionDefnWindow::addParameter()
{
    dataEntryWindow = new DataEntryDialog("SSOOTLIB~FCTN_PARAM",
    (UIW_WINDOW *) this,
    (void(UIW_WINDOW::*)()) &MemFunctionDefnWindow::completeParamAdd);
    *windowManager + dataEntryWindow;


}

void MemFunctionDefnWindow::completeParamAdd()
{
    ParamDefinition param;
    UIW_STRING *theString = (UIW_STRING *) dataEntryWindow->Get("PARAM_TYPE");
    param.typeSpecifiers = theString->DataGet();
    theString = (UIW_STRING *) dataEntryWindow->Get("PARAM_NAME");
    param.name = theString->DataGet();
    theString = (UIW_STRING *) dataEntryWindow->Get("PARAM_DEF_VALUE");
    param.defaultValue = theString->DataGet();
    param.defaultValue.Trim();
    UIW_TEXT *theText = (UIW_TEXT *) dataEntryWindow->Get("PARAM_DEFN");
    param.description = theText->DataGet();
    ParamList &paramList = aFunctionEntry->getParams();
    paramList.add(param);
    changedParamList = ::true;
#ifdef _Windows
    Event(S_REDISPLAY);
#endif
}

// Delete a parameter from the function

void MemFunctionDefnWindow::delParameter()
{

    ParamList &paramList = aFunctionEntry->getParams();
    UIW_VT_LIST *theList = (UIW_VT_LIST *) Get("MEM_FCTN_PARM_LST");
    int i = theList->Index(theList->Current());
    if (i < paramList.total() && i >= 0)
    {
        paramList.seek(i);
```

```
        ParamDefinition param = paramList.current();
        string paramSpec = ((param.typeSpecifiers + ` `)+ param.name);
        DIALOG_WINDOW dialog("Confirm", "QUESTION",
        DIF_YES|DIF_NO,
              "Delete Parameter:\r\n\r\n%s ?", paramSpec.ptr());
        if (dialog.Response() == DIALOG_NO)
            return;

        paramList.remove();
    }
    changedParamList = ::true;
    updateParamList();
}


///////////////////////////////////////////////////////////////////////
// Listing  : 10-30
// Filename : FnDefWin.HPP
// Purpose  : Function Definiton Window
///////////////////////////////////////////////////////////////////////
#include <alloc.h>
#ifndef FNDEFWIN_HPP
#define FNDEFWIN_HPP
#include "defnfile.h"
///////////////////////////////////////////////////////////////////////
// Author        : David Brumbaugh
// Class Name    : FunctionDefnWindow
// Creation Date: 11/92
// Catagories    : User Interface
// Purpose       : Allows creation and editing of data in the
//                 FunctionDefinition
//
// Major Public Methods:
//  Event - Handles event processing in this window
//  FunctionDefnWindow - Constructor
//
//
// Major Data Items:
//  aFunctionEntry - The function entry being edited.
///////////////////////////////////////////////////////////////////////

#include <ui_win.hpp>
#define USE_FUNC_DEF
#include "ssootlib.hpp"
#undef USE_FUNC_DEF
#include "Entry.H"
#include "dediag.h"
class LibMainWindow;


// Librarian Function Definiton Window Event Constants -
// These constants match the Menu item values in the
// SSOOTLIB.DAT FUNC_DEF resource.
```

```
// File Menu Events
const int ToSourceEvent = 10001;
const int MakeTemplateEvent = 10002;
const int MakeFromSourceEvent = 10003;
const int ReserveEvent = 10004;
const int PrintEntryEvent = 10005;

// Options Menu Events
const int UseCommentsEvent = 20011;

// Buttons
const int OKBtn = 3001;
const int CancelBtn = 3000;
const int AddParamBtn = 20010;
const int EditParamBtn = 20020;
const int DelParamBtn = 20030;
const int SpecFctnBtn = 20040;

class FunctionDefnWindow : public UIW_WINDOW
{
    protected:
        FunctionEntry *aFunctionEntry;
        HeaderFileDefn *aHeaderFileDefn;
        Boolean needToDelete;
        LibMainWindow  *mainWindow;
        DataEntryDialog *dataEntryWindow;
        Boolean changedParamList;
        Boolean wantsComments;
        // Data Transfer
        virtual void entryToWindow();
        virtual void windowToEntry();

        // File Menu
        virtual void toSource();
        virtual void makeFromSource();
        virtual void makeTemplate();
        virtual void reserve() {}
        // Options Menu
        virtual void useComments();
        // Buttons
        virtual void handleCancel() {eventManager->Put(S_CLOSE);}
        virtual void handleOK();
        virtual void editParameter();
        virtual void addParameter();
        virtual void delParameter();
        virtual void specifyFunction();
        // Support
        virtual void completeSpecify();
        virtual void completeParamEdit();
        virtual void completeParamAdd();
        virtual void updateParamList();
        virtual void completeMakeFromSource();

    public:
```

```
        virtual EVENT_TYPE Event(const UI_EVENT &event);
        FunctionDefnWindow (LibMainWindow *lmw,
        FunctionEntry *fe = NULL) :
        UIW_WINDOW("SSOOTLIB~FUNC_DEF"),mainWindow(lmw)
        {
#ifndef _Windows
   UI_WINDOW_OBJECT::errorSystem->ReportError(UI_WINDOW_OBJECT::windowManager,
      WOS_NO_STATUS, "FuncDef Core left %ld.", coreleft());
#endif
        changedParamList = ::true;
        wantsComments = false;
        aHeaderFileDefn = NULL;
        if ( ! fe)
        {
            needToDelete = ::true;
            aFunctionEntry = new FunctionEntry;
        }
        else
        {
            needToDelete = false;
            aFunctionEntry = fe;
        // originalEntry = *fe;
        }
    }
        virtual ~FunctionDefnWindow() {
#ifndef _Windows
   UI_WINDOW_OBJECT::errorSystem->ReportError(UI_WINDOW_OBJECT::windowManager,
     WOS_NO_STATUS, "~FuncDef Core left %ld.", coreleft());
#endif
        if (needToDelete) delete aFunctionEntry;
        if (aHeaderFileDefn) delete aHeaderFileDefn;
    }
};


#endif


/////////////////////////////////////////////////////////////////////
// Listing  : 10-31
// Filename : FnDefWin.CPP
// Purpose  : Source code for function Definition Window
/////////////////////////////////////////////////////////////////////

#include "FNDEFWIN.HPP"
#include "LIBMWIN.HPP"
#include "DEDIAG.H"
#include "dialog.hpp"
#include <fstream.h>


/////////////////////////////////////////////////////////////////////
// Author: David Brumbaugh
// Method Name: Event
```

```
// Creation Date: 11/92
// Purpose: Handles Event processing for the FunctionDefnWindow
//
// Return Value: Event type to process
// Parameters: Event to be processed
//
////////////////////////////////////////////////////////////////////

EVENT_TYPE FunctionDefnWindow::Event(const UI_EVENT &event)
{
    switch(event.type)
    {
    // File Menu Events
        case ToSourceEvent:
            toSource();
        break;
        case MakeTemplateEvent:
            makeTemplate();
        break;
        case MakeFromSourceEvent:
            makeFromSource();
        break;
        case ReserveEvent:
            reserve();
        break;
    // Option Menu Events
        case UseCommentsEvent:
            useComments();
        break;
        case OKBtn:
            handleOK();
        break;
        case CancelBtn:
            handleCancel();
        break;
        case AddParamBtn:
            addParameter();
        break;
        case EditParamBtn:
            editParameter();
        break;
        case DelParamBtn:
            delParameter();
        break;
        case SpecFctnBtn:
            specifyFunction();
        break;
        case S_INITIALIZE:
            if (aFunctionEntry)
                entryToWindow();
        case S_CURRENT:
        case S_REDISPLAY:
            if (changedParamList)
            {
```

```
                    updateParamList();
                }
        default:
            return UIW_WINDOW::Event(event);
    }
    return event.type;
}

//////////////////////////////////////////////////////////////////////
// Author: David Brumbaugh
// Method Name: windowToEntry
// Creation Date: 11/92
// Purpose: Transfer data from the window to the aFunctionEntry data
//          member.
//
// Return Value: None
// Parameters: None
//
//////////////////////////////////////////////////////////////////////

void FunctionDefnWindow::windowToEntry()
{
    UIW_STRING *theString = (UIW_STRING *) Get("FCTN_NAME");
    aFunctionEntry->setName(theString->DataGet());

    theString = (UIW_STRING *) Get("FCTN_RTN_TYP");
    aFunctionEntry->setTypeSpec(theString->DataGet());

    theString = (UIW_STRING *) Get("FCTN_RTN_VAL");
    aFunctionEntry->setReturnValue(theString->DataGet());

    theString = (UIW_STRING *) Get("HEADER_FILE_PATH");
    aFunctionEntry->setLocation(theString->DataGet());

    theString = (UIW_STRING *) Get("SRC_PATH");
    aFunctionEntry->setSourcePath(theString->DataGet());

    UIW_TEXT *theText = (UIW_TEXT *) Get("FCTN_DESC");
    aFunctionEntry->setDescription(theText->DataGet());

    UIW_INTEGER *theInt = (UIW_INTEGER *) Get("FCTN_VERS");
    aFunctionEntry->setVersion(theInt->DataGet());

}
//////////////////////////////////////////////////////////////////////
// Author: David Brumbaugh
// Method Name: updateParamList
// Creation Date: 12/92
// Purpose: Updates the parameter list on the screen
//
// Return Value: None
// Parameters: None
//
//////////////////////////////////////////////////////////////////////
```

```
void FunctionDefnWindow::updateParamList()
{
    ParamList &paramList = aFunctionEntry->getParamList();
    ParamDefinition param;
    string theParam;
    UIW_VT_LIST *theList = (UIW_VT_LIST *) Get("FCTN_PARM_LST");
    theList->Destroy();
    UI_EVENT event;
    for(int i = 0; i < paramList.total(); ++i)
    {
        param = paramList[i];
        theParam = param.typeSpecifiers;
        theParam += " ";
        theParam += param.name;
        if (param.defaultValue.Len())
        {
            theParam += " = ";
            theParam += param.defaultValue;
        }
        theList->Add(new UIW_STRING(0,0,51,theParam.ptr(),
        -1, STF_NO_FLAGS, WOF_VIEW_ONLY));
    }
    changedParamList = ::false;
    theList->Event(UI_EVENT(S_REDISPLAY));

}


///////////////////////////////////////////////////////////////////
// Author: David Brumbaugh
// Method Name: toSource
// Purpose: Writes the function to a header file template
//
///////////////////////////////////////////////////////////////////

void FunctionDefnWindow::toSource()
{
    windowToEntry();
    string sourcePath =     aFunctionEntry->getLocation();
    sourcePath.Trim();
    if (sourcePath.Len() == 0)
    {
        DIALOG_WINDOW dialog("Incomplete Data", "ASTERISK",
        DIF_OK,    "You need a valid file name in the Header File field.");
        dialog.Response();
        return;
    }
    ofstream out(sourcePath.ptr(),ios::app|ios::out);
    aFunctionEntry->toSource(out);
}

///////////////////////////////////////////////////////////////////
// Author: David Brumbaugh
// Method Name: makeTemplate
```

```
// Creation Date: 12/92
// Purpose: Makes source template
//
///////////////////////////////////////////////////////////////////////

void FunctionDefnWindow::makeTemplate()
{
    windowToEntry();
    string sourcePath;
    aFunctionEntry->getSourcePath(sourcePath);
    sourcePath.Trim();
    if (sourcePath.Len() == 0)
    {
        DIALOG_WINDOW dialog("Incomplete Data", "ASTERISK",
        DIF_OK,    "You need a valid file name in the Source File field.");
        dialog.Response();
        return;
    }
    ofstream out(sourcePath.ptr(),ios::app|ios::out);
    string descrip;
    aFunctionEntry->getDescription(descrip);
    aFunctionEntry->makeTemplate(out,wantsComments,descrip.ptr());
}


///////////////////////////////////////////////////////////////////////
// Author: David Brumbaugh
// Method Name: makeFromSource and completeMakeFromSource
// Creation Date: 12/92
// Purpose: Creates a function from the source file.
//
///////////////////////////////////////////////////////////////////////

void FunctionDefnWindow::makeFromSource()
{
    dataEntryWindow = new DataEntryDialog("SSOOTLIB~FCTN_HDR_LST_WIN",
    (UIW_WINDOW *) this,
    (void(UIW_WINDOW::*)()) &FunctionDefnWindow::completeMakeFromSource);

    UIW_VT_LIST *theList = (UIW_VT_LIST *) dataEntryWindow->Get("FCTN_LST");
    windowToEntry();
    string sourcePath = aFunctionEntry->getLocation();
    sourcePath.Trim();
    if (sourcePath.Len() == 0)
    {
        DIALOG_WINDOW dialog("Incomplete Data", "ASTERISK",
        DIF_OK,    "You need a valid file name in the Header File field.");
        dialog.Response();
        return;
    }
    if (aHeaderFileDefn)
        delete aHeaderFileDefn;
    aHeaderFileDefn = new HeaderFileDefn(sourcePath.ptr());
    FunctOSList *functionList = aHeaderFileDefn->getFunctionList();
    string theFunct;
```

```
    for (int i = 0; i < functionList->total(); ++i)
    {
        theFunct = (*functionList)[i].name+
        (*functionList)[i].parameters.toString(::true,::true);
        theList->Add(new UIW_STRING(0,0,50,theFunct.ptr()));
    }
    *windowManager + dataEntryWindow;
}


void FunctionDefnWindow::completeMakeFromSource()
{
    FunctOSList *functionList = aHeaderFileDefn->getFunctionList();

    UIW_VT_LIST *theList = (UIW_VT_LIST *) dataEntryWindow->Get("FCTN_LST");
    int i = theList->Index(theList->Current());
    long offset = (*functionList)[i].offset;
    iostream *anIoStream =        aHeaderFileDefn->getIoStream();
    anIoStream->clear();
    anIoStream->unsetf(ios::skipws);
    anIoStream->seekg(offset, ios::beg);
    anIoStream->seekp(offset, ios::beg);
    aFunctionEntry->fromSource(*anIoStream);
    delete aHeaderFileDefn;
    aHeaderFileDefn = NULL;
    entryToWindow();
    changedParamList = ::true;
    Event(S_REDISPLAY);
}

////////////////////////////////////////////////////////////////////
// Author: David Brumbaugh
// Method Name: various
// Creation Date: 11/92
// Purpose: Handle button messages
//
// Return Value: None
// Parameters: None
//
////////////////////////////////////////////////////////////////////

void FunctionDefnWindow::handleOK()
{
    windowToEntry();
    Catalog *theCatalog = mainWindow->getCatalog();
    theCatalog->setEntry(*aFunctionEntry);
    mainWindow->refreshCatList();
    eventManager->Put(S_CLOSE);
}

void FunctionDefnWindow::specifyFunction()
{
    dataEntryWindow = new DataEntryDialog("SSOOTLIB~FCTN_SPC_WIN",
    (UIW_WINDOW *) this,
    (void(UIW_WINDOW::*)()) &FunctionDefnWindow::completeSpecify);
```

```cpp
    UIW_TEXT *theText = (UIW_TEXT *) dataEntryWindow->Get("FCTN_SPC");
    theText->DataSet((char *)aFunctionEntry->getSpecification());
    *windowManager + dataEntryWindow;

    // This is completed in "completeSpecify"
}

void FunctionDefnWindow::completeSpecify()
{
    UIW_TEXT *theText = (UIW_TEXT *) dataEntryWindow->Get("FCTN_SPC");
    aFunctionEntry->setSpecification(theText->DataGet());
}

// Transfer data from entry to the window.

void FunctionDefnWindow::entryToWindow()
{
    UIW_STRING *theString = (UIW_STRING *) Get("FCTN_NAME");

    theString->DataSet((char *) aFunctionEntry->getName());
    // I'm deliberatly bypassing the saftey provided by a "const char *"

    theString = (UIW_STRING *) Get("FCTN_RTN_TYP");
    theString->DataSet((char *) aFunctionEntry->getTypeSpec());

    theString = (UIW_STRING *) Get("FCTN_RTN_VAL");
    string theRval;
    aFunctionEntry->getReturnValue(theRval);
    theString->DataSet(theRval.ptr());

    theString = (UIW_STRING *) Get("HEADER_FILE_PATH");
    theString->DataSet((char *) aFunctionEntry->getLocation());

    theString = (UIW_STRING *) Get("SRC_PATH");
    string theSourcePath;
    aFunctionEntry->getSourcePath(theSourcePath);
    theString->DataSet(theSourcePath.ptr());

    UIW_TEXT *theText = (UIW_TEXT *) Get("FCTN_DESC");
    string descrip;
    aFunctionEntry->getDescription(descrip);
    theText->DataSet(descrip.ptr());

    UIW_INTEGER *theInt = (UIW_INTEGER *) Get("FCTN_VERS");
    int i = aFunctionEntry->getVersion();
    theInt->DataSet(&i);

}

// Edit a parameter

void FunctionDefnWindow::editParameter()
{
    dataEntryWindow = new DataEntryDialog("SSOOTLIB~FCTN_PARAM",
```

```
        (UIW_WINDOW *) this,
        (void(UIW_WINDOW::*)()) &FunctionDefnWindow::completeParamEdit);

    UIW_VT_LIST *theList = (UIW_VT_LIST *) Get("FCTN_PARM_LST");
    int i = theList->Index(theList->Current());
    ParamList &paramList = aFunctionEntry->getParamList();
    ParamDefinition param = paramList[i];

    UIW_STRING *theString = (UIW_STRING *) dataEntryWindow->Get("PARAM_TYPE");
    theString->DataSet(param.typeSpecifiers.ptr());
    theString = (UIW_STRING *) dataEntryWindow->Get("PARAM_NAME");
    theString->DataSet(param.name.ptr());
    theString = (UIW_STRING *) dataEntryWindow->Get("PARAM_DEF_VALUE");
    theString->DataSet(param.defaultValue.ptr());
    UIW_TEXT *theText = (UIW_TEXT *) dataEntryWindow->Get("PARAM_DEFN");
    theText->DataSet(param.description.ptr());

    *windowManager + dataEntryWindow;

}

void FunctionDefnWindow::completeParamEdit()
{
    ParamDefinition param;

    UIW_STRING *theString = (UIW_STRING *) dataEntryWindow->Get("PARAM_TYPE");
    param.typeSpecifiers = theString->DataGet();
    theString = (UIW_STRING *) dataEntryWindow->Get("PARAM_NAME");
    param.name = theString->DataGet();
    theString = (UIW_STRING *) dataEntryWindow->Get("PARAM_DEF_VALUE");
    param.defaultValue = theString->DataGet();
    param.defaultValue.Trim();
    UIW_TEXT *theText = (UIW_TEXT *) dataEntryWindow->Get("PARAM_DEFN");
    param.description = theText->DataGet();

    UIW_VT_LIST *theList = (UIW_VT_LIST *) Get("FCTN_PARM_LST");
    int i = theList->Index(theList->Current());
    ParamList &paramList = aFunctionEntry->getParamList();
    paramList[i] = param;
    changedParamList = ::true;
#ifdef _Windows
    Event(S_REDISPLAY);
#endif
}

// Add a parameter

void FunctionDefnWindow::addParameter()
{
    dataEntryWindow = new DataEntryDialog("SSOOTLIB~FCTN_PARAM",
    (UIW_WINDOW *) this,
    (void(UIW_WINDOW::*)()) &FunctionDefnWindow::completeParamAdd);
    *windowManager + dataEntryWindow;
```

```
}

void FunctionDefnWindow::completeParamAdd()
{
    ParamDefinition param;
    UIW_STRING *theString = (UIW_STRING *) dataEntryWindow->Get("PARAM_TYPE");
    param.typeSpecifiers = theString->DataGet();
    theString = (UIW_STRING *) dataEntryWindow->Get("PARAM_NAME");
    param.name = theString->DataGet();
    theString = (UIW_STRING *) dataEntryWindow->Get("PARAM_DEF_VALUE");
    param.defaultValue = theString->DataGet();
    param.defaultValue.Trim();
    UIW_TEXT *theText = (UIW_TEXT *) dataEntryWindow->Get("PARAM_DEFN");
    param.description = theText->DataGet();
    aFunctionEntry->addParameter(param);
    changedParamList = ::true;
#ifdef _Windows
    Event(S_REDISPLAY);
#endif
}

// Delete a parameter

void FunctionDefnWindow::delParameter()
{

    ParamList &paramList = aFunctionEntry->getParamList();
    UIW_VT_LIST *theList = (UIW_VT_LIST *) Get("FCTN_PARM_LST");
    int i = theList->Index(theList->Current());
    if (i < paramList.total() && i >= 0)
    {
        paramList.seek(i);
        ParamDefinition param = paramList.current();
        string paramSpec = ((param.typeSpecifiers + ' ')+ param.name);
        DIALOG_WINDOW dialog("Confirm", "QUESTION",
        DIF_YES|DIF_NO,
                "Delete Parameter:\r\n\r\n%s ?", paramSpec.ptr());
        if (dialog.Response() == DIALOG_NO)
            return;

        paramList.remove();
    }
    changedParamList = ::true;
    updateParamList();
}

// True if the user wants comments.

void FunctionDefnWindow::useComments()
{
    UIW_PULL_DOWN_MENU *mnu = (UIW_PULL_DOWN_MENU *) Get("FUNC_MENU");
    UIW_PULL_DOWN_ITEM *item = (UIW_PULL_DOWN_ITEM *) mnu->Get("OPTN_ITM");
    UIW_POP_UP_ITEM *popup = (UIW_POP_UP_ITEM *) item->Get("USE_CMNT");
    if (! wantsComments)
```

```
        {
            popup->woStatus |= WOS_SELECTED;
            wantsComments = ::true;
        }
        else
        {
            popup->woStatus &= ~WOS_SELECTED;
            wantsComments = false;
        }
}


#include "searchwi.h"
#include "dialog.hpp"
////////////////////////////////////////////////////////////////////////
// Listing  : 10-32
// Filename : SearchWi.Cpp
// Purpose  : The window to allow the user to find the appropriate entry.
////////////////////////////////////////////////////////////////////////


////////////////////////////////////////////////////////////////////////
// Author: David Brumbaugh
// Method Name: windowToQuery
// Purpose: Generates a query string from the information in window
//
// Return Value: True if string is built
//
////////////////////////////////////////////////////////////////////////

Boolean EntrySearchWindow::windowToQuery()
{
    UIW_GROUP *theGroup;
    UIW_BUTTON *theButton;
    UIW_STRING *theString;
    // Extract Data Type From Window
    char *classes[4] = { "class", "function", "struct", "union" };
    int noEntryTypes = 0;
    string entryType = '(';
    theGroup =(UIW_GROUP *) Get("ENTRY_TYP_GRP");
    theButton = (UIW_BUTTON *) theGroup->First();
    do
    {
        if (theButton->woStatus & WOS_SELECTED)
        {
            if (noEntryTypes > 0)
                entryType += " || ";
            entryType += (string("EntryType == '") +
            string(classes[noEntryTypes++]) +"'");
        }
    } while ((theButton = (UIW_BUTTON *) theGroup->Next()) == NULL);
    entryType += ')';
    // Enforce one or more Entry type
    if (noEntryTypes == 0)
```

```
        {
            DIALOG_WINDOW dialog("Incomplete", "ASTERISK",
            DIF_OK,    "You must select an Entry Type.");
            dialog.Response();
            return false;
        }
        // Extract Name & Description
        theString = (UIW_STRING *) Get("NAME_CONTAINS");
        string name = theString->DataGet();
        theString = (UIW_STRING *) Get("DESC_CONTAINS");
        string description = theString->DataGet();
        name.Trim();
        description.Trim();
        // We must have at least one of these
        if (name.Len() == 0 && description.Len() == 0)
        {
            DIALOG_WINDOW dialog("Incomplete", "ASTERISK",
            DIF_OK,    "You must have a name, description or both.");
            dialog.Response();
            return false;
        }
        // Extract AND or OR
        theGroup = (UIW_GROUP *) Get("AND_OR_GRP");
        theButton = (UIW_BUTTON *) theGroup->Get("AND_BTN");
        Boolean and;
        if (theButton->woStatus & WOS_SELECTED)
            and = ::true;

        buildQueryString(entryType,name,description,and);
        return ::true;
}


/////////////////////////////////////////////////////////////////////
// Author: David Brumbaugh
// Method Name: buildQueryString
// Purpose: Builds query string
//
/////////////////////////////////////////////////////////////////////

void EntrySearchWindow::buildQueryString(string &entryType,
 string &name, string &description, Boolean and)
{
    // Entry types
    queryString += entryType;
    queryString += " && ";

    // name term
    if (name.Len())
    {
        // Allow wild card searches
        string nameTerm = "(Name ? '*";
        nameTerm += name + "*')";
        if (description.Len() && and)
            nameTerm += " && ";
```

```
        else if (description.Len())
            nameTerm += " || ";
        queryString += nameTerm;
    }
    if (description.Len())
    {
        string descripTerm = "(Description ? '*";
        descripTerm += description + "')";
        queryString += descripTerm;
    }

}
/////////////////////////////////////////////////////////////////////
// Author: David Brumbaugh
// Method Name: executeFind
// Purpose: Performs find on catalog based on the query string.
//
/////////////////////////////////////////////////////////////////////

void EntrySearchWindow::executeFind()
{
    Catalog *catalog = theMainWin->getCatalog();
    eventManager->DeviceState(E_MOUSE,DM_WAIT);
    long start = theMainWin->currentCatListPos();

    long old_current = catalog->tell();
    catalog->top();

    if (catalog->find(queryString.ptr()))
    {
        int where = catalog->tell();
        eventManager->DeviceState(E_MOUSE,DM_VIEW);
        eventManager->Put(S_CLOSE);

        theMainWin->scrollCatList(where - start);
        eventManager->Put(EditEntryEvent);

    }
    else
    {
        DIALOG_WINDOW dialog("Not Found", "ASTERISK",
        DIF_OK,    "No Entry meets your search criteria.");
        dialog.Response();
        catalog->seek(old_current);
    }

}
/////////////////////////////////////////////////////////////////////
// Author: David Brumbaugh
// Method Name: executeSelect
// Purpose: Executes a select on the catalog based on the query
//          string.
/////////////////////////////////////////////////////////////////////
```

```
void EntrySearchWindow::executeSelect()
{
    Catalog *catalog = theMainWin->getCatalog();
    eventManager->DeviceState(E_MOUSE,DM_WAIT);

    long old_current = catalog->tell();
    catalog->select(queryString.ptr());
    catalog->set_order("IDVersion");

    if (catalog->total() > 0)
    {
        // catalog->top();
        eventManager->DeviceState(E_MOUSE,DM_VIEW);
        eventManager->Put(S_CLOSE);
        theMainWin->refreshCatList();

    }
    else
    {
        DIALOG_WINDOW dialog("Not Found", "ASTERISK",
        DIF_OK,    "No Entry meets your search criteria.");
        dialog.Response();
        catalog->clear_select();
        catalog->seek(old_current);
    }

}

//////////////////////////////////////////////////////////////////////
// Author: David Brumbaugh
// Method Name: Event
// Creation Date:
// Purpose: Handles events for the window.
//////////////////////////////////////////////////////////////////////

EVENT_TYPE EntrySearchWindow::Event(const UI_EVENT & event)
{
    switch(event.type)
    {
        case OKBtn:
            if (! windowToQuery())
                break;
            if (find)
                executeFind();
            else
                executeSelect();
        break;
        case CancelBtn:
            eventManager->Put(S_CLOSE);
        break;
        default:
            return UIW_WINDOW::Event(event);

    }
```

```
        return event.type;
}

/////////////////////////////////////////////////////////////////////
// Author: David Brumbaugh
// Method Name: EntrySearchWindow
// Purpose: Constructor
/////////////////////////////////////////////////////////////////////

 EntrySearchWindow::EntrySearchWindow(LibMainWindow *mainWin,
 Boolean is_find):UIW_WINDOW("SSOOTLIB~SEARCH_WINDOW")
{
    theMainWin = mainWin;
    find = is_find;
}




/////////////////////////////////////////////////////////////////////
// Listing  : 10-33
// Filename : SearchWin.H
// Purpose  : Definition of Search Window
/////////////////////////////////////////////////////////////////////

#ifndef SEARCHWIN_H
#define SEARCHWIN_H

#include <ui_win.hpp>
#include "STR.H"
#define USE_SEARCH_WINDOW
#include "ssootlib.hpp"
#undef USE_SEARCH_WINDOW
#include "libmwin.hpp"
// Buttons
/*
const int OKBtn = 3001;
const int CancelBtn = 3000;
*/


class LibMainWindow;
/////////////////////////////////////////////////////////////////////
// Author        : David Brumbaugh
// Class Name    : EntrySearchWindow
// Creation Date : 1/93
// Catagories    : User interface
// Purpose       : Allows user to search for catalog entries
//
/////////////////////////////////////////////////////////////////////

class EntrySearchWindow : public UIW_WINDOW
{
    protected:
        string queryString;
```

```
        LibMainWindow *theMainWin;
        virtual Boolean windowToQuery();
        virtual void buildQueryString(string &entryTypes,
        string &name, string &description, Boolean and);
        virtual void executeFind();
        virtual void executeSelect();
        Boolean find; // It's a find or a select
    public:
        virtual EVENT_TYPE Event(const UI_EVENT &event);
        EntrySearchWindow(LibMainWindow *aMainWin, Boolean is_find);

};
#endif


////////////////////////////////////////////////////////////////////////
// Listing  : 10-34
// Filename : LibMain.CPP
// Purpose  : Main for SSOOT CASE Librarian
////////////////////////////////////////////////////////////////////////


////////////////////////////////////////////////////////////////////////
// Author: David Brumbaugh
// Funcion Name: Main or WinMain as the CASE may be (snicker...)
// Creation Date: 11/92
////////////////////////////////////////////////////////////////////////

#include <ui_win.hpp>
#include <string.h>


#include "LIBMWIN.hpp"


#ifdef ZIL_MSWINDOWS

int PASCAL WinMain(HANDLE hInstance, HANDLE hPrevInstance, LPSTR, int nCmdShow)
{
    UI_DISPLAY *display = new UI_MSWINDOWS_DISPLAY(hInstance, hPrevInstance,
nCmdShow);

    HINSTANCE theDll = LoadLibrary("PRE_B.DLL");
    if (theDll < HINSTANCE_ERROR)
    {
        MessageBox(NULL,"theDll Not Loaded", "HINSTANCE_ERROR",MB_OK);
        return 0;
    }
#else

main(int argc, char **argv)
{
    // Initialize the display (compiler dependent).
```

```
#if defined(__BCPLUSPLUS__) | defined(__TCPLUSPLUS__)
    UI_DISPLAY *display = new UI_BGI_DISPLAY;
#endif
#ifdef __ZTC__
    UI_DISPLAY *display = new UI_FG_DISPLAY;
#endif
#ifdef _MSC_VER
    UI_DISPLAY *display = new UI_MSC_DISPLAY;
#endif

    // Install a text display if no graphics capability.
    // Or /t option selected
    if (!display->installed || ((argc > 1) && !strcmp(argv[1],"/t")) )
    {
        delete display;
        display = new UI_TEXT_DISPLAY;
    }

#endif

    // Create the event manager and add devices.
    UI_EVENT_MANAGER *eventManager = new UI_EVENT_MANAGER(display);
    *eventManager
        + new UID_KEYBOARD
        + new UID_MOUSE
        + new UID_CURSOR;

    // Create the window manager.
    UI_WINDOW_MANAGER *windowManager = new UI_WINDOW_MANAGER(display,
        eventManager);

    // Initialize the help and error systems.
    UI_WINDOW_OBJECT::errorSystem = new UI_ERROR_SYSTEM;
/*    UI_WINDOW_OBJECT::helpSystem = new UI_HELP_SYSTEM("hello.dat",
        windowManager, HELP_GENERAL);
 */

    UI_STORAGE *storage = new UI_STORAGE("ssootlib.dat", UIS_READ);
    UI_WINDOW_OBJECT::defaultStorage = storage;

    // Add two windows to the window manager.
    LibMainWindow *window1 = new LibMainWindow("SSOOTLIB.DB");
    *windowManager
        + window1;

    // Wait for user response.
    EVENT_TYPE ccode;
    do
    {
        // Get input from the user.
        UI_EVENT event;
        eventManager->Get(event);

        // Send event information to the window manager.
```

```
        ccode = windowManager->Event(event);
    } while (ccode != L_EXIT && ccode != S_NO_OBJECT);

    // Clean up.
    /*
    delete UI_WINDOW_OBJECT::helpSystem;
    */
    delete UI_WINDOW_OBJECT::errorSystem;

    delete windowManager;
    delete eventManager;
    delete display;

#ifdef ZIL_MSWINDOWS
    FreeLibrary(theDll);
#endif

    return (0);
}


Listing 11-1 ssootlib.db
create ssootlib.db
addtab * Entry "Entry in the SSOOT CASE Library Catalog"
addcol * * Identity "Specific Indentifier" "%s" NULL "String NoNulls Indexed"
addcol * * Version "Version of Identifier" "%s" NULL "Integer NoNulls Indexed"
addkey * * IDVersion +Identity+Version Unique
addcol * * Name "Entry Name" "%s" NULL "String Indexed NoNulls"
addcol * * Description "Entry Description" "%s" NULL "String"
addcol * * CheckedOut "Checked In or Out" NULL NULL "Integer"
addcol * * DateAdded "Date Entry Entered" NULL NULL "Integer"
addcol * * ChangedBy "Person who changed" "%s" NULL "String NoNulls Indexed"
addcol * * AddedBy "Person who added this entry" "%s" NULL "String"
addcol * * EntryType "Is it a Class or Function Entry?" "%s" NULL "String"
addcol * * DateChecked "Date Last Checked In/Out" NULL NULL "Integer"
addcol * * WhereLocated "File path to source" "%s"  NULL "String"
addcol * * MustInclude "File path to header" "%s" NULL "String"
addcol * * Active "If 1, Entry  active version" "%d" NULL "Integer Indexed"

addtab * FunctionEntry "Additonal Function Data"
addcol * * Identity "Specific Indentifier" "%s" NULL "String NoNulls Indexed"
addcol * * Version "Version of Identifier" "%s" NULL "Integer NoNulls Indexed"
addkey * * IDVersion +Identity+Version Unique
addcol * * Parameters "List of parameters" "%s" NULL "String"
addcol * * ReturnType "Return type" "%s" NULL "String"
addcol * * ReturnVal "The meaning of the return value" "%s" NULL "String"
addcol * * SourcePath "File Path to Source Code" "%s" NULL "String"
addcol * * Specification "Specification if it's a function" "%s" NULL "String"
addcol * * ParamDescriptions "Parameter descriptions" "%s" NULL "String"

addtab * ClassEntry "Additional Class Data"
addcol * * Identity "Specific Indentifier" "%s" NULL "String NoNulls Indexed"
addcol * * Version "Version of Identifier" "%s" NULL "Integer NoNulls Indexed"
addkey * * IDVersion +Identity+Version Unique
```

```
addcol * * BaseClasses "List of base classes" "%s" NULL "String"
addcol * * ClassSpec "class,struct or union" "%s" NULL "String"

addtab * ClassMember "Member Data (Function & Data)"
addcol * * Identity "Specific Indentifier" "%s" NULL "String NoNulls Indexed"
addcol * * Version "Version of Identifier" "%s" NULL "Integer NoNulls Indexed"
addkey * * IDVersion +Identity+Version
addcol * * Name       "Name of class member" "%s" NULL "NoNulls String"
addcol * * OwningClass "Name of class that owns this one" "%s" NULL "String NoNulls"
addcol * * AccessSpecifier "public, private, etc." "%s" NULL "String NoNulls
                    Indexed"
addcol * * TypeSpecifiers "const, int, virtual, etc." "%s" NULL "String Indexed"
addcol * * MemberType "Function or Data" "%s" NULL "String Indexed"
addcol * * PtrSpec "Pointer Specifications" "%s" NULL "String"
addcol * * Suffix "Function Member Only" "%s" NULL "String"
addcol * * Specification "Specification if it's a function" "%s" NULL "String"
addcol * * Parameters "List of parameters (Fn Member Only)" "%s" NULL "String"
addcol * * ReturnVal "The meaning of the typespecifier (Fn Mem)" "%s" NULL "String"
addcol * * Description "Description of Member" "%s" NULL "String"
addcol * * SourcePath "File Path to Source Code" "%s" NULL "String"


exit
```

Bibliography

Used but not cited
Borland C++ 3.0 Programmer's Guide
1991, Borland International
Scotts Valley, CA

[Booch]
Booch, Grady
Object-Oriented Design With Applications
1991, The Benjamin/Cummings Publishing
    Company, Inc.
Redwood City, CA

[Brumbaugh 1992]
Brumbaugh, David
Porting C Libraries to C++
January 1992, C Users Journal, R & D
    Publications
Lawrence, KS

[Brumbaugh 1990]
Brumbaugh, David
Object-Oriented Programming in C
July 1990, C Users Journal, R & D Publications
Lawrence, KS

[Bulman 1989]
Bulman, David
An Object-Based Development Model
August 1989, Computer Language, Miller
    Freeman Publications
San Francisco, CA

[Bulman 1991]
Bulman, David
Refining Candidate Objects
January 1991, Computer Language, Miller
    Freeman Publications
San Francisco, CA

[Coad, Yourdon 1990, 91]
Coad, Peter; Yourdon, Ed
Object-Oriented Analysis 2nd Edition
1990, 1991, Prentice Hall
Englewood Cliffs, NJ

[Coad, Yourdon 1991]
Coad, Peter; Yourdon, Ed
Object-Oriented Design
1991, Prentice Hall
Englewood Cliffs, NJ

Used but not cited
Dewhurst, Stephen; Stark, Kathy
Programming in C++
1989, Prentice Hall
Englewood Cliffs, NJ

[Fisher]
Fisher, Alan S.
1988
CASE, Using Software Development Tools
John Wiley & Sons, Inc.
New York, NY

Used but not cited
Khoshafian, Setrag; Abnous Razmik
1990
*Object Orientation Concepts, Languages,
    Databases, User Interfaces*
John Wiley & Sons, Inc.
New York, NY

Used but not cited
Lippman, Stanley B.
C++Primer
1991, Addison Wesley Publishing Company
Reading, MA

[Plum, Saks]
Plum, Thomas; Saks, Dan
C++ Programming Guidelines
1991, Plum Hall
Kamuela, HI

Used but not cited
Stevens, AL
Teach Yourself . . . C++
1990, MIS Press
Portland, OR

[Wasserman, 1991]
Wasserman, Anthony
Object-Oriented Thinking
Sept/Oct 1991, Object Magazine, SIGS
    Publications, Inc.
New York, NY

[Wasserman, Pircher, Muller]
Wasserman, Anthony; Pircher, Peter; Muller,
    Robert
The Object-Oriented Structured Design Notation
March 1990, Computer, IEEE
Los Almitos, CA

Used but not cited
Winder, Russel
Developing C++ Software
1991, John Wiley & Sons, Inc.
New York, NY

[Yourdon 1992]
Yourdon, Ed
The Decline and Fall of the American Programmer
1992, Prentice-Hall, Inc.
Englewood Cliffs, NJ

Index

Index to Source Code